The Freelance
Photographer's
Market Handbook
2008

D1332341

The Freelance Photographer's Market Handbook 2008

Edited by John Tracy
& Stewart Gibson

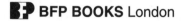 BFP BOOKS London

A catalogue record for this book is available from the British Library

ISBN-10: 0-907297-59-5
ISBN-13: 978-0-907297-59-8

24th Edition

Published for the Bureau of Freelance Photographers by BFP Books, Focus House, 497 Green Lanes, London N13 4BP. Typesetting and page layout by BFP Books. Text set in New Century Schoolbook. Printed in Great Britain by Biddles Ltd.

CONTENTS

PREFACE

As far as activity in the magazine publishing world is concerned, the past 12 months has been very quiet indeed. Some may recall that this is very much what we said in the preface to our 2007 edition, so it is becoming clear that this may be the pattern for the future.

There have been far fewer significant magazine launches during the past year than in any previous year we can recall, and thus fewer new entries in our listings here.

Publishers themselves are now admitting what has been becoming obvious for some time – that the British magazine market is effectively saturated.

Every niche now has its established players but, more importantly, in the battle for the mass market, there are just too many titles chasing an increasingly elusive consumer.

Many, of course, point to the Internet and suggest that readers are decamping to websites for the sort of fix they used to get from magazines. Some may be, but the picture is not as simple as that.

It's true that many of the most high profile mass market sectors are in sharp decline. In particular, men's magazines and women's weeklies, which for a time were the greatest success stories, are now seeing sales figures in freefall. Even the once-glittering celebrity market seems to be losing its lustre.

But, perhaps surprisingly, at the same time there have also been far fewer notable closures during the past year. Spectacular closures there have been, but most of these have gone within a year of their launch.

Indeed, if there has been one notable trend during the past year, it is that publishers are no longer prepared to invest time and money in keeping a title going if it is not an immediate success. Some will go for a complete revamp after just a few months, but most are simply closed. The days when a publisher would take the time to establish a new offering over a lengthy period seem to be over.

Meanwhile, though high profile titles are seeing their sales figures slump, the overall level of readership across all magazines remains remarkably steady. Undeniably, what we are seeing is an unusually stable and "mature" market. That means stability for the freelance too, with less risk of losing a lucrative market overnight.

Much the same can be said for picture agencies. Again, fewer newcomers and fewer closure than for some years, though the trend to consolidation continues as larger agency groups continue to buy up selected smaller specialists.

An encouraging trend though, is that those smaller agencies that are bought up are being allowed to retain their identity and specialist offering. There does seem to be more recognition that picture buyers often prefer to deal with a niche source with a finite subject range, rather than being overwhelmed by the offerings of the giant, all-purpose agencies.

"May you live in interesting times" was the old Chinese curse. Well, as far as the freelance market is concerned, we don't. So we should all be quite content.

ABOUT THE BFP

Founded in 1965, the Bureau of Freelance Photographers is today the major body for the freelance photographer. It has a worldwide membership, comprising not only full-time freelances, but also serious amateur and semi-professional photographers. Being primarily a service organisation, membership of the Bureau is open to anyone with an interest in freelance photography.

The most important service offered to members is the *Market Newsletter,* a confidential monthly report on the state of the freelance market. A well-researched and highly authoritative publication, the *Newsletter* keeps freelances in touch with the market for freelance work, mainly by giving information on the type of photography currently being sought by a wide range of publications and other outlets. It gives full details of new magazines and their editorial requirements, and generally reports on what is happening in the publishing world and how this is likely to affect the freelance photographer.

The *Newsletter* also includes in-depth interviews with editors, profiles of successful freelances, examples of successful pictures, and other general features to help freelances in understanding and approaching the marketplace.

The *Newsletter* is considered essential reading for the freelance and aspiring freelance photographer, and because it pinpoints launches and changes in the marketplace as they occur, it also acts as a useful supplement to the *Handbook*. The *Handbook* itself is an integral part of BFP membership services; members paying the full annual fee automatically receive a copy every year as it is published.

Other services provided to members for the modest annual subscription include:

● Advisory Service. Individual advice on all aspects of freelancing is available to members.

● Mediation Service. The Bureau tries to protect its members' interests in every way it can. In particular, it is often able to assist individual members in recovering unpaid fees and in settling copyright or other disputes.

● Exclusive items and special offers. The Bureau regularly offers books and other useful items to members, usually at discount prices.

● In the Services section of this *Handbook* can be found a number of companies providing special discounts to BFP members on production of a current membership card. Amongst various services members can obtain comprehensive photographic insurance cover at competitive rates.

For further details and an application form, write to Bureau of Freelance Photographers, Focus House, 497 Green Lanes, London N13 4BP, telephone 020 8882 3315, e-mail mail@thebfp.com, or visit the BFP website at www.thebfp.com. Or if you wish to join right away, you'll find an application form at the back of this book, after the main index, on page 247.

HOW TO USE THIS BOOK

Anyone with the ability to use a camera correctly has the potential to make money from their pictures. Taking saleable photographs isn't difficult; the difficulty lies in finding the market. It isn't enough for you, the photographer in search of a sale, to find what you think *might* be a suitable market; rather you must find *exactly* the right magazine, publisher, agency or whatever for your particular type of work. Many a sale is lost when work which is, in itself, technically perfect fails to fulfil the total requirements of the buyer.

The Freelance Photographer's Market Handbook has been designed to help resolve these difficulties. It puts you in touch with major markets for your work, telling you exactly what each is looking for, together with hints and tips on how to sell to them and, wherever possible, an idea of the rates they pay.

The *Handbook* covers five big markets for your pictures: magazines (by far the largest), newspapers, book publishers, picture agencies, and companies producing cards, calendars, posters and other print products. There are three ways of using the book, depending on the way you need or wish to work:

1. If you are out to sell to magazines and you can offer coverage on a theme particularly applicable to a certain type of publication (eg gardening, angling, sport) turn to the magazine section and look for the subject. The magazines are listed under 36 categories, each of which has a broad heading covering specific magazines. The categories are in alphabetical order, as are the magazines within those categories. You need only read through them to discover which is best for your type of work.

2. If you have a set of pictures that fall into a specific photographic category (landscapes, children, celebrities etc), turn to the subject index on page 21.

Look up your chosen subject and there you will find a list of all the magazines with a strong interest in that particular type of picture. You then have only to look up each one mentioned in the appropriate section for precise details of their requirements. (If in doubt as to where to find a particular magazine consult the general index at the back of the book.) There are separate subject indexes for book publishers and agencies on pages 162 and 187 respectively.

3. If you are looking for the requirements of a specific magazine, book publisher, agency, card or calendar publisher, whose name is already known to you, simply refer to the general index at the back of the book.

Some points to remember

With this wealth of information open to you, and with those three options for finding the right market, there is no reason why you shouldn't immediately start earning good cash from your camera. But before you rush off to submit your images, here are some points worth bearing in mind and which will help you to more successful sales:

1. The golden rule of freelancing: don't send people pictures they don't want. Read the requirements listed in the various parts of this directory and obey them. When, for instance, a Scottish magazine says they want pictures of all things Scottish with the exception of kilts and haggis, you can be sure they are over-stocked with these subjects. They are not going to make an exception just for you, however good you think your pictures might be.

2. Digital images supplied on CD are usually acceptable, but always check preferred image file format and size with your chosen market in advance. If working with colour film, and unless the listing states otherwise, always supply transparencies rather than prints. Unless otherwise stated, it can be assumed that any size of transparency can be accepted.

3. When submitting pictures, make sure they are accompanied by detailed captions. And don't forget to put your own name and address on each photograph/CD.

4. If you have an idea for a picture or feature for a particular publication, don't be afraid to telephone or e-mail first to discuss what you have in mind. Nearly every editor or picture buyer approached when the *Handbook* was being com-

piled said they would much prefer to hear from potential freelances in advance, rather than have inappropriate pictures or words landing on their desks.

5. If seeking commissions, always begin by making an appointment with the appropriate person in order to show your portfolio and/or cuttings. Do not turn up at a busy editor's office unannounced and expect to be met with open arms.

6. Enclose a stamped addressed envelope if you want a posted submission returned if unsuccessful.

APPROACHING THE MARKET

You've chosen your market, taken the pictures and written the captions. Full of hope and expectation, you put your work in the post. A week later, it comes back with a formal rejection slip. Why? Where did you go wrong?

You have only to look through the pages of this book to see that there are a lot of markets open to the freelance photographer, yet the sad fact remains that a great many of those who try their hand at editorial freelancing fail the first few times, and many never succeed at all. That isn't meant to be as discouraging as it might sound. On the contrary, because so many freelances fail, *you*, with the inside knowledge gleaned from these pages, stand a better chance of success than most. What's more you can gain from the experience of others.

So let's take a look at some of the areas where the inexperienced freelance goes wrong. Knowing the common mistakes, you can avoid them and consequently stand the best chance of success with your own work.

The first big mistake made by the novice is in the actual format of pictures supplied. The easiest types of photograph to take and produce today are digital or colour print. Unfortunately, both can be difficult to sell.

Images taken with digital cameras are acceptable to most markets, but need to be produced on a well-specified digital SLR in order to provide the quality parameters necessary for high-quality reproduction. They must also be of a suitable resolution (usually 300dpi) and file size.

In the case of prints, larger, high-quality prints may be acceptable. But if you are shooting on film, bear in mind that most buyers in the publishing world much prefer colour slides (transparencies) or digital files scanned from slides or negatives. The only exception here is newspapers, which may accept prints if digital files are unavailable.

Most publications are all-colour, but a number of smaller magazines still use some black and white, while many up-market titles like to use a proportion of high-quality monochrome imagery. In this case, high-quality black and white prints will usually be required.

A few markets – such as calendars and greetings cards, or certain specialist picture libraries – continue to prefer film, often in the form of larger format transparencies for ultimate reproduction quality. If your chosen market stipulates a larger format, don't send 35mm.

The quality of your work must be first class. Images should be pin-sharp and perfectly exposed to give strong, saturated colours. Slight underexposure of around one-third to half a stop may be acceptable, but overexposure never. *Never* send over-exposed, washed-out pictures.

While most markets now accept images in digital form, each will have specific technical requirements or preferences that should be ascertained before submission. File format and image size preferences do vary, so always check with your chosen market for their precise requirements in each case.

Unless otherwise stated in an individual entry, it can be assumed that all the markets listed here accept both digital and film submissions.

So much for picture format, but what of the actual subject of your pictures? Here again, a lot of fundamental mistakes are made. The oldest rule in the freelancing book is this: don't take pictures, then look for markets; find a market first and then shoot your pictures specifically with that market in mind.

Every would-be freelance knows that rule; yet the many who ignore it is frankly staggering. Remember that rule and act accordingly. First find your market, analyse it to see the sort of pictures it uses, then go all out to take *exactly* the right type of picture.

Editors see a lot of pictures every day, and the vast majority are totally unsuited to their market. Of those that are suited, many are still rejected because, despite being the right *type* of pictures, the subjects are still uninspiring. They are subjects the editor has seen over and over again; and the type that the magazine will already have on file. So once again, the work gets rejected.

Remember this and learn from it. Most of the pictures that fall on an editor's desk are pretty ordinary. If you want to make yours sell, you have to show them something different. It might be a fairly straightforward view of an unusual subject, or it might be a more common subject, seen and photographed from a new angle. Either way, it will be different.

So when you set out to take your pictures, really look at your subject and, even before you press the shutter, ask yourself, why am I taking this picture? Why will an editor want to buy it? What's so different or unusual about it? How can I make a few changes here and now to give it a better chance of success?

Good, traditional picture composition also plays a part in a picture's chances. Many would-be freelances submit pictures of people in which the principal subject is far too small and surrounded by a wealth of unwanted, distracting detail. So make a point, whenever you shoot, of moving in close and really filling the viewfinder with your subject.

Many potentially saleable landscapes are ruined by a flat perspective. So watch out for, and try to include, foreground interest in such pictures.

People at work on a craft or a hobby can be good sellers, but a good many pictures depicting such subjects are shot candidly without the necessary thought needed to really show the subject to its best. Always pose pictures like these before you take them.

Finally, a word about presentation. It's true that a good picture can often find a sale, no matter how badly it is presented; but it is equally true that bad presentation can have a negative influence on an editor or picture buyer and so ruin your chances of success. So why make things difficult for yourself?

When you send prints or CDs, make sure they are stiffly packed between thick cardboard or in cardboard envelopes. Present slides in plastic filing wallets and make them easy to view with the minimum of fuss.

With digital submissions, an editor will appreciate a print-out of thumbnail images for quick reference.

If you are sending words – either captions to pictures or a full-blown article – always type them, rather than writing them by hand. Text for articles should be printed on one side of the paper only with double spacing between lines and with good margins on each side. If submitting text on disk, always include a "hard copy" print-out as well.

Send your submission with a brief covering letter, not with pages of explanations about the work. The sale will stand or fall by your pictures and/or words, never by the excuses you offer as to why certain pictures might not be too good. If they're not good enough, they won't sell.

Give your editor what he or she wants. Give them originality and sparkle, and present the whole package in the best way you can. Learn the rules and you'll be on your way to a good many picture sales.

But don't think that anyone is going to break those rules just for you. If your pictures don't measure up to what is required, there will always be another envelope right behind full of pictures that do. And there are no prizes for guessing which submission is going to make the sale.

MAGAZINES

The British magazine market is vast. Anyone who doubts that has only to look at the racks of periodicals in any major newsagent. And this is only the tip of the iceberg, the largest section of the consumer press. Beneath the surface there is the trade press, controlled circulation magazines and many smaller publications that are never seen on general sale. At the last count more than 8,000 magazines were being published on a regular basis in Britain.

In this section you will find detailed listings of magazines which are looking for freelances. Some pay a lot, others are less generous, but all have one thing in common – they are here because they need freelance contributions on a regular basis and they are willing to pay for them.

When you come to start looking at these listings in detail, you might be surprised by the number of magazines of which you have never heard. Don't let that put you off. What the newcomer to freelancing often fails to realise is that there are as many, if not more, trade magazines or small specialist titles as there are major consumer publications, and very few of these are ever seen on general sale.

Trade magazines, as the term implies, are aimed at people whose business is making money from the particular subject concerned. As such, their requirements are usually totally different to their consumer counterparts.

As an example, consider boating. A consumer magazine on that subject will be aimed at the boat owner or enthusiast and could contain features on boats and the way they are handled. A trade magazine on the same subject is likely to be more interested in articles about the profits being made by the boating industry and pictures of shop displays of boating accessories.

Trade magazines do not necessarily have a separate section to themselves. If the subject is a common one, such as the example above in which there are both trade and consumer publications, they have been listed for your convenience under a common heading. Despite that, however, there *is* a section specifically for trade. This contains trade magazines that have no consumer counterparts, as well as magazines whose subject is actually trade itself and trading in general.

As you go through these listings, therefore, it is important for you to realise that there is a very real difference between the two sides of the subject, but it is a difference which is explained under each publication's requirements. So don't ignore trade magazines of whose existence you were not previously aware. Very often such a magazine will have just as big a market for your pictures and the fees will be just as good, if not better, than those offered by the consumer press.

It is often a good idea for the freelance to aim at some of the more obscure publications listed here, be they trade magazines or the smaller hobbyist magazines. Simply because they are a little obscure they may not have been noticed by other freelances and, as such, your sales potential may well be higher even if fees paid by some of these publications are relatively low.

When you are looking through the entries, don't stop at the section on illustrations. Read what the magazine needs in the way of text too. A publication that might appear to have a very small market for individual pictures often has a larger potential for illustrated articles, and all you need to do to make a sale is add a few words.

You will also find that many publications talk about needing mainly commissioned work. Don't be misled by this. The commissions are given to freelances and, although this means they won't consider your work on spec, they could well be interested in giving you a commission if you can prove you are worth it. That's where previous experience comes in. When trying for commissions, you should always have examples of previously published work to show an editor.

Many of the larger magazines employ a specific editor to deal with picture submissions and with photographers. They may go under various titles – picture editor, art editor, art director – but this is the person directly responsible for picture selection and for commissioning photographers for specific jobs. This, therefore, is the person you should approach when sending pictures or seeking photographic assignments. When sending written material though – illustrated or not – your approach is best made direct to the editor.

The magazine market is one of the largest available to the freelance. You might not receive as large a fee per picture as you would from, say, the calendar market, or for certain sales that might be made on your behalf by an agency, but what this field does offer is a *steady* income, especially once you have made a breakthrough with one or more titles.

There are so many magazines, covering so many different subjects, that freelances who have their wits about them would be hard put *not* to find one to which their own style and interests can be adapted. Make yourself known to a few chosen magazine editors, let them see that you can turn out good quality work on the right subject, at the right time, and there is no reason why this market shouldn't make you a good, regular income, either part time or full time.

New Listings, Changes & Deletions

The following is designed to alert readers to possible new markets as well as to important changes that have taken place since the last edition of the *Handbook*.

'New Listings' includes magazines that have been launched since the last edition appeared as well as established titles that appear in the *Handbook* for the first time. 'Title Changes' lists publications that have changed their names (previous titles in brackets). 'Deletions' lists publications that appeared in the previous edition but are omitted from this one. Publications under this heading have not necessarily ceased publication – they may have been deleted because they no longer offer a worthwhile market for the contributor.

To find the page number for any particular magazine, refer to the main index at the back of the book.

New Listings

Active Life
Classic Plant & Machinery
Coast
Digital Photo Pro
Digital SLR Photography
Digital SLR User
Fieldsports
Go Flying!
Look
Meat Trades Journal
Travel & Leisure
Your Home

Title Changes

Jaguar Heritage Archive Magazine
   (*Jaguar Heritage*)
WI Life (*WI Home & Country*)

Deletions

Attitude
British Railway Modelling
Children Now
Company Car
Digital Photography Techniques
Echoes
The English Garden
Fire and Rescue
First Down
Florida
4Homes
Homes Worldwide
Homestyle
Ice
Location, Location, Location
Meat & Poultry News
Roustabout Energy International
Spanish Magazine

The Subpostmaster
VW Motoring

You Are What You Eat
Zero

Subject Index

Only magazines are included in this index, but it should be noted that many of these subjects are also required by agencies, book publishers and card and calendar publishers.

Separate subject indexes for book publishers and picture agencies appear in the appropriate sections, on pages 162 and 187 respectively.

To find the page number for any magazine, refer to the main index at the back of the book.

Agriculture

The Countryman
Crops
Dairy Farmer
Eurofruit Magazine
Farmers Guardian
Farmers Weekly
Fresh
Organic Life
Poultry World
Waitrose Food Illustrated
World Tobacco

Aircraft

Aeroplane
Air International
Airforces Monthly
Airliner World
Aviation News
Defence Helicopter
Flight International
Flyer
Flypast
Go Flying!
Jane's Defence Weekly
Pilot
Today's Pilot

Arts/Crafts

Best of British
Classic Stitches
Crafts Beautiful
Furniture & Cabinetmaking
Good Woodworking
Knitting
The Lady
This England
Woodcarving
Woodturning
The Woodworker

Birds

BBC Wildlife
Bird Watching
Birds Illustrated
Birdwatch
The Falconers & Raptor Conservation
  Magazine
Parrots
Racing Pigeon Pictorial

Boats/Nautical

Boat International
Canal Boat & Inland Waterways
Canals & Rivers
Classic Boat
Coast
Containerisation International
International Boat Industry
Jet Skier & PW
Marine Engineers Review
Motor Boat and Yachting
Motor Boats Monthly
RYA Magazine
Rowing & Regatta
Sailing Today
Sportsboat & RIB Magazine
Towpath Talk
Traditional Boats & Tall Ships
Water Craft
Waterways World
Yachting Monthly
Yachting World
Yachts and Yachting

Buildings

Architecture Today
BD
Build It
Country Homes and Interiors
The English Home

FX
Glass Age
House Beautiful
Housebuilder
House & Garden
Icon
Municipal Journal
Period Living
Planning
RIBA Journal
SelfBuild & Design
Stadium & Arena Management
World of Interiors

Business

Accountancy Age
CA Magazine
CNBC European Business
Computer Weekly
Director
EN
The Economist
Financial Management
MEED
Marketing
People Management

Celebrities

Bella
Best
Closer
First
Glamour
Grazia
Heat
Hello!
Look
Mizz
More
Now
OK!
Radio Times
Red
Reveal
Saga
Sneak
The Stage
Sugar
TV Times
Woman
Woman and Home

Children

Mother & Baby
Nursery World
Prima Baby
Right Start
Scholastic Magazines
Scouting

Domestic/Farm Animals

Dairy Farmer
Dogs Today
Farmers Guardian
Horse
Horse & Pony
Horse & Rider
K9 Magazine
The Lady
Our Cats
Your Cat
Your Dog

Fashion

Arena
Bella
Best
Company
Condé Nast Customer Publishing
Drapers
Elle
Esquire
Essentials
FHM
Front
GQ
Glamour
Good Housekeeping
Grazia
Harper's Bazaar
The Lady
Loaded
Look
Marie Claire
Maxim
Mizz
More
Ms London
Prima
Red
Refresh

She
Woman
Woman's Own
Woman's Weekly

Flowers/Plants

BBC Gardeners' World
BBC Good Homes
Country Homes & Interiors
The Garden
Garden Answers
Garden News
Garden Trade News
Gardens Illustrated
Gardens Monthly
Good Housekeeping
Homes & Gardens
Horticulture Week
House Beautiful
House & Garden
The Lady
Woman and Home

Food/Drink

Bella
Best
British Baker
Caterer & Hotelkeeper
Country Homes & Interiors
Decanter
Essentials
Eurofruit Magazine
Food & Travel
France
French Magazine
Fresh
Good Housekeeping
Greece
Homes & Gardens
House Beautiful
House & Garden
Italia UK
Italian Magazine
Lifescape
Olive
Organic Life
Prima
Publican
Red
Restaurant
Scottish Licensed Trade News
Waitrose Food Illustrated

Glamour/Erotic

Club International
Desire
Escort
FHM
Front
Loaded
Mayfair
Men Only
Nuts
Zoo Weekly

Homes/Interiors

BBC Good Homes
Best
Build It
Coast
Country Homes & Interiors
Elle Decoration
The English Home
Essentials
Glamour
Good Housekeeping
Homes & Gardens
House Beautiful
House & Garden
Ideal Home
Period Living
Prima
Red
SelfBuild & Design
25 Beautiful Homes
Woman and Home
World of Interiors
Your Home

Industry

Chemist & Druggist
Director
Education in Chemistry
The Engineer
Engineering
Financial Management
Industrial Diamond Review
People Management
Planning
Post Magazine
Professional Engineering
Urethanes Technology
Utility Week
Works Management

Landscapes

Amateur Photographer
Best of British
Bird Watching
Buckinghamshire Countryside
Camping
Cheshire Life
Coast
Cotswold Life
Country Homes & Interiors
Country Life
Country Walking
The Countryman
Cumbria
Dalesman
Dorset
Dorset Life
The Great Outdoors
Hertfordshire Countryside
The Lady
Lake District Life
Lancashire Life
Lincolnshire Life
Outdoor Photography
Photography Monthly
Practical Photography
The Scots Magazine
Somerset Life
Sussex Life
TGO – The Great Outdoors
This England
Trail
Walk
Waterways World
Yorkshire Life

Military

Air International
Airforces Monthly
Defence Helicopter
Jane's Defence Weekly

Motor Vehicles

American Car World
Auto Express
Autocar
The Automobile
Automotive Management
Boys Toys
Classic American
Classic Cars

Classic & Sports Car
Classic Plant & Machinery
Classics Monthly
Coach and Bus Week
Commercial Motor
Driving Magazine
Evo
4x4
Fleet News
Jaguar
Jaguar Heritage Archive Magazine
Land Rover Monthly
Land Rover Owner
Maxpower
Motor Trader
Motoring & Leisure
Motor Sport
911 & Porsche World
Octane
Performance Ford
Redline
Roadway
Top Gear Magazine
Total911
Tractor
Triumph World
Truck and Driver

Motorcycles

Back Street Heroes
Bike
Classic Bike
The Classic Motor Cycle
Dirt Bike Rider
Moto Magazine
Motor Cycle News
Redline
Ride
Scootering
Superbike
Two Wheels Only

Pop/Rock

Blues and Soul
Heat
Kerrang!
Keyboard Player
Loaded
Metal Hammer
MixMag

Mojo
New Musical Express
Q
Rhythm
Total Guitar

Railways

Engineering in Miniature
Heritage Railway
International Railway Journal
Rail
Rail Express
Railnews
The Railway Magazine
Steam Railway
Today's Railways UK
Traction

Sport

All Out Cricket
Athletics Weekly
Badminton
Boat International
Boxing Monthly
Cycle Sport
Cycling Plus
Cycling Weekly
Darts World
Dirt Bike Rider
Esquire
F1 Racing
Fieldsports
FourFourTwo
Front
GQ
Golf Monthly
Golf World
Horse & Hound
International Rugby News
Loaded
Martial Arts Illustrated
Match
Maxim
Men's Health
Motor Boats Monthly
Motor Cycle News
Motor Sport
Mountain Biking UK
Nuts
Redline
Rowing & Regatta

Rugby World
Running Fitness
Shooting Gazette
Shooting Times & Country Magazine
Ski & Board
The Skier & Snowboarder Magazine
Snooker Scene
Snowboard UK
Spin
Sports Boat & RIB Magazine
Stadium & Arena Management
Swimming Times
Today's Golfer
Two Wheels Only
Windsurf Magazine
The Wisden Cricketer
Yachts and Yachting
Zoo

Travel

A Place in the Sun
Active Life
Australia & New Zealand
Business Life
Business Traveller
Coach and Bus Week
Condé Nast Customer Publishing
Condé Nast Traveller
Food & Travel
France
French Magazine
Geographical
Good Housekeeping
Greece
Italia
Italian Magazine
Italy
The Lady
Living France
Motorhome Monthly
Motoring & Leisure
Olive
Portugal
Real Travel
Saga Magazine
Spain
Sunday Times Travel Magazine
Travel & Leisure
The Traveller
Wanderlust
Woman and Home
Yours

Wildlife

Amateur Photographer
BBC Wildlife
Bird Watching
Birds Illustrated
Birdwatch
Coast
Country Life
Country Walking
The Countryman
Cumbria
Dalesman
Devon Today

Dorset
The Falconers & Raptor Conservation
  Magazine
The Field
Geographical
The Lady
Natural World
Outdoor Photography
Photography Monthly
Practical Photography
The Scottish Sporting Gazette
The Shooting Gazette
Shooting Times and Country Magazine
Sporting Shooter

Angling

ANGLER'S MAIL
IPC Media Ltd, Blue Fin Building, 110 Southwark Street, London SE1 0SU.
Tel: 020 3148 4150. E-mail: tim_knight@ipcmedia.com
Editor: Tim Knight.
Weekly publication with news and features for followers of coarse and sea fishing in the UK.
Illustrations: Digital files preferred. Topical news pictures of successful anglers with their catches.
Captions should give full details concerning weight and circumstances of capture. Covers: pictures of anglers with exceptional specimen fish or catches.
Text: Features on coarse and sea fishing topics only. Up to 800 words.
Overall freelance potential: Minimal for non-angling freelances.
Editor's tips: Contributors really need knowledge and experience of the subject; pictures and text seen from non-anglers are rarely acceptable.
Fees: By agreement.

ANGLING TIMES
EMAP Active Ltd, Bushfield House, Orton Centre, Peterborough PE2 5UW.
Tel: 01733 232600. Fax: 01733 465844. E-mail: richard.lee@emap.com
Editor: Richard Lee.
Weekly newspaper format publication covering mainly coarse angling. Includes news, features and general instruction.
Illustrations: General angling images, especially newsworthy catches, action and scenics. Covers: "stunning" action shots featuring anglers in the environment.
Text: Illustrated features on all aspects of the hobby. Up to 800 words.
Overall freelance potential: A good percentage used each week.
Fees: By agreement.

COARSE FISHERMAN
Metrocrest Ltd, 2 Harcourt Way, Meridian Business Park, Leicester LE19 1WP.
Tel: 0116 289 4567. E-mail: info@conceptdesignltd.co.uk
Editor: Stuart Dexter.
Monthly magazine covering all aspects of coarse fishing.
Illustrations: Pictures of anglers in action or riverside/lakeside scenes where coarse angling takes place. Covers: colour pictures showing anglers displaying particularly fine catches.
Text: Articles of 1,000–2,000 words, most usually first person accounts of angling experiences.
Overall freelance potential: Excellent scope for angling specialists.
Fees: Pictures from £10 upwards. £25 per 1,000 words for text.

FLY FISHING & FLY TYING
Rolling River Publications Ltd, The Locus Centre, The Square, Aberfeldy, Perthshire PH15 2DD.
Tel: 01887 829868. Fax: 01887 829856. E-mail: markb.ffft@btinternet.com
Editor: Mark Bowler.
Monthly for the fly fisherman and fly-tyer.
Illustrations: Digital files preferred. Shots of fly fishermen in action, scenics of locations, flies and fly-tying, and appropriate insect pictures.
Text: Illustrated articles on all aspects of fly fishing.

Are you working from the latest edition of The Freelance Photographer's Market Handbook? It's published on 1 October each year. Markets are constantly changing, so it pays to have the latest edition

---

Overall freelance potential: Fairly good.
Editor's tips: Make an effort to avoid bland backgrounds, especially at watersides.
Fees: Colour from £24–£58; covers £50. Text £50 per 1,000 words.

IMPROVE YOUR COARSE FISHING
EMAP Active Ltd, Bushfield House, Orton Centre, Peterborough PE2 5UW.
Tel: 01733 237111. Fax: 01733 465658. E-mail: kevin.green@emap.com
Editor: Kevin Green.
Monthly, inspirational, "hints and tips" style magazine for coarse fishing enthusiasts.
Illustrations: Digital files preferred. Photographs depicting all aspects of coarse fishing.
Text: Ideas for illustrated features from experienced angling writers always considered. 2,500 words; submit a synopsis first.
Overall freelance potential: Limited; much of the editorial content is produced in-house.
Editor's tips: Always query the editor before submitting.
Fees: £50 per picture unless supplied with article; articles £100 – £200 inclusive of pictures.

SEA ANGLER
EMAP Active Ltd, Bushfield House, Orton Centre, Peterborough PE2 5UW.
Tel: 01733 465702. Fax: 01733 465658. E-mail: mel.russ@emap.com
Editor: Mel Russ.
Monthly magazine dealing with the sport of sea angling from both boat and beach.
Illustrations: Good sea fishing and shore fishing pictures, scenic coastline pictures from around the country, and proud anglers with good catches. Covers: Head shots of individual sea fish and anglers displaying an exceptional catch (must be a fresh catch).
Text: Instructional features, fishing expeditions, match articles, etc. 1,000 words.
Overall freelance potential: 50 per cent of published material comes from freelance sources.
Fees: By negotiation; good rates for the right kind of material.

TROUT & SALMON
EMAP Active Ltd, Bushfield House, Orton Centre, Peterborough PE2 5UW.
Tel: 01733 237111. Fax: 01733 465820. E-mail: andrew.flitcroft@emap.com
Editor: Andrew Flitcroft.
Monthly magazine for game fishermen.
Illustrations: Digital files preferred. Photographs of trout or salmon waters, preferably with an angler included in the picture. Close-up and action shots to illustrate particular techniques. Captioned news pictures showing anglers with outstanding catches. Covers: attractive pictures of game fishing waters, always with an angler present.
Text: Instructional illustrated articles on all aspects of game fishing.
Overall freelance potential: Excellent for those who can produce the right sort of material.
Fees: Pictures inside according to use. Cover shots, £80. Text according to length.

TROUT FISHERMAN
EMAP Active Ltd, Bushfield House, Orton Centre, Peterborough PE2 5UW.
Tel: 01733 237111. Fax: 01733 465658. E-mail: russell.hill@emap.com
Editor: Russell Hill.
Monthly magazine for the trout fishing enthusiast.
Illustrations: Colour. Photographs depicting any aspect of angling for trout – outstanding catches, angling locations, techniques, flies and equipment.
Text: Illustrated articles on all aspects of trout fishing, around 1,500 words.
Overall freelance potential: Excellent scope for top quality material.
Editor's tips: Too much angling photography is dull and uninteresting; an original and lively approach would be welcome.
Fees: On a rising scale according to size of reproduction or length of text.

Animals & Wildlife

BBC WILDLIFE
Bristol Magazines Ltd, 14th Floor, Tower House, Fairfax Street, Bristol BS1 3BN.
Tel: 0117 927 9009. Fax: 0117 934 9008. E-mail: sophiestafford@bbcmagazinesbristol.com/
wandasowry@bbcmagazinesbristol.com
Editor: Sophie Stafford. **Art Editor:** Simon Bishop. **Picture Researcher:** Wanda Sowry.
Heavily-illustrated magazine for readers with a serious interest in wildlife and environmental
matters. 13 issues per year.
Illustrations: Digital files preferred. Top-quality wildlife and environmental photography of all
kinds, mostly to illustrate specific features. Lists of available stock imagery should be sent to picture
researcher; suggestions for special portfolios or illustrated features to editor. See
www.bbcwildlifemagazine.com for submission guidelines.
Text: Feature suggestions considered from contributors who have a genuine knowledge of their
subject.
Overall freelance potential: Only for the very best quality work.
Fees: Pictures from £50 (under quarter-page) to £150 (dps); covers £300.

BIRD WATCHING
EMAP Active Ltd, Media House, Lynchwood, Peterborough PE2 6EA.
Tel: 01733 282601. E-mail: kevin.wilmot@emap.com
Editor: Kevin Wilmot.
Monthly magazine devoted to bird watching and ornithology.
Illustrations: Digital files preferred. Top quality photographs of birds in the wild, both in the UK
and overseas. Prefer to use pictures that illustrate specific aspects of bird behaviour. Also, landscape
shots of British bird-watching sites.
Text: Illustrated features on all aspects of birds and bird watching.
Overall freelance potential: Excellent scope for wildlife specialists.
Fees: By negotiation.

BIRDS ILLUSTRATED
Buckingham Press, 55 Thorpe Park Road, Longthorpe, Peterborough PE3 6LJ.
Tel: 01733 566815. E-mail: editor@buckinghampress.com
Editor: David Cromack.
Quarterly subscription-only magazine showcasing all aspects of bird life, birding, wildlife art and
photography.
Illustrations: Digital files preferred. "Classic Images" feature requires pictures that are exceptional
in aesthetic terms or which show unusual bird behaviour. Proposals for word and picture packages
on individual species, birdwatching locations or bird behaviour are welcome. Also readers' pictures
section. No images of captive birds.
Text: Articles on places to see birds, individual species or groups of birds, up to 3,000 words.
Gallery-type profiles of bird photographers and artists, profiles of birding personalities.
Overall freelance potential: Excellent scope for wildlife specialists.
Fees: By agreement. No fees paid for readers' gallery.

BIRDWATCH
Solo Publishing Ltd, B403A The Chocolate Factory, 5 Clarendon Road, London N22 6XJ.
Tel: 020 8881 0550. E-mail: editorial@birdwatch.co.uk
Editor: Dominic Mitchell. **Picture Editor:** Steve Young.
Monthly for all birdwatchers. Includes a strong emphasis on the photographic side of the hobby.
Illustrations: Digital files only. Good photographs of British and European birds in their natural
habitat. Those with collections of such material should send lists of subjects available.

Text: Well-illustrated features on birdwatching topics, including practical articles on bird photography. 1,000–1,200 words, but send a synopsis first.
Overall freelance potential: Average.
Fees: According to use.

DOGS TODAY
Pet Subjects Ltd, 2 The Barns, Pennypot Lane, Chobham, Surrey GU24 8DJ.
Tel: 01276 858880. Fax: 01276 858860. E-mail: enquiries@dogstodaymagazine.co.uk
Editor: Beverley Cuddy.
Monthly magazine for the pet dog lover.
Illustrations: Digital files preferred. News pictures or shots showing dogs in action, in specific situations, and interacting with people (especially children). Will also consider exciting or amusing photo sequences and pictures of celebrities with their dogs. No simple dog portraits unless displaying a strong element of humour or sentiment. Shots of crossbreeds always needed.
Text: General illustrated features about dogs. Should be positive and have a "human interest" feel.
Overall freelance potential: Excellent for the right material.
Fees: According to use.

THE FALCONERS & RAPTOR CONSERVATION MAGAZINE
PW Publishing Ltd, Arrowsmith Court, Station Approach, Broadstone, Dorset BH18 8PW.
Tel: 0845 803 1979. Fax: 01202 659950. E-mail: steve@pwpublishing.ltd.uk
Editor: Peter Eldrett. **Art Editor:** Stephen Hunt.
Quarterly magazine devoted to falconry and birds of prey.
Illustrations: B&W and colour. Digital files preferred. Usually only required to illustrate specific articles. Covers: Striking images of birds of prey.
Text: Articles on falconry and related topics. 1,000–5,000 words.
Overall freelance potential: Little scope for individual photographs, but complete illustrated articles always welcome.
Editor's tips: Free author's guide available on request.
Fees: By negotiation.

K9 MAGAZINE
K9 Media Solutions, 21 High Street, Warsop, Mansfield, Notts NG20 0AA.
Tel: 08700 114 115. E-mail: mail@k9magazine.com
Editor: Ryan O'Meara.
Quarterly magazine plus extensive website (www.k9magazine.com), described as the only lifestyle magazine for British dog lovers.
Illustrations: Colour. Digital files preferred. High quality dog images – breeds, puppies, dogs with people, dogs in action, etc. Submit low-res samples via e-mail in the first instance. Some commissions available to experienced animal photographers.
Text: Illustrated features on aspects of dog behaviour and dog ownership.
Overall freelance potential: Only top quality material considered.
Fees: By negotiation.

As a member of the Bureau of Freelance Photographers, you'll be kept up-to-date with markets through the BFP Market Newsletter, published monthly. *For details of membership, turn to page 9*

NATURAL WORLD
The Wildlife Trusts, The Kiln, Waterside, Mather Road, Newark, Nottinghamshire NG24 1WT.
Tel: 0870 0367711. Fax: 0870 0360101.
Editor: Rupert Paul.
The magazine of The Wildlife Trusts, concerned with all aspects of wildlife and countryside conservation in the UK. Published three times per year.
Illustrations: Interesting shots of British mammals, amphibians, insects, flowers and trees. Subjects must be wild; no pets or zoo animals.
Text: Short photo-features on wildlife or conservation topics particularly connected with local Wildlife Trusts. Around 300 words.
Overall freelance potential: Limited.
Fees: £35 minimum.

OUR CATS
Our Dogs Publishing Co Ltd, 1 Lund Street, Manchester M16 9EJ.
Tel: 0870 7311 6505. Fax: 0870 731 6501. E-mail: editorial@ourcats.co.uk
Editor: Vince Hogan.
Fortnightly publication aimed at the serious cat breeder and exhibitor and all cat lovers.
Illustrations: Digital files preferred. Newsy photographs of interest to serious cat lovers. All pictures must be accompanied by informative captions.
Text: Limited scope for knowledgeable features.
Overall freelance potential: Limited to the coverage of serious cat matters.
Editor's tips: If the subject concerns cats, take a chance and submit it.
Fees: By negotiation.

YOUR CAT
BPG (Stamford) Ltd, Roebuck House, 33 Broad Street, Stamford, Lincs PE9 1RB.
Tel: 01780 766199. Fax: 01780 766416. E-mail: s.parslow@bournepublishinggroup.co.uk
Editor: Sue Parslow.
Monthly magazine for all cat lovers. Covers every type of cat including the household moggie and pedigree cats.
Illustrations: Transparencies preferred; digital only if of the highest quality. Mostly by commission to accompany features as below. Some scope for interesting, unusual or humorous single pictures.
Text: Illustrated news items and features on the widest variety of topics relating to cats: famous cats, cats in the news, readers' cats, rare cats, cats that earn a living, etc. Also authoritative articles on practical matters: behaviour, grooming, training, etc.
Overall freelance potential: Reasonable; the magazine is heavily illustrated.
Fees: By negotiation.

YOUR DOG
BPG (Stamford) Ltd, Roebuck House, 33 Broad Street, Stamford, Lincs PE9 1RB.
Tel: 01780 766199. Fax: 01780 766416. E-mail: s.wright@bournepublishinggroup.co.uk
Editor: Sarah Wright.
Monthly magazine for "the everyday dog owner", with the emphasis on care and training.
Illustrations: Digital files preferred. Top quality pictures showing dogs and their owners in a practical context, i.e. walking, training, grooming; dogs in the news; amusing pictures. For covers pictures must be of the highest technical quality.
Text: Illustrated news stories, practical features, and articles on any interesting canine subject, i.e. working dogs, dog charities, celebrities and their dogs, etc. Always contact editor before submitting.
Overall freelance potential: Fair.
Editor's tips: Make sure that pictures are recent and not just something dug up from the back of the filing cabinet.
Fees: According to size of reproduction and by negotiation.

Architecture & Building

ARCHITECTURE TODAY
Architecture Today plc, 161 Rosebery Avenue, London EC1R 4QX.
Tel: 020 7837 0143. Fax: 020 7837 0155. E-mail: mark.l@architecturetoday.co.uk
Editors: Ian Latham, Chris Foges.
Independent monthly for the architectural profession. Covers the most important projects in the UK and Europe, from art galleries to social housing and from interiors to urban design.
Illustrations: Most photography is commissioned, but interesting pictures of current architectural projects are always of interest on spec.
Text: Illustrated articles of genuine interest to a professional readership; submit ideas only first. 800–2,000 words.
Overall freelance potential: Some scope for specialists.
Editor's tips: Potential contributors must contact the editors before submitting anything.
Fees: £100 per 1,000 words; photography by arrangement.

BD
CMP Information, Ludgate House, 245 Blackfriars Road, London SE1 9UY.
Tel: 020 7921 8200. Fax: 020 7921 8244. E-mail: abaillieu@cmpinformation.com
Editor: Amanda Baillieu.
Weekly newspaper for architects and architectural technicians.
Illustrations: Digital files preferred. News pictures may be considered on spec but most photography commissioned to illustrate major stories and features. Photographers should have a proven record in architectural photography and a demonstrable understanding of what it should capture. Submit samples of work along with details of experience.
Text: News pieces and features on all aspects of building design, by those with real understanding of the subject matter. Always make contact before submitting.
Overall freelance potential: Good for those with the requisite expertise.
Fees: Pictures variable according to use etc. Text around £160 per 1,000 words.

BUILD IT
Ocean Media Group Ltd, 19th Floor, 1 Canada Square, Canary Wharf, London E14 5AP.
Tel: 020 7772 8300. Fax: 020 7772 8584. E-mail: pippa.collins@oceanmedia.co.uk
Editor: Pippa Collins. **Art Editor:** Kirsten Seymour.
Monthly devoted to the self-build market – those people building a one-off home or converting old barns, chapels, etc.
Illustrations: Commissions available to experienced photographers to cover architecture, renovations and interiors. Some interest in relevant stock photographs of housing and interior decoration subjects.
Text: Authoritative features on building, landscaping and interior design, plus specialised articles on finance, legal issues, weatherproofing, etc.
Overall freelance potential: Excellent for the experienced contributor in the architecture and interiors field.
Fees: Good rates for photographers; text negotiable.

BUILDERS' MERCHANTS JOURNAL
Faversham House Group, Faversham House, 232A Addington Road, South Croydon CR2 8LE.
Tel: 020 8651 7100. Fax: 020 8651 7117. E-mail: fionarussellhorne@fav-house.com
Editor: Fiona Russell Horne.
Monthly business to business magazine for the builders merchants industry – wholesale distributors of building products, including heating, bathroom and kitchen fixtures.
Illustrations: Mostly colour. Always interested in unusual photography of merchants' yards,

computers, showrooms and vehicles. Ongoing requirement for shots of house building/refurbishment work. Possible scope for creative still life shots of items such as bricks, blocks, timber, etc. Commissions also available, depending on geographic location – write in with details of experience and rates.

Text: Limited scope for freelance articles on suitable subjects – send business card and samples of published work in the first instance.

Overall freelance potential: Limited.

Editor's tips: Most commissions here tend to be rather mundane, usually involving quite general shots of a merchant's yard. Need photographers who can provide a more creative approach. Write in the first instance – do not telephone.

Fees: Photographs by negotiation. Text around £125 per 1,000 words.

BUILDING SERVICES JOURNAL

CMP Information Ltd, Ludgate House, 245 Blackfriars Road, London SE1 9LN.
Tel: 020 7560 4000. Fax: 020 7560 4020. E-mail: bsjeditorial@cmpi.biz
Editor: Andrew Pearson. **Art Editor:** Jason Harris.
Monthly publication for engineers and senior management involved with installing heating, air conditioning, ventilation, lighting, lifts, hot and cold water systems etc into buildings.

Illustrations: Good quality news or stock pictures of building services installations. Pictures used for caption stories and for stock. Covers usually commissioned.

Text: No scope.

Overall freelance potential: Good, since very few pictures of this subject are offered.

Fees: By negotiation.

FX

Wilmington Business Information, 6-14 Underwood Street, London N17JQ.
Tel: 020 7490 0049. Fax: 020 7549 2578. E-mail: tdowling@wilmington.co.uk
Editor: Theresa Dowling. **Art Editor:** Wesley Mitchell.
Monthly interior design business magazine for the retail, hotel and commercial sectors. Aimed at architects, designers and their clients.

Illustrations: By commission only; experienced architectural and interiors photographers with fresh ideas always welcome.

Text: Articles on commercial design matters and related business issues, only from those with real expertise in these areas.

Overall freelance potential: Good for the experienced worker.

Editor's tips: The magazine is very receptive to original ideas. Articles should be hard-hitting and possibly contentious.

Fees: Photography around £200–£250 per day. £160 per 1,000 words.

GLASS AGE

CMP Information Ltd, Ludgate House, 245 Blackfriars Road, London SE1 9UY.
Tel: 020 7560 4247. Fax: 020 7560 4017. E-mail: dbentham@cmpi.biz
Editor: Dominic Bentham.
Monthly magazine for the flat glass and fenestration industries. Aimed at builders, architects, glaziers, shopfitters, glass merchants, stained glass artists and all glass-related workers.

Illustrations: Particularly interested in pictures of glass in new buildings. Detailed captions essential.

Text: Features on glass in construction.

Overall freelance potential: Good opportunities for high quality architectural photography.

Editor's tips: Make contact before submitting any material.

Fees: On a rising scale according to the size of reproduction or length of feature.

H&V NEWS
EMAP Trenton, 19th Floor, Leon House, 233 High Street, Croydon CR0 9XT.
Tel: 020 8649 9665. Fax: 020 8277 5434. E-mail: simon.duddy@emap.com
Editor: Simon Duddy.
Weekly for those who purchase or specify heating, ventilating and air conditioning equipment.
Illustrations: Pictures of installations and equipment in active use, preferably with a human interest element.
Text: News stories, installation stories regarding heating, ventilating and air conditioning equipment, stories on companies and people. 200–300 words. Longer features by negotiation.
Overall freelance potential: Good scope for newsworthy material.
Editor's tips: The more current the information supplied the better its chance of success.
Fees: £12 per 100 words; pictures by negotiation.

HOUSEBUILDER
Housebuilder Publications Ltd, Byron House, 7-9 St James's Street, London SW1A 1DW.
Tel: 020 7960 1638. Fax: 020 7960 1631. E-mail: allison.heller@house-builder.co.uk
Editor: Allison Heller.
Monthly journal of the House Builders Federation. Aimed at key decision makers, managers, technical staff, marketing executives, architects and local authorities.
Illustrations: Digital files preferred. Some scope for housebuilding coverage, but only by prior consultation with the editor.
Text: Features on marketing, land and planning, government liaison, finance, materials, supplies, etc. Always to be discussed before submission. 1,000 words.
Overall freelance potential: Around 50 per cent comes from freelances.
Editor's tips: Authoritative articles and news stories only. No PR "puffs".
Fees: £150 per 1,000 words; pictures by agreement.

ICON
Media Ten Ltd, National House, High Street, Epping, Essex CM16 4BD.
Tel: 01992 570030. Fax: 01992 570031. E-mail: justin@icon-magazine.co.uk
Editor: Justin McGuirk. **Art Editor:** Rob Timm. **Picture Researcher:** Clare Limpus.
Monthly magazine covering architecture and design, aimed at both professionals and interested consumers.
Illustrations: Top quality architectural and design photography, mostly by commission. Submit ideas and samples in the first instance. Also runs a regular monthly photographers' showcase.
Text: Suggestions considered, but contributors must really know their subject.
Overall freelance potential: Fair.
Editor's tips: Potential contributors should really study the magazine first in order to "tune in" to what it is trying to do.
Fees: By negotiation.

LANDSCAPE
Wardour Publishing & Design, Elsley Court, 20-22 Great Titchfield Street, London W1P 8BB.
Tel: 020 7016 2555. E-mail: joe@wardour.co.uk
Editor/Art Director: Joe Gardiner.
Official magazine of The Landscape Institute. Aimed at professionals either producing or commissioning landscape architecture and designed to showcase the best work in the field.
Illustrations: Mostly by commission only; always happy to hear from photographers who can offer high-level skills in architectural work.
Text: Ideas for features will be considered.
Overall freelance potential: Good scope for experienced workers.
Editor's tips: Requirements are very specific, so in the first instance submit only a couple of samples as an indication of style.
Fees: By negotiation.

PRESTIGE INTERIORS
(Two separate titles covering CORPORATE and HOTEL & HIGH STREET interiors)
Albatross Publications, PO Box 523, Horsham, West Sussex RH12 4WL.
Tel: 01293 871201. Fax: 01293 871301. E-mail: newsdesk123@aol.com
Editor: Carol Andrews.
Quarterly publications covering interior design in the commercial sectors specified above. Aimed at managers concerned with interiors in the fields of hotels and restaurants, office spaces, retail and catering, and the designers serving them.
Illustrations: Colour only. Digital files preferred. Pictures only accepted as part of an illustrated feature on topics such as interesting new interiors and developments, examples of good (or bad) design and decor, lighting, and specific problems encountered in individual projects.
Text: News stories and profiles of relevant individual projects, but always contact the editor with suggestions first.
Overall freelance potential: Fair.
Editor's tips: Remember that these are professional publications for business people and interior designers.
Fees: By negotiation.

RIBA JOURNAL
RIBA Journals Ltd, Ludgate House, 245 Blackfriars Road, London SE1 9UY.
Tel: 020 7560 4120. Fax: 020 7560 4191. E-mail: hpearman@cmpinformation.com
Editor: Hugh Pearman. **Art Editor:** Mark Bergin.
Monthly magazine of the Royal Institute of British Architects. Covers general aspects of architectural practice as well as criticisms of particular buildings, profiles and interviews.
Illustrations: Digital files preferred. Pictures of buildings, old, new and refurbished. Covers: colour pictures connected with main feature inside. Best to send list of subjects initially.
Text: Illustrated features on architectural subjects and criticisms of particular buildings.
Overall freelance potential: Fair.
Fees: By arrangement.

SELFBUILD & DESIGN
Waterways World Ltd. Editorial: The Mill House, Bache Mill, Diddlebury, Shropshire FY7 9JX.
Tel/fax: 01584 841417. E-mail: r.stokes@easynet.co.uk
Editor: Ross Stokes.
Monthly practical consumer magazine covering self-build housing, including conversions and major extensions.
Illustrations: Striking photographs of recently completed self-builds (interiors and exteriors), particularly those of an innovative design or in unusual or visually appealing locations. Coverage of new builds by celebrities also welcomed.
Text: Authoritative and well illustrated articles covering all aspects of building and renovation, including brief items of a quirky, amusing or informative nature. Telephone to discuss ideas before submission.
Overall freelance potential: Good.
Fees: By negotiation.

STADIUM & ARENA MANAGEMENT
Alad Ltd. Editorial: 4 North Street, Rothersthorpe, Northants NN7 3JB.
Tel: 01604 832149. E-mail: mark.webb@tesco.net
Editor: Mark Webb.
Bi-monthly, international news magazine covering all aspects of stadium and arena design, construction and management.
Illustrations: Digital files preferred. Photographs of new stadia or arenas internationally, but especially in Europe, preferably at the construction stage. Also newsworthy images involving stadia.
Text: News items always considered.

Overall freelance potential: Fair.
Editor's tips: Always make contact before undertaking a shoot; it may be possible to link the pictures to a feature story.
Fees: By negotiation.

Arts & Entertainment

CLUB MIRROR
Alchemy Media Solutions Ltd, Aaron House, 2-6 Bardolph Road, Richmond TW9 2CS.
Tel: 020 8288 7400. E-mail: editorial@clubmirror.co.uk
Editor: Sean Ferris.
Published 10 times a year for officials, committee members and stewards of registered clubs throughout the UK; proprietary club owners and managers; and discotheque owners and managers.
Illustrations: Interior pictures of new clubs, new club openings, interesting general pictures of club activities.
Text: Articles on new club openings, new clubs planned, news stories on clubs, special features on successful clubs. Also features on the club trade, catering services etc.
Overall freelance potential: Good; 90 per cent from freelance sources.
Fees: By arrangement.

HEAT
EMAP Performance Network, Endeavour House, 189 Shaftesbury Avenue, London WC2H 8JG.
Tel: 020 7295 5000. Fax: 020 7817 8847. E-mail: russ.o'connell@emap.com
Editor: Mark Frith. **Picture Director:** Russ O'Connell.
Popular entertainment weekly with news, reviews and heavy celebrity content.
Illustrations: Digital files preferred. Interested in hearing from photographers covering live events throughout the UK. Assignments available to shoot performances and behind-the-scenes coverage. Some scope for stock pictures of contemporary music and the entertainment industries, and paparazzi-type material.
Text: No scope.
Overall freelance potential: Good.
Fees: By negotiation.

RADIO TIMES
BBC Worldwide Publishing, Woodlands, 80 Wood Lane, London W12 0TT.
Tel: 020 8433 2000. Fax: 020 8433 3160. E-mail: roger.dickson@bbc.co.uk
Editor: Gill Hudson. **Picture Editor:** Roger Dickson.
Weekly TV and radio listings magazine, containing news and features on mainly BBC productions and personalities.
Illustrations: Coverage of broadcasting events, BBC productions, and TV personalities, usually by commission.
Text: Commissioned features on TV personalities or programmes of current interest.
Overall freelance potential: Fair for commissioned work.
Fees: Various.

THE STAGE
The Stage Newspaper Ltd, 47 Bermondsey Street, London SE1 3XT.
Tel: 020 7403 1818. Fax: 020 7357 9287. E-mail: editor@thestage.co.uk
Editor: Brian Attwood.
Weekly newspaper for professionals working in the performing arts and the entertainment industry.
Illustrations: News pictures concerning people and events in the theatre and television worlds.
Text: Features on the theatre and light entertainment. 800 words.

Overall freelance potential: Limited.
Fees: Pictures by agreement, text £100 per 1,000 words.

TV TIMES
IPC Media Ltd, Blue Fin Building, 110 Southwark Street, London SE1 0SU.
Tel: 020 3148 5570. Fax: 020 3148 8115. E-mail: elaine_mccluskey@ipcmedia.com
Editor: Ian Abbott. **Art Director:** Penny Miles. **Picture Editor:** Elaine McCluskey.
Weekly television programme listings magazine, plus features on major programmes.
Illustrations: Usually commissioned or requested from specialist sources. Mainly quality colour portraits or groups specific to current programme content.
Text: Articles on personalities and programmes.
Overall freelance potential: Between 50 and 75 per cent each week is freelance, but mostly from recognised contributors.
Fees: Negotiable.

Aviation

AEROPLANE
IPC Media Ltd, Blue Fin Building, 110 Southwark Street, London SE1 0SU.
Tel: 020 3148 4100. E-mail: aeroplane_monthly@ipcmedia.co.uk
Editor: Michael Oakey.
Monthly aviation history magazine, specialising in the period 1909–1960. Occasional features on modern aviation.
Illustrations: Colour; B&W archive material. Photographs for use in their own right or for stock. Main interests – veteran or vintage aircraft, including those in museums; preserved airworthy aircraft; unusual pictures of modern aircraft. Action shots preferred in the case of colour material – air-to-air, ground-to-air, or air-to-ground. Covers: high quality air-to-air shots of vintage or veteran aircraft. Transparencies 6x6cm minimum.
Text: Short news stories concerning preserved aircraft, new additions to museums and collections, etc. Not more than 300 words.
Overall freelance potential: Most contributions are from freelance sources, but specialised knowledge and skills are often necessary.
Editor's tips: The magazine is always in the market for sharp, good quality colour images of preserved aircraft in the air.
Fees: Colour photographs: full page £80; centre spread £100; covers £180. B&W from £10 upwards.

AIR INTERNATIONAL
Key Publishing Ltd, PO Box 100, Stamford, Lincolnshire PE9 1XQ.
Tel: 01780 755131. Fax: 01780 757261. E-mail: malcolm.english@keypublishing.com
Editor: Malcolm English.
Monthly general aviation magazine covering both modern military aircraft and the civil aviation industry. Includes some historical topics. Aimed at both enthusiasts and industry professionals.
Illustrations: Digital files preferred. Topical single pictures or picture stories on aviation subjects worldwide, e.g. aircraft in active war zones, airliners in new livery, new aircraft at Heathrow, etc. Overseas material welcomed. Air show coverage rarely required.
Text: Illustrated features on topics as above, from writers with in-depth knowledge of the subject. Length variable.
Overall freelance potential: Very good for suitable material.
Editor's tips: Remember the magazine is read by professionals and is not just for enthusiasts.
Fees: B&W from £10; colour based on page rate of £75. Covers, up to £120 for full-bleed sole reproduction. Text £50 per 1,000 words.

AIRFORCES MONTHLY
Key Publishing Ltd, PO Box 100, Stamford, Lincolnshire PE9 1XQ.
Tel: 01780 755131. Fax: 01780 751323. E-mail: afm@keypublishing.com
Editor: Alan Warnes.
Monthly magazine concerned with modern military aircraft.
Illustrations: Mostly colour. Interesting, up-to-date pictures of military aircraft from any country. Must be current; archive material rarely used.
Text: Knowledgeable articles concerning current military aviation. No historical matter.
Overall freelance potential: Good for contributors with the necessary knowledge and access.
Fees: £25 minimum for colour; £10 minimum for B&W; covers £120. Text by negotiation.

AIRLINER WORLD
Key Publishing Ltd, PO Box 100, Stamford, Lincs PE9 1XQ.
Tel: 01780 755131. Fax: 01780 757261. E-mail: tony.dixon@keypublishing.com
Editor: Tony Dixon.
Heavily-illustrated monthly for civil aviation enthusiasts.
Illustrations: Colour, some B&W. Always interested in topical photos covering the commercial airline scene, including business jets – new aircraft being rolled out, new liveries, new airlines, airport developments, etc. International coverage. Some archive material used; send stock lists.
Text: Will consider ideas for articles on any civil aviation theme, around 2,000 words. Contributors must have in-depth knowledge of their subject.
Overall freelance potential: Excellent.
Fees: Pictures from £20; text £50 per 1,000 words.

AIRPORT WORLD
Insight Media Ltd, Sovereign House, 26-30 London Road, Twickenham TW1 3RW.
Tel: 020 8831 7507. Fax: 020 8891 0123. E-mail: joe@airport-world.com
Editor: Joe Bates.
Bi-monthly trade journal published for the Airports Council International, circulated to airport operators worldwide.
Illustrations: Recent photographs taken in airports and airport terminals in any part of the world – must be high quality pictures with a creative approach. Before submitting photographers should first send details of airports they have on file.
Text: No scope.
Overall freelance potential: Fair.
Fees: By negotiation.

AIRPORTS INTERNATIONAL
Key Publishing Ltd, PO Box 100, Stamford, Lincs PE9 1XQ.
Tel: 01780 755131. Fax: 01780 757261. E-mail: tom.allett@keypublishing.com
Editor: Tom Allett.
Published nine times a year, dealing with all aspects of airport construction, management, operations, services and equipment worldwide.
Illustrations: Photographs related to airport operational affairs. Particularly interested in high quality images for cover use, and coverage of "exotic" overseas locations. Always contact the editor before submitting.
Text: Possible scope for overseas material, depending on region; Middle East, Asia-Pacific, South America and Africa of particular interest.
Overall freelance potential: Fair.
Fees: By negotiation.

AVIATION NEWS

HPC Publishing, Drury Lane, St Leonards on Sea, East Sussex TN38 9BJ.
Tel: 01424 720477. Fax: 01424 443693. ISDN: 01424 721727. E-mail:editor@aviation-news.co.uk
Editor: David Baker.
Monthly magazine covering aviation in general, both past and present. Aimed at both the industry and the enthusiast.
Illustrations: Colour; B&W archive material. Photographs of all types of aircraft, civil and military, old or new. Captioned news pictures of particular interest, but no space exploration or aircraft engineering.
Text: News items about current aviation matters. Historical contributions concerning older aircraft.
Overall freelance potential: About 45 per cent is contributed by freelances.
Fees: On a rising scale according to size of reproduction or length of text.

DEFENCE HELICOPTER

The Shephard Press Ltd, 111 High Street, Burnham, Bucks SL1 7JZ.
Tel: 01628 606965. Fax: 01628 669808. E-mail: ad@shephard.co.uk
Editor: Andrew Drwiega.
Bi-monthly publication concerned with military and public service helicopters.
Illustrations: Pictures of military and public service (police, coastguard, etc) helicopters anywhere in the world. Must be accurately captioned. Covers: high quality pictures of appropriate helicopters. Should preferably be exclusive and in upright format. No "sterile" pictures; must be action shots.
Text: News stories and features on helicopters in service use and helicopter technology. Up to 1,500 words.
Overall freelance potential: Moderate.
Fees: By negotiation.

FLIGHT INTERNATIONAL

Reed Business Information Ltd, Quadrant House, The Quadrant, Sutton, Surrey SM2 5AS.
Tel: 020 8652 3842. Fax: 020 8652 3840.
Editor: Murdo Morrison. **Group Art Editor:** James Mason.
Weekly aviation magazine with worldwide circulation, aimed at aerospace professionals in all sectors of the industry.
Illustrations: Mostly colour; digital only by prior arrangement. Weekly requirement for news pictures of aviation-related events. Feature illustrations on all aspects of aerospace, from airliners to satellites. Covers: clean, uncluttered pictures of aircraft – civil and military, light and business. Medium format preferred.
Text: News items always welcomed. Features by prior arrangement only; submit ideas in the first instance.
Overall freelance potential: Limited for those without contacts in the industry.
Editor's tips: News material should be submitted on spec. Pictures should always be as new as possible or have a news relevance.
Fees: B&W, £19.61; colour, £56.38 up to 30 sq.in., £65.93 to £106.93 30–60 sq. in.; £223.30 for cover. News reports, minimum £7.07 per 100 words; commissioned features by negotiation.

FLYER

Seager Publishing Ltd, 9 Riverside Court, Lower Bristol Road, Bath BA2 3DZ.
Tel: 01225 481440. Fax: 01225 481262. E-mail: philip@flyermag.co.uk
Editor: Philip Whiteman.
Monthly magazine for private pilots.
Illustrations: Digital files preferred. Attractive and striking photographs of light aircraft of the type commonly used by the private pilot. Details of material available should be sent first, rather than speculative submissions.
Text: News items and illustrated articles from those with proper knowledge of the subject.

Overall freelance potential: Limited – mainly provided by established contributors.
Editor's tips: All contributors should have a genuine understanding of the flying scene.
Fees: By negotiation.

FLYPAST
Key Publishing Ltd, PO Box 100, Stamford, Lincs PE9 1XQ.
Tel: 01780 755131. Fax: 10780 757261. E-mail: flypast@keypublishing.com
Editor: Ken Ellis.
Monthly magazine devoted to aviation heritage.
Illustrations: Mostly colour. Digital files preferred. Photographs of interesting old aircraft or aircraft collections from anywhere in the world, but always contact the editor before submitting.
Text: Articles on collections, museums, aircraft operators and personal accounts of past flying experiences.
Overall freelance potential: Good for those with access to suitable material.
Fees: £20 for colour; £10 B&W. Text £50 per 1,000 words.

GO FLYING!
Archant Specialist, The Mill, Bearwalden Business Park, Wendens Ambo, Essex CB11 4GB.
Tel: 01799 544200. Fax: 01799 544201. E-mail: stephen.bridgewater@archant.co.uk
Editor: Stephen Bridgewater.
Picture-led magazine aimed at all pilots of light aircraft, both amateur and professional, but especially at those still at the learning and training stage. Distributed free at airfields, flying clubs and schools, as well as being sent direct to aircraft owners.
Illustrations: Always interested in striking images and unusual news pictures featuring flying, pilots and light aircraft. Especially seeking spectacular images or different and unusual angles.
Text: Will always consider illustrated news items, features and profiles likely to be of interest to the readership.
Overall freelance potential: Very good for those with access to the flying scene.
Fees: by negotiation.

PILOT
Archant Specialist, The Mill, Bearwalden Business Park, Wendens Ambo, Essex CB11 4GB.
Tel: 01799 544200. Fax: 01799 544201. E-mail: nick.bloom@pilotweb.co.uk
Editor: Nick Bloom.
Monthly publication for the general aviation (i.e. business and private flying) pilot.
Illustrations: Digital files preferred. Pictures on topics associated with this field of flying.
Text: Features, preferably illustrated, on general aviation. 2,000–4,000 words.
Overall freelance potential: Excellent. Virtually all of the editorial matter in the magazine is contributed by freelances.
Editor's tips: Read a copy of the magazine before submitting and study style, content, subject and coverage.
Fees: £150–£800 for features. Pictures inside £30; covers £250.

TODAY'S PILOT
Key Publishing Ltd, PO Box 100, Stamford, Lincs PE9 1XQ.
Tel: 01780 755131. Fax: 01780 757261.E-mail: dave.unwin@keypublishing.com
Editor: David Unwin.
Monthly aimed at both private and commercial pilots, those learning to fly, and general

---

Are you working from the latest edition of The Freelance Photographer's Market Handbook? It's published on 1 October each year. Markets are constantly changing, so it pays to have the latest edition

aviation enthusiasts.
Illustrations: Digital files preferred. Will consider any news-based or unusual photographs likely to be of interest to the readership.
Text: Always interested in well-illustrated, authoritative articles on any aspect of private or commercial flying, ranging from travelogues to technical pieces. Submit suggestions only in the first instance
Overall freelance potential: Good scope for illustrated articles.
Fees: By negotiation.

Boating & Watersport

BOARDS
Yachting Press Ltd, 196 Eastern Esplanade, Southend-on-Sea, Essex SS1 3AB.
Tel: 01702 582245. Fax: 01702 588434. E-mail: editorial@boards.co.uk
Editor: Bill Dawes.
Monthly magazine devoted to boardsailing and windsurfing.
Illustrations: Good clear action shots of boardsailing or windsurfing; pictures of attractive girls in a boardsailing context; any other visually striking material relating to the sport. Covers: good colour action shots always needed.
Text: Articles and features on all aspects of the sport.
Overall freelance potential: Very good for high quality material.
Editor's tips: Action shots must be clean, clear and crisp.
Fees: By negotiation.

BOAT INTERNATIONAL
Edisea Ltd, Ward House, 5–7 Kingston Hill, Kingston upon Thames, Surrey KT2 7PW.
Tel: 020 8547 2662. Fax: 020 8547 9731. E-mail: amandam@boatinternational.co.uk
Editor: Amanda McCracken.
Monthly glossy magazine focusing on the top, luxury level of sailing and power vessels.
Illustrations: Digital files or transparencies. Will consider images of world class yacht racing and luxury cruising.
Text: Mostly staff produced or commissioned from top writers in the field.
Overall freelance potential: Excellent for the best in boating photography and marine subjects.
Editor's tips: Only the very best quality is of interest.
Fees: By negotiation.

BOATING BUSINESS
Mercator Media Ltd, The Old Mill, Lower Quay, Fareham, Hants PO16 0RA.
Tel: 01329 825335. Fax: 01329 825220. E-mail: editor@boatingbusiness.com
Editor: Peter Nash.
Monthly magazine for the leisure marine trade.
Illustrations: News pictures relating to the marine trade, especially company and overseas news. Some scope for commissioned work.
Text: Features on marine trade topics; always consult the editor first.
Overall freelance potential: Limited.
Fees: Photographs from £20; text £100 per 1,000 words.

CANAL BOAT & INLAND WATERWAYS
Archant Specialist Publishing, The Mill, Bearwalden Business Park, Wendens Ambo, Essex CB11 4GB.
Tel: 01799 544200. Fax: 01799 544201. E-mail: editorial@canalboatmag.co.uk
Editor: Kevin Blick.

Monthly specialist title covering inland boating especially on canals, looking at boats, boat ownership and cruising.
Illustrations: Digital files preferred. Photographs depicting colourful boats, attractive waterways, scenery and seasonal elements, but mainly published as part of an illustrated article.
Text: Good opportunities for illustrated features on canal boats and boating personalities.
Overall freelance potential: Good opportunities for good freelance photojournalists.
Editor's tips: Good ideas will be enthusiatically received, but study the magazine before making contact.
Fees: According to use of material.

CANALS & RIVERS

A E Morgan Publications Ltd. Editorial: PO Box 618, Norwich NR7 0QT.
Tel: 01603 708930. E-mail: chris@themag.fsnet.co.uk
Editor: Chris Cattrall.
Monthly publication aimed at inland waterway enthusiasts and canal holidaymakers.
Illustrations: Digital files preferred. Photographs of all inland waterway subjects. Covers: colour pictures of attractive waterways subjects, preferably with an original approach.
Text: Illustrated articles on canals, rivers, boats and allied subjects.
Overall freelance potential: Good, especially for material with an original approach.
Fees: By negotiation.

CLASSIC BOAT

IPC Country & Leisure Group, Leon House, 233 High Street, Croydon CR9 1HZ.
Tel: 020 8726 8000. Fax: 020 8774 0943. E-mail: cb@ipcmedia.com
Editor: Dan Houston. **Art Editor:** Peter Smith.
Monthly magazine for the enthusiast interested in traditional or traditional-style boats from any part of the world. Emphasis on sailing boats, but also covers traditional power boats, steam vessels and modern reproductions of classic styles.
Illustrations: Digital files accepted, but transparencies preferred. Pictures to accompany features and articles. Single general interest pictures with 100 word captions giving full subject details. Particular interest in individual boat photo essays. Covers: spectacular sailing images, but exceptional boat building shots may be used. Upright format with space for logo and coverlines.
Text: Well-illustrated articles covering particular types of boat and individual craft, combining well-researched historical background with hard practical advice about restoration and maintenance. Some scope for humorous pieces and cruising articles involving classic boats. Always send a detailed synopsis in the first instance.
Overall freelance potential: Good for those with specialist knowledge or access.
Editor's tips: Well-documented and photographed practical articles do best. Contributors' notes available on request, or see website www.classicboat.com.
Fees: £90-£100 per page pro rata; covers £200.

INTERNATIONAL BOAT INDUSTRY

IPC Country & Leisure Media Ltd, Leon House, 233 High Street, Croydon CR9 1HZ.
Tel: 020 8726 8134. Fax: 020 8726 8196. E-mail: ed_slack@ipcmedia.com
Editor: Ed Slack.
Business publication dealing with the marine leisure industry worldwide. Eight issues a year.
Illustrations: Pictures of boat building and moulding, chandlery shops, showrooms, new boats and equipment. Also marinas.
Text: News items about the boat industry are always of interest.
Overall freelance potential: Good for those in touch with the boat trade.
Editor's tips: This is strictly a trade magazine – general pictures of cruising or racing are not required.
Fees: Linear scale – £100 per page down.

JET SKIER & PW

CSL Publishing Ltd, Alliance House, 49 Sydney Street, Cambridge CB2 3JF.
Tel: 01223 460490. Fax: 01223 315960. E-mail: spicer@jetskier.co.uk
Editor: Tim Spicer.
Monthly magazine devoted to small, powered water craft and related sports activity. Features jet skis, wetbikes and other personal watercraft.
Illustrations: Spectacular action shots and pictures of unusual individual craft and uses. Events coverage usually by commission.
Text: Some scope for illustrated articles from those with good knowledge of the subject. Submit ideas only in the first instance.
Overall freelance potential: Good.
Fees: By negotiation.

MOTOR BOAT & YACHTING

IPC Media Ltd, Blue Fin Building, 110 Southwark Street, London SE1 0SU.
Tel: 020 3148 4651. Fax: 020 3148 8128. E-mail: mby@ipcmedia.com
Editor: Hugo Andreae. **Art Editor:** Caroline Creighton-Metcalf.
Monthly magazine for owners and users of motor cruisers.
Illustrations: Digital files preferred. Pictures of motor cruisers at sea, harbour scenes, workboats. Covers: Pictures of people having fun on motor boats at sea. Also good harbour scenes, showing exceptional composition and/or lighting.
Text: Features on interesting, unusual or historic motor boats; first-person motor boat cruising accounts; technical motor boating topics. 1,500–2,500 words.
Overall freelance potential: Around 40 per cent of features and 20 per cent of pictures are freelance contributed.
Fees: Good; on a rising scale according to size of reproduction or length of article.

MOTOR BOATS MONTHLY

IPC Inspire, Blue Fin Building, 110 Southwark Street, London SE1 0SU.
Tel: 020 3148 4664. Fax: 020 3148 8128. E-mail: mbm@ipc.co.uk
Editor: Carl Richardson. **News Editor:** Stewart Campbell.
Monthly magazine for all motorboating enthusiasts, but mainly aimed at owners of boats of up to 60 feet. Covers all aspects, from top level powerboat racing to inland waterway cruising.
Illustrations: Digital files preferred. News pictures, motor boat action, and shots of cruising locations, both in UK and overseas.
Text: Illustrated articles on any motorboat-related topic, UK and worldwide.
Overall freelance potential: Fairly good.
Fees: On a rising scale according to size of reproduction or length of text.

PRACTICAL BOAT OWNER

IPC Magazines Ltd, Westover House, West Quay Road, Poole, Dorset BH15 1JG.
Tel: 01202 440820. Fax: 01202 440860. E-mail: pbo@ipcmedia.com
Editor: Sarah Norbury. **Art Editor:** Kevin Slater.
Monthly magazine for yachtsmen, sail and power.
Illustrations: Digital files preferrred. Up to date pictures of boats, harbours and anchorages. Covers: Action shots of cruising boats up to about 40ft (preferably sail) showing people enjoying themselves. Must have strong colours.
Text: Features and associated illustrations of real use to the people who own boats. Subjects can cover any aspect of boating, from buying a boat through to navigation, seamanship, care and maintenance.
Overall freelance potential: About 75 per cent bought from contributors.
Fees: On a rising scale according to size of reproduction or length of feature.

RYA MAGAZINE
Royal Yachting Association, RYA House, Ensign Way, Hamble, Southampton SO31 4YA.
Tel: 0845 3450400. E-mail: deborah.cornick@rya.org.uk
Editor: Deborah Cornick.
Quarterly publication for personal members of the RYA, affiliated clubs and class associations.
Illustrations: Digital files preferred. Pictures of boats, yachting events and personalities, used either in their own right or as illustrations for reports and articles. Covers: seasonal/topical shots of yachting subjects.
Text: Reports and articles on yachting.
Overall freelance potential: Moderate.
Fees: By arrangement.

ROWING & REGATTA
Amateur Rowing Association, 6 Lower Mall, London W6 9DJ.
Tel: 0870 060 7100. Fax: 0870 060 7101. E-mail: sarah.chapman@ara-rowing.org
Editor: Sarah Chapman.
Covers rowing and sculling – competitive, recreational and technical. 10 editions annually.
Illustrations: Digital files preferred. Any coverage of the subject considered, especially action pictures of rowing and rowing in scenic settings.
Text: Short, illustrated articles on all aspects of rowing. Technical topics such as coaching, training and boat-building.
Overall freelance potential: Good.
Fees: By arrangement with editor.

SAILING TODAY
Madforsport Ltd, Swanwick Marina, Lower Swanwick, Southampton SO31 1ZL.
Tel: 01489 585225. Fax: 01489 565054. E-mail: stewart.wheeler@sailingtoday.co.uk
Editor: Duncan Kent. **Art Editor:** Stewart Wheeler.
Practical monthly for active sail cruising enthusiasts.
Illustrations: Digital files preferred. Dynamic action shots of people involved in active sailing situations. Ideally compositions should be closely cropped in to focus on the sailor(s) involved, who should be clearly enjoying themselves. Scope for location photo shoots and step-by-step boat improvement projects.
Text: Well-illustrated features on boat improvements and cruising round the British Isles. Should have a modern, upbeat and original approach.
Overall freelance potential: Good.
Fees: By negotiation.

SPORTSBOAT & RIB MAGAZINE
CSL Publishing Ltd, Alliance House, 49 Sydney Street, Cambridge CB2 3HX.
Tel: 01223 460490. Fax: 01223 315960. E-mail: editor@sportsboat.co.uk
Editor: Alex Smith.
Monthly publication covering sports boats from 14–50 feet.
Illustrations: Digital files preferred. Top quality action shots of small sports boats. Also stylish pictures that show boats as glamorous and exciting. Commissions may be available to illustrate major features. Covers: colour action shots with plenty of impact.
Text: Illustrated articles on all aspects of sports boats and waterskiing will always be considered. 500–3,000 words.
Overall freelance potential: Excellent.
Fees: By negotiation.

TRADITIONAL BOATS & TALL SHIPS
Poundbury Publishing Ltd, Middle Farm, Middle Farm Way, Poundbury, Dorchester DT1 3RS.
Tel: 01305 266360. Fax: 01305 262760. E-mail: tallships@poundbury.co.uk
Editor: Stephen Swann.
Bi-monthly for enthusiasts of traditional sailing boats, with an emphasis on tall ships and other larger sea-going vessels.
Illustrations: Mainly colour; archive B&W. Digital files preferred, prints acceptable. Always interested in striking photographs of traditional vessels under full sail. Must have excellent definition, light and colour for often large-scale reproduction. Detailed captions also essential.
Text: Well-illustrated articles on traditional sailboats, including restoration projects and historical features.
Overall freelance potential: Excellent; the magazine relies on freelance contributors.
Editor's tips: Pictures that come with a story or interesting context stand the best chance of being used.
Fees: From £20–£90 depending on size of reproduction.

WATER CRAFT
Pete Greenfield Publishing, Bridge Shop, Gweek, Helston, Cornwall TR12 6UD.
Tel: 01326 221424. Fax: 01326 221728. E-mail: ed@watercraft-magazine.com
Editor: Pete Greenfield.
Bi-monthly magazine devoted to traditional small boats and boat building.
Illustrations: Photographs mainly required as part of complete feature packages, but interesting or unusual singles and sequences considered if accompanied by detailed caption information.
Text: Well-illustrated features on suitable subjects
Overall freelance potential: Limited at present; much is produced by regular contributors.
Fees: Around £60 per published page inclusive of pictures.

WATERWAYS WORLD
Waterways World Ltd, 151 Station Street, Burton-on-Trent DE14 1BG.
Tel: 01283 742952. Fax: 01283 742957. E-mail: richard.fairhurst@wwonline.co.uk
Editor: Richard Fairhurst.
Monthly magazine that covers all aspects of canal and river navigations (not lakes) in Britain and abroad. Aimed at inland waterway enthusiasts and holiday boaters.
Illustrations: No scope for stand-alone pictures except for cover use. Covers: colourful canal or river scenes with boating activity prominently in the foreground; medium format transparencies preferred.
Text: Well-illustrated features on inland waterways, 500–2,000 words. Send s.a.e. or e-mail for contributors' guide.
Overall freelance potential: Around 20 per cent freelance contributed.
Fees: Covers £75.

WINDSURF MAGAZINE
Arcwind Ltd, The Blue Barns, Tew Lane, Wootton, Woodstock, Oxon OX20 1HA.
Tel: 01993 811181. Fax: 01993 811481. E-mail: mark@windsurf.co.uk
Editor: Mark Kasprowicz. **Features Editor:** Chris Addison.
Published ten times a year. Aimed at the enthusiast and covering all aspects of windsurfing.
Illustrations: Sequences and singles of windsurfing action. Top quality shots always considered.
Text: Illustrated articles on any aspect of windsurfing.
Overall freelance potential: Excellent.
Fees: £5–£15 for B&W; up to £35 for full-page colour; £60 for centre-spread; £60 for covers.

YACHTING MONTHLY
IPC Media Ltd, Blue Fin Building, 110 Southwark Street, London SE1 0SU.
Tel: 020 3148 4872. Fax: 020 3148 8128. E-mail: holly_ramsay@ipcmedia.com
Editor: Paul Gelder. **Features Editor:** Dick Durham. **Art Editor:** Holly Ramsay.
Monthly magazine for cruising yachtsmen.
Illustrations: Colour. News pictures considered for immediate use; location pictures for stock;
pictures illustrating seamanship, navigation and technical subjects to illustrate features. Top
quality images also considered for regular "Opening Shot" double-page spread and for covers (people
working boats at sea; cruising boats at sea; yachts in harbour).
Text: Articles relevant to cruising yachtsmen, and short accounts of cruising experiences.
1,000–2,250 words. Submit synopsis to features editor in the first instance.
Overall freelance potential: Around 40 per cent comes from outside contributors, but most are
experienced specialists.
Fees: Dependent upon size of reproduction or length of feature. Normally around £50–£110 for
colour; £200 for covers. Text from £75 per 1,000 words.

YACHTING WORLD
IPC Media Ltd, Blue Fin Building, 110 Southwark Street, London SE1 0SU.
Tel: 020 3148 4835. Fax: 020 3148 8128. E-mail: ywpictures@ipcmedia.com
Editor: Andrew Bray. **Picture Editor:** Vanda Woolsey.
Monthly magazine for informed yachtsmen.
Illustrations: Digital files only. Pictures of general yachting techniques or types of boat; pictures of
events and occasions; location shots and mood pictures. Major feature photography commissioned
from known specialists. Covers: top quality pictures of yachts in 35ft+ range – action pictures on
board, at sea.
Text: Informative or narrative yachting articles; technical yachting features; short humorous
articles; and news. 1,000–1,500 words and 2,000–2,500 words. Send for writers' guidelines.
Overall freelance potential: Around 30 per cent comes from freelances.
Editor's tips: Contributors must know the subject and know the market. The most successful
photographers we use are the ones who work the hardest.
Fees: Inside pictures according to size, from £37–£280 (dps), covers £585. Text up to £148 per 1,000
words.

YACHTS & YACHTING
Yachting Press Ltd, 196 Eastern Esplanade, Southend-on-Sea, Essex SS1 3AB.
Tel: 01702 582245. Fax: 01702 588434. E-mail: photos@yachtsandyachting.com
Editor: Gael Pawson.
Fortnightly publication covering all aspects of racing, including dinghies and offshore racers.
Illustrations: Pictures of racing dinghies, yachts and general sailing scenes. Covers: colour action
shots of relevant subjects.
Text: Features on all aspects of the race sailing scene. 1,000–2,000 words.
Overall freelance potential: Quite good.
Fees: Negotiable.

Business

ACCOUNTANCY AGE
VNU Business Publications, 32–34 Broadwick Street, London W1A 2HG.
Tel: 020 7316 9000. Fax: 020 7316 9250. E-mail: accountancy_age@vnu.co.uk
Editor: Damien Wild.
Weekly publication for qualified accountants.
Illustrations: All commissioned, but new photographers are always welcome.

Text: News and features coverage for accountants. Synopsis preferred in first instance. 1,200 words.
Overall freelance potential: Fairly good for commissioned photography. About 50 per cent of the features come from freelances.
Editor's tips: To gain acceptance, articles must contribute something which cannot be provided by the in-house staff.
Fees: By agreement.

CA MAGAZINE
Connect Communications Ltd, Studio 2001, Mile End, Paisley PA1 1JS.
Tel: 0141 560 3045. Fax: 0141 501 0400. E-mail: camag@connectcommunications.co.uk
Editor: Rob Outram. **Art Editor:** John Pender.
Scottish financial and management magazine incorporating monthly journal of The Institute of Chartered Accountants of Scotland.
Illustrations: B&W and colour. Digital files preferred. Creative and innovative images which can be related to the subject and which attract readers' attention.
Text: Articles on accounting and auditing, company law, finance, taxation, management topics, company/personal profiles, the financial and management scene in the UK and overseas, investment, computer science, etc. Length: 1,200–3,000 words.
Overall freelance potential: Fair for business specialists.
Fees: By arrangement.

CNBC EUROPEAN BUSINESS
Future Inc Ltd, 141-143 Shoreditch High Street, London E1 6JE.
Tel: 020 7613 8777. Fax: 020 7613 8776. E-mail: tim.white@ink-publishing.com
Editor: Richard Lofthouse. **Picture Editor:** Tim White.
London-based business monthly offering an entirely European perspective on business in Europe. Allied with CNBC Europe, the only pan-European television network devoted to financial and business news.
Illustrations: European-based business images, but mainly people-oriented, focusing on the individuals behind businesses rather than the companies themselves. Some stock material used but prefer not to use standard "grey suit" business imagery. Photographers available for shoots overseas should contact picture editor in the first instance.
Text: Will consider relevant articles from those who know about business and can write in a lively style. Articles are kept fairly short and have to be written so that they are easy to comprehend for non-native English speakers. Contact the editor with details of experience in the first instance.
Overall freelance potential: Good, especially for freelances based on or regularly visiting the Continent.
Editor's tips: Try to get away from "grey suits" and show business people in a more original and stimulating way.
Fees: By negotiation.

DIRECTOR
Director Publications Ltd, 116 Pall Mall, London SW1Y 5ED.
Tel: 020 7766 8950. Fax: 020 7766 8840. E-mail: director-ed@iod.co.uk
Editor: Joanna Higgins. **Picture Editor:** Jane Moss.
Monthly journal for members of the Institute of Directors.
Illustrations: B&W and colour. Top quality portraits of company chairmen or major business personalities. Covers: portraits as above or top quality business/industry subjects. More creative, avant-garde illustrations also used.
Text: Interviews; management advice; company profiles; business controversies; EC affairs.
Overall freelance potential: Good.
Fees: By negotiation.

EN
Entrepreneur Business Publishing, Portland Buildings, 127-129 Portland Street, Manchester M1 4PZ.
Tel: 0161 236 2782. Fax: 0161 236 2783. E-mail: mike.fahy@excelpublishing.co.uk
Editor: Mike Fahy.
Glossy business monthly for entrepreneurs, with separate editions for the North West and Yorkshire regions, aimed at owner-managed companies with turnover between £0.5m–£40m.
Illustrations: Captioned news pictures about developments in private businesses as above. General business/industrial photography by commission, mainly portraiture but some general business/industrial work.
Text: Topical articles of interest to business people in the region – hard-edged, readable, jargon-free. Newsy items only.
Overall freelance potential: Quite good for the freelance with a professional and creative approach.
Editor's tips: Prefer a creative, even off-the-wall, style. Happy to consider newcomers as long as they are thoroughly professional and reliable.
Fees: By negotiation.

FINANCIAL MANAGEMENT
Caspian Publishing Ltd, 198 King's Road, London SW3 5XX.
Tel: 020 7368 7177. Fax: 020 7368 7201. E-mail: rp1@caspianpublishing.co.uk
Editor: Ruth Prickett.
Monthly publication for financial managers. Published for the Chartered Institute of Management Accountants.
Illustrations: B&W and colour. Regular profile photography to accompany business articles.
Text: Occasional freelance market for articles on management/accountancy subjects.
Overall freelance potential: Good.
Fees: By agreement.

MEED (MIDDLE EAST ECONOMIC DIGEST)
EMAP Communications, 151 Rosebery Avenue, London EC1R 4GB.
Tel: 020 7505 6600. Fax: 020 7505 6969. E-mail: gavin.gaughan@meed.com
Editor: Richard Thompson. **Art Director:** Gavin Gaughan.
Weekly business journal covering the affairs of Middle Eastern countries.
Illustrations: Digital files preferred. Pictures of current major construction projects in the Middle East and stock shots of important personalities (politicians, leading businessmen) in the region. Recent general views of particular locations occasionally used. Covers: colour pictures of contemporary Middle East subjects, preferably with an obvious business flavour. Also, high-quality colour abstracts.
Text: Specialist articles on relevant business matters.
Overall freelance potential: Limited.
Fees: On a rising scale according to size of reproduction or length of text.

MARKETING
Haymarket Business Publications Ltd, 174 Hammersmith Road, London W6 7JP.
Tel: 020 8267 4341. Fax: 020 8267 4504. E-mail: craig.smith@haymarket.com
Editor: Craig Smith. **News Editor:** Jeremy Lee.
Weekly publication for marketing management, both client and agency.
Illustrations: Requires only experienced business photographers for commissioned coverage of subjects relating to marketing.
Text: News and features with a marketing angle and objective case histories.
Overall freelance potential: Limited; for business specialists only.
Editor's tips: Photographers must be able to work accurately to a brief.
Fees: Negotiable.

NORTH EAST TIMES
North East Times Ltd, 5-11 Causey Street, Gosforth, Newcastle-upon-Tyne NE3 4DJ.
Tel: 0191 284 9994. Fax: 0191 284 9915. E-mail: info@accentmagazines.co.uk
Editor: Richard Holmes.
Monthly up-market business magazine.
Illustrations: Digital files preferred. Any general interest pictures connected with the North East of England.
Text: Features on business, fashion, property, motoring, wining and dining, sport, etc, all with North East connections. Around 750 words with two pictures.
Overall freelance potential: Fully committed to freelances.
Fees: By agreement.

PEOPLE MANAGEMENT
Personnel Publications Ltd, 17 Britton Street, London EC1M 5TP.
Tel: 020 7880 6200. Fax: 020 7336 7635. E-mail: claire.handley@redactive.co.uk
Editor: Steve Crabb. **Picture Editor:** Claire Handley.
Fortnightly magazine of the Chartered Institute of Personnel and Development. Covers all aspects of staff management and training.
Illustrations: Digital files preferred. Photographs of people at work in business and industry, particularly any depicting staff education and training. Detailed lists of subjects available welcomed. Some commissions may be available to experienced workers.
Text: Ideas for articles always welcome; submit a short written proposal first.
Overall freelance potential: Quite good – a lot of stock pictures are used. Contributions here might also be used in Supply Management, a similar title produced by the same team for the Chartered Institute of Purchasing and Supply.
Fees: By negotiation.

POST MAGAZINE
Incisive Media Plc, Haymarket House, 28-29 Haymarket, London SW1Y 4RX.
Tel: 020 7316 9321. Fax: 020 7484 9992. E-mail: jonathan.swift@incisivemedia.com
Editor: Jonathan Swift. **Art Editor:** Nicky Brown.
Weekly publication covering insurance at home and abroad.
Illustrations: Digital files preferred. Pictures of traffic, houses, offices, building sites, damage (including fire and motoring accidents), shipwrecks or aviation losses, etc. Also political and industry personalities.
Text: News and features on insurance, including general insurance, reinsurance, financial services, investment, marketing, technology, offices and personnel areas.
Overall freelance potential: Most news and features are contributed by freelances.
Fees: By negotiation.

PROMOTIONS & INCENTIVES
Haymarket Marketing Publications Ltd, 174 Hammersmith Road, London W6 7JP.
Tel: 020 8267 4152. Fax: 020 8267 4442. E-mail: bhavna.mistry@haymarket.com
Editor: Bhavna Mistry.
Monthly publication for brand managers, SP managers, incentive managers etc. Concerned with incentive ideas for staff motivation and sales promotion campaigns, aids and general marketing themes.
Illustrations: B&W and colour. Pictures limited to the marketing and/or promotions profession. Covers: highly creative colour pictures, usually linked to the main feature inside.
Text: Authoritatively written articles on technical aspects of the marketing and/or promotions profession. 1,500–2,000 words.
Overall freelance potential: Up to 30 per cent bought from freelances.
Editor's tips: Contact the magazine first.
Fees: Negotiable.

Camping & Caravanning

CAMPING & CARAVANNING
The Camping and Caravanning Club, Greenfields House, Westwood Way, Coventry CV4 8JH.
Tel: 02476 475274. Fax: 02476 475413. E-mail: magazine@campingandcaravanningclub.co.uk
Editor: Nick Harding.
Monthly magazine concerning all aspects of camping and caravanning, exclusive to C&CC members.
Illustrations: Colour. Usually only required in conjunction with feature articles.
Text: Illustrated features on camping and caravanning in Britain, around 1,200 words. Contact the editor with ideas only in the first instance.
Overall freelance potential: Fair.
Fees: By agreement.

CAMPING
Warners Group Publications plc, The Maltings, West Street, Bourne, Lincs PE10 9PH.
Tel: 01778 392442. Fax: 01778 392422. E-mail: cliveg@warnersgroup.co.uk
Editor: Clive Garrett.
Monthly magazine covering all aspects of camping. Emphasises the range of activities that camping makes available.
Illustrations: Digital files preferred. Photographs showing campers engaged in various activities. Also landscapes and tourist attractions to illustrate specific area guides; assignments may be available. Covers: Strong images of campers obviously enjoying themselves on a family or lightweight camping holiday.
Text: Picture-led features that show camping as "a means to an end" and illustrate the range of people and lifestyles that camping embraces, travel features focusing on particular areas in the UK or the Continent. Always check with the editor before submitting.
Overall freelance potential: Excellent.
Editor's tips: Pictures should not be dominated by tents and camping clutter.
Fees: £70 per published page.

CARAVAN
IPC Focus Network, Leon House, 233 High Street, Croydon CR9 1HZ.
Tel: 020 8726 8000. Fax: 020 8726 8299. E-mail: steve_rowe@ipcmedia.com
Editor: Steve Rowe.
Monthly magazine for all caravanners.
Illustrations: Digital files preferred. Occasional need for general illustrations of touring and caravan-related subjects to illustrate features. Send list of subjects and loew-res samples in the first instance. Some opportunities for commissioned work, though in-house photographers handle much of this.
Text: Well-illustrated accounts of touring in specific areas, or more general caravanning-related items with a human interest angle. Call or write with ideas first.
Overall freelance potential: Fair, but most content is supplied by regulars.
Fees: By negotiation.

CARAVAN INDUSTRY
A.E.Morgan Publications Ltd, 8a High Street, Epsom, Surrey KT19 8AD.
Tel: 01372 741411. Fax: 01372 744493. E-mail: teamwork@ukonline.co.uk
Editor: David Ritchie.
Monthly publication for manufacturers, traders, suppliers and park operators in the caravan industry.
Illustrations: Digital files preferred. News pictures of interest to the industry – new caravan park developments, new models, new dealer depots, etc.
Text: Company profiles on park owners and their businesses, traders and manufacturers. 900–1,200 words.

Overall freelance potential: Up to 30 per cent of the content comes from freelance contributors.
Fees: By agreement.

MOTORHOME MONTHLY
Stone Leisure Ltd, Andrew House, 2a Granville Road, Sidcup, Kent DA14 4BN.
Tel: 020 8302 6150/6069 and 020 8300 2316. Fax: 020 8300 2315. E-mail: mhm@stoneleisure.com
Editor: Bob Griffiths.
Monthly magazine about motorhomes and their use. Covers travel, lifestyle, etc.
Illustrations: Digital files preferred. Photographs related to above subjects.
Text: Illustrated features on travel and motorhoming. 500–1,000 words. Also reports on shows or
other relevant events.
Overall freelance potential: Good.
Editor's tips: Preference for copy that requires a minimum of subbing or rewriting.
Fees: Around £50 for illustrated articles.

OUT & ABOUT
Warners Group Publications plc, The Maltings, West Street, Bourne, Lincs PE10 9PH.
Tel: 01778 393313. Fax: 01778 425437. E-mail: valc@warnersgroup.co.uk
Editor: Val Chapman. **Deputy Editor:** Bernard Horton.
Monthly magazine aimed at both caravan and motorhome enthusiasts, based around aspects of
touring.
Illustrations: Pictures only required to illustrate feature packages as below.
Text: Will consider illustrated packages on any relevant topic, such as site reports, routes,
attractions to visit, etc. Features may be quite long and heavily illustrated, ranging from
2,000–4,000 words with 3–4 pictures per page.
Overall freelance potential: Good for the experienced contributor in this field.
Editor's tips: Contributions will be considered on spec, but best to submit an outline and a couple
of sample images in the first instance.
Fees: By negotiation.

PARK HOME & HOLIDAY CARAVAN
IPC Focus Network, Leon House, 233 High Street, Croydon CR9 1HZ.
Tel: 020 8726 8252. Fax: 020 8726 8299. E-mail: em_bartlett@ipcmedia.com
Editor: Emma Bartlett.
Monthly covering residential park homes and caravan holiday homes.
Illustrations: Digital files preferred. Always interested in good photographs of park homes, static
holiday caravans (not touring caravans), residential and holiday parks.
Text: Illustrated features on the above.
Overall freelance potential: Fair.
Fees: According to use.

PRACTICAL CARAVAN
Haymarket Publishing Ltd, 60 Waldegrave Road, Teddington, Middlesex TW11 8LG.
Tel: 020 8267 5629. Fax: 020 8267 5725. E-mail: practical.caravan@haymarket.com
Editor: David Motton. **Art Editor:** Sarah Mountford.
Monthly for caravanning holidaymakers.
Illustrations: Transparencies or digital files. Mostly commissioned to accompany specific features,
but interesting or unusual caravanning images may be considered on spec.
Text: Feature ideas and first-person stories always considered.
Overall freelance potential: Only for those with experience.
Fees: Commissions £250–£350 per day; other material negotiable.

PRACTICAL MOTORHOME
Haymarket Publishing Ltd, Teddington Studios, Broom Road, Teddington, Middlesex TW11 9BE.
Tel: 020 8267 5614. Fax: 020 8267 5725. E-mail: practical.motorhome@haymarket.com
Editor: Carl Rodgerson. **Art Editor:** Martin Gannon.
Monthly for all motorhome holidaymakers and enthusiasts.
Illustrations: Colour. Transparency only; medium format preferred. Mostly commissioned to accompany specific features, but interesting or motorhome images may be considered on spec.
Text: Feature ideas and first-person stories always considered.
Overall freelance potential: Only for those with experience.
Fees: Commissions £250–£350 per day; other material negotiable.

Children & Teenage

GUIDING MAGAZINE
Girlguiding UK, 17-19 Buckingham Palace Road, London SW1W 0PT.
Tel: 020 7834 6242. Fax: 020 7828 5791. E-mail: guiding@girlguiding.org.uk
Editor: Wendy Kewley.
Monthly official magazine of The Guide Association.
Illustrations: Action pictures of girls and young women, indoors and outdoors. Those depicted don't necessarily have to be Guides. E-mail with suggestions in the first instance.
Text: Articles and activity ideas; freelances who feel they could contribute should contact magazine for more information.
Overall freelance potential: Suitable material from freelances always considered.
Fees: By arrangement.

MIZZ
Panini UK, Coach & Horses Passage, The Pantiles, Tunbridge Wells TN2 5UJ.
Tel: 01892 500100. Fax: 01892 545666. E-mail: mizz@panini.co.uk
Editor: Karen Brown. **Picture Researcher:** Kirsty Grant.
Fortnightly magazine aimed at girls in the 10–14 age group.
Illustrations: Digital files preferred. Youth celebrity pictures always of interest (young TV stars, boy/girl bands, etc). Most other photography by commission for specific features, but some scope for stock images that could illustrate "real life" situations encountered by teenage girls. Some scope for single captioned pictures of a humorous nature.
Text: Lively illustrated features on almost any topic that could be of interest to the the target age group. Text should be informative as well as entertaining. A detailed synopsis should always be submitted in the first instance.
Overall freelance potential: Good for the experienced contributor.
Fees: By negotiation.

SCOUTING MAGAZINE
The Scout Association, Gilwell Park Chingford, London E4 7QW.
Tel: 020 8433 7100. Fax: 020 8433 7103. E-mail: scouting.magazine@scout.org.uk
Editors: Chris James, Hilary Galloway, Matt Oakes.
Monthly publication offering practical programme and activity ideas for Scout Groups, plus articles of general interest to members of the Scout Movement as well as those involved in youth work and active lifestyles.
Illustrations: Digital files preferred. Pictures of Scouting activities, preferably action shots. Covers: action and head and shoulder shots of Beaver Scouts, Cub Scouts, Scouts, Explorer Scouts, Scout Network and Scout Fellowship members.
Text: Features on activities, competitions and interesting and unusual news stories suitable for a national readership. All material should be Scouting related or relevant to Scouting.

Overall freelance potential: A high proportion of pictures and text comes from Scout Association members.
Editor's tips: Note that where uniform is used, it should be the correct uniform; new uniforms were introduced from July 2001 and these are preferred in photos. Also, if pictures are of adventurous or hazardous activities, the correct safety rules must be seen to be observed and the correct safety equipment and precautions must be evident.
Fees: By agreement.

SUGAR
Hachette Filipacchi (UK) Ltd, 64 North Row, London W1K 7LL.
Tel: 020 7150 7000. Fax: 020 7150 7001. E-mail: deborah.hughes@hf-uk.com
Editor: Annabel Brog. **Art Director:** Deborah Hughes.
Monthly for teenage girls.
Illustrations: Fashion, beauty, still-life and portraiture, all commissioned for specific features. Some scope for celebrity stock.
Text: No scope.
Overall freelance potential: Only for experienced specialists.
Fees: Basic rate £350 per day.

County & Country

BUCKINGHAMSHIRE COUNTRYSIDE
Beaumonde Publications, PO Box 5, Hitchin, Herts SG5 1GJ.
Tel: 01462 422014. Fax: 01462 422015. E-mail: martin_small@btconnect.com
Editor: Sandra Small.
Bi-monthly county magazine for the named area.
Illustrations: Mostly colour. Transparencies preferred. People, places, and events in the county. Covers: colourful local countryside views.
Text: Topical articles, of a cultural nature, on any aspect of the county.
Overall freelance potential: Limited because much is supplied by regular freelance contributors.
Fees: By negotiation.

CHESHIRE LIFE
Archant Life, 3 Tustin Court, Portway, Preston PR1 8UR.
Tel: 01772 722022. Fax: 01772 760905. E-mail: patrick.o'neill@cheshirelife.co.uk
Editor: Patrick O'Neill.
Monthly up-market county magazine specialising in regional features.
Illustrations: Prints and digital files accepted. Pictures of the Cheshire region, mainly to accompany features on topics such as property, antiques, wildlife, society, arts and crafts, sport. Picture postcard scenes of Cheshire also of interest – landscapes, towns villages, heritage, etc.
Text: Articles and features on regional topics. Always consult the editor in the first instance.
Overall freelance potential: Good.
Fees: By negotiation.

COTSWOLD LIFE
Archant Life, Archant House, 3 Oriel Road, Cheltenham GL50 1BB.
Tel: 01242 216050. Fax: 01242 255116. E-mail: mike.lowe@archant.co.uk
Editor: Mike Lowe.
Monthly showcasing "the best of the Cotswolds".
Illustrations: Pictures of local scenes and events, preferably with some life in them. Covers: Medium format colour of lively local scenes, with clear space at top for title logo.

Text: Illustrated articles of varying lengths, on local people, places, events, etc.
Overall freelance potential: Most material comes from regular freelance contributors but new contributors always considered.
Fees: Cover shots £50. Articles and other illustrations negotiable.

COUNTRY LIFE
IPC Media Ltd, Blue Fin Building, 110 Southwark Street, London SE1 0SU.
Tel: 020 3148 4428. Fax: 020 3148 8129. E-mail: steve_tydeman@ipcmedia.com
Editor: Mark Hedges. **Art Editor:** Steve Tydeman.
Weekly magazine for a general readership.
Illustrations: All formats acceptable. Pictures of British countryside, wildlife, interiors, country pursuits. Covers: Top quality pictures of landscapes, rural and urban.
Text: No scope.
Overall freelance potential: Limited; around 80 per cent of the magazine comes from regular suppliers.
Fees: Good; on a rising scale according to size of reproduction. Covers, £300–350.

COUNTRY QUEST
Cambrian News Ltd, Unit 7, Cefn Illan Scence Park, Aberystwyth SY23 3AH.
Tel: 01970 615000. Fax: 01970 624699. E-mail: julie@cambrian-news.co.uk
Editor: Beverly Davies.
Monthly country and lifestyle magazine for Wales and the border counties.
Illustrations: Print, transparency or digital. Photographs focusing on the history, buildings, people and culture of the region. Eye-catching lifestyle pictures always required for cover use.
Text: Illustrated articles on the above subjects, usually around 1,000 words.
Overall freelance potential: Very good; all contributions are freelance.
Fees: Variable, depending on what is offered.

COUNTRY WALKING
EMAP Active Ltd, Media House, Lynchwood, Peterborough PE2 6EA.
Tel: 01733 468000. E-mail: jonathan.manning@emap.com
Editor: Jonathan Manning.
Monthly magazine for all walkers who enjoy great days out in the countryside.
Illustrations: Pictures depicting walkers in attractive locations, who must be wearing proper outdoor gear. Also top quality landscapes of suitable parts of the country, historic locations, landscapes with elements of walking interest (eg. stile, path), nature and wildlife. Covers: seasonal pictures of very attractive landscape settings. Medium format preferred.
Text: Well-illustrated articles and features on any walking or countryside topics. Strong emphasis on inspiration and entertainment and capturing the essence of why people walk.
Overall freelance potential: Good, though much is produced by regulars.
Editor's tips: The emphasis is always on getting enjoyment from walking and the countryside.
Fees: By negotiation.

THE COUNTRYMAN
Country Publications Ltd, The Water Mill, Broughton Hall, Skipton, North Yorkshire BD23 3AG.
Tel: 01756 701381. Fax: 01756 701326. E-mail: editorial@thecountryman.co.uk
Editor: Paul Jackson.
Monthly covering all matters of countryside interest other than blood sports.
Illustrations: Mainly colour. Digital files preferred. Sequences of pictures about particular places, crafts, customs, farming practices, kinds of wildlife, etc. Must be accompanied by ample caption material. Only limited scope for single stock pictures, but always seeking high-quality wildlife/countryside images for covers.
Text: Well-illustrated articles of 800–1,200 words, on such subjects as mentioned above. Must be accurate, and usually based on the writer's own experience.

Overall freelance potential: Excellent; almost all photographs, and most articles, are from freelance contributors.
Fees: £30 upwards for photographs inside; £150 for cover. Text according to length and merit.

CUMBRIA
Country Publications Ltd, The Water Mill, Broughton Hall, Skipton, North Yorkshire BD23 3AG.
Tel: 01756 701381. Fax: 01756 701326. E-mail: editorial@dalesman.co.uk
Editor: Terry Fletcher. **Picture Editor:** Kevin Hopkinson.
Monthly countryside magazine for Cumbria and the surrounding area.
Illustrations: Digital files preferred. Attractive shots of local landscapes, rural characters, wildlife, country pursuits and heritage.
Text: Illustrated articles on any aspect of Lakeland country life. 800–1,200 words.
Overall freelance potential: Excellent.
Fees: Half-page £20; full-page £30; covers £100.

DALESMAN
Country Publications Ltd, The Water Mill, Broughton Hall, Skipton, North Yorkshire BD23 3AG.
Tel: 01756 701381. Fax: 01756 701326. E-mail: editorial@dalesman.co.uk
Editor: Terry Fletcher. **Picture Editor:** Mark Whitley.
Monthly countryside magazine for Yorkshire.
Illustrations: Digital files preferred. Attractive shots of local landscapes, local characters, wildlife and heritage.
Text: Illustrated articles on any aspect of Yorkshire life. 800–1,200 words.
Overall freelance potential: Excellent.
Fees: Half-page £20; full-page £30; covers £100.

DEVON TODAY
Westcountry Publications Ltd, Heron Road, Sowton, Exeter EX2 7NF.
Tel: 01392 442211. Fax: 01392 442473. E-mail: devontoday@westcountrypublications.co.uk
Editor: Lynne Turner.
Glossy monthly for the county of Devon.
Illustrations: Images to illustrate features about life in Devon, especially plants and wildlife. Submit only lists of subjects in the first instance.
Text: Illustrated features on lifestyle topics including fitness, health treatments, travel and leisure. Submit ideas and samples of previously published work in the first instance.
Overall freelance potential: Limited for pictures as the magazine has a regular photographer.
Fees: By negotiation.

DORSET
Archant Life, 3a Poundbury Business Centre, Poundbury, Dorchester DT1 3WE.
Tel: 01305 211840. Fax: 01305 211841. E-mail: bridget.swann@archant.co.uk
Editor: Bridget Swann.
Monthly for people who like to explore the Dorset region.
Illustrations: Digital files preferred. Good stock photographs of the region: people, places, landscapes, natural history, culture and heritage.
Text: Local news and illustrated articles on subjects as above, around 1,200 words.
Overall freelance potential: Good.
Fees: Pictures from £25–£45; text £100 per 1,000 words.

As a member of the Bureau of Freelance Photographers, you'll be kept up-to-date with markets through the BFP Market Newsletter, published monthly. For details of membership, turn to page 9

DORSET LIFE
Dorset County Magazines Ltd, 7 The Leanne, Sandford Lane, Wareham, Dorset BH20 4BY.
Tel: 01929 551264. Fax: 01929 552099. E-mail:office@dorsetlife.co.uk
Editor: John Newth.
Monthly magazine for the Dorset area.
Illustrations: Interesting and original photographs of the region, but usually required as part of an article, not in isolation. Covers: Attractive local scenes, suitable for upright reproduction. Must be original.
Text: Well-illustrated articles on any topic relating to Dorset, around 1,000 words.
Overall freelance potential: Most contributions come from regular freelance contributors but new contributors always considered.
Fees: According to size of reproduction and length of text.

THE FIELD
IPC Media Ltd, Blue Fin Building, 110 Southwark Street, London SE1 0SU.
Tel: 020 3148 4777. Fax: 020 3148 8179. E-mail: rebecca_hawtrey@ipcmedia.com
Editor: Jonathan Young. **Art Editor:** Rebecca Hawtrey.
Monthly publication concerned with all rural and country sports interests.
Illustrations: Digital files required. Good pictures illustrating relevant topics as below. Most used for article illustration but good single pictures always considered for cover use. Commissions available to specialists.
Text: Illustrated features on country and country sporting subjects, especially shooting, fly-fishing, working dogs (gundogs, terriers). Length according to article, in the range 1,000–2,000 words.
Overall freelance potential: Around 80 per cent comes from outside contributors, many of whom are specialists, but opportunities are good for the right material.
Fees: According to merit.

HERTFORDSHIRE COUNTRYSIDE
Beaumonde Publications, PO Box 5, Hitchin, Herts SG5 1GJ.
Tel: 01462 422014. Fax: 01462 422015. E-mail: martin_small@btconnect.com
Editor: Sandra Small.
Monthly county magazine for the named area.
Illustrations: B&W and colour. Transparencies/prints preferred. People, places, and events in the county. Covers: colourful local countryside views.
Text: Topical articles, of a cultural nature, on any aspect of the county.
Overall freelance potential: Limited because much is supplied by regular freelance contributors.
Fees: By negotiation.

LAKE DISTRICT LIFE
Archant Life, 3 Tustin Court, Port Way, Preston PR2 2YQ.
Tel: 01772 722022. Fax: 01772 760905. E-mail: roger.borrell@lakedistrict-life.co.uk
Editor: Roger Borrell.
Monthly up-market county magazine covering contemporary life as well as past heritage.
Illustrations: Digital files preferred. Pictures of the Lake District, mainly to accompany town and village features, society events and the local environment. Pictures of nationally known personalities with a Lake District connection. Covers: top quality regional scenes.
Text: Articles and features on regional topics, both contemporary and nostalgic. Always consult the editor in the first instance.
Overall freelance potential: Good for the right material.
Editor's tips: Unlikely to be interested unless there is a definite regional angle.
Fees: By negotiation.

LANCASHIRE LIFE
Archant Life, 3 Tustin Court, Port Way, Preston PR2 2YQ.
Tel: 01772 722022. Fax: 01772 736496. E-mail: roger.borrell@lancashirelife.co.uk
Editor: Roger Borrell.
Monthly up-market county magazine specialising in regional features.
Illustrations: Digital files preferred. Pictures of the Lancashire region, mainly to accompany features. Pictures of nationally known personalities with a Lancashire connection. Covers: top quality regional scenes.
Text: Articles and features on regional topics. Always consult the editor in the first instance.
Overall freelance potential: Good; around 40 per cent is from freelance sources.
Editor's tips: Unlikely to be interested unless there is a definite Lancashire angle.
Fees: By negotiation.

LINCOLNSHIRE LIFE
County Life Ltd, County House, 9 Checkpoint Court, Sadler Road, Lincoln LN6 3PW.
Tel: 01522 527127. Fax: 01522 842000. E-mail: editorial@lincolnshirelife.co.uk
Editor: Josie Thurston.
Monthly magazine, dealing with county life past and present from the Humber to the Wash.
Illustrations: B&W and colour. Digital files preferred. Pictures of people and places within the county of Lincolnshire Covers: portrait format colour pictures of local landscapes, architecture, people, street scenes, etc. Submissions for annual calendar also accepted.
Text: Features on people and places within the appropriate area. No more than 1,600 words. Contact editor first to discuss.
Overall freelance potential: Fifty per cent of the magazine comes from freelance sources.
Fees: £50 for covers, other material by agreement.

THE SCOTS MAGAZINE
D. C. Thomson and Co. Ltd, 2 Albert Square, Dundee DD1 9QJ.
Tel: 01382 223131. Fax: 01382 322214. E-mail: mail@scotsmagazine.com
Editor: John Methven. **Picture Editor:** Ian Neilson.
Monthly magazine for Scots at home and abroad, concerned with Scottish subjects.
Illustrations: Digital files preferred. Scottish scenes, but avoid the obvious. Non-Highland subjects particularly welcome. Scenics with one or more figures preferred to "empty pictures". Ongoing requirement for good vertical scenes for possible front cover use.
Text: Features on all aspects of Scottish life past and present. 1,500–2,500 words.
Overall freelance potential: Around 80 per cent of the magazine comes from freelances.
Editor's tips: Do not cover sport, politics, household, beauty or fashion.
Fees: Variable.

SCOTTISH FIELD
Craigcrook Castle, Craigcrook Road, Edinburgh EH4 3PE.
Tel: 0131 312 4550. Fax: 0131 312 4551. E-mail: editor@scottishfield.co.uk
Editor: Archie Mackenzie.
Monthly magazine reflecting the quality of life in Scotland today for Scots at home and abroad.
Illustrations: Varied subjects of Scottish interest; must be accompanied by appropriate text.
Text: Illustrated features with a Scottish dimension. 850–1,200 words. Submit only ideas initially, rather than completed articles.
Overall freelance potential: There are only limited openings for new contributors.
Editor's tips: Market study is essential.
Fees: Negotiable.

SOMERSET LIFE
Archant Life, Archant House, Babbage Road, Totnes, Devon TQ9 5JA.
Tel: 01803 860914. Fax: 01803 860926. E-mail: nicki.lukehurst@archant.co.uk
Editor: Nicki Lukehurst.
Monthly magazine for Somerset and Bristol area.
Illustrations: Mainly colour. Interesting and original photographs of the area, usually only required as part of a words and pictures package. Covers: always on the lookout for portrait-format shots that will carry the title and coverlines, preferably seasonal pictures of recognisable Somerset scenes.
Text: Well-illustrated articles on any topic relating to Somerset, around 1,000 words.
Overall freelance potential: Keen to find new contributoros with photographic skills.
Fees: £75 for illlustrated articles; cover pictures by arrangement.

SUSSEX LIFE
Sussex Life Ltd, Baskerville Place, 28 Teville Road, Worthing, West Sussex BN11 1UG.
Tel: 01903 604208. Fax: 01903 820193. E-mail: jonathan.keeble@sussexlife.co.uk
Editor: Jonathan Keeble.
Monthly county magazine.
Illustrations: Digital files preferred. Stock photographs always welcomed, but complete illustrated articles are preferred. Covers: medium format transparencies of Sussex scenes, usually depicting landscapes, but houses, activities, interiors and personalities from Sussex also welcome.
Text: Well illustrated features on any topic relevant to the county. 1,000–2,000 words.
Overall freelance potential: Quite good.
Fees: 1,000-word article plus pics, £150.

TGO – THE GREAT OUTDOORS
Newsquest Magazines, 200 Renfield Street, Glasgow G2 3PR.
Tel: 0141 302 7700. Fax: 0141 302 7799. E-mail: cameron.mcneish@tgomagazine.co.uk
Editor: Cameron McNeish.
Monthly magazine for walkers in the UK. Covers hill and mountain walking, and related topics.
Illustrations: Digital files preferred. Material required for stock – mostly landscapes featuring walkers; no towns or churches. Plus pictures to illustrate features. Covers: colour pictures in upright format considered independently of internal content. Photographs of walkers, backpackers and fell walkers in landscape settings. Must be contemporary, well-equipped people in photos; action shots preferred.
Text: Features on the subjects mentioned above. 2,000 words.
Overall freelance potential: Most of the magazine comes from freelance sources.
Editor's tips: Too many freelances send material which is outside the scope of the magazine – not interested in low level rambling. Send e-mail for guidelines.
Fees: Articles, £150–£450 depending on length and number of illustrations; covers, around £200.

THIS ENGLAND
This England International Ltd, PO Box 52, Cheltenham, Gloucestershire GL50 1YQ.
Tel: 01242 537900. Fax: 01242 537901. E-mail: editor@thisengland.co.uk
Editor: Roy Faiers.
Quarterly magazine on England, mainly its people, places, customs and traditions. Aimed at those who love England and all things English.

As a member of the Bureau of Freelance Photographers, you'll be kept up-to-date with markets through the BFP Market Newsletter, published monthly. For details of membership, turn to page 9

Illustrations: Mostly colour, transparencies preferred. Town, country and village scenes, curiosities, craftsmen at work, nostalgia, patriotism. Prefer people in the picture, but dislike modernity etc. Pictures for stock or use in their own right.
Text: Illustrated articles on all things traditionally English. 1,000–1,500 words.
Overall freelance potential: Around 50 per cent comes from freelance sources.
Editor's tips: Send SAE for contributor guidelines.
Fees: By negotiation.

TRAIL

EMAP Active Ltd, Bretton Court, Bretton, Peterborough PE3 8DZ.
Tel: 01733 264666. Fax: 01733 282653. E-mail: trail@emap.com
Editor: Matt Swaine.
Monthly magazine aimed at the more adventurous walker, plus rock climbers and mountain bikers.
Illustrations: Digital files preferred. Well-composed pictures of walkers, backpackers, climbers and mountain bikers in attractive and dramatic landscapes, UK or overseas, high viewpoints preferred. Walkers seen close up should be wearing proper outdoor gear. Covers: "stunning" colour shots as above.
Text: Illustrated articles on any aspect of hill walking, backpacking and overseas trekking, including diet, fitness, etc. Only accepted from contributors who clearly understand what the magazine is about and what the readers need. Always discuss ideas with the editor in the first instance.
Overall freelance potential: Very good for high quality material.
Editor's tips: It is essential that people in pictures be wearing proper walking/climbing clothes and shoes – no jeans and trainers.
Fees: From £25–£150 (DPS). Text £80 per 1,000 words.

WALK

The Ramblers' Association, 2nd Floor, Camelford House, 87-90 Albert Embankment, London SE1 7TW.
Tel: 020 7339 8500. Fax: 020 7339 8501. E-mail: denisen@london.ramblers.org.uk
Editor: Chris Ord. **Picture Editor:** Denise Noble.
Quarterly journal for members of the Ramblers' Association.
Illustrations: Digital files preferred. Scenic views of the countryside, preferably but not necessarily with walkers in shot. Also pictures of difficulties encountered when walking in the countryside, eg damaged bridges, locked gates, obstructed footpaths, etc.
Text: Little scope for text as most articles are commissioned from regulars.
Overall freelance potential: Quite good for pictures.
Editor's Tips: Pictures usually only used in the service of commissioned articles and features; contact editor to check on upcoming requirements.
Fees: By agreement.

YORKSHIRE LIFE

Archant Life, 1200 Century Way, Thorpe Park, Leeds LS15 8ZA.
Tel: 01772 722022. Fax: 01772 760905. E-mail: esther.leach@yorkshirelife.co.uk
Editor: Esther Leach.
Monthly up-market county magazine for Yorkshire.
Illustrations: Pictures of the Yorkshire region, mainly to accompany features. Pictures of nationally known personalities with a Yorkshire connection, and local society events, but most by commission. Covers: top quality regional scenes; medium format preferred.
Text: Articles and features on regional topics, from those with a truly professional approach. Always consult the editor in the first instance.
Overall freelance potential: Fair.
Fees: By negotiation.

Cycling & Motorcycling

BACK STREET HEROES
Inside Communications Ltd, One Canada Square, Canary Wharf, London E14 5AP.
Tel: 020 7772 8300. Fax: 020 7772 8585. E-mail: bsh-magazine@yahoo.com
Editor: Stu Garland.
Monthly magazine for custom bike enthusiasts.
Illustrations: Pictures of individual customised or one-off machines, and coverage of custom bike meetings and events. The style of photography must be tailored to fit the style of the magazine.
Text: Limited freelance market.
Overall freelance potential: Good for those who can capture the flavour and style of the custom bike scene.
Editor's tips: This is something of a lifestyle magazine, and it is essential that the stylistic approach be absolutely right.
Fees: By negotiation.

BIKE
EMAP Automotive Ltd, Media House, Lynchwood, Peterborough PE2 6EA.
Tel: 01733 468000. Fax: 01733 468196. E-mail: bike@emap.com
Editor: Steve Rose.
Monthly motorcycling magazine aimed at all enthusiasts.
Illustrations: Digital files preferred. Interesting or unusual topical pictures always required for news section. Sporting pictures for file. Top quality action pictures, "moody" statics and shots that are strong on creative effects. Reportage/documentary shots of events/people.
Text: Interesting or unusual news items. Scope for features on touring, personalities, icons etc; 1,000–3,000 words.
Overall freelance potential: Good for those with experience.
Editor's tips: Always looking for new photographers and styles.
Fees: By agreement.

CLASSIC BIKE
EMAP Automotive Ltd, Media House, Lynchwood, Peterborough PE2 6EA.
Tel: 01733 468465. Fax: 01733 468466. E-mail: classic.bike@emap.com
Editor: Hugo Wilson.
Monthly magazine dealing with thoroughbred and classic motorcycles from 1896 to 1990.
Illustrations: Digital files preferred. Pictures of rallies, races, restored motorcycles.
Text: Technical features, histories of particular motorcycles, restoration stories, profiles of famous riders, designers etc. 500–2,000 words.
Overall freelance potential: Most photography is freelance.
Editor's tips: Contact the editor before submitting.
Fees: By agreement and on merit.

THE CLASSIC MOTORCYCLE
Mortons Motorcycle Media Ltd, PO Box 99, Horncastle, Lincs LN9 6LZ.
Tel: 01507 529405. Fax: 01507 529495. E-mail: jrobinson@mortons.co.uk
Editor: James Robinson.
Monthly magazine covering veteran, vintage and post-war motor cycles and motorcycling.
Illustrations: Mostly colour. Pictures that cover interesting restoration projects, unusual machines, personalities with a background story, etc. Covers: colour pictures, usually a well-restored and technically interesting motor cycle, always related to editorial.
Text: Features on subjects detailed above. 1,500–2,500 words.
Overall freelance potential: Around 50 per cent of the magazine comes from freelances, but much of it is commissioned.

Editor's tips: Potential contributors must have a good technical knowledge of the subject.
Fees: Good; on a rising scale according to size of reproduction or length of article.

CYCLE SPORT
IPC Focus Network, Leon House, 233 High Street, Croydon CR9 1HZ.
Tel: 020 8726 8000. Fax: 020 8774 0952. E-mail: robert_garbutt@ipcmedia.com
Editor: Robert Garbutt.
Monthly devoted to professional cycle sport, offering a British perspective on this essentially Continental sport.
Illustrations: High quality, topical photographs relating to professional cycle racing.
Text: Illustrated features on the professional scene, but always query the editor before submitting. 1,500–4,000 words.
Overall freelance potential: Good for those with access to the professional scene, but most coverage comes from specialists based on the Continent.
Editor's tips: Most interested in "the news behind the news".
Fees: Pictures according to nature and use. Text £100–£200 per 1,000 words.

CYCLING PLUS
Future Publishing Ltd, Beauford Court, 30 Monmouth Street, Bath BA1 2BW.
Tel: 01225 442244. Fax: 01225 732310. E-mail: warren.rossiter@futurenet.co.uk
Editor: Mat Brett. **Art/Picture Editor:** Warren Rossiter.
Monthly magazine aimed at recreational cyclists, concentrating on touring and leisure/fitness riding. Some racing coverage.
Illustrations: Digital files preferred. Photographs that capture the excitement and dynamics of cycle sport. Speculative submissions welcomed; commissions also available.
Text: Little freelance scope; most is produced by a team of regular writers.
Overall freelance potential: Good for photographers.
Fees: By negotiation.

CYCLING WEEKLY
IPC Media Ltd, Leon House, 233 High Street, Croydon CR9 1HZ.
Tel: 020 8726 8000. Fax: 020 8774 0952. E-mail: cycling@ipcmedia.com
Editor: Robert Garbutt.
News-based weekly magazine covering all aspects of cycling; aimed at the informed cyclist.
Illustrations: Digital files preferred. Good photographs of cycle racing, plus any topical photographs of interest to cyclists. Covers: striking colour photographs of cycle racing; must be current.
Text: Well-illustrated articles on racing and technical matters. Around 1,500 words.
Overall freelance potential: Fairly good.
Fees: According to use.

DIRT BIKE RIDER
L&M Newspapers. Editorial: 12 Victoria Street, Morecambe, Lancs LA4 4AG.
Tel: 01524 834077. Fax: 01524 425469. E-mail: sean.lawless@dirtbikerider.co.uk
Editor: Sean Lawless.
Monthly covering all forms of off-road motorcycle sport, aimed at competitors and those who aspire to compete.
Illustrations: Current pictures of off-road events, bikes and riders.
Text: Illustrated features on all aspects of off-road motorcycling and racing. Contact editor with suggestions in the first instance.
Overall freelance potential: Good.
Fees: Negotiable.

MOTO MAGAZINE
4130 Publishing Ltd, Unit 8D, Arena Business Centre, Holyrood Close, Poole, Dorset BH17 7FP.
Tel: 01202 606118. E-mail: jeff@motomagazine.co.uk
Editor: Jeff Perrett.
Bi-monthly magazine covering motocross from an international perspective.
Illustrations: Colour and B&W. Will consider any topical and relevant images on spec. Has two regular photographers covering main events but commissions may be available.
Text: Possible scope for features on leading riders - contact editor with suggestions.
Overall freelance potential: Quite good for specialists.
Fees: By negotiation.

MOTOR CYCLE NEWS
EMAP Automotive Ltd, Media House, Lynchwood, Peterborough PE2 6EA.
Tel: 01733 468000. Fax: 01733 468028. E-mail: mcn@emap.com
Editor: Marc Potter.
Weekly tabloid for all road-riding and recreational motorcyclists. Also covers motorcycle sport.
Illustrations: Digital files preferred. Rarely use on-spec material, but frequently require freelances for assignments. Seek competent photographers with keen news sense, able to work closely to a given brief yet able to incorporate their own visual ideas. Successful applicants are added to a nationwide contact list and may be approached to cover stories at any time.
Text: Illustrated news stories on all aspects of motorcycling always considered. Lively tabloid style required.
Overall freelance potential: Good.
Editor's tips: Assignments are often at short notice and to tight deadlines – photographers who can work quickly and flexibly stand the best chance of success. Commission fees include copyright assignment to MCN, though permission for re-use by the photographer is rarely denied.
Fees: Single pictures from £50; day rate £200 plus expenses.

MOUNTAIN BIKING UK
Future Publishing Ltd, Beauford Court, 30 Monmouth Street, Bath BA1 2BW.
Tel: 01225 442244. Fax: 01225 822790. E-mail: danny.walter@futurenet.co.uk
Editor: Danny Walter.
Monthly magazine devoted to the sport of mountain biking.
Illustrations: Digital files preferred. Spectacular or unusual shots of mountain biking, action pictures that convey a sense of both movement and height. General coverage of events and individual riders may be of interest.
Text: Well-illustrated articles that show good knowledge of the sport.
Overall freelance potential: Good scope for individual and original photography.
Fees: By negotiation.

RIDE
EMAP Automotive, Media House, Lynchwood, Peterborough Business Park, Peterborough PE2 6EA.
Tel: 01733 468081. Fax: 01733 468092. E-mail: dave.miller@emap.com
Editor: TBA. **News Editor:** David Miller.
Monthly magazine for the motorcycling enthusiast.

Are you working from the latest edition of The Freelance Photographer's Market Handbook? It's published on 1 October each year. Markets are constantly changing, so it pays to have the latest edition

---

Illustrations: Always interested in expanding network of photographers, for reader shots, news pictures etc. Commissions available to produce coverage for road tests and general features, but only for those with prior experience of motor sport or similar action photography.
Text: Little scope.
Overall freelance potential: Limited.
Fees: Around £250 per day.

SCOOTERING
PO Box 99, Horncastle, Lincs LN9 6LZ.
Tel/fax: 01507 524004. E-mail: editorial@scootering.com
Editor: Andy Gillard.
Monthly magazine for motor scooter enthusiasts.
Illustrations: Mostly colour. Pictures of motor scooters of the Lambretta/Vespa type – shows, meetings, "runs", racing, special paint jobs, "chopped" scooters, etc. Covers: usually staff-produced, but a good freelance shot might be used.
Text: Original ideas considered. Contributors should be aware of the particular lifestyle and terminology attached to the scooter scene.
Overall freelance potential: Potential scope for those who know the current scooter scene and its followers, but most is produced by staff or regular contributors.
Editor's tips: Be aware that the readers have a very good knowledge of this specialised subject.
Fees: By negotiation.

SUPERBIKE
IPC Focus Network, Leon House, 233 High Street, Croydon CR9 1HZ.
Tel: 020 8726 8000. Fax: 020 8726 8499. E-mail: kenny_pryde@ipcmedia.com
Editor: Kenny Pryde.
Monthly for sports motorcycle enthusiasts. Specialising in new model tests and old model reviews, motorcycle Grand Prix, World Superbike and UK racing scene.
Illustrations: Pictures of unusual motorcycles, road-racing, drag-racing and other sports pictures of unusual interest or impact; crash sequences; motorcycle people.
Text: Features of general or specific motorcycle interest. Editorial style is humorous, irreverent. 1,500–3,000 words.
Overall freelance potential: Around 30 per cent of the magazine is contributed from outside sources.
Fees: Dependent on size and position in magazine.

TWO WHEELS ONLY
Magicalia Media, Berwick House, 8-10 Knoll Rise, Orpington, Kent BR6 0EL.
Tel: 01689 899200. E-mail: john@two.tv
Editor: John Cantle.
Wide-ranging glossy monthly for all motorcycling enthusiasts. Covers road bikes, racing, touring and scooters.
Illustrations: Digital files preferred. Any strong and interesting images connected with any aspect of motorcycling and the biking lifestyle – unusual bikes or biking situations, good race action, celebrities with bikes, etc. Most major feature photography is handled by a regular team but commissions may be available to those with experience.
Text: Limited scope, but original ideas considered.
Overall freelance potential: Good for the specialist.
Editor's tips: Images from the sidelines of the motorcycling scene may be of more interest than action or straight shots of bikes.
Fees: Negotiable, depending on what is offered.

Electronics & Computing

COMPUTER WEEKLY
Reed Business Information, Quadrant House, The Quadrant, Sutton, Surrey SM2 5AS.
Tel: 020 8652 8642. Fax: 020 8652 8979. E-mail: computer.weekly@rbi.co.uk
Editor: Brian McKenna.
Weekly news magazine aimed at IT directors.
Illustrations: B&W and colour. News pictures, plus general shots of people involved in computer usage situations for general illustration purposes.
Text: Illustrated features on professional and business applications and issues in information technology. Length around 1,200 words.
Overall freelance potential: Main scope is for specialists.
Fees: By negotiation.

PRACTICAL WIRELESS
PW Publishing Ltd, Arrowsmith Court, Station Approach, Broadstone, Dorset BH18 8PW.
Tel: 0845 803 1979. Fax: 01202 659950. E-mail: steve@pwpublishing.ltd.uk
Editor: Rob Mannion. **Art Editor:** Stephen Hunt.
Monthly magazine covering all aspects of radio of interest to the radio amateur and enthusiast.
Illustrations: B&W and colour. Digital files preferred. Usually only required to illustrate specific articles. Covers: radio-related subjects, B&W or colour.
Text: Articles on amateur radio or short wave listening, or on aspects of professional radio systems of interest to the enthusiast. 1,000–5,000 words.
Overall freelance potential: Little scope for individual photographs, but complete, illustrated articles always welcome.
Fees: By negotiation.

PRO SOUND NEWS
CMP Information, 7th Floor, Ludgate House, 245 Blackfriars Road, London SE1 9UR.
Tel: 020 7921 8319. Fax: 020 7921 8302. E-mail: david.robinson@cmpinformation.com
Editor: Dave Robinson.
Monthly news magazine for professionals working in the European sound production industry. Covers recording, live sound, post-production, mastering and broadcasting.
Illustrations: News pictures on all aspects of the industry, from equipment manufacture to live sound shows and concert performances to recording studios.
Text: Illustrated news items and features (800–1,000 words) on any aspect of the industry, but always check with the editor before submitting.
Overall freelance potential: Good for those with contacts in the audio and music business.
Fees: £140 per 1,000 words for text; photographs from £25.

RADIO USER
PW Publishing Ltd, Arrowsmith Court, Station Approach, Broadstone, Dorset BH18 8PW.
Tel: 0845 803 1979. Fax: 01202 659950. E-mail: elaine@pwpublishing.ltd.uk
Editor: Elaine Richards.
Monthly magazine for anyone interested in the world of radio communications.
Illustrations: B&W and colour. Pictures connected with the world of radio and communications including ships, aircraft and vehicles, but usually only required to illustrate specific articles.
Text: Features on radio systems or on other aspects of radio of interest to the enthusiast. News and reviews of equipment, clubs, etc. 1,000–2,000 words.
Overall freelance potential: Between 50 and 75 per cent comes from freelances.
Editor's tips: The magazine is always on the lookout for features on new and novel uses for radio communications. Visual articles on all aspects of communications welcome.
Fees: £40 per published page.

WHAT SATELLITE & DIGITAL TV
Future Publishing Ltd, 2 Balcombe Street, London NW1 6NW.
Tel: 020 7042 4000. Fax: 020 7042 4471. E-mail: alex.lane@futurenet.co.uk
Editor: Alex Lane.
Monthly magazine for satellite TV system buyers and users. Contains tests on receivers and dishes, general features, programme listings, reviews and the latest satellite news.
Illustrations: B&W and colour. Photographs of satellite systems in situ, family/people shots with equipment in use.
Text: Technical topics, plus programme reviews and personality pieces. 500–1,200 words.
Overall freelance potential: Around 50 per cent from such sources.
Fees: By agreement.

Equestrian

EQUESTRIAN TRADE NEWS
Equestrian Management Consultants Ltd, Stockeld Park, Wetherby, West Yorkshire LS22 4AW.
Tel: 01937 582111. Fax: 01937 582778. E-mail: editor@equestriantradenews.com
Editor: Elizabeth Peplow.
Monthly publication for business people and trade in the equestrian world.
Illustrations: Digital files preferred. Pictures covering saddlery, feedstuffs, new riding schools and business in the industry. Also news pictures of people connected with the industry – people retiring, getting married, etc.
Text: Features on specialist subjects and general articles on retailing, marketing and business. 1,000 words.
Overall freelance potential: Around 50 per cent comes from freelances.
Editor's tips: Only stories with a business angle will be considered. No scope for general horsey or racing material.
Fees: Text, £25 per 1,000 words; pictures by arrangement.

HORSE
IPC Media Ltd, Blue Fin Building, 110 Southwark Street, London SE1 0SU.
Tel: 020 3148 5000. E-mail: joanna_pyatt@ipcmedia.com
Editor: Jo Pyatt. **Picture Editor:** Vanessa Milburn.
Monthly aimed at the serious leisure rider.
Illustrations: Digital files preferred. All photography by commission only to illustrate specific features. Experienced workers should send an introductory letter with examples of previously published work.
Text: No scope.
Overall freelance potential: Limited and only for the experienced equestrian specialist.
Fees: By negotiation.

HORSE & HOUND
IPC Media, Blue Fin Building, 110 Southwark Street, London SE1 0SU.
Tel: 020 3148 4562. Fax: 020 3148 8128 . E-mail: emma_mccall@ipcmedia.com
Editor: Lucy Higginson. **Picture Editor:** Emma McCall.
Weekly news magazine covering all equestrian sports.
Illustrations: Digital files preferred. News and feature pictures considered on spec for immediate use or for stock, covering racing, point-to-pointing, showjumping, eventing, polo, hunting, driving and showing. Commissions available to experienced equestrian/countryside photographers; make appointment with the picture editor to show portfolio.
Text: Possible opportunities for those with knowledge and experience of the above disciplines.
Overall freelance potential: Good for those who can show skill in this field; enquiries from

photographers are encouraged.
Fees: Single pictures according to size of reproduction. Commission rates £200 per day (all rights); £135 per day (first use).

HORSE & PONY
BPG (Stamford) Ltd, Roebuck House, 33 Broad Street, Stamford, Lincs PE9 1RB.
Tel: 01780 766199. Fax: 01780 766416. E-mail: s.whittington@bournepublishinggroup.co.uk
Editor: Sarah Whittington.
Monthly equestrian magazine for the younger rider and equestrian enthusiast.
Illustrations: Digital files preferred. Will consider quality images from top class riding events and of professional riders. Some opportunities for experienced equestrian photographers to obtain commissions; write to the editor in the first instance with examples of previous work.
Text: Ideas for illustrated articles always considered, but writers must bear in mind that text needs to be tailored for the younger reader.
Overall freelance potential: Only for material with genuine appeal for the younger reader.
Fees: By negotiation.

HORSE & RIDER
D. J. Murphy (Publishers) Ltd, Headley House, Headley Road, Grayshott, Surrey GU26 6TU.
Tel: 01428 601020. Fax: 01428 601030. E-mail: djm@djmurphy.co.uk
Editor: Alison Bridge.
Monthly magazine aimed at adult horse-riders.
Illustrations: Digital files preferred. Off-beat personality shots and pictures for photo stories illustrating equestrian subjects, eg plaiting up, clipping, etc. May also consider general yard pictures, riding pictures, people and horses, but only by prior arrangement.
Text: Illustrated instructional features on stable management, grooming, etc, from contributors with real knowledge of the subject. Submit ideas only in the first instance.
Overall freelance potential: Only for freelances who have a real understanding of the market.
Editor's tips: Material must be technically accurate – riders must be shown wearing the correct clothes, especially hats; horses must be fit and correctly tacked.
Fees: Pictures £25–£60. Text £65 per 1,000 words.

Farming

CROPS
Reed Farmers Publishing Group, Quadrant House, The Quadrant, Sutton, Surrey SM2 5AS.
Tel: 020 8652 3500. Fax: 020 8652 8928. E-mail: charles.abel@rbi.co.uk
Editor: Charles Abel.
Fortnightly magazine catering exclusively for the arable farmer.
Illustrations: News pictures depicting anything of topical, unusual or technical interest concerning crop farming and production. Captions must be precise and detailed.
Text: Limited scope for short topical articles written by specialists.
Overall freelance potential: Good for farming specialists.
Fees: By negotiation.

DAIRY FARMER
CMP Information Ltd, Riverbank House, Angel Lane, Tonbridge, Kent TN9 1SE.
Tel: 01732 377273. Fax: 01732 377543. E-mail: phollinshead@cmpibiz.com
Editor: Peter Hollinshead.
Monthly journal for dairy farmers.
Illustrations: Digital files preferred. Captioned pictures, technical or possibly historical. Also humourous or unusual pictures concerning the dairy industry. Some assignments to visit

farms available.
Text: In-depth, technical features to help dairy farmers run their businesses more profitably.
Overall freelance potential: Limited, but open to suggestions.
Fees: By arrangement.

FARMERS GUARDIAN
CMP Information Ltd, Unit 4, Fulwood Park, Caxton Road, Fulwood, Preston PR2 9NZ.
Tel: 01772 799445. Fax: 01772 654987. E-mail: teveson@cmpi.biz
Editor: Elizabeth Falkingham. **Picture Editor:** Theresa Eveson.
Weekly news publication for all farmers, with the emphasis on commerce.
Illustrations: Digital files preferred. Current farming, rural and equestrian news pictures accompanied by story or extended captions.
Text: News items always of interest. Possible scope for articles on current agricultural and rural issues.
Overall freelance potential: Fair.
Fees: According to use.

FARMERS WEEKLY
Reed Business Information, Quadrant House, The Quadrant, Sutton, Surrey SM2 5AS.
Tel: 020 8652 4080. Fax: 020 8652 4005. E-mail: farmers.weekly@rbi.co.uk
Editor: Jane King.
Weekly publication covering all matters of interest to farmers.
Illustrations: Digital files preferred. News pictures relating to the world of farming and picture stories on technical aspects. Some opportunities for assignments.
Text: Tight, well-written copy on farming matters and anything that will help farmers run their business more efficiently.
Overall freelance potential: Good.
Fees: By negotiation.
Editor's tips: News pages are started on Monday and close for press on Wednesday afternoon, so news material should be submitted during that period. Copy and pics can be received by e-mail.

POULTRY WORLD
Reed Business Information, Quadrant House, The Quadrant, Sutton, Surrey SM2 5AS.
Tel: 020 8652 3500. Fax: 020 8652 4042. E-mail: poultry.world@rbi.co.uk
Editor: Richard Allison.
Monthly publication aimed at the UK, EU and worldwide commercial poultry industries. Covers egg production as well as chickens, turkeys, ducks and geese. Includes Pure Breeds section.
Illustrations: Prints or digital files preferred. News pictures and good general stock relating to the poultry industry, both in UK and overseas.
Text: News stories and ideas for features always considered; breeding, processing, packing, marketing, etc.
Overall freelance potential: Limited.
Fees: By negotiation.

Food & Drink

DECANTER
IPC Inspire, Blue Fin Building, 110 Southwark Street, London SE1 0SU.
Tel: 020 3148 5000. Fax: 020 3148 8524. E-mail: decanterpictures@decanter.com
Editor: Guy Woodward. **Picture Editor:** Victoria Hall.

Monthly magazine for the serious wine enthusiast, featuring producer and regional profiles, tastings, and related food and travel features.
Illustrations: Digital files preferred. Stock images of wine-producing regions occasionally needed to illustrate features, including attractive travel images of the region, not necessarily specifically wine-related. Send details of coverage available in the first instance.
Text: Illustrated articles on topics as above; submit synopsis first.
Overall freelance potential: Limited.
Fees: By negotiation.

FRESH
Trojan Publishing Ltd, Ground Floor, 211 Old Street, London EC1V 9NR.
Tel: 020 7608 6433. Fax: 020 7608 6320. E-mail: editorial@livingfresh.co.uk
Editor: Angelina Manzano.
Monthly aimed at an upmarket readership in the 25–40 age group, with the focus on easy-to-cook recipes for busy professionals rather than "dinner party" food. Particular emphasis on fresh ingredients and locally-sourced British produce.
Illustrations: Digital files preferred. Mostly commissioned to illustrate specific features or recipes. Experienced photographers should write in the first instance with samples of previous work.
Text: Will consider ideas for features on food production and home growing.
Overall freelance potential: Good possibilities for the specialist.
Editor's tips: First look at the magazine to see what we are about; then e-mail some examples of your work if you think it fits.
Fees: By negotiation.

ITALIA UK
Italia UK Limited, 3 Brooklands Place, Brooklands Road, Sale, Manchester M33 3SD.
Tel: 0161 976 1212. Fax: 0161 976 2888. E-mail: gr@italiauk.net
Editor: Glenn Routledge.
Anglo-Italian publication distributed through catering and food retail outlets.
Illustrations: Digital files preferred. Images of Italian food, drink, restaurants, travel and culture. Send details of subjects available in the first instance.
Text: Will always consider quality restaurant reviews (with pictures) from main UK cities, and general feature suggestions.
Overall freelance potential: Average.
Editor's tips: Bear in mind readership is pro-Italian and already has a reasonable knowledge of Italy.
Fees: By negotiation.

LIFESCAPE
Madafu Publishing Ltd, 353 Shenley Road, Borehamwood, Herts WD6 1TN.
Tel: 01707 859805. E-mail: rajasana@lifescapemag.com
Editor: Rajasana Otiende.
Magazine designed as a complete resource for vegetarians, covering not just food but also holidays, fair trade fashion/beauty and the use of organic products generally.
Illustrations: Agency pictures often used but the editor would prefer to use freelance stock or even commission images. In-house photographer produces most beauty coverage but possible opportunities for fashion work.
Text: Approaches from writers with expert knowledge of health subjects always welcomed.

Are you working from the latest edition of The Freelance Photographer's Market Handbook? It's published on 1 October each year. Markets are constantly changing, so it pays to have the latest edition

Overall freelance potential: Fair.
Editor's tips: Would rather pay for something unique than rely on agencies, though it does have to be within budget.
Fees: By negotiation.

OLIVE
BBC Worldwide Publishing, Woodlands, 80 Wood Lane, London W12 0TT.
Tel: 020 8433 1769 2000. Fax: 020 8433 3499. E-mail: elizabeth.galbraith@bbc.co.uk
Editor: Christine Hayes. **Creative Director:** Elizabeth Galbraith.
Monthly food and travel magazine for a young, upmarket readership.
Illustrations: Digital files preferred. Almost all by commission to illustrate major features.
Experienced workers should make an an appointment to show portfolio to the creative director.
Those with relevant stock collections should send lists.
Text: Will consider ideas from experienced contributors, especially for travel-related material, but no on spec submissions.
Overall freelance potential: Opportunities for specialists only.
Fees: By negotation.

PUBLICAN
United Business Media, Ludgate House, 245 Blackfriars Road, London SE1 9UY.
Tel: 020 7955 3711. E-mail: cnodder@cmpinformation.com
Editor: Caroline Nodder.
Weekly independent newspaper for publicans and pub companies throughout the UK.
Illustrations: Topical pictures concerning pubs and publicans, brewery and pub company management, and the drinks trade generally. Must be newsworthy or have some point of unusual interest, and preferably include people. Call before submitting.
Text: News items and picture stories about publicans – humorous, unusual, or controversial. Stories that have implications for the whole pub trade, or that illustrate a problem; original ways of increasing trade. News items up to 250 words; features around 500–800 words, but discuss proposal before submitting.
Overall freelance potential: Good for original material, especially from outside London and the South East.
Editor's tips: Forget charity bottle smashes, pub openings, and pictures of people pulling or holding pints – hundreds of these are received already.
Fees: On a rising scale according to size of reproduction or length of text.

RESTAURANT
William Reed Hospitality Ltd, 6th Floor, 103 Regent Street, London W1B 4HL.
Tel: 020 7534 3750. E-mail: editorial@restaurantmagazine.co.uk
Editor: Joe Warwick. **Art Director:** Joe McAllister. **Picture Editor:** Suzanne Mitchell.
Fortnightly magazine for the restaurant trade, with coverage ranging from top London restaurants to high street operations. Also designed to appeal to serious food lovers and restaurant-goers.
Illustrations: Mostly by commission to shoot food, interiors, portraiture, reportage, still life and travel. Some scope for those with in-depth stock collections on suitable subjects. On-spec opportunities for coverage of restaurant openings, events and informal shots of trade personalities.
Text: Will consider ideas on any relevant subject.
Overall freelance potential: Good for experienced freelances.
Fees: By negotiation.

SCOTTISH LICENSED TRADE NEWS
Peebles Media Group, Berguis House, Clifton Street, Glasgow G3 7LA.
Tel: 0141 567 6000. Fax: 0141 331 1395. E-mail: scott.wright@peeblesmedia.com
Editor: Scott Wright.
Fortnightly publication for Scottish publicans, off-licensees, hoteliers, caterers, restaurateurs,

drinks executives, drinks companies.
Illustrations: Digital files preferred. News pictures connected with the above subjects.
Text: News and features of specific interest to the Scottish trade.
Overall freelance potential: Limited.
Fees: By agreement.

WAITROSE FOOD ILLUSTRATED

John Brown Publishing, 136-142 Bramley Road, London W10 6SR.
Tel: 020 7565 3000. Fax: 020 7565 3076. E-mail: food@johnbrowngroup.co.uk
Editor: William Sitwell. **Art Director:** Brian Saffer. **Picture Editor:** Tabitha Hawkins.
Picture-led monthly concentrating on the "culture of food" as well as recipes and cookery.
Illustrations: Colour transparencies only. Very high quality food photography, plus coverage of food
producers, gourmet travel, restaurants and chefs. Much commissioned from established specialists;
those with suitable skills should initally submit some examples of previous work. Limited use of top
quality specialist stock; send lists to picture editor. Commissions for interior/food shots for
restaurant reviews around the UK are frequently sought.
Text: Scope for well-experienced food and drink writers.
Overall freelance potential: Excellent, but only for the experienced worker in the field.
Fees: By negotiation.

Gardening

BBC GARDENERS' WORLD MAGAZINE

BBC Worldwide Publishing, Room AG167, 80 Wood Lane, London W12 0TT.
Tel: 020 8433 3959. Fax: 020 8433 3986. E-mail: abigail.dodd@bbc.co.uk
Editor: Adam Pasco. **Creative Director:** Abigail Dodd. **Art Editor:** Guy Bennington.
Monthly magazine for gardeners at all levels of expertise.
Illustrations: Digital files preferred. No speculative submissions. Photographers with specialist
gardening collections should send lists of material available. Commissions may be available to
photograph individual gardens; the editor will always be pleased to hear from photographers who
can bring potential subjects to his attention. Also photographers prepared to set up small studios
with lights on location: good studio, portrait and reportage photography also commissioned.
Text: All text is commissioned.
Overall freelance potential: Mainly for specialists.
Editor's tips: Always looking for interesting "real" gardens for possible coverage. Small gardens,
patios and container gardening of particular interest.
Fees: By negotiation.

THE GARDEN

RHS Publications, 4th Floor, Churchgate, New Road, Peterborough PE1 1TT.
Tel: 01733 775775. Fax: 01733 775819. E-mail: thegarden@rhs.org.uk
Editor: Ian Hodgson.
Monthly Journal of the Royal Horticultural Society. Publishes articles on plants and specialist
aspects and techniques of horticulture.
Illustrations: Top quality photographs of identified plants, general horticultural subjects and
specific gardens.

---

*As a member of the Bureau of Freelance Photographers, you'll be
kept up-to-date with markets through the BFP Market Newsletter,
published monthly. For details of membership, turn to page 9*

Text: Some freelance market; submit suggestions first.
Overall freelance potential: Some potential opportunities.
Fees: £40–£100 according to size of reproduction; cover £150.

GARDEN ANSWERS
EMAP Active Ltd, Bushfield House, Orton Centre, Peterborough PE3 5UW.
Tel: 01733 237111. E-mail: justine.thompson@emap.com
Editor: Justine Thompson.
Monthly magazine for the enthusiastic gardener.
Illustrations: Digital files preferred. Little scope for speculative submissions, but always interested in receiving lists of subjects available from photographers. Do not send transparencies unless requested.
Text: Experienced gardening writers may be able to obtain commissions.
Overall freelance potential: Limited to the experienced gardening contributor.
Editor's tips: Practical gardening pictures are required, rather than simple shots of plants. Must be accompanied by detailed and accurate captions.
Fees: By arrangement.

GARDEN NEWS
EMAP Active Ltd, Bushfield House, Orton Centre, Peterborough PE3 5UW.
Tel: 01733 237111. E-mail: jane.cutteridge@emap.com
Editor: Neil Pope. **Deputy Editor:** Jane Blackford. **Picture Researcher:** Jane Cutteridge.
Weekly consumer newspaper for gardeners.
Illustrations: Digital files preferred, or medium format transparencies. Pictures of general horticultural subjects. Practical photographs to illustrate gardening techniques, top quality colour portraits of trees, shrubs, flowers and vegetables, and coverage of quality small/medium sized gardens.
Text: Short practical features of interest to gardeners. 600–800 words.
Overall freelance potential: Fair.
Fees: By agreement.

GARDEN TRADE NEWS
The Garden Communication and Media Company, Churchgate, New Road, Peterborough PE1 1TT.
Tel: 01733 7775700. Fax: 01733 775838. E-mail: info@gardentradenews.uk.com
Editor: Mike Wyatt.
Monthly business publication containing news, features and advice for retailers, wholesalers, manufacturers and distributors of horticultural products.
Illustrations: Digital files preferred. Pictures to illustrate news items or features.
Text: Illustrated news stories or articles concerning garden centres, nurseries and garden shops. Maximum 600 words.
Overall freelance potential: Limited.
Fees: £12.50 per 100 words; pictures from £17.50–£50 according to size of reproduction.

GARDENS ILLUSTRATED
Bristol Magazines Ltd, 14th Floor, Tower House, Fairfax Street, Bristol BS1 3BN.
Tel: 0117 314 8770. Fax: 0117 934 9008. E-mail: davidgrenham@originpublishing.co.uk
Editor: Juliet Roberts. **Art Director:** David Grenham.
Heavily-illustrated monthly with a practical and inspirational approach.
Illustrations: Usually commissioned, but high quality submissions may be considered on spec. Photography should have a narrative and journalistic slant rather than just pretty pictures of gardens. The gardens should be depicted in relation to the landscape, houses and the people who own or work them. Coverage from outside UK welcome.
Text: Scope for experienced gardening writers – submit samples of previously published work first.
Overall freelance potential: Very good for the right material.

Editor's tips: Quality is key. Material previously published in the UK is not of interest.
Fees: By negotiation.

GARDENS MONTHLY
Magicalia Media, Berwick House, 8-10 Knoll Rise, Orpington, Kent BR6 0EL.
Tel: 01689 899228. Fax: 01689 899266. E-mail: liz.dobbs@encanta.co.uk
Editor: Liz Dobbs.
Monthly aimed at gardeners of all levels, with an emphasis on easy to achieve success.
Illustrations: Digital files preferred. Stock images of gardening subjects may be needed – send detailed list of subjects available in the first instance.
Text: Will consider short, well-illustrated articles on gardening and garden design ideas; submit suggestions first.
Overall freelance potential: Fair.
Fees: From £15, to £100 for full page or cover.

HORTICULTURE WEEK
Haymarket Media Ltd, 174 Hammersmith Road, London W6 4JP.
Tel: 020 8267 4977. Fax: 020 8267 4987. E-mail: hortweek@haymarket.com
Editor: Kate Lowe. **Art Editor:** Chris Dias.
Weekly news magazine for commercial growers of plants and those employed in landscape work, garden centres, public parks and gardens.
Illustrations: Digital files preferred. Captioned news and feature pictures relating to commercial horticulture, landscaping, public parks, garden centres. Stock botanical images often needed – send details of material available. Some commissions available.
Text: Short news items about happenings affecting the trade. Longer articles may be considered – discuss ideas with the editor. 500–1,500 words.
Overall freelance potential: Limited.
Fees: By arrangement.

PROFESSIONAL LANDSCAPER & GROUNDSMAN
Albatross Publications, PO Box 523, Horsham, West Sussex RH12 4WL.
Tel: 01293 871201. Fax: 01293 871301. E-mail: newsdesk123@aol.com
Editor: Carol Andrews.
Quarterly magazine for landscapers, contractors, foresters, environmental designers, groundsmen and local authorities. Covers both hard and soft landscape creation.
Illustrations: Digital files preferred. Pictures depicting subjects as below, usually only accepted as part of a complete illustrated feature.
Text: Well-illustrated articles or case histories dealing with technical or practical landscaping matters, horticulture, and general environmental and conservation issues. 1,200–1,500 words.
Overall freelance potential: Limited.
Fees: By negotiation.

General Interest

ACTIVE LIFE
Millennium Ltd. Editorial: 16 Ennismore Avenue, London W4 1SF.
Tel: 020 8994 3144. E-mail: hhodge@btclick.com
Editor: Helene Hodge.
Bi-monthly general interest magazine for the over-50s.
General interest magazine for the over-50s, covering health, travel, food, finance, gardening, crafts and celebrities.
Illustrations: Lively, upbeat stock images of older people and the retired lifestyle always

of interest.
Text: Topical and seasonal illustrated features always considered, in particular "case studies" of older individuals who are doing something positive, interesting or unusual.
Overall freelance potential: Limited.
Fees: By negotiation.

BEST OF BRITISH
Church Lane Publishing Ltd, Bank Chambers, 27a Market Place, Market Deeping, Lincs PE6 8EA. Tel/fax: 01778 342814. E-mail: mail@british.fsbusiness.co.uk
Editor: Ian Beacham.
Monthly magazine covering all aspects of British heritage and nostalgia, but with a strong emphasis on 1940s/1950s/1960s.
Illustrations: Mainly colour; B&W for archive pictures from earlier eras. Digital media preferred. Top quality coverage of all British heritage subjects, from landscapes and museums to craftspeople and collectors; send details of material available in the first instance.
Text: Illustrated articles offering a positive view of aspects of Britain, past and present. Also profiles of people with unusual passions, humorous pieces about the British people and interviews with celebrities about aspects of Britain they love. Submit ideas or an outline first.
Overall freelance potential: Excellent.
Editor's tips: Pictures with good captions are always more interesting than those without. Material should always reflect a positive view of Britain. Nostalgic pictures always welcome. See website at www.bestofbritishmag.co.uk.
Fees: By negotiation with editor.

BIZARRE
Dennis Publishing Ltd, 30 Cleveland Street, London W1T 4JD.
Tel: 020 7907 6000. Fax: 020 7907 6020. E-mail: bizarre.pictures@dennis.co.uk
Editor: Alex Godfrey. **Picture Editor:** Tom Broadbent.
Monthly magazine specialising in alternative (fetish and subversive) lifestyles. Heavily illustrated, including special 14-page photo section.
Illustrations: Digital files preferred. Will consider pictures depicting anything that broadly falls within the above parameters, with a heavy emphasis on shocking reportage photography. "Weird, disturbing and downright bizarre photos from around the world, the more unique the better." Prefer material that has not been previously published.
Text: Little freelance scope unless the contributor is a genuine expert in a specific subject.
Overall freelance potential: Very good.
Editor's tips: Always call first with details of what you have to offer. Please no "ghost" photos.
Fees: By negotiation and dependent on what is being offered.

CHOICE
1st Floor, 2 King Street, Peterborough PE1 1LT.
Tel: 01733 555123. E-mail: editorial@choicemag.co.uk
Editor: Norman Wright. **Art Editor:** Gill Shaw.
General interest monthly for the over-50s.
Illustrations: Digital files preferred. Photographs mainly used to illustrate specific features. Photography, especially of people, occasionally commissioned all over the UK; send cards or tearsheets in the first instance. Top quality British travel shots may be of interest, but send lists of subjects/locations available in the first instance.
Text: Ideas for articles on any suitable topic always welcome, especially when accompanied by relevant photos. Contact editor in the first instance.
Overall freelance potential: Good.
Fees: By negotiation.

COAST

The National Magazine Company Ltd, 72 Broadwick Street, London W1F 9EP.
Tel: 020 7439 5000. Fax: 7439 6880. E-mail: jasmine.grigg@natmags.co.uk
Editor: Clare Gogerty. **Art Editor:** Amanda Scope. **Picture Editor:** Jasmine Grigg.
Monthly glossy that celebrates the best of British coastal and seaside living.
Illustrations: High-quality seaside imagery, including coastal landscapes, seascapes, marine
wildlife, etc, either for use in their own right with captions or to illustrate features. Mainly
interested in hearing from photographers who can offer good coverage of specific coastal locations or
subjects. Initial approach should be by e-mail with a small selection of low-res images. Also some
opportunities for commissions, mainly for homes and interiors work – contact art editor in the first
instance.
Text: Illustrated articles and features on suitable subjects always considered.
Overall freelance potential: Excellent for quality material.
Editor's tips: Keep in mind that requirements vary from month to month according to what
features and locations are being included in each issue.
Fees: By negotiation.

CONDÉ NAST CUSTOMER PUBLISHING

6-8 Bond Street, London W1S 0AD.
Tel: 020 7499 9080 (switchboard); 020 7152 3015 (pictures). E-mail: sophie.corben@condenast.co.uk
Group Picture Editor: Sophie Corben.
Contract publishing division of Condé Nast. Produces titles for corporate clients such as House of
Fraser, the Maybourne Group and Mandarin Oriental.
Illustrations: Mainly colour. Digital files preferred. Opportunities for experienced photographers to
obtain commissions in the fields of fashion, portraiture, travel, lifestyle and still life. Contact picture
editor by e-mail with details of previous experience and examples of work.
Text: N/A.
Overall freelance potential: Scope for photographers producing the highest quality work.
Fees: By negotiation.

DESIRE

Moondance Media Ltd, PO Box 282, London SW4 0QQ.
Tel: 020 7820 8844. Fax: 020 7820 9944. E-mail: editorial@moondancemedia.co.uk
Editor: Ian Jackson.
Bi-monthly magazine providing erotic entertainment for both men and women.
Illustrations: B&W and colour. Digital files preferred. Quality erotic photography of all kinds,
especially portraying couples. Both single pictures and sets.
Text: Features celebrating sex and sensuality as a mutual, shared experience; study the magazine
before submitting.
Overall freelance potential: Good.
Editor's tips: Seek material that is a cut above the usual standard of the more explicit top shelf.
Prospective contributors can obtain a free copy of the magazine on request by enclosing four 1st
class stamps.
Fees: Negotiable, but "competitive".

ORGANIC LIFE

GMC Publications Ltd, 86 High Street, Lewes, East Sussex BN7 1XN.
Tel: 01273 477374. Fax: 01273 402836. E-mail: paulq@thegmcgroup.com
Editor: Helen Vintner. **Deputy Editor:** Paul Quinn.
Monthly consumer magazine devoted to organic and sustainable living, not just in food but in all
aspects of lifestyle. Also covers farming and rural issues.
Illustrations: Digital files only. Mostly commissioned, with opportunities for photographers around
the country. Opportunities for experienced food photographers who are prepared to travel to the
publisher's offices in East Sussex to undertake shoots. Initial approach should be by e-mail,

preferably with a few sample images attached.
Text: Suggestions for profiles and feature articles always welcomed. Also seek real life stories about people living the organic lifestyle.
Overall freelance potential: Very good.
Editor's tips: Particularly keen to find regional freelances outside London. Often need people to produce profiles of farmers, local producers and people living an organic lifestyle.
Fees: According to use.

READER'S DIGEST
The Reader's Digest Association Ltd, 11 Westferry Circus, Canary Wharf, London E14 4HE.
Tel: 020 7715 8029. Fax: 020 7715 8716.
Editor-in-Chief: Katherine Walker. **Picture Researcher:** Roberta Mitchell.
British edition of the monthly magazine for a general interest readership.
Illustrations: Mostly colour. Digital files preferred. Pictures to illustrate specific general interest features. Some commission possibilities for experienced specialist workers.
Text: High quality features on all topics.
Overall freelance potential: Limited opportunities for new freelance contributors.
Fees: By agreement.

SAGA MAGAZINE
Saga Publishing Ltd, The Saga Pavilion, Enbrook Park, Sandgate, Folkestone CT20 3SE.
Tel: 01303 771523. Fax: 01303 776699.
Editor: Emma Soames. **Art Director:** Paul Hayes-Watkins.
Monthly, subscription-only, general interest magazine aimed at readers over 50.
Illustrations: Colour. Photography is mainly commission only, but some top quality photo features sometimes accepted.
Text: Will consider wide range of articles – human interest, "real life" stories, intriguing overseas interest (not travel), celebrity interviews, some natural history – all relevant to 50+ readership.
Overall freelance potential: Limited, but possible for carefully-targeted ideas exclusive to UK.
Fees: Good, but by negotiation.

TRAVEL & LEISURE
Editorial: 16 Ennismore Avenue, London W4 1SF.
Tel: 020 8994 3144. E-mail: hhodge@btclick.com
Editor: Helene Hodge.
Family-oriented quarterly, covering not just travel but also motoring, health, interiors, gardens, food and drink.
Illustrations: Always interested in seeing potential front cover shots. These are always seasonal in nature and most frequently feature happy families in a seasonal setting.
Text: Some scope for illustrated articles, mainly on the travel side and for the magazine's regular sections – intending contributors should ask for a copy of the magazine so that they can see the usual format of the sections. Rarely take speculative pieces but often ask freelances to write on specific locations or topics.
Overall freelance potential: Limited.
Fees: By negotiation.

WORLD ILLUSTRATED
World Illustrated Ltd, 29-31 Saffron Hill, London EC1N 8SW.
Tel: 020 7421 6000. Fax: 020 7421 6006. E-mail: charles.taylor@photoshot.com

---

Are you working from the latest edition of The Freelance Photographer's Market Handbook? It's published on 1 October each year. Markets are constantly changing, so it pays to have the latest edition

---

Editor: Charles Taylor. **Picture Editor:** Tim Bishop.
Picture-led magazine depicting aspects of the world through photographs. Also sells prints of published images with commission paid to photographer.
Illustrations: B&W and colour. Digital files preferred. High-quality photo essays and photojournalism from all parts of the world. Major regular themes include news, reportage, travel, people, events and sport.
Text: Only a small amount used in support of images.
Overall freelance potential: Good for really top-quality material.
Editor's tips: Sets of images need to tell a story and have contemporary relevance.
Fees: By negotiation.

YOURS
EMAP Esprit Ltd, Bretton Court, Peterborough PE3 8DZ.
Tel: 01733 264666. Fax: 01733 465266. E-mail: yours@emap.com
Editor: Valery McConnell. **Managing Editor** (pictures): Sharon Reid.
Fortnightly publication aimed at the over-50s. Aims to be entertaining as well as informing the retired generation of their rights and entitlements. It also campaigns on behalf of retired people.
Illustrations: Colour (plus B&W pictures from the past). Good stock shots of mature people engaged in a variety of activities, or depicted in varying moods (happy, worried, thoughtful, etc), always needed for general illustration purposes. The latter should be model-released. Send list of subjects and a few samples first. For commissions, requires experienced photographers around the country able to take strong, sympathetic shots to accompany news items and real life stories.
Text: Positive stories about older people's achievements and general features likely to be of particular interest to an older readership. 950–1,400 words.
Overall freelance potential: Very good.
Fees: By negotiation.

Health & Medical

DOCTOR/HOSPITAL DOCTOR
Elsevier Healthcare, Quadrant House, The Quadrant, Sutton, Surrey SM2 5AS.
Tel: 020 8652 8723. Fax: 020 8652 8701. E-mail: aimee.blumsom@rbi.co.uk
Editors: Charles Creswell/Rob Finch. **Picture Editor:** Aimee Blumsom.
Weekly newspapers for GPs and hospital doctors respectively.
Illustrations: Digital files preferred. News pictures of interest to the medical profession: health ministers, conferences, and GPs, consultants and hospitals in the news. Limited scope for stock shots of hospital exteriors, waiting rooms, signs, surgical staff, A&E wards, etc. Some commissions available; contact picture desk and be prepared to show portfolio.
Text: News stories always welcomed.
Overall freelance potential: Good.
Fees: Pictures according to use, text £160 per 1,000 words.

GP
Haymarket Medical Ltd, 174 Hammersmith Road, London W6 7JP.
Tel: 020 8267 4849. Fax: 020 8267 4866. E-mail: jason.lancy@haymarket.com
Editor: Bronagh Miskelly. **Picture Editor:** Jason Lancy.
Weekly newspaper for family doctors.
Illustrations: Pictures of general practitioners involved in news stories, and clinical/scientific pictures for features.
Text: News stories, up to 400 words, preferably by prior arrangement. Features considered, by prior arrangement with the features editor.

Overall freelance potential: The paper uses a lot of pictures from freelances.
Fees: By negotiation, but around £200-£300 per 1,000 words, and £100 for half-day photographic session.

H&E NATURIST MONTHLY

New Freedom Publications Ltd, Burlington Court, Carlisle Street, Goole, East Yorkshire DN14 5EG.
Tel: 01405 760298. Fax: 01405 763815. E-mail: editor@henaturist.co.uk
Editor: Sara Backhouse.
Monthly naturist/nudist magazine.
Illustrations: Mainly colour; some B&W. Digital files preferred. Attractive photos of naturists in landscapes, on beaches, in countryside. Couples and singles, male and female, any age from 16 –70. Also travel and scenic shots used.
Text: Illustrated articles up to 1,200 words about naturist lives and resorts, and off the beaten track naturism.
Overall freelance potential: Excellent.
Editor's tips: Contributors' guidelines are available on request.
Fees: Cover £150; £20 per quarter page inside.

HEALTH & FITNESS

Future Publishing Ltd, 2 Balcombe Street, London NW1 6NW.
Tel: 020 7042 4000. Fax: 020 7042 4471. E-mail: mary.comber@futurenet.co.uk
Editor: Mary Comber.
Glossy monthly covering all aspects of fitness, health and nutrition, aimed at women.
Illustrations: Captioned news pictures, and photographs for use in illustrating articles and features. Covers: outstanding and striking colour shots, usually featuring an obviously healthy young woman in close-up.
Text: Articles and features on suitable topics, with an appeal to women generally. Always query the editor before submitting.
Overall freelance potential: Good.
Fees: By negotiation.

PULSE

CMP Information Ltd, Ludgate House, 245 Blackfriars Road, London SE1 9UY.
Tel: 020 7921 8102. Fax: 020 7921 8248. E-mail: mcollard@cmpi.biz
Editor: Jo Haynes. **Group Picture Editor:** Marie Louise Collard.
Weekly newspaper for family doctors covering all aspects of general practice medicine.
Illustrations: Digital files preferred. Topical pictures with captions, involving GPs or illustrating relevant news stories. Commissions available for high quality portraiture, especially outside the London area. Pictures are also commissioned for the Pulse Picture Library, a specialist collection of life and medicine in general practice.
Text: News and topical features about general practice and GPs.
Overall freelance potential: Good, especially for portrait specialists.
Editor's tips: Most interested in photographers who can produce original and creative portrait work.
Fees: Negotiable. £100 per half day for commissions.

---

*Are you working from the latest edition of The Freelance Photographer's
Market Handbook? It's published on 1 October each year. Markets are
constantly changing, so it pays to have the latest edition*

Hobbies & Craft

CLASSIC STITCHES
D C Thomson & Company Ltd, 80 Kingsway East, Dundee DD4 8SL.
Tel: 01382 575120. Fax: 01382 452491. E-mail: editorial@classicstitches.com
Editor: Bea Neilson.
Bi-monthly embroidery magazine which looks at the work of designers and their lifestyles. Includes project-based features.
Illustrations: Digital files preferred. Photography generally required only to accompany features, though feature ideas are often generated by photographs. Commissions available to experienced workers to shoot still life and room sets.
Text: Illustrated embroidery-related articles and specific projects, up to 1,000 words. Look at previous issues for style.
Overall freelance potential: Good; 70% of content is freelance.
Editor's tips: Make sure any submissions are relevant. For photographs, lighting and focus are paramount.
Fees: By negotiation.

CLOCKS
Splat Publishing Ltd, Elizabeth House, Royal Elizabeth Yard, Dalmeny EH29 9RT.
Tel: 0131 331 3200. Fax: 0131 331 3213. E-mail: editor@clocksmagazine.com
Editor: John Hunter.
Monthly magazine for clock enthusiasts generally, those interested in building, repairing, restoring and collecting clocks and watches.
Illustrations: Digital files preferred. Pictures of anything concerned with clocks, e.g. public clocks, clocks in private collections or museums, clock movements and parts, people involved in clock making, repairing or restoration. Detailed captions essential.
Text: Features on clockmakers, repairers or restorers; museums and collections; clock companies. 1,000–2,000 words.
Overall freelance potential: Around 90 per cent of the magazine is contributed by freelances.
Editor's tips: Pictures unaccompanied by textual descriptions of the clocks, or articles about them, are rarely used.
Fees: By arrangement.

COLLECT IT!
Warners Group Publications, The Maltings, West Street, Bourne PE10 9PH.
Tel: 01778 391124. Fax: 01778 423063. E-mail: jeanhodge@warnersgroup.co.uk
Editor: Jean Hodge.
Monthly for collectors in all fields, concentrating on "affordable" collectable objects ranging from Royal Doulton china to toys and wine labels.
Illustrations: Digital files preferred. Mostly by commission to illustrate specific collections around the country, with most opportunities for photographers outside the South East Region.
Text: Original ideas always considered. Submit an outline and a sample picture in the first instance.
Overall freelance potential: Excellent.
Fees: By negotiation.

CRAFTS BEAUTIFUL
Aceville Publications Ltd, 25 Phoenix Court, Hawkins Road, Colchester, Essex CO1 1TH.
Tel: 01206 505974. Fax: 01206 505985. E-mail: editorial@crafts-beautiful.com
Editor: Sarah Crosland.
Glossy monthly covering all types of arts and crafts. Aimed primarily at women, beginners to experts.

Illustrations: Commissions available to illustrate specific features. Medium or larger format equipment essential. Send samples of work in the first instance.
Text: Step-by-step illustrated features dealing with crafts which appeal to women, i.e. cross stitch, decoupage, silk painting, etc. 1,500–2,000 words.
Overall freelance potential: Good for those with suitable expertise.
Fees: Photography by negotiation. Features around £80 per 1,200 words.

ENGINEERING IN MINIATURE
TEE Publishing Ltd, The Fosse, Fosse Way, Radford Semele, Leamington Spa CV31 1XN.
Tel: 01926 614101. Fax: 01926 614293. E-mail: info@teepublishing.com
Editor: Chris Deith.
Monthly magazine concerned with model engineering and working steam models.
Illustrations: B&W and colour. Digital images preferred. Photographs only used in conjunction with specific news items or articles. No stock photos required. Covers: colour of model steam locomotives, engines or other model engineering subjects. A4 portrait format.
Text: Well-illustrated articles and features on all aspects of model engineering and serious modelling, and on full size railways and steam road vehicles. Must be of a serious and technical nature.
Overall freelance potential: Some 80 per cent of contributions come from freelances.
Editor's tips: Ideally engines depicted should be true steam-operated, not electric steam outline. There is no coverage of model railways below "0" gauge, or of plastic models. Telephone contact is preferred in the first instance.
Fees: Negotiable.

FURNITURE & CABINETMAKING
GMC Publications Ltd, 86 High Street, Lewes, East Sussex BN7 1XN.
Tel: 01273 477374. Fax: 01273 402849. E-mail: coline@thegmcgroup.com
Editor: Colin Eden-Eadon.
Monthly magazine for the serious furniture maker.
Illustrations: Mostly by commission to illustrate step-by-step projects and features on individual craftsmen – write with details of experience and samples of work. Good stock shots of fine furniture often required to illustrate specific styles. Topical single pictures may be considered if accompanied by detailed supporting text.
Text: Ideas for illustrated features always welcome. Submit a synopsis and one sample picture in the first instance.
Overall freelance potential: Good for experienced workers.
Fees: £25 per single picture inside; illustrated articles £50–£70 per page.

GIBBONS STAMP MONTHLY
Stanley Gibbons Publications, 7 Parkside, Christchurch Road, Ringwood, Hampshire BH24 3SH.
Tel: 01425 472363. Fax: 01425 470247. E-mail: hjefferies@stanleygibbons.co.uk
Editor: Hugh Jefferies.
Monthly magazine for stamp collectors.
Illustrations: Mainly colour. Digital files preferred. Pictures inside only as illustrations for articles. Covers: colour pictures of interesting or unusual stamps relating to editorial features.
Text: Features on stamp collecting. 500–3,000 words.
Overall freelance potential: Most of the editorial comes from freelance contributors.
Fees: From £40 per 1,000 words.

GOOD WOODWORKING
Magicalia Media, Berwick House, 8-10 Knoll Rise, Orpington, Kent BR6 0EL.
Tel: 01689 899256. E-mail: dave.roberts@magicalia.com
Editor: Dave Roberts.
Four weekly magazine for the serious amateur woodworker.

Illustrations: By commission only. Assignments available to cover specific projects.
Text: Ideas and suggestions welcome, but writers must have good technical knowledge of the subject. Commissions available to interview individual woodworkers.
Overall freelance potential: Good for those with experience of the subject.
Fees: Photography by negotiation. Text around £150 per 1,000 words.

KNITTING

Guild of Master Craftsman Publications Ltd, 86 High Street, Lewes, East Sussex BN8 4TH.
Tel: 01273 402824. Fax: 01273 487692. E-mail katet@thegmcgroup.com
Editor: Kate Taylor.
Monthly magazine for hand knitting enthusiasts.
Illustrations: Digital files preferred. Seek interesting, unusual and colourful images of people knitting from around the world. Must be accompanied by detailed captions, up to 500 words. Images of celebrities knitting welcomed.
Text: Will consider features on knitting events, stitch 'n' bitch groups, new wool shops, and how-to articles about knitting and crochet. Up to 1500 words with about 10 pictures. Ideas always welcomed.
Overall freelance potential: Good.
Fees: By negotiation.

MODEL BOATS

Magicalia Media, Berwick House, 8–10 Knoll Rise, Orpington, Kent BR6 0PS.
Tel: 01689 899200. Fax: 01689 886666. E-mail: editor@modelboats.co.uk
Editor: Paul Freshney.
Monthly magazine that covers any facet of model boating plus occasional material on full-size subjects of interest to modellers.
Illustrations: All model boating subjects, including regattas.
Text: News items, illustrated articles and plans on wide range of ship and boat modelling, e.g. scale, electric, internal combustion, steam, sail, etc. Other maritime subjects considered if there is some connection with modelling. Up to 3,000 words.
Overall freelance potential: Good; 30 per cent bought from outside contributors.
Fees: According to use.

MODEL ENGINEER

Magicalia Media, Berwick House, 8-10 Knoll Rise, Orpington, Kent BR6 0EL.
Tel: 01689 899200. Fax: 01689 876438. E-mail: dcarpenter@magicalia.com
Editor: David Carpenter.
Fortnightly magazine aimed at the serious model engineering enthusiast.
Illustrations: B&W and colour. No stock shots required; all pictures must be part of an article. Covers: medium format transparencies depicting models of steam locomotives and traction engines; metalworking equipment and home workshop scenes; some full size vintage vehicles.
Text: Well-illustrated articles from specialists.
Overall freelance potential: Considerable for the specialist.
Fees: Negotiable.

PARROTS

Imax Ltd, The Old Cart House, Applesham Farm, Coombes, West Sussex BN15 0RP.
Tel: 01273 464777. Fax: 01273 463999. E-mail: editorial@imaxweb.co.uk
Editor: Gilly Lloyd.
Monthly magazine for the parrot enthusiast.
Illustrations: High quality photographs of specific types of parrots and parakeets. Must be well-posed and well lit, showing clear details of plumage. Full and accurate caption information (preferably including scientific names) also essential. Limited scope for amusing pictures involving parrots.

Text: Articles aimed at the parrot enthusiast.
Overall freelance potential: Good for top-quality material.
Editor's tips: Do not submit unidentified generic pictures of the "parrot on a branch" variety, or shots taken from long distances in zoos or bird parks. Only properly thought out, close-up shots will be considered.
Fees: Dependent on quality.

PRACTICAL FISHKEEPING
EMAP Active Ltd, Bushfield House, Orton Centre, Peterborough PE3 5UW.
Tel: 01733 237111. E-mail:karen.youngs@emap.com
Editor: Karen Youngs.
Monthly magazine for all tropical freshwater, marine, pond and coldwater fishkeepers, aimed at every level from hobbyist to expert.
Illustrations: Digital files preferred. Pictures of all species of tropical, marine and coldwater fish, plants, tanks, ponds and water gardens. Fish diseases, pond and tank maintenance, and pictures of things that have "gone wrong" are especially welcome. Prefer to hold material on file for possible future use.
Text: Emphasis on instructional articles on the subject. 1,000–2,000 words.
Overall freelance potential: Most is supplied by contributors with a specific knowledge of the hobby, but freelance material is considered on its merit at all times.
Editor's tips: Telephone first to give a brief on the intended copy and/or photographs available. Caption all fish clearly and get names right.
Fees: Negotiable.

THE ROUTER
GMC Publications, 86 High Street, Lewes, East Sussex BN7 1XN.
Tel: 01273 477374. Fax: 01273 487692.
Editor: Stuart Lawson.
Bi-monthly for router machine tool users, both hobbyists and professionals.
Illustrations: Digital files preferred. Detailed illustrations of the use of the tool and its application to projects, mostly as part an article package or by commission to illustrate the work of writers. For the latter, photographers must have the ability to take detailed technical shots of wood and metal parts, as well as headshots.
Text: Will always consider well-illustrated articles covering use of the router, techniques and tips, and individual projects.
Overall freelance potential: Fair for those with a good understanding of this type of work.
Editor's tips: Most pictures are close-up and well-detailed so photographers need to have the skill to achieve this.
Fees: £70 per published page, inclusive of photos.

TEDDY BEAR SCENE
Warners Group Publications plc, The Maltings, West Street, Bourne, Lincs PE10 9PH.
Tel: 01778 392048. Fax: 01778 392079. E-mail: kathym@warnersgroup.co.uk
Editor: Kathy Martin.
Monthly for collectors of teddy bears and other "furry friends".
Illustrations: Digital files preferred. Pictures of interesting individual bears or of specialist collectors, supported by detailed captions or a story.
Text: Well-illustrated features on notable bear makers or collectors. Raise ideas with the editor in the first instance.
Overall freelance potential: Fair.
Editor's tips: Always on the lookout for fresh and original contributions.
Fees: From £25 per page; negotiable for special material.

TREASURE HUNTING
Greenlight Publishing, The Publishing House, 119 Newland Street, Witham, Essex CM8 1NF.
Tel: 01376 521900. Fax: 01376 521901. E-mail: greg@acguk.com
Editor: Greg Payne.
Monthly magazine for metal detecting and local history enthusiasts.
Illustrations: Colour prints or digital files preferred. Usually only as illustrations for features detailed below, but captioned news pictures may be of interest. Covers: colour pictures of people using metal detectors in a countryside or seaside setting.
Text: Illustrated stories and features on individual finds, club treasure hunts, lost property recovery, local history, etc. However, fees nominal.
Overall freelance potential: Approximately 50 per cent of the magazine comes from freelances.
Editor's tips: Advisable to telephone the magazine before attempting a cover.
Fees: Covers, £50; features £20 per 1,000 words.

WOODCARVING
Guild of Master Craftsman Publications Ltd, 86 High Street, Lewes, East Sussex BN7 1XN.
Tel: 01273 477374. Fax: 01273 487692. E-mail: stuartl@thegmcgroup.com
Editor: Stuart Lawson.
Magazine published six times per year and aimed at both amateur and professional woodcarvers.
Illustrations: Mostly to illustrate specific articles, but some scope for news pictures and shots of interesting pieces of work accompanied by detailed captions. Covers: striking colour shots of exceptional woodcarvings or woodcarvers in action, relating to article inside.
Text: Illustrated articles on all aspects of serious woodcarving, including profiles of individual craftsmen.
Overall freelance potential: Good for the right material.
Fees: Negotiable for one-off reproductions inside. £70 per published page for articles, including photos.

WOODTURNING
Guild of Master Craftsman Publications Ltd, 86 High Street, Lewes, East Sussex BN7 1XN.
Tel: 01273 477374. Fax: 01273 486300. E-mail: colins@thegmcgroup.com
Editor: Colin Simpson.
Monthly magazine aimed at both amateur and professional woodturners.
Illustrations: Digital files preferred. Mostly to illustrate specific articles, but some scope for unusual or interesting single pictures with full captions. Covers: striking colour shots of turned items, relating to article inside.
Text: Illustrated articles on all aspects of woodturning, including profiles of individual craftsmen.
Overall freelance potential: Good for the right material.
Fees: £25 for one-off reproductions inside. £50 per published page for articles, including photos.

THE WOODWORKER
Magicalia Media, Berwick House, 8-10 Knoll Rise, Orpington, Kent BR6 0EL.
Tel: 01442 831128. E-mail: mark.chisholm@magicalia.com
Editor: Mark Chisholm.
Monthly magazine for all craftspeople in wood. Readership includes schools and woodworking businesses, as well as individual hobbyists.
Illustrations: Digital files preferred. Pictures relating to wood and wood crafts, mostly as illustrations for features. Covers: colour pictures of fine furniture.
Text: Illustrated features on all facets of woodworking crafts. 1,500 words.
Overall freelance potential: Good, about 75 per cent bought from outside contributors.
Editor's tips: Clear, concise authoritative writing in readable, modern style essential.
Fees: Negotiable, but around £50–55 per published page.

Home Interest

BBC GOOD HOMES
BBC Worldwide Publishing, Woodlands, 80 Wood Lane, London W12 0TT.
Tel: 020 8433 2000. Fax: 020 8433 2691. E-mail: georgia.hibberdine@bbc.co.uk
Editor: Bernie Herlihy. **Art Director:** Georgia Hibberdine.
Glossy monthly aimed at people who love their homes and love to decorate. Maintains some links with BBC TV programmes on home topics.
Illustrations: Digital files preferred. Top quality photography of interiors, gardens, home products, etc, all by commission. Photographers who have previously worked on top quality homes publications should write with details of their experience.
Text: No scope.
Overall freelance potential: Limited to those experienced in producing the highest standard of work.
Editor's tips: Not interested in hearing from photographers who have not done editorial interiors work before, no matter how skilled in other fields.
Fees: Standard day rate £450.

COUNTRY HOMES & INTERIORS
Southbank Publishing Group, Blue Fin Building, 110 Southwark Street, London SE1 0SU.
Tel: 020 3148 7190. E-mail: petra_manley-leach@ipcmedia.com
Editor: Rhoda Parry. **Art Director:** Petra Manley-Leach.
Monthly magazine concerning up-market country homes, interiors and gardens.
Illustrations: Top quality coverage of architecture, interiors, gardens and landscapes. Mostly by commission, but speculative submissions of picture features on specific country houses or gardens, or other country-based topics, may be considered if of the highest quality. Covers: always related to a major feature inside.
Text: Top level coverage of country home and lifestyle subjects, only by commission.
Overall freelance potential: Excellent for photographers who can provide the right sort of material.
Fees: Negotiable from a minimum of £100.

ELLE DECORATION
Hachette Filipacchi (UK) Ltd, 64 North Row, London W1K 7LL.
Tel: 020 7150 7000. Fax: 020 7150 7001. E-mail: david.golden@hf-uk.com
Editor: Michelle Ogundehin. **Art Director:** David Golden. **Picture Editor:** Anna Wilkins.
Monthly interior decoration magazine aimed at a trend-setting readership.
Illustrations: Mostly colour. By commission only, but always interested in hearing from photographers experienced in this field.
Text: Ideas for features always of interest.
Overall freelance potential: Plenty of scope for the experienced freelance.
Editor's tips: Particular projects must always be discussed in detail beforehand to ensure that the magazine's specific styling requirements are observed.
Fees: Photography according to commission.

THE ENGLISH HOME
Archant Specialist, Jubilee House, 2 Jubilee Place, London SW3 3TQ.
Tel: 020 7751 4831. Fax: 020 7751 4848. E-mail: sharon.parsons@archant.co.uk
Editor: Sharon Parsons.
Bi-monthly home interest title emphasising traditional English style.
Illustrations: Colour. Mainly by commission. Opportunities for experienced architectural and interiors photographers to obtain assignments. Suggestions, with sample pictures, of suitable homes or places to feature always welcome.

Text: Illustrated features on traditional English homes, decoration, UK travel, and style. Submit ideas in the first instance.
Overall freelance potential: Good.
Fees: By negotiation.

HOMES & GARDENS

IPC Media Ltd, Blue Fin Building, 110 Southwark Street, London SE1 0SU.
Tel: 020 3148 5000. E-mail: caroline_harrington@ipcmedia.com
Editor: Deborah Barker. **Art Director:** Caroline Harrington.
Monthly glossy magazine devoted to quality interior design and related matters.
Illustrations: High quality commissioned coverage of interior decoration, design, architecture, gardens, furnishings, food and travel. Emphasis on homes decorated in a tasteful style, up-market and attractive rather than wacky. Ideas for coverage always welcome.
Text: Heavily-illustrated features as above.
Overall freelance potential: Good for really top quality work.
Editor's tips: Out of London material particularly welcome.
Fees: By negotiation.

HOUSE & GARDEN

Condé Nast Publications Ltd, Vogue House, Hanover Square, London W1S 1JU.
Tel: 020 7499 9080. Fax: 020 7629 2907. E-mail: name.surname@condenast.co.uk
Editor: Susan Crewe. **Art Director:** Jenny Lister. **Picture Editor:** Owen Gale.
Monthly glossy magazine devoted to high quality homes and associated subjects.
Illustrations: Digital, transparency or print. Almost entirely by commission. Photographs of interior decoration, architecture, furnishings, food and wine, and gardens. Complete picture features depicting a house or apartment of interest and quality.
Text: Features on subjects as above, invariably commissioned.
Overall freelance potential: Reasonable scope for experienced architectural and interiors photographers to obtain commissions. Some scope for non-commissioned features on houses, gardens and food.
Fees: By negotiation.

HOUSE BEAUTIFUL

National Magazine Company Ltd, 72 Broadwick Street, London W1F 9EP.
Tel: 020 7439 5642. Fax: 020 7437 6886. E-mail: chris.thurston@natmags.co.uk
Editor: Julia Goodwin. **Art Director:** Chris Thurston. **Picture Researcher:** Pascale Rowan.
Monthly magazine with the emphasis on practical home decorating ideas.
Illustrations: Usually by commission. Photographs of houses, interior decoration, furnishings, cookery and gardens. Complete picture features depicting houses and interiors of interest.
Text: Features on subjects as above, invariably commissioned, but possible scope for speculative features on suitable subjects.
Overall freelance potential: Quite good for experienced contributors in the home interest and interiors field.
Fees: By negotiation.

IDEAL HOME

IPC Media Ltd, Blue Fin Building, 110 Southwark Street, London SE1 0SU.
Tel: 020 3148 5000. E-mail: warren_filmer@ipcmedia.com
Editor: Susan Rose. **Picture Editor:** Warren Filmer.
Monthly devoted to interiors and decorating.
Illustrations: Colour; print and digital files accepted. Major feature photography always by commission; make appointment to show portfolio. Some scope for good general home style and decorating images for stock and general illustration.

Text: No scope.
Overall freelance potential: Very good for experienced workers.
Editor's tips: Research past issues to see what subjects have already been covered and to anticipate the types of issues likely to be covered in the future.
Fees: By negotiation.

PERIOD LIVING
Centaur Special Interest Media, St Giles House, 50 Poland Street, London W1V 4AX.
Tel: 020 7970 4433. Fax: 020 7970 4438. E-mail: period.living@centaur.co.uk
Editor: Sarah Whelan. **Art Editor:** Puishun Li.
Monthly magazine featuring homes from any period pre-1939, and traditional-style living.
Illustrations: Commissions available to experienced architectural and interiors photographers, who should make appointment to show portfolios in the first instance.
Text: No scope.
Overall freelance potential: Good.
Fees: By negotiation.

25 BEAUTIFUL HOMES
IPC Media Ltd, Blue Fin Building, 110 Southwark Street, London SE1 0SU.
Tel: 020 3148 7154. Fax: 020 3148 8117. E-mail: john_smigielski@ipcmedia.com
Editor: John Smigielski.
Interior design magazine featuring 25 individual homes per issue.
Illustrations: High-res digital files or medium format transparencies. Top quality interiors photography illustrating specific homes. Always looking for homes to feature: initially send a selection of recce snaps showing each room, plus an exterior shot, with brief details about the home and its owners; a commission to produce a full feature may follow.
Text: Features as above.
Overall freelance potential: Very good for the experienced interiors photographer.
Fees: Fee for complete feature package of words and pictures normally around £1,200.

THE WORLD OF INTERIORS
The Condé Nast Publications Ltd, Vogue House, Hanover Square, London W1S 1JU.
Tel: 020 7152 3831. Fax: 020 7493 4013. E-mail: mark.lazenby@condenast.co.uk
Editor-in-Chief: Rupert Thomas. **Art Director:** Mark Lazenby.
Monthly magazine showing the best interior decoration of all periods and in all countries.
Illustrations: Mainly colour, occasional B&W. Subjects as above. Extra high standard of work required.
Text: Complete coverage of interesting houses; occasionally public buildings, churches, shops, etc. 1,000–2,000 words.
Overall freelance potential: Much of the work in the magazine comes from freelances.
Fees: Negotiable.

YOUR HOME
Hubert Burda Media UK, The Tower, Phoenix Square, Colchester, Essex CO4 9HU.
Tel: 01206 851117. Fax: 01206 849078. E-mail: sarah@essentialpublishing.co.uk
Production Editor: Sarah Gallagher.
Monthly magazine concerned with home and home improvement projects.
Illustrations: Commissions available for experienced workers in the home or DIY fields to illustrate features as below.
Text: Scope for contributors who can write knowledgeably and enjoyably on specific subjects. Illustrated features on real life reader stories and room by room makeovers.
Overall freelance potential: Very good for those with some experience in the field.
Fees: By negotiation.

Industry

CLASSIC PLANT & MACHINERY
Kelsey Publishing Group. Editorial: 1 Longview Cottage, Bodle Street Green, East Sussex BN27 4RA.
Tel: 01323 833125. E-mail: peterlove@kelsey.co.uk
Editor: Peter Love.
Monthly magazine covering vintage construction and mining plant and ancillary equipment.
Illustrations: Digital files preferred. Pictures of collectable, classic and vintage machinery, including dumptrucks, excavators, forklifts, road making and mining machinery. Must be accompanied by detailed and accurate captions. Contact editor before preparing a submission.
Text: Suggestions from those with suitable knowledge of these subjects always welcomed.
Overall freelance potential: Good.
Fees: By arrangement.

ELECTRICAL TIMES
Purple Media Solutions, 2nd Floor, 207-215 High Street, Orpington, Kent BR6 0PF.
Tel: 01689 899170. E-mail: ben.cronin@purplems.com
Editor: Ben Cronin.
Monthly publication for electrical contractors in the public and private sectors, wholesalers, architects, commercial and industrial users of electricity and the electricity supply industry.
Illustrations: Digital files preferred. Pictures of new technical products, site installation work, electrical-related exhibitions, personalities, equipment, etc.
Text: Some openings for business-related articles on the electrical industry. 750–1,000 words.
Overall freelance potential: Limited.
Fees: By negotiation.

ENERGY IN BUILDINGS & INDUSTRY
Pinede Publishing Ltd, PO Box 825, Guildford, Surrey GU4 8WQ.
Tel/fax: 01483 452854. E-mail: mark.thrower@btinternet.com
Editor: Mark Thrower.
Monthly magazine concerned with the use and conservation of energy in large buildings and the industrial environment.
Illustrations: Digital files preferred. Pictures of relevant and interesting installations.
Text: Some scope for writer/photographers who have good knowledge of the energy business.
Overall freelance potential: Limited unless contributors have connections within the field.
Fees: £30–£40 per picture; £140 per 1,000 words for text.

ENGINEERING
Gillard Welch Ltd, 6a New Street, Warwick CV34 4RX.
Tel: 01926 408244. Fax: 01926 408206. E-mail: steve@engineeringnet.co.uk
Managing Editor: Steve Welch.
Monthly magazine dealing with all areas of manufacturing engineering from a design viewpoint.
Illustrations: Photographs depicting all aspects of design in industrial engineering, from aerospace and computers to energy management and waste disposal. Much from manufacturers but some by commission. Covers: Abstract and "artistic" photography.
Text: Short illustrated news items up to major design features. 250–2,000 words.

Are you working from the latest edition of The Freelance Photographer's Market Handbook? It's published on 1 October each year. Markets are constantly changing, so it pays to have the latest edition

Overall freelance potential: Good for commissioned work.
Fees: £100 per published page for text. Covers £300–£400. Other commissioned photography around £120 per day.

INDUSTRIAL DIAMOND REVIEW
Odeon House, 146 College Road, Harrow, Middlesex HA1 1BH.
Tel: 020 8422 5891. E-mail: martin.jennings@idr-online.com
Editor: Martin Jennings.
Quarterly publication designed to promote a wider and more efficient use of diamond tools, i.e. grinding wheels, drill bits, saw blades, etc. in all branches of engineering.
Illustrations: B&W and colour. Pictures of any type of diamond tool in action.
Text: Case histories on the use of diamond tools in engineering, mining, etc. Up to 2,000 words for finished feature.
Overall freelance potential: Excellent but highly specialised.
Editor's tips: Technical case histories are welcome, but check acceptance with editor before submitting material. Potential contributors are requested to consult the editor before submitting.
Fees: by arrangement, but generally excellent..

INDUSTRIAL FIRE JOURNAL
Hemming Information Services, No 8, The Old Yarn Mills, Westbury, Sherborne, Dorset DT9 3RG.
Tel: 01935 816030. Fax: 01935 817200. E-mail: aylene@kennedycommunications.co.uk
Editor: Jose Sanchez-De Moniain.
Quarterly magazine concerning firefighting in the industrial sector.
Illustrations: Pictures of anything concerning or involving firefighting services in an industrial context, including firefighting personnel in action. Covers: powerful colour images of the same.
Text: No scope for non-specialists.
Overall freelance potential: Fair.
Editor's tips: Seek editor's agreement before submitting. No photos of ordinary car fires or firefighters/engines at domestic home/high street fires. Look for racy, exciting and explicit shots to interest and educate a readership of fire professionals who've "seen it all before".
Fees: Negotiable. Up to £200 for a really good cover picture.

MANUFACTURING CHEMIST
Wilmington Media Ltd, Wilmington House, Maidstone Road, Sidcup, Kent DA14 5HZ.
Tel: 020 8269 7744. Fax: 020 8269 7860. E-mail: hayshford@wilmington.co.uk
Editor: Hilary Ayshford.
Monthly journal for the pharmaceutical industry. Read by senior management involved in research, development, manufacturing and marketing of pharmaceuticals.
Illustrations: Colour. Digital files preferred. Pictures of any aspect of the pharmaceutical industry. 35mm acceptable, but digital format preferred.
Text: Features on any aspect of the pharmaceutical industry as detailed above. 1,000–2,000 words.
Overall freelance potential: Approximately 30 per cent is contributed by freelances.
Fees: Text, £170 per 1,000 words for features, £15 per 100 words for news stories; pictures by agreement.

MARINE ENGINEERS REVIEW
Institute of Marine Engineering, Science & Technology, 80 Coleman Street, London EC2R 5BJ.
Tel: 020 7382 2600. Fax: 020 7382 2670. E-mail: mer@imarest.org
Editor: John Barnes.
Monthly publications for marine engineers.
Illustrations: Interesting topical photographs of ships and marine machinery.
Text: Articles on shipping and marine engineering, including naval and offshore topics.
Overall freelance potential: Good, but enquire before submitting.
Fees: By negotiation.

NEW CIVIL ENGINEER

EMAP Construct, Greater London House, Hampstead Road, London NW1 7EJ.
Tel: 020 7505 6677. Fax: 020 7505 6667. E-mail: anthony.oliver@emap.com
Editor: Anthony Oliver.
Weekly news magazine for professional civil engineers.
Illustrations: Digital files preferred. Up-to-date pictures depicting any civil engineering project. Must be well captioned and newsworthy.
Text: By commission only.
Overall freelance potential: Limited.
Fees: On a rising scale according to size of reproduction or length of text.

NEW DESIGN

Gillard Welch Ltd, 6a New Street, Warwick CV34 4RX.
Tel: 01926 408244. Fax: 01926 408206. E-mail: info@newdesignmagazine.co.uk
Editor: Steve Welch.
Monthly for professional designers and manufacturers, covering developments in industrial and product design.
Illustrations: Photographs depicting new or current product, industrial and interior design, including architecture, theatre, textile, medical and transport design. Pictures should either have a news angle or be particularly strong images in their own right that might be used for covers.
Text: Illustrated news stories or features on any aspect of contemporary commercial design.
Overall freelance potential: Good.
Fees: Dependent on use, up to £300–£400 for covers.

PROFESSIONAL ENGINEERING

Professional Engineering Publishing, Institution of Mechanical Engineers, 1 Birdcage Walk, London SW1H 9JJ.
Tel: 020 7973 1299. Fax: 020 7973 0462. E-mail: pe@pepublishing.com
Editor: John Pullin.
Fortnightly publication for members of the Institution of Mechanical Engineers and decision-makers in industry.
Illustrations: Digital files preferred. Pictures of relevant people, locations, factories, processes and specific industries.
Text: Features with a general engineering bias at a fairly high management level, eg management techniques, new processes, materials applications, etc. 1,500 words maximum.
Overall freelance potential: Limited, and usually commissioned specifically.
Fees: Not less than around £200 per 1,000 words; pictures by agreement.

URETHANES TECHNOLOGY

Crain Communications Ltd, 3rd Floor, 21 St Thomas Street, London SE1 9RY.
Tel/fax: 020 7457 1400. E-mail: lwhite@crain.co.uk
Editor: Liz White.
Bi-monthly publication for the polyurethane producing, processing, and using industries.
Illustrations: Digital files preferred. Pictures of production, equipment, and application of polyurethane materials. Also news pictures and shots of trade personalities. Covers: top quality and graphically striking medium format colour of polyurethane-related subjects.
Text: Features on new applications of polyurethanes; new products; new equipment and processing. Business, marketing, personnel and technical news items. Up to 2,000 words.
Overall freelance potential: Good scope for those with access to the industries involved.
Fees: By arrangement.

UTILITY WEEK
Reed Business Information Ltd, Quadrant House, The Quadrant, Sutton, Surrey SM2 5AS.
Tel: 020 8652 3806. Fax: 020 8652 8906. E-mail: steve.hobson@rbi.co.uk
Editor: Steve Hobson.
Weekly business magazine for the three major supply utilities: electricity, gas and water.
Illustrations: Digital files preferred. News pictures concerning the major utilities. Possible scope for good stock coverage of industry subjects. Commissions available to experienced portrait and business/industry workers.
Text: Contributors with expert knowledge always welcomed. Submit details of experience in the first instance.
Overall freelance potential: Very good for industrial specialists.
Fees: By negotiation.

WORKS MANAGEMENT
Findlay Publications Ltd, Hawley Mill, Hawley Road, Dartford, Kent DA2 7TJ.
Tel: 01322 221144. Fax: 01322 221188. E-mail: crowlands@findlay.co.uk
Editor: Chris Rowlands. **Art Editor:** Neil Young.
Monthly publication for managers and engineers who directly control or perform the works management function in selected manufacturing concerns.
Illustrations: Mainly colour. Occasional need for regional coverage of managers and workers in realistic work situations in factories. Mostly pictures are used only to illustrate features.
Text: Illustrated features of interest to management, eg productivity, automation in factories, industrial relations, employment law, finance, energy, maintenance, handling and storage, safety and welfare. Around 1,500 words.
Overall freelance potential: Up to 30 per cent is contributed by freelances.
Fees: By agreement.

WORLD TOBACCO
DMG World Media, Westgate, 120-130 Station Road, Redhill, Surrey RH1 1ET.
Tel: 01737 855221. Fax: 01737 855467. E-mail: duncanmacowan@dmgworldmedia.com
Editor: Duncan MacOwan.
Bi-monthly aimed at international manufacturers, dealers and suppliers to the tobacco processing and manufacturing industries.
Illustrations: Digital files preferred. Pictures of tobacco growing, processing or manufacture from any part of the world, or general smoking-related images. Main scope is for striking cover images.
Text: Limited scope depending on the country.
Overall freelance potential: Fair.
Editor's tips: Pictures from remote parts of the world are particularly welcome.
Fees: By arrangement.

Local Government & Services

FIRE PREVENTION & FIRE ENGINEERS JOURNAL
Fire Protection Association, London Road, Moreton in Marsh, Gloucestershire GL56 0RH.
Tel: 01608 812518. Fax: 01608 812501. E-mail: rgilbey@thefpa.co.uk
Editor: Rupert Gilbey.
Monthly technical publication on fire safety. Aimed at fire brigades, fire equipment manufacturers, architects, insurance companies, and those with responsibility for fire safety in public sector bodies, commerce and industry.
Illustrations: Digital files preferred. Pictures of large and small fires to illustrate reports. Pictures

showing different types of occupancy (offices, commercial premises, warehouses, etc) also welcome.
Text: Technical articles and news items on fire prevention and protection. Features 1,000–2,000 words.
Overall freelance potential: Good pictures of fires and unusual fire safety experiences are always welcome.
Fees: Pictures, negotiable from £15. Text, negotiable from £110 per 1,000 words.

JANE'S POLICE REVIEW

Jane's Information Group, Sentinel House, 163 Brighton Road, Coulsdon, Surrey CR5 2YH.
Tel: 020 8276 4701. Fax: 020 7287 4765. E-mail: anthony.foot@janes.com
Editor: Chris Herbert. **Art Editor:** Anthony Foot.
Weekly news magazine for the police service.
Illustrations: All aspects of the police service. Particular interest in up-to-date news pictures covering the previous seven days (e-mail policereviewnews@janes.com). Some commissioned work available, with a need for more photographers to carry out regional work. Contact art editor first to show portfolio.
Text: Limited scope because of specialist subject matter, but will consider any subject of contemporary interest to police officers, 1,000–1,500 words.
Overall freelance potential: Good.
Editor's tips: The magazine is published on Friday with a Tuesday morning deadline for news pictures. Photographs for features should be good photojournalism and reportage; not interested in "publicity-style" photos.
Fees: Negotiable, minimum £50.

LEGAL ACTION

The Legal Action Group, 242 Pentonville Road, London N1 9UN.
Tel: 020 7833 2931. Fax: 020 7837 6094. E-mail: vwilliams@lag.org.uk
Editor: Valerie Williams.
Monthly publication for lawyers, advice workers, law students and academics.
Illustrations: B&W only. Pictures of lawyers and judges, especially other than the standard head and shoulders shot. Plus stock pictures to illustrate features covering a wide range of subjects (e.g. housing, police, immigration, advice services).
Text: Features on legal services and professional issues, including the courts. High technical detail required. Also information for news and feature material that can be written in-house.
Overall freelance potential: Always interested in hearing from photographers holding suitable material.
Fees: By negotiation.

MUNICIPAL JOURNAL

Hemming Group Ltd, 32 Vauxhall Bridge Road, London SW1V 2SS.
Tel: 020 7973 6400. Fax: 020 7233 5051.
Editor: Michael Burton.
Weekly publication for senior local government officers, councillors, Whitehall departments and academic and other institutions.
Illustrations: B&W and colour. News pictures; relevant personalities, vehicles, buildings, etc;

As a member of the Bureau of Freelance Photographers, you'll be kept up-to-date with markets through the BFP Market Newsletter, published monthly. For details of membership, turn to page 9

general stock shots of local government subjects and situations to illustrate features.
Text: Features on local government issues. 750–1,000 words.
Overall freelance potential: Very good.
Fees: Good; on a rising scale according to the size of reproduction or length of feature.

PLANNING
Haymarket Business Publications Ltd, 174 Hammersmith Road, London W6 7JP
Tel: 020 8267 4928. Fax: 020 8267 4013. E-mail: planning@haymarket.com
Editor: Huw Morris. **News Editor:** Susanna Gillman.
Weekly news magazine for all involved with town and country planning and related issues. Official journal of the Royal Town Planning Institute.
Illustrations: News pictures always of interest, on specific planning issues. Also good generic shots of subjects planning touches on, e.g. conservation, transport, rivers, waste disposal, housing, energy, industry, retailing, etc. Some commissions available to illustrate major features.
Text: Illustrated news stories and longer features from contributors with good knowledge of planning issues, up to 1,500 words. Must be relevant to planners.
Overall freelance potential: Good for genuinely relevant topical material.
Editor's tips: Photos can be of general or specific interest.
Fees: Photography according to use or assignment; text £100 per 1,000 words.

SCHOLASTIC MAGAZINES
Scholastic Ltd, Villiers House, Clarendon Avenue, Leamington Spa CV32 5PR.
Tel: 01926 887799. Fax: 01926 883331.
Design/Picture Editor: Sally King.
Range of monthly publications for teachers in primary and nursery education.
Illustrations: Digital files preferred. News pictures and good, unposed pictures of school children from 3-12 years, in classrooms and other school situations. Cover pictures as above often commissioned. Pictures are retained within a large in-house library.
Text: No scope.
Overall freelance potential: Good.
Fees: By agreement.

THE TEACHER
National Union of Teachers, Hamilton House, Mabledon Place, London WC1H 9BD.
Tel: 020 7380 4708. Fax: 020 7383 7230. E-mail: teacher@nut.org.uk
Editor: Ellie Campbell-Barr.
Official magazine of the National Union of Teachers. Published eight times a year.
Illustrations: Digital files preferred. News pictures concerning any educational topic, especially those taken in schools and colleges. Coverage of union activities, personalities, demonstrations, etc.
Text: Short articles and news items on educational matters.
Overall freelance potential: Limited; interested in good pictures though.
Editor's tips: Consult the editor before submitting.
Fees: According to use.

YOUNG PEOPLE NOW
Haymarket Publishing Ltd, 174 Hammersmith Road, London W6 7JP.
Tel: 020 8267 4707. Fax: 020 8267 4728. E-mail: ypn.editorial@haymarket.com
Editor: Ravi Chandiramani. **Art Editor:** David McCullough.
Weekly publication for youth workers, social workers, careers officers, teachers, counsellors and others working in the youth affairs field.

Illustrations: Digital files preferred. Mainly commissioned shoots to cover youth work and youth workers around the country. Contact art editor with details and samples in the first instance.
Text: Small proportion of copy is from freelance contributors.
Overall freelance potential: Occasional news pictures and one or two features using freelance photos per issue.
Fees: According to use.

Male Interest

ARENA
EMAP Elan Men's Group, 189 Shaftesbury Avenue, London WC2H 8JG.
Tel: 020 7437 9011. Fax: 020 7520 6500. E-mail: editorial@arenamag.co.uk
Editor: Giles Hattersley. **Art Director:** Tom Usher.
Monthly general interest magazine for fashion-conscious men in the 20–40 age group.
Illustrations: Mainly colour; some high-quality B&W. By commission only, to illustrate features on fashion, design, sport, travel, etc. Photographers with an original approach always welcome.
Text: Features and profiles aimed at the intelligent and style-conscious man. Up to 3,000 words.
Overall freelance potential: Fairly good, but only for the experienced contributor.
Fees: Photography by negotiation; text around £200 per 1,000 words.

BOYS TOYS
Freestyle Publications Ltd, Alexander House, Ling Road, Poole, Dorset BH12 4NZ.
Tel: 01202 735090. Fax: 01202 733969. E-mail: tperkins@freestyle-group.com
Editor: TBA. **Assistant Editor:** Tom Perkins.
Monthly for young men, covering all lifestyle topics but with an emphasis on desirable products and technology.
Illustrations: Mainly colour. Mostly commissioned in the fields of sport, fashion, motoring, technology and portraiture. Portfolios can be viewed in London. On spec material also considered if it fits the magazine's style.
Text: Ideas always considered.
Overall freelance potential: Excellent.
Fees: By negotiation.

CLUB INTERNATIONAL
Paul Raymond Publications Ltd, 2 Archer Street, London W1D 7AW.
Tel: 020 7292 8000. Fax: 020 7734 5030. E-mail: mattb@paul-raymond.com
Editor: Matt Berry.
Popular glamour monthly for men.
Illustrations: 35mm transparencies or digital files. Requires top quality glamour sets of very attractive girls (aged 18 – 25).
Text: Articles on sexual or humorous topics, or factual/investigative pieces. 1,000–2,000 words.
Overall freelance potential: Most of the published glamour material comes from freelances, but they are normally experienced glamour photographers.
Editor's tips: Study the magazine to appreciate style. As well as being very attractive, girls featured must look contemporary and fashionable.
Fees: £650 for glamour sets. Text up to £200 per 1,000 words.

ESCORT
Paul Raymond Publications Ltd, 2 Archer Street, London W1D 7AW.
Tel: 020 7292 8000. Fax: 020 7734 5030. E-mail: escort@pr-org.co.uk
Editor: James Hundleby.
Monthly glamour magazine; less sophisticated than the other Paul Raymond publications, Men Only

and Club International.
Illustrations: 35mm Kodachrome preferred. Looks for glamour sets of "normal, healthy, girl-next-door" types. Each issue contains about 10 glamour sets running to 2–5 pages each.
Text: Purely "readers' contributions".
Overall freelance potential: Good.
Fees: £400+ for glamour sets, or from £25 per picture.

ESQUIRE
The National Magazine Company Ltd, 72 Broadwick Street, London W1F 9EP.
Tel: 020 7439 5000. Fax: 020 7439 5675. E-mail: henny.manley@natmags.co.uk
Editor: Jeremy Langmead. **Art Director:** David McKendrick. **Picture Editor:** Henny Manley.
Up-market general interest monthly for intelligent and affluent men in the 25–44 age group.
Illustrations: Mainly colour. Top-quality material only, invariably by commission. Mostly portraiture, fashion and photojournalism.
Text: Scope for "name" writers only.
Overall freelance potential: Good for photographers, but restricted to those experienced at the highest level of magazine work.
Fees: By negotiation.

FHM
EMAP Elan Men's Group, Mappin House, 4 Winsley Street, London W1W 8HF.
Tel: 020 7182 8014. Fax: 020 7182 8021. E-mail: regina.wolek@emap.com
Editor-in-Chief: Anthony Noguera. **Photo Director:** Regina Wolek.
Monthly lifestyle and fashion magazine for young men.
Illustrations: Mainly colour. Main feature and fashion photography always by commission. Stock images relating to subjects of major interest (sports, travel, adventure, cars, sex) often required – send details of coverage available.
Text: Will consider interesting short items of interest to a young male readership, and feature ideas from experienced workers.
Overall freelance potential: Good for the experienced contributor.
Fees: By negotiation.

FRONT
Flip Media, 19 Waterside, 44-48 Wharf Road, London N1 7UX.
Tel: 020 7689 3916. E-mail: joe.barnes@frontmag.co.uk
Editor: Joe Barnes. **Picture Editor:** Sophie Palmer.
Monthly for 18-24 year old men.
Illustrations: Digital files preferred. Wide range of stock pictures always required – glamour, sport, music, fashion, reportage, etc – plus "weird and bizarre" images of all kinds. Some commissions available; make appointment to show portfolio.
Text: Picture-based features always of interest.
Overall freelance potential: Good.
Fees: By negotiation.

GQ
Condé Nast Publications Ltd, Vogue House, Hanover Square, London W1S 1JU.
Tel: 020 7499 9080. Fax: 020 7629 2093. E-mail: james.mullinger@condenast.co.uk
Editor: Dylan Jones. **Photo Editor:** James Mullinger.
Up-market general interest magazine for men in the 20–45 age group.
Illustrations: Mainly colour. Top-quality illustrations for articles on a range of topics, invariably

by commission.

Text: Top level investigative, personality, fashion and style features, plus articles on other subjects likely to be of interest to successful and affluent men.

Overall freelance potential: Only for the contributor experienced at the top level of magazine work.

Editor's tips: See from the magazine itself what sort of style and quality is required.

Fees: By negotiation.

LOADED

IPC Media Ltd, Blue Fin Building, 110 Southwark Street, London SE1 0SU.

Tel: 020 3148 6818. E-mail: sam_riley@ipcmedia.com

Editor: Martin Daubney. **Picture Editor:** Sam Riley.

General interest monthly for men in their 20s. Covers music, sport, humour, fashion and popular culture in a down-to-earth and irreverent manner.

Illustrations: Mainly colour. Mostly by commission to accompany features, but speculative submissions always considered. Submit only dupes or photocopies in the first instance.

Text: Fashion features, reportage (clubs, drugs, crime, etc), interviews, humour and "anything off the wall".

Overall freelance potential: Always open to fresh and original photography and ideas.

Fees: By negotiation.

MAXIM

Dennis Publishing Ltd, 30 Cleveland Street, London W1P 5FF.

Tel: 020 7907 6410. Fax: 020 7907 6439. E-mail: derek_harbinson@dennis.co.uk

Editor: Derek Harbinson. **Picture Editor:** Jason Timson.

General interest lifestyle magazine aimed at sophisticated men in the 20–30 age group.

Illustrations: Commissioned coverage of male fashion, grooming, sport, cars, etc – make appointment to show portfolio. Also some high quality reportage work on topical issues, colour or B&W.

Text: Limited scope, but ideas from experienced contributors always considered.

Overall freelance potential: Good for the experienced worker.

Editor's tips: An original approach could pay off.

Fees: Variable according the nature of the work.

MAYFAIR

Paul Raymond Publications Ltd, 2 Archer Street, London W1D 7AW.

Tel: 020 7292 8000. Fax: 020 7437 8788. E-mail: mayfair@pr-org.co.uk

Editor: David Spenser. **Art Editor:** Nick Barclay.

Glamour-based monthly for men.

Illustrations: 35mm transparencies or digital files. Only top quality material will be considered. Glamour sets taken in up-market surroundings and real-life locations, such as a luxury furnished flat. Outdoor material needs strong sunlight.

Text: No scope.

Overall freelance potential: Only for high-quality material; much is produced by regular contributors.

Editor's tips: For glamour thought should be given to the erotic use of clothing and suggestion of sex appeal or sexual situation, together with striking but simple colour co-ordination. Always call before submitting.

Fees: £250–£1,000 for glamour sets, or dependent on use. Covers: from £50.

MEN ONLY

Paul Raymond Publications Ltd, 2 Archer Street, London W1D 7AW.

Tel: 020 7292 8000. Fax: 020 7734 5030. E-mail: mattb@paul-raymond.com

Editor: Matt Berry.

Sophisticated erotic monthly for men.
Illustrations: 35mm transparencies or digital files. Imaginative glamour sets featuring "the most beautiful women". Models must be young, fresh, athletic and natural. Sets welcomed from new photographers as well as established contributors. Also picture-led supporting features.
Text: Laid-back humour, sport, male interests etc.
Overall freelance potential: Excellent.
Editor's tips: Attention to detail in clothes and make-up, a wide variety of poses, and imaginative locations will always set you apart. New ideas and faces always welcome.
Fees: £500–£1,000 for glamour sets. Other pictures by negotiation.

MEN'S HEALTH
NatMag Rodale Ltd, 72 Broadwick Street, London W1F 9EP.
Tel: 020 7339 4400. Fax: 020 7339 4444. E-mail: gary.cadogan@natmag-rodale.co.uk
Editor: Morgan Rees. **Art Director:** Gary Cadogan.
Magazine published 10 times per year and covering sports, fitness, grooming and other aspects of male lifestyle.
Illustrations: Mainly colour. Mostly by commission, though possible scope for good generic stock shots of fitness etc. subjects.
Text: Articles on male lifestyle subjects, especially health and fitness. Write with ideas and details of experience in the first instance.
Overall freelance potential: Only for the experienced contributor.
Fees: By negotiation.

NUTS
IPC Ignite, Blue Fin Building, 110 Southwark Street, London SE1 0SU.
Tel: 020 3148 6937. Fax: 020 3148 8107. E-mail: nutspictures@ipcmedia.com
Editor: Dominic Smith. **Picture Editor:** John Gooch.
Weekly general interest magazine for young men.
Illustrations: Digital files preferred. Always interested in "amazing, spectacular and extreme" images for "True Stories" picture feature section – single pictures or series of pictures used over double-page spreads, usually 4–5 per issue. Must have obvious appeal to the target market, anything from spectacular sports shots to unusual animal pics. Also relevant news pictures (sport, celebrities) which have not been seen elsewhere. Limited opportunities for commissioned work, but will consider approaches from experienced photographers working in suitable areas.
Text: Little scope.
Overall freelance potential: Excellent.
Fees: Dependent on the individual image and how it is used, as well as on level of exclusivity.

REFRESH
Wild Publishing Ltd, 22a Iliffe Yard, Kennington, London SE17 3QA.
Tel: 020 7277 4517. Fax: 020 7703 8718. E-mail: david@wildpublishing.com
Editor: David Tickner.
Monthly magazine for affluent gay men.
Illustrations: Digital files preferred. Mostly by commission, but opportunities often available. Main scope is for fashion shoots, both studio and location. Some portraiture, interiors and travel. E-mail samples with a CV in the first instance.
Text: Ideas for features always considered.
Overall freelance potential: Good – always looking to broaden the range of photographers used.
Fees: By negotiation.

ZOO
EMAP Performance Network, 4 Winsley Street, London W1W 8HF.
Tel: 020 7208 3797. Picture desk: 020 7208 3767. E-mail: zoopictures@emap.com
Editor: Ben Todd. **Features Editor:** Matt Mason. **Picture Editor:** Steve Nash.

Weekly general interest magazine for young men.
Illustrations: Digital files preferred. Always need topical, unusual and visually striking images for the magazine's news section – several double-page spreads per issue displaying spectacular or unusual images of all kinds. Also unusual or exclusive sports images. Commissions in relevant areas may be available.
Text: Will consider ideas for topical features and real life stories. Material should have a laddish/humorous approach but be backed with genuine knowledge of the subject. Submit suggestions to features editor in the first instance.
Overall freelance potential: Excellent.
Fees: Negotiable, dependent on the nature of images and their exclusivity.

Motoring

AMERICAN CAR WORLD
CH Publications Ltd, Nimax House, 20 Ullswater Crescent, Ullswater Business Park, Coulsdon, Surrey CR5 2HR.
Tel: 020 8655 6400. Fax: 020 8763 1001. E-mail; chp@chpltd.com
Editor: Richard Nicholls.
Monthly magazine covering custom cars and hot rods based on pre-1975 vehicles, British or American; and American cars, standard and modified, up to present day.
Illustrations: Newsy and well-captioned single pictures depicting happenings on the UK custom and American car scene. Other pictures usually as part of a story/picture package on subjects detailed below. Prefers British-sourced material.
Text: Well-illustrated features on completed cars, step-by-step illustrated material on how to do it, track tests of modified cars and coverage of shows and events. Always phone or write first to discuss ideas.
Overall freelance potential: Good for the right sort of material.
Editor's tips: Not interested in front-wheel drive or post-1980 vehicles.
Fees: £50 for news items; text £125 per 1,000 words.

AUTO EXPRESS
Dennis Publishing, 30 Cleveland Street, London W1T 4JD.
Tel: 020 7907 6000. Picture library: 020 7907 6132. Fax: 020 7917 5556. E-mail: editorial@autoexpress.co.uk
Editor: David Johns. **Picture Editor:** Dawn Tennant.
Popular weekly magazine, aimed at the average motorist rather than the car enthusiast.
Illustrations: Digital files preferred. Hard news pictures and topical motoring subjects with impact may be considered on spec, but most is by commission.
Text: Features on any motoring topic, to appeal to a general readership. May be practical but should not be too technical. 1,000–2,000 words. Always submit a synopsis in the first instance.
Overall freelance potential: Limited for the non-specialist.
Editor's tips: Although a popular non-technical title, accuracy is essential.
Fees: Photographs according to size of reproduction. Text usually £200 per 1,000 words.

AUTOCAR
Haymarket Publishing Ltd, Teddington Studios, Broom Road, Teddington, Middlesex TW11 9BE.
Tel: 020 8267 5630. Fax: 020 8267 5759. E-mail: paul.yelland@haymarket.com
Editor: Chas Hallett. **Group Art Editor:** Paul Yelland.
High quality general interest motoring weekly. Includes road tests, new car descriptions, international motor sport, motor shows, etc.
Illustrations: Digital files preferred. Mostly by commission for top quality general car coverage, test reports, performance cars, industry picture stories and portraits – submit CV/portfolio to the

Art Editor. Always interested in scoop pictures of pre-production models under test or any other exclusive motor industry photo items.
Text: Illustrated features on motoring subjects, by prior arrangement with the editor. 1,000–2,000 words.
Overall freelance potential: Good for those with experience.
Editor's tips: Technical accuracy and full information on the cars featured is essential. Familiarise yourself with the magazine first; too much material received is unsuitable.
Fees: Features by negotiation.

THE AUTOMOBILE
Enthusiast Publishing Ltd. Editorial: Herons Lodge, Herons Gate, Rickmansworth WD3 5DH.
Fax: 01923 284379. E-mail: mhlbowler@boltblue.com
Editor: Michael Bowler.
Monthly publication featuring veteran, vintage, and pre-1960s motor vehicles.
Illustrations: Digital files preferred. Not much scope for single pictures unless of particular interest. The main requirement is for well-illustrated articles concerning any pre-1960s motor vehicle; not only cars but also commercial vehicles. Also limited room for coverage of race meetings, exhibitions or other events at which old motor vehicles are present.
Text: Informative illustrated articles as above. Of particular interest are good restoration features, with both "before" and "after" pictures showing what can be achieved.
Overall freelance potential: Although limited there is scope for illustrated features – consult the editor before starting on feature.
Editor's tips: Do not submit material concerning post-1960s vehicles.
Fees: By negotiation.

CAR & ACCESSORY TRADER
Haymarket Publishing Ltd, Teddington Studios, Broom Road, Teddington, Middlesex TW11 9BE.
Tel: 020 8267 5992. Fax: 020 8267 5993. E-mail: cat.eds@haymarket.com
Editor: Dan Anderson.
Monthly magazine for traders involved in the selling of car parts and accessories.
Illustrations: B&W and colour. Captioned news pictures concerning new products, openings of new premises, handover of sales awards, etc. Much is commissioned. Covers: excellent relevant photographs considered.
Text: Varied subjects of interest to the trade, by commission only.
Overall freelance potential: About 50 per cent of contributions are from freelance sources.
Fees: £100 per £1,000 words. Photographs negotiable.

CLASSIC & SPORTS CAR
Haymarket Publishing Ltd, Teddington Studios, Broom Road, Teddington, Middlesex TW11 9BE.
Tel: 020 8267 5399. Fax: 020 8267 5318. E-mail: james.elliott@haymarket.com
Editor: James Elliott.
Monthly magazine covering mainly post-1945 classic cars, generally of a sporting nature. Strong coverage of the owners' scene.
Illustrations: Colour; B&W archive material. Mainly interested in coverage of club or historic car gatherings, unless staff photographer is present. Feature photography always commissioned.
Text: Articles of interest to the classic car enthusiast and collector, up to 2,500 words.
Overall freelance potential: Small, as much material is staff produced.
Editor's tips: Always get in touch before submitting.
Fees: According to merit.

CLASSIC AMERICAN
Trader Media Group, Optimum House, Clippers Quay, Salford Quays, Manchester M50 3XP.
Tel: 0161 836 4406. Fax: 0161 872 6238. E-mail: email@classic-american.com
Editor: Ben Klemenzson. **Art Editor:** Tony Crowther.

Monthly magazine concerning American cars mainly of the '50s, '60s and '70s.
Illustrations: Digital files preferred. Striking or unusual pictures of classic US vehicles. However, much of the photography is commissioned from regulars or staff-produced.
Text: Illustrated articles on specific cars or bikes and their owners, plus features on other aspects of American-style youth culture such as clothing, music, sport, etc. 1,000–2,000 words. Always check with the editor before submitting.
Overall freelance potential: Car coverage welcome, but best scope is for lifestyle features.
Fees: Pictures by negotiation. £150 per 1,000 words for text.

CLASSIC CARS
EMAP Automotive Ltd, Media House, Lynchwood, Peterborough Business Park, Peterborough PE2 6EA.
Tel: 01733 468000. Fax: 01733 468888. E-mail: classic.cars@emap.com/tony.turner@emap.com
Editor: Phil Bell. **Deputy Editor:** Mike Goodbun. **Picture Researcher:** Tony Turner.
Glossy, heavily-illustrated monthly covering classic cars of all eras.
Illustrations: Digital files preferred. Will consider on-spec reportage-style coverage of classic car gatherings around the country. Major feature photography mostly handled by a team of regulars. E-mail picture researcher in the first instance.
Text: Limited scope, but suggestions considered.
Overall freelance potential: Very good for the right sort of material.
Editor's tips: Detailed captions and a contact number for each car's owner are essential.
Fees: On a rising scale according to size of reproduction, up to £150 for a full-bleed page.

CLASSICS MONTHLY
Future Publishing Ltd, Beauford Court, 30 Monmouth Street, Bath BA1 2BW.
Tel: 01225 442244. E-mail: classicsmonthly@futurenet.co.uk
Editor: Gary Stretton.
Practical monthly for classic car owners.
Illustrations: Digital files preferred. Captioned pictures of newsworthy cars and events, including relevant motorsport coverage, always considered on spec. Also scope for commissions to do photo shoots of featured cars; send samples of previous work in the first instance.
Text: Well-illustrated features about restoring classic cars; reports from events.
Overall freelance potential: Good.
Editor's tips: Look at mag carefully before submitting work, particularly the editorial profile and style. Always interested in hearing about cars which might make a good feature subject. Send a sample shot with some details about the car and a commission to shoot may be offered.
Fees: Pictures, typically £100 per feature; £120 per 1,000 words; commissioned photography, £200 per day.

DRIVING MAGAZINE
Safety House, Beddington Farm Road, Croydon CR0 4XZ.
Tel: 0845 345 5151. Fax: 020 8665 5565. E-mail: drivingmagazine@driving.org
Editor: Graham Fryer.
Bi-monthly road safety publication for advanced drivers, road safety educationists and driving instructors.
Illustrations: Prints or digital files preferred. Pictures of home or overseas motorists/driving school vehicles in unusual surroundings or circumstances. Humorous incidents, traffic accidents of an unusual nature, unusual road signs, humorous signs or those in extraordinary positions.
Text: Features on road safety, driver training occasionally accepted. 500–2,000 words.
Overall freelance potential: Modest.
Fees: Photographs from £15–£20, variable according to subject and quality.

EVO
Evo Publications Ltd, Tower Court, Irchester Road, Wollaston, Wellingborough NN29 7PJ.
Tel: 020 7907 6310. E-mail: eds@evo.co.uk
Editor: Harry Metcalfe. **Art Editor:** Chee-Chiu Lee.
Glossy monthly covering the high-performance end of the car market.
Illustrations: Digital files preferred. All by commission. Interested in hearing from freelances who can produce good action photography of cars on the move, preferably with an individual and "cutting edge" style. Some portrait work also available.
Text: No scope.
Overall freelance potential: Good for the experienced car photographer.
Fees: By negotiation.

FLEET NEWS
EMAP Automotive Ltd, Media House, Lynchwood, Peterborough Business Park, Peterborough PE2 6EA.
Tel: 01733 468000. Fax: 01733 468296. E-mail: fleetnews@emap.com
Editor: Martyn Moore.
Weekly newspaper aimed at those responsible for running company car and light commercial vehicle fleets.
Illustrations: Captioned news pictures concerning company car operations, handover of car fleets to companies, appointments in the trade, etc.
Text: News, articles on business car management and related subjects.
Overall freelance potential: Excellent.
Editor's tips: Always write or e-mail first.
Fees: Negotiable.

4x4
IPC Focus Network, Leon House, 233 High Street, Croydon CR9 1HZ.
Tel: 020 8726 8374. Fax: 020 8726 8398. E-mail: john_carroll@ipcmedia.co.uk
Editor: John Carroll.
Monthly magazine devoted to four-wheel-drive vehicles.
Illustrations: Digital files preferred. Pictures of new vehicles, travel and other "off road" events. Must be captioned with full details of driver, event and location.
Text: Illustrated articles concerning four-wheel-drive vehicles and off-road activities. 1,000–2,000 words.
Overall freelance potential: Limited, but there is room for new contributors.
Fees: By negotiation.

JAGUAR
Haymarket Publishing Ltd, Teddington Studios, Broom Road, Teddington, Middlesex TW11 9BE.
Tel: 020 8267 5947. Fax: 020 8267 5872. E-mail: jaguar-magazine@haymarket.com
Editor: Jonathan Evans.
Glossy general interest quarterly for owners of Jaguar cars.
Illustrations: High quality commissioned photography of Jaguar cars, travel and general lifestyle subjects. Opportunities only for experienced workers with medium format equipment.
Text: Strongly-illustrated articles on travel and lifestyle subjects. All work is by commission, no unsolicited work is accepted.
Overall freelance potential: Good for experienced workers, though limited by the publishing frequency.
Fees: Photography by negotiation. Articles around £400; pictures, £600.

JAGUAR HERITAGE ARCHIVE MAGAZINE

Jaguar Daimler Heritage Trust, Browns Lane, Allesley, Coventry CV5 9DR.
Tel: 02476 202141. E-mail: editor@jdhtsales.co.uk
Editor: François Prins.
Concentrates on the history of the Jaguar company and of individual cars bearing the Jaguar, Daimler or Lanchester marques.
Illustrations: Colour; archive B&W. Most interested in coverage of individual classic models that are still in good running order, especially if they have an interesting story attached. Will also consider interesting older photographs, from 1896 on, though a good deal of material is sourced from the Heritage Trust archive. Commissions may be available to experienced car photographers.
Text: Feature packages about unusually interesting classics and restoration projects always of considerable interest. Submit suggestions and ideas in the first instance, by letter or e-mail.
Overall freelance potential: Good.
Fees: Pictures according to use; text usually £50 per 1,000 words.

LAND ROVER MONTHLY

Golden Gate Production Co Ltd, The Publishing House, 2 Brickfields Business Park, Woolpit, Suffolk IP30 9QS.
Tel: 01359 240066. Fax: 01359 244221. E-mail: editorial@lrm.co.uk
Managing Editor: Richard Howell-Thomas.
Monthly magazine for Land Rover enthusiasts.
Illustrations: Digital files preferred. Little scope for individual photographs unless accompanied by extended captions or background text.
Text: Well-illustrated articles on all matters relating to Land Rover, Range Rover, Discovery and Freelander vehicles; travel/adventure stories, features on interesting individual vehicles and off-roading personalities, competition and club event reports. Limited scope for vehicle test reports.
Overall freelance potential: Excellent for those who can add words to their pictures, and have good knowledge of Land Rover products.
Fees: By negotiation.

LAND ROVER OWNER

EMAP Automotive Ltd, Media House, Lynchwood, Peterborough Business Park, Peterborough PE2 6EA.
Tel: 01733 468000. Fax: 01733 468238. E-mail; rob.mccabe@emap.com
Editor-in-Chief: John Pearson.
Magazine for Land Rover owners and enthusiasts. 13 issues a year.
Illustrations: Digital files or transparencies. Interesting or unusual pictures of Land Rovers, Range Rovers, Freelanders, Defenders and Discoverys. Celebrities pictured with such vehicles.
Text: Illustrated articles on overland expeditions using Land Rovers. Length 1,000 words, plus around six pictures.
Overall freelance potential: Good.
Fees: Text, £100 per 1,000 words; pictures by negotiation.

MAX POWER

EMAP Automotive Ltd, Media House, Lynchwood, Peterborough Business Park, Peterborough PE2 6EA.
Tel: 01733 468000. Fax: 01733 468001. E-mail: simon.penson@emap.com
Editor: Simon Penson.
Monthly for young men heavily involved with fast cars and modifying them.
Illustrations: Pictures of smart and well-modified cars; also "sheds" (particularly badly modified cars). Also picture stories of likely interest to the target readership, including coverage of car gatherings.
Text: Ideas for features of interest to "lads" in their twenties always considered.
Overall freelance potential: Good for those in touch with this scene.

Editor's tips: Freelances need to be able to recognise the particular type of "cool" car that is featured here, and be aware of the general mood of the magazine.
Fees: Picture stories around £200–£300; single pictures according to use.

MOTOR SPORT
Stratfield Ltd, 26-30 Old Church Street, Chelsea, London SW3 5BY.
Tel: 020 7349 3180. Fax: 020 7349 3160. E-mail: editorial@motorsportmagazine.co.uk
Editor-in-Chief: Andrew Frankel. **Deputy Editor:** Gordon Cruikshank. **Picture Editor:** Ian Marshall.
Monthly devoted to motor sport and sports cars, both old and new.
Illustrations: Colour; B&W archive material. Will always consider coverage of classic or vintage sports car meetings and racing. Archive collections always of interest.
Text: No scope.
Overall freelance potential: Fair.
Fees: From around £35 upwards.

MOTOR TRADER
Nexus Media Communications, Media House, Azalea Drive, Swanley, Kent BR8 8HU.
Tel: 01322 660070. Fax: 01322 616378. E-mail: curtis.hutchinson@nexusmedia.com
Editor: Curtis Hutchinson.
Weekly trade newspaper, controlled circulation and subscription, read by dealers & manufacturers in the car and component industries, garage owners, body shop workers.
Illustrations: B&W and colour. News pictures on anything connected with the motor trade.
Text: News and features relevant to the motor trade and industry. 300–1,000 words.
Overall freelance potential: Good for those in touch with the trade.
Editor's tips: This is the trade's only weekly newspaper; it is particularly interested in hard news. Call to discuss with editor or deputy before submitting material.
Fees: Negotiable.

MOTORING & LEISURE
Csma Ltd, Britannia House, 21 Station Street, Brighton BN1 4DE.
Tel: 01273 744744. Fax: 01273 744761. E-mail: magazine@csma.uk.com
Editor: David Arnold.
Monthly journal of the Civil Service Motoring Association, covering motoring, travel and leisure activities.
Illustrations: General car-related subjects and Continental travel.
Text: Illustrated articles on motoring, travel, camping and caravanning. 750–1,000 words.
Overall freelance potential: Limited.
Fees: By arrangement.

911 & PORSCHE WORLD
CH Publications Ltd, Nimax House, 20 Ullswater Crescent, Ullswater Business Park, Coulsdon, Surrey CR5 2HR.
Tel: 020 8655 6400. Fax: 020 8763 1001. E-mail: chp@chpltd.com
Editor: Steve Bennett.
Magazine published nine times a year and devoted to Porsche or Porsche-derived cars.
Illustrations: Mostly colour. All commissioned, with opportunities for those who have original ideas and can produce top quality car photography.
Text: Ideas for articles always of interest; write with details in the first instance.
Overall freelance potential: Very good for specialist coverage.
Fees: Photography by arrangement; around £100 per 1,000 words.

OCTANE
Dennis Publishing Ltd, Tower Court, Irchester Road, Wollaston, Northants NN29 7PJ.
Tel: 020 7907 6585. E-mail: rob@octane-magazine.co.uk
Editor: Robert Coucher. **Art Editor:** Robert Gould.
Monthly covering both contemporary high-performance cars and prestige classics from all eras.
Illustrations: Colour and historic B&W. Digital files preferred. Mostly by commission with good opportunities for experienced car photographers. Possible on-spec scope for picture stories covering specific events such as meets, rallies, races, etc. Relevant archive material also of interest.
Text: Suggestions always considered.
Overall freelance potential: Good.
Fees: By negotiation.

PERFORMANCE FORD
Unity Media Communications Ltd, Becket House, Vestry Road, Sevenoaks, Kent TN14 5EJ.
Tel: 01732 748000. Fax: 01732 748001. E-mail: dmoore@unity-media.com
Editor: Dave Moore.
Monthly magazine devoted to Ford and Ford-based vehicles, with the emphasis on high-performance road use.
Illustrations: Digital files preferred. Pictures commissioned to illustrate features, or topical single pictures of particular quality, i.e. prototypes, one-offs, etc.
Text: Illustrated articles on maintenance and modification of Ford-based cars. Personality profiles with a direct relevance to Ford products.
Overall freelance potential: Fair.
Editor's tips: Always raise ideas with the editor before submitting material.
Fees: Pictures according to size of reproduction or day rate by arrangement; text £120 per 1,000 words.

REDLINE
Future Publishing Ltd, Beauford Court, 30 Monmouth Street, Bath BA1 2BW.
Tel: 01225 442244. Fax: 01225 822793. E-mail: tim.durant@futurenet.co.uk
Editor: Dan Lewis. **Art Editor:** Tim Durant.
Motoring monthly for young men who want to get the best out of their modified cars.
Illustrations: Exciting and dramatic pictures of modified cars, sporting and speed events, unusual vehicles and fast lifestyles. Commissions available for car shoots, also some glamour; make appointment with the art editor.
Text: Will always consider suggestions for illustrated articles on suitable subjects, such as touring trips, unusual events, weird car-based experiences, etc.
Overall freelance potential: Moderate.
Editor's tips: Although photographers should know how to light and shoot cars, non-specialists are welcome if they can produce something exciting and different.
Fees: Single pictures £25–£250; page rate ££50–£125; day rate £150–£300.

TOP GEAR MAGAZINE
BBC Magazines, Room AG192, Woodlands, 80 Wood Lane, London W12 0TT.
Tel: 020 8433 2000. Fax: 020 8576 3754. E-mail: queries.tgmag@bbc.co.uk
Editor: Michael Harvey.
General interest motoring magazine designed to complement the BBC TV programme.
Illustrations: All by commission and much from known specialists, but photographers with a fresh approach and a good portfolio are welcomed. Send samples and details of previous experience in the first instance, or call for appointment. Stock images of pre-1990 cars often needed to illustrate articles.
Text: Motoring-related features considered, preferably out of the ordinary.
Overall freelance potential: Good opportunities for talented car photographers.
Fees: By negotiation.

TOTAL 911
9 Publishing, PO Box 6815, Matlock, Derbyshire DE4 4WZ.
Tel: 0845 450 6964. E-mail: phil@9publishing.co.uk
Editor: Philip Raby.
Monthly for Porsche 911 car enthusiasts, covering both classic and modern models.
Illustrations: All by commission only. Interested in hearing from professional car photographers who can offer something different. Write first enclosing samples of work.
Text: Ideas from professional motoring writers always welcome – apply in writing only.
Overall freelance potential: Good.
Editor's tips: Study the magazine before getting in touch.
Fees: Negotiable, but from around £150 for photo assignments, £100 per 1,000 words for text.

TRIUMPH WORLD
Kelsey Publishing Group, PO Box 13, Westerham, Kent TN16 3WT.
Tel: 01895 623612. Fax: 01895 623613. E-mail: tw.ed@kelsey.co.uk
Editor: Ted Connolly.
Bi-monthly for Triumph car (not motorcycle) enthusiasts.
Illustrations: B&W and colour. Digital files preferred. Photographs of newsworthy or unusual Triumph cars, especially the "classics" such as Heralds, TRs, Spitfires and Stags. Some opportunities for experienced photographers to produce commissioned work for major features.
Text: Illustrated articles likely to appeal to the dedicated enthusiast. Phone first to discuss ideas.
Overall freelance potential: Good.
Fees: Pictures by negotiation and according to use. Text £120 per 1,000 words.

Music

BLUES & SOUL
Blues & Soul Ltd, 153 Praed Street, London W2 1RL.
Tel: 020 7402 6869. Fax: 020 7224 8227. E-mail: editorial@bluesandsoul.com
Editor: Bob Kilbourn.
Fortnightly publication covering soul, R&B, funk, fusion, jazz, house, garage, urban dance – all forms of black music excepting reggae.
Illustrations: B&W and colour. Digital files preferred. Will always consider original and exclusive pictures of black music performers.
Text: Small amount of scope for exclusive articles or interviews.
Overall freelance potential: Limited.
Editor's tips: Think of the readership, and the format, in order to produce something really striking and eye-catching.
Fees: By negotiation.

CLASSICAL MUSIC
Rhinegold Publishing Ltd, 241 Shaftesbury Avenue, London WC2H 8TF.
Tel: 020 7333 1742. Fax: 020 7333 1769. E-mail: classical.music@rhinegold.co.uk
Editor: Keith Clarke.
Fortnightly news and feature magazine for classical music professionals and the interested general public.
Illustrations: Digital files preferred. Very limited scope as most pictures are supplied by promoters, etc, but always happy to look at portfolios, subject to appointment. Occasional urgent need for a musician or group in the news – most easily met if freelances can supply lists of photographs they hold.
Text: Short news items and news stories about events in the music/arts world, including politics and performance, up to 800 words. Longer background features about musicians, usually relating to a

forthcoming event, up to 2,000 words. All work is commissioned.
Overall freelance potential: Limited for photographers, but most text is from commissioned freelance sources.
Fees: Pictures by negotiation; text from £100 per 1,000 words.

FROOTS
Southern Rag Ltd, PO Box 337, London N4 1TW.
Tel: 020 8340 9651. Fax: 020 8348 5626. E-mail: froots@frootsmag.com
Editor: Ian Anderson.
Monthly publication concerned with folk and world roots music.
Illustrations: B&W and colour. Pictures to be used in conjunction with interviews, reviews of records or reports on events. Mostly commissioned.
Text: Interviews and reviews concerned with folk and world music.
Overall freelance potential: Limited for the contributor unknown in this field. The magazine favours its regular contributors.
Fees: By agreement.

KERRANG!
EMAP Performance Network, Mappin House, 4 Winsley Street, London W1W 8HF.
Tel: 020 7436 1515. Fax: 020 7312 8910. E-mail: kerrang@emap.com
Editor: Paul Brannigan. **News Editor:** Simon Young.
Weekly magazine covering a wide range of hard rock.
Illustrations: Pictures of relevant bands. On-stage performance shots preferred, with the emphasis on action. Some posed shots and portraits of top performers also used.
Text: Little freelance market.
Overall freelance potential: Very good. The magazine is heavily illustrated.
Fees: According to size of reproduction.

KEYBOARD PLAYER
Bookrose Ltd, 100 Birkbeck Road, Enfield, Middlesex EN2 0ED.
Tel: 020 8245 5840. E-mail: steve@keyboardplayer.com
Editor: Steve Miller.
Monthly magazine for players of all types of keyboard instrument. Covers pianos, organs, keyboards and synthesisers; and all forms of music, from pop to classical.
Illustrations: B&W and colour. Photographs of keyboard instruments and their players, preferably accompanied by a newsy caption. Covers: striking colour pictures of keyboard instruments.
Text: Articles of around 1,000 words on any topic of interest to keyboard players.
Overall freelance potential: Fairly limited, but scope is there for the right type of material.
Editor's tips: Run-of-the-mill pictures of players seated at their instruments will not be met with much enthusiasm – a strikingly different approach is required.
Fees: By negotiation.

METAL HAMMER
Future Publishing Ltd, 2 Balcombe Street, London NW1 6NW.
Tel: 020 7042 4000. Fax: 020 7042 4471. E-mail: jamie.hibbard@futurenet.co.uk
Editor: Jamie Hibbard. **Art Editor:** James Isaacs.
Monthly for heavy metal and hard rock fans.
Illustrations: Mostly colour. Good action and group portrait photographs of hard rock or heavy metal performers – send lists of subjects available. Commissions available to experienced rock photographers.
Text: Illustrated articles, interviews and reviews. Submit suggestions only in the first instance.
Overall freelance potential: Excellent for those in touch with this scene.
Fees: By negotiation.

MIXMAG
Development Hell, 90-92 Pentonville Road, London N1 9HS.
Tel: 020 7520 8625. Fax: 020 7833 9900. E-mail: mixmag@mixmag.net
Editor: Nick de Cosemo.
Monthly covering the dance music and clubbing scene.
Illustrations: Photographs of clubs and clubbers throughout the country; portraits of musicians; photo features. Fresh young photographers always welcome.
Text: Reports from clubs nationwide; young writers welcome.
Overall freelance potential: Very good.
Editor's tips: Contributors don't have to have experience, just a good sense of what the dance scene is about.
Fees: By negotiation.

MOJO
EMAP Performance Network, Mappin House, 4 Winsley Street, London W1W 8HF.
Tel: 020 7312 8207. Fax: 020 7312 8296. E-mail: matt.turner@emap.com
Editor-in-Chief: Phil Alexander. **Picture Editor:** Matt Turner.
Monthly rock music magazine aimed at fans of all ages.
Illustrations: Colour and archive B&W. Photographs of leading rock artists, both contemporary and from earlier eras. Archive material from the '50s, '60s and '70s always of interest. Good opportunities for commissioned work.
Text: In-depth profiles of individual artists and bands, but scope mainly for established writers.
Overall freelance potential: Good.
Editor's tips: Previously unpublished or unseen photographs, or those that have not been used for some years, are of particular interest.
Fees: According to use.

NEW MUSICAL EXPRESS
IPC Media Ltd, Blue Fin Building, 110 Southwark Street, London SE1 0SU.
Tel: 020 3148 6864. Fax: 020 3148 8107. E-mail: nmepics@ipcmedia.com
Editor: Conor McNicholas. **Art Director:** Mark Jones. **Picture Editor:** Marian Paterson.
Weekly tabloid covering all aspects of popular music and allied youth culture.
Illustrations: Mostly colour. All aspects of contemporary popular music, but see below.
Text: Scope for exclusive news stories or interviews with rock musicians, film stars, or other personalities of interest to a young and aware readership. Always write or phone with suggestions first.
Overall freelance potential: Good, but very dependent on subject matter.
Editor's tips: NME only covers those parts of the music scene considered worthwhile by the editorial team – study recent issues.
Fees: On a rising scale according to size of reproduction.

Q
EMAP Performance Network, Mappin House, 4 Winsley Street, London W1W 8HF.
Tel: 020 7436 1515. Fax: 020 7182 8547. E-mail: qpictures@emap.com
Editor: Paul Rees. **Picture Director:** Steve Peck.
Monthly rock music magazine aimed at the 18–35 age group.
Illustrations: Mostly colour. Most pictures staff-produced or commissioned from a pool of regular contributors, but suitable stock pictures of relevant personalities will always be considered.
Text: Top quality profiles, interviews and feature articles of interest to a rock-oriented readership, invariably by commission.
Overall freelance potential: 50 per cent is commissions; good for library/stock shots.
Fees: By negotiation.

RHYTHM
Future Publishing Ltd, Beauford Court, 30 Monmouth Street, Bath BA1 2BW.
Tel: 01225 442244. Fax: 01225 732285. E-mail: phil.ascott@futurenet.co.uk
Editor: Phil Ascott.
Monthly magazine for drummers and percussionists in the rock and pop music field.
Illustrations: Mostly colour. Interesting photographs relating to contemporary percussion instruments and their players, including the use of electronic and computer-aided equipment.
Text: Illustrated profiles, interviews and features about leading contemporary drummers and percussionists. Articles on technique and programming from knowledgeable contributors.
Overall freelance potential: Limited.
Fees: £110 per 1,000 words for text; photographs according to use.

TOTAL GUITAR
Future Publishing Ltd, Beauford Court, 30 Monmouth Street, Bath BA1 2BW.
Tel: 01225 442244. Fax: 01225 462986. E-mail: totalguitar@futurenet.co.uk
Editor: Stephen Lawson. **Art Editor:** Graham Dalzell.
Monthly magazine for guitar players at all levels, concentrating on practical advice.
Illustrations: Mostly commissioned to accompany features and reviews. Stock shots of well-known players and individual instruments always of interest; send lists first.
Text: Profiles and interviews with leading guitarists, and practical articles. Submit ideas only in the first instance.
Overall freelance potential: Limited.
Fees: By negotiation.

Parenting

MOTHER & BABY
EMAP Esprit, Greater London House, Hampstead Road, London NW1 7EJ.
Tel: 020 7874 0200. Fax: 020 7347 1888. E-mail: mother&baby@emap.com
Editor: Elena Dalrymple.
Monthly aimed at pregnant women and mothers of young children.
Illustrations: High quality photographs of mothers with babies, or babies (under one year) on their own. Medium format transparencies preferred.
Text: Articles on all subjects related to pregnancy, birth, baby care and the early years.
Overall freelance potential: Limited, since the magazine is frequently overstocked.
Editor's tips: Only top quality pictures will be considered.
Fees: From £30 upwards for single pictures.

NURSERY WORLD
Haymarket Publishing Ltd, 22 Bute Gardens, London W6 7HN.
Tel: 020 8267 8412. E-mail: kate.watson@haymarket.com
Editor: Liz Roberts. **Picture Editor:** Kate Watson.
Weekly publication on child care. Aimed at professional baby and child care workers such as teachers, nursery nurses and nannies.
Illustrations: Digital files preferred. Pictures of babies and young children (up to five years old) involved in various activities in childcare settings. Covers: Location shots of children, always linked to a feature inside.
Text: Features on child care, education, health, and any aspect of bringing up children, e.g. physical, intellectual, emotional etc. Ideas for nurseries and playgroups.
Overall freelance potential: Many features come from freelance contributors.
Fees: By arrangement.

PREGNANCY & BIRTH

EMAP Esprit Ltd, Greater London House, Hampstead Road, London NW1 7EJ.
Tel: 020 7874 0200. Fax: 020 7874 0201. E-mail: dani.corbett@emap.com
Editor: Sarah Hart. **Art Editor:** Dani Corbett.
Monthly covering pregnancy from conception to birth.
Illustrations: Mostly by commission. Opportunities for experienced photographers to produce cover shots, mother and baby fashion, and "real life" material; contact art editor in the first instance. Always interested in hearing of good specialist stock collections.
Text: No scope.
Overall freelance potential: Good for experienced workers.
Editor's tips: Photographers need to be capable of working with real people rather than models.
Fees: By negotiation.

PRIMA BABY

National Magazine Company, 72 Broadwick Street, London W1F 9EP.
Tel: 020 7439 5000. Fax: 020 7312 3744. E-mail: lisa.durows@natmags.co.uk
Editor: Elaine Griffiths. **Art Director:** Lisa Durows.
Glossy monthly covering pregnancy, babies and toddlers up to three years.
Illustrations: Digital files preferred. Top quality pictures of babies and toddlers, with/without parents, in situations, engaged in activities, etc. Also pictures relating to aspects of childcare, health, fashion and home life. Must be warm, natural lifestyle images rather than posed "stock" shots. Write with details in the first instance. Some commissions available, mainly for reportage and studio photographers; call first to discuss possibilities.
Text: Limited freelance scope.
Overall freelance potential: Very good for quality material.
Fees: Variable; day rate around £400.

RIGHT START

McMillan Scott plc, 9 Savoy Street, London WC2E 7HR.
Tel: 020 7878 2338. Fax: 020 7379 6261. E-mail: lynette@rightstartmagazine.co.uk
Editor: Lynette Lowthian.
Bi-monthly magazine for parents of pre-school and primary school age children, covering health, behaviour, education and family life.
Illustrations: B&W and colour. Mostly by commission but some scope for good stock coverage of children in educational and learning situations; send only lists or details of coverage available in the first instance.
Text: Opportunities for education and child care specialists. Approach with details of ideas and previous experience.
Overall freelance potential: Limited.
Fees: By negotiation.

Photography & Video

AV MAGAZINE

Haymarket Specialist, 174 Hammersmith Road, London W6 7NH.
Tel: 020 8267 8005. Fax: 020 8267 8008. E-mail: peter.lloyd@haymarket.com
Editor: Peter Lloyd.
Monthly magazine for managers in industry and commerce, public services, government etc who use audiovisual communication techniques, eg slides, film, video, overhead projection and filmstrips, plus the new technologies of computer graphics and telecommunication.
Illustrations: B&W and colour. Digital files preferred. Pictures of programmes being shown to audiences, preferably supported by case history details; relevant news; new products or location

107

shooting pictures. All must be backed with solid information. Covers: colour pictures of same, but check before submitting.
Text: Case histories of either shows, conferences or studies of a particular company's use of AV techniques. Good location/conference stories always welcome. 1,000–2,500 words.
Overall freelance potential: Up to 25 per cent comes from freelances.
Fees: Text, £180-£200 per 1,000 words; pictures by agreement.

AMATEUR PHOTOGRAPHER
IPC Inspire, Blue Fin Building, 110 Southwark Street, London SE1 0SU.
Tel: 020 3148 4138. Fax: 020 3148 8123. E-mail: amateurphotographer@ipcmedia.com
Editor: Damien Demolder.
Weekly magazine for all photographers, from beginners to experienced enthusiasts.
Illustrations: B&W and colour. Pictures to illustrate specific photo techniques and general photo features. General portfolios in B&W and colour. Send no more than 20 pictures, prints unmounted, slides in a plastic slide wallet.
Text: No scope.
Overall freelance potential: Good.
Fees: £50 per published page, pictures and text, except "Gallery".

BLACK & WHITE PHOTOGRAPHY
GMC Publications Ltd, 86 High Street, Lewes, East Sussex BN7 1XN.
Tel: 01273 477374. Fax: 01273 402849. E-mail: ailsam@thegmcgroup.com
Editor: Ailsa McWhinnie.
Published 13 times a year, the magazine is devoted to showcasing the best in black and white photography.
Illustrations: B&W only. Features and portfolios showcasing the work of individual photographers, usually a cohesive body of work on a specific subject or theme. Regular "Reader Gallery" feature devotes up to two pages per reader/contributor. Photojournalistic work of particular interest, especially long-term projects produced over an extended period. Also step by step features showing all stages from a straight print to the final print. Digital techniques also covered. Little scope for single images. Also runs annual Black & White Photographer of the Year competition.
Text: Illustrated articles on printing techniques, film/paper combinations, equipment choices, etc. Submit sample prints and synopsis in the first instance.
Overall freelance potential: Excellent for the dedicated B&W worker.
Fees: £100 for "Gallery" feature; other fees according to subject and use.

THE BRITISH JOURNAL OF PHOTOGRAPHY
Incisive Media, 32–34 Broadwick Street, London W1A 2HG.
Tel: 020 7316 9658. Fax: 020 7316 9003. E-mail: bjp.features@bjphoto.co.uk
Editor: Simon Bainbridge. **Deputy Editor:** Diane Smyth. **News Editor:** Katie Scott.
Weekly publication for professional and semi-professional photographers, technicians, etc., and all those engaged in professional photography.
Illustrations: B&W and colour. Digital files preferred. Portfolios along with some biographical notes about the photographer concerned. Contact deputy editor in the first instance.
Text: Interested in anything related to professional photography, particularly the more unusual and technical aspects.
Overall freelance potential: Good for bringing freelances to the attention of potential clients.
Editor's tips: Contributors do need to offer something special. Remember the magazine is aimed at those engaged in professional and semi-professional photography – technical features must therefore be of the highest calibre.
Fees: Portfolios not normally paid for; exposure in the magazine frequently leads to commissions elsewhere. Negotiable for text.

DIGITAL CAMERA MAGAZINE

Future Publishing Ltd, Beauford Court, 30 Monmouth Street, Bath BA1 2BW.
Tel: 01225 442244. Fax: 01225 732295. E-mail: editor.dcm@futurenet.co.uk
Editor: Marcus Hawkins.
Monthly for the mid-market of digital camera users, those mainly using digital SLRs in the
£600–£1400 price range.
Illustrations: B&W and colour. Good single images required to illustrate seasonal subjects and
topical events, and as examples of creative digital manipulations/compositions. Should be
accompanied by detailed captions.
Text: Well-illustrated "how to" articles on digital photography and image editing. Contributors need
to have some prior experience of producing such material.
Overall freelance potential: Good.
Editor's tips: Contributors should supply as much background detail about their images as they
can.
Fees: Single images by negotiation and according to use; features £80 per published page.

DIGITAL PHOTO

EMAP Active Ltd, Media House, Lynchwood, Peterborough PE2 6EA.
Tel: 01733 468000. E-mail: jon.adams@emap.com
Editor: Jon Adams.
Monthly aimed at photographers keen to use their computer to enhance their pictures.
Illustrations: B&W and colour. Need for high-quality – technically and pictorially – original images
that inspire readers to produce similar work. Ideally submissions should be accompanied by step-by-
step screengrabs and words illustrating the thought processes and the stages involved in producing
the work. Creative work always needed for the portfolio pages; require ten outstanding digitally
manipulated images.
Text: Good potential for quality, step-by-step tutorials, but the final image must be outstanding and
relevant. Contact editor in the first instance.
Overall freelance potential: Excellent for step-by-step tutorials.
Editor's tips: Look at and read the magazine first, then e-mail ideas and low-resolution JPEGs to
illustrate. If submitting on CD always enclose high-quality inkjet prints too.
Fees: Negotiable, but typically £60 per page or £120 per 1,000 words.

DIGITAL PHOTO PRO

Bright Publishing Ltd, Bright House, 82 High Street, Sawston, Cambridge CB2 4HJ.
Tel: 01223 499450. Fax: 01223 839953. E-mail: terryhope@bright-publishing.com
Editor: Terry Hope. **News & Features Editor:** Charlotte Griffiths.
Monthly for professional and aspiring professional photographers, with the emphasis on business
matters.
Illustrations: Only required as illustrations to major features as below.
Text: Much is staff-produced or from regular contributors., but suggestions for artcles on aspects of
pro photography always considered.
Overall freelance potential: Limited.
Fees: By negotiation.

DIGITAL PHOTOGRAPHER

Imagine Publishing Ltd, Richmond House, 33 Richmond Hill, Bournemouth BH2 6EZ.
Tel: 01202 586249. Fax: 01202 299955. E-mail: debbi.allen@imagine-publishing.co.uk
Editor: Debbi Allen.
Digital photography magazine for the more advanced user, aimed at serious enthusiasts and
professionals.
Illustrations: Pictures mainly required to illustrate features on contemporary digital photography.
Opportunities best for photographers using digital for specialist subjects (landscape, wildlife,
portraiture, etc) or those experienced in Photoshop techniques.

Text: Practical illustrated articles and features on topics as above.
Overall freelance potential: Good for those with well-developed skills in digital work.
Fees: Negotiable, depending on what is on offer.

DIGITAL SLR PHOTOGRAPHY

Halo Publishing, 6 Swan Court, Cygnet Park, Hampton, Peterborough PE7 8FD.
Tel: 01733 567401. Fax: 01733 352650. E-mail: jo.smith@digitalslrphoto.com
Editor: Daniel Lezano. **Editorial Co-ordinater:** Jo Smith.
Monthly for all photographers who use digital SLRs.
Illustrations: Regular requirement for high-quality images produced on digital SLRs. Most interested in seeing portfolios of between 20-100 images. For all submissions, supply TIFFs or maximum-quality JPEGs on CD/DVD, with thumbnail printouts (maximum 20 images per A4 sheet).
Text: Mostly produced by regulars, but ideas always considered.
Overall freelance potential: Excellent.
Editor's tips: See website at www.digitalslrphoto.com for a flavour of the content of the magazine along with details of picture requirements and submission guidelines.
Fees: On a standard scale according to use.

DIGITAL SLR USER

Bright Publishing Ltd, Bright House, 82 High Street, Sawston, Cambridge CB2 4HJ.
Tel: 01223 499450. Fax: 01223 839953. E-mail: terryhope@bright-publishing.com
Editor: Terry Hope. **News & Features Editor:** Charlotte Griffiths.
Monthly for all digital SLR camera enthusiasts, both existing users and those who are buying into this market for the first time.
Illustrations: high-quality images prodcued on digital SLRs, but usually only used within illustrated features as below.
Text: Mostly staff-produced or from regular contributors.
Overall freelance potential: Limited.
Fees: According to use.

DIGITAL VIDEO

Future Publishing Ltd, 2 Balcombe Street, London NW1 6NW.
Tel: 020 7042 4000. Fax: 020 7042 4471. E-mail: rob.hull@futurenet.co.uk
Editor: Robert Hull. **Group Art Editor:** John Rook.
Monthly magazine for buyers and users of camcorders and digital video, with a practical bias.
Illustrations: General shots to illustrate technique and advice features. Good colour pictures of camcorders in use at various locations especially welcomed, e.g. on the beach, at sports events, at social occasions, on expeditions. Also pictures of editing and post-production equipment in use. Spectacular location shots may also be considered.
Text: Technique articles on producing better movies, tests on machines and accessories, action and application features, equipment reviews and personality interviews.
Overall freelance potential: Excellent. Around 50 per cent from such sources.
Fees: By agreement.

EOS MAGAZINE

Robert Scott Publishing Ltd, The Old Barn, Ball Lane, Tackley, Kidlington, Oxon OX5 3AG.
Tel: 01869 331741. Fax: 01869 331641. E-mail: editorial@eos-magazine.com
Editor: Angela August.
Quarterly magazine for users of Canon EOS cameras.
Illustrations: Mostly colour, but B&W considered. Digital files preferred. Top quality photographs of any subject taken with Canon EOS cameras. Should demonstrate some aspect of photographic technique or the use of equipment. Comparison shots always of interest.
Text: Contributions are welcomed.

Overall freelance potential: Very good.
Editor's tips: Up-to-date details of photo requirements available on e-mail request. Telephone or e-mail (with "editorial requirements" in subject box) to discuss ideas for written contributions.
Fees: Minimum fee for pictures is £15, but most are paid at between £20 and £60 depending on usage. Cover and dps, £100-£250. Text £90–£150 per 1,000 words (higher rates are for technique material which is comprehensive and well researched).

HOTSHOE INTERNATIONAL
World Illustrated Ltd, 29-31 Saffron Hill, London EC1N 8SW.
Tel: 020 7421 6000. Fax: 020 7421 6006. E-mail: melissa.dewitt@photoshot.com
Editor: Melissa De Witt.
Bi-monthly contemporary photography magazine covering all genres.
Illustrations: B&W and colour. Digital files preferred. High-quality photography and portfolios of all kinds, including fine art, documentary, reportage, photojournalism and creative photography.
Text: Only in support of material as above.
Overall freelance potential: Very good for high-quality, original material.
Editor's tips: Contributions need to be of real interest to other working photographers.
Fees: By negotiation.

MARKET NEWSLETTER
Bureau of Freelance Photographers, Focus House, 497 Green Lanes, London N13 4BP.
Tel: 020 8882 3315. Fax: 020 8886 3933. E-mail: eds@thebfp.com
Editor: John Tracy.
Monthly journal of the BFP, mainly devoted to detailing markets for photography. For members only.
Illustrations: B&W and colour. Photographs required for "Pictures that Sell" feature – photographs taken by BFP members that have proven commercial success, having earned high fees and/or having sold to a wide range of markets.
Text: Photographer profiles in which a successful photographer outlines his or her freelance activities, or general features on aspects of selling photography, backed up with examples of successful pictures and hints and tips to encourage others. Around 1,000 words.
Overall freelance potential: Limited.
Fees: £35 for "Pictures that Sell", £150 for photographer profile.

MASTER PHOTO>DIGITAL
Icon Publications Ltd, Maxwell Lane, Kelso, Roxburghshire TD5 7BB.
Tel: 01573 226032. Fax: 01573 26000. E-mail: iconmags@btconnect.com
Editor: David Kilpatrick.
Magazine for the UK's commercial and studio photographers, with the emphasis on photographing people for profit. Official journal of the Master Photographers Association (MPA). Eight issues per year.
Illustrations: B&W and colour. Digital files preferred. Only required to accompany and illustrate specific articles mainly relating to commercial studio or events photography.
Text: Illustrated articles and features on topics as above, mainly profiles/interviews with successful practitioners. Some technical articles.
Overall freelance potential: Limited; most material is contributed on a voluntarary basis by MPA members.
Fees: Interviews and technical material, £60-£90 per published page.

As a member of the Bureau of Freelance Photographers, you'll be kept up-to-date with markets through the BFP Market Newsletter, published monthly. For details of membership, turn to page 9

OUTDOOR PHOTOGRAPHY

GMC Publications, 86 High Street, Lewes, East Sussex BN7 1XN.
Tel: 01273 477374. Fax: 01273 478606. E-mail: keithw@thegmcgroup.com
Editor: Keith Wilson.
Monthly devoted to the photography of all types of outdoor subject matter.
Illustrations: Mainly colour. Top-quality photographs of British landscapes, countryside, wildlife, gardens, architecture and travel abroad. Scope for good single images in the "Reader's Pictures" gallery section, but prefer packages of both words and pictures.
Text: Well-illustrated articles on all aspects of outdoor photography, accompanied by full background details on location or subject.
Overall freelance potential: Excellent; the magazine relies on freelances contributors.
Editor's tips: The magazine is seasonally-led, so subject matter needs to be relevant to the month of publication.
Fees: By negotiation.

PENTAX USER

Unit 31/32 The Turbine, Shireoaks Business Park, Coach Close, Shireoaks S81 8AP.
Tel: 01909 512147. Fax: 01909 512147. E-mail: peter@pentaxuser.co.uk
Editor: Peter Bargh.
Exclusive magazine for members of the Pentax User club. Features techniques reviews and how-to articles on all areas of photography with an emphasis on Pentax camera equipment.
Illustrations: B&W and colour. Digital files preferred. Images mainly required for cover – any image that is taken on a Pentax, with space available to allow logo to appear top right and tasters bottom left. Other images usually only as part of a complete package of words and pictures.
Text: Well-illustrated articles on all aspects of photography with an emphasis on Pentax camera equipment. How-to articles on using modes of compacts and SLRs particularly sought after, along with techniques on using flash, lenses, filters etc. Please submit suggestions in writing in first instance. The editor will then phone or reply to discuss commission.
Overall freelance potential: Most of the magazine is based on articles from club members or freelances.
Fees: £50 per published page.

PHOTOGRAPHY MONTHLY

Archant Specialist, The Mill, Bearwalden Business Park, Wendens Ambo, Essex CB11 4GB.
Tel: 0845 650 1065. E-mail: photography.monthly@photographymonthly.co.uk
Editor: William Cheung.
Magazine for the camera enthusiast, with the emphasis on helping readers improve their own photography using the latest imaging techniques and equipment.
Illustrations: B&W and colour. High quality photography of all types – action, portraits, still life, architecture, travel, wildlife, etc. Also images to illustrating photographic techniques, use of specific equipment, comparison shots, image manipulation, special film effects, etc.
Text: Mostly produced by regular contributors but ideas always considered.
Overall freelance potential: Excellent.
Fees: According to use, from £10–£80 per picture.

PRACTICAL PHOTOGRAPHY

EMAP Active Ltd, Media House, Lynchwood, Peterborough PE2 6EA.
Tel: 01733 468000. E-mail: practical.photography@emap.com
Editor: Andrew James. **Features Editor:** Ben Hawkins.
Monthly magazine aimed at all photographers, with news, interviews, equipment tests, etc. Growing emphasis on digital imaging techniques.
Illustrations: B&W and colour. Photographs of any subject considered for general illustration and

for the magazine's files. Images should have strong impact and be original, also illustrating some aspect of photographic technique – use of filters, shooting at the right time of day, camera viewpoint, etc. Colour and B&W portfolios regularly featured.
Text: Some potential, but contact editor in the first instance. Will use writers who can offer something the staff writers can't.
Overall freelance potential: Excellent for pictures and digital techniques; fewer opportunities for words but ideas still welcome.
Editor's tips: Read the magazine and study the pictures; if you can produce comparable work, send it in.
Fees: Negotiable but typically £80 per page and £120 per 1,000 words.

PROFESSIONAL PHOTOGRAPHER
Archant Specialist, The Mill, Bearwalden Business Park, Wendens Ambo, Essex CB11 4GB.
Tel: 01799 544200. Fax: 01799 544202. E-mail: ian.farrell@archant.co.uk
Editor: Ian Farrell.
Monthly magazine for professional photographers.
Illustrations: B&W and colour. Digital files preferred. Only with features as below.
Text: Techniques, equipment, business skills and general issues of interest to professional photographers. Check with the editor before submitting.
Overall freelance potential: Good – for the right material appropriately written.
Editor's tips: The magazine appeals to readers who find other magazines too superficial. It is therefore more important than ever that potential contributors study recent issues.
Fees: From £200 per article, words and pictures.

WHAT DIGITAL CAMERA
IPC Inspire, Blue Fin Building, 110 Southwark Street, London SE1 0SU.
Tel: 020 3148 4796. Fax: 020 3148 8123. E-mail: wdc@ipcmedia.com
Editor: Nigel Atherton.
Monthly consumer magazine for digital photography enthusiasts.
Illustrations: Digital files preferred. Will consider original, creative, digital images and portfolios, either digitally originated or manipulations from conventional film.
Text: Illustrated features about the techniques and applications of digital cameras. Contact editor with suggestions first.
Overall freelance potential: Good.
Fees: Pictures by negotiation and according to use. Text £100 per 1,000 words.

Politics & Current Affairs

THE BIG ISSUE
1-5 Wandsworth Road, London SW8 2LN.
Tel: 020 7526 3200. Fax: 020 7526 3241. E-mail: sam.freeman@bigissue.com
Editor: Charles Howgego. **Art Director:** Sam Freeman.
Current affairs weekly sold in support of the homeless.
Illustrations: B&W and colour. Broad range of mainly news-based images covering politics, social issues and the arts. For hard news pictures contact the news desk; for general feature photography contact the art director.
Text: Suitable reportage-type features always considered. usually around 1,200 with with 2-3 illustrations.
Overall freelance potential: Very good for the right sort of material.
Fees: By negotiation.

THE ECOLOGIST
Unit 102D, Lana House Studios, 116-118 Commercial Road, London E1 6NF.
Tel: 020 7422 8100. E-mail: editorial@theecologist.org
Editor: Zac Goldsmith.
Monthly magazine covering all ecological and environmental topics.
Illustrations: Mainly colour. News pictures and images to illustrate features on current environmental or ethical concerns.
Text: News items and articles on relevant topical issues. Contributors must have good, in-depth knowledge of their subject.
Overall freelance potential: Fair.
Fees: According to use.

THE ECONOMIST
The Economist Newspaper Ltd, 25 St James's Street, London SW1A 1HG.
Tel: 020 7830 7000. Fax: 020 7830 7130. E-mail: celinadunlop@economist.com
Editor: John Micklethwait. **Picture Editor:** Celina Dunlop.
Weekly publication covering world political, business and scientific affairs.
Illustrations: Digital files preferred. Pictures of politicians, businessmen, social conditions (housing, health service, etc), major industries (coal, steel, oil, motor, agriculture, etc). Always prepared to keep digital images for stock.
Text: All staff-produced.
Overall freelance potential: Only for serious and experienced photojournalists. Commissions not available.
Editor's tips: Telephone picture editor in the first instance.
Fees: On a rising scale according to size of reproduction inside.

JANE'S DEFENCE WEEKLY
Jane's Information Group, Sentinel House, 163 Brighton Road, Coulsdon, Surrey CR5 2YH.
Tel: 020 8700 3700. Fax: 020 8763 1007. E-mail: jdw@janes.com
Editor: Peter Felstead.
News magazine concentrating on developments in all military fields.
Illustrations: Mainly colour. Digital files preferred. News pictures of defence subjects worldwide – exercises, deployments, equipment, etc. Contact the news editor initially.
Text: News items and informed articles on the military, industrial and political aspects of global defence.
Overall freelance potential: Limited for those without contacts in the forces or defence industry, but work submitted here may also be published in the various annuals produced by the Jane's Information Group.
Fees: Photographs £40 inside; covers negotiable; text from £200 per 1,000 words.

JEWISH CHRONICLE
Jewish Chronicle Newspapers Ltd, 25 Furnival Street, London EC4A 1JT.
Tel: 020 7415 1616. Fax: 020 7405 9040. E-mail: jclib@thejc.com
Editor: David Rowan.
Weekly newspaper publishing news and features concerning, and of interest to, the British Jewish community.
Illustrations: B&W and colour. Digital files preferred. Any topical pictures related to the purpose stated above. Also material for the paper's wide range of supplements that deal with subjects such as holidays, fashion, interior decoration, regional development, etc.
Text: Features on topics detailed above. 600–2,500 words.
Overall freelance potential: At least 30 per cent of the content comes from freelance sources.
Fees: By negotiation.

LIBERAL DEMOCRAT NEWS
Liberal Democrats, 4 Cowley Street, London SW1P 3NB.
Tel: 020 7227 1361. Fax: 020 7222 7904. E-mail: ldn@libdems.org.uk
Editor: Deirdre Razzall.
Weekly tabloid newspaper of the Liberal Democrats.
Illustrations: B&W and colour. Prints or digital files accepted (no transparencies). Pictures of Liberal Democrat activities around the country and general political news pictures.
Text: News and features: politics, current affairs.
Overall freelance potential: Limited.
Fees: By negotiation.

THE MIDDLE EAST
IC Publications Ltd, 7 Coldbath Square, London EC1R 4LQ.
Tel: 020 7713 7711. Fax: 020 7713 7970. E-mail: p.lancaster@africasia.com
Editor: Pat Lancaster.
Monthly publication directed at senior management, governmental personnel and universities. Covers Middle Eastern current affairs of a political, cultural and economic nature.
Illustrations: B&W and colour. Digital files preferred. Pictures of all topical Middle Eastern subjects, personalities and scenes.
Text: Features on Middle Eastern subjects or world subjects that relate to the area. 1,000–3,000 words.
Overall freelance potential: Most of the pictures come from freelances and around 75 per cent of the overall editorial.
Fees: B&W pictures £15–£35; covers by agreement. Text, from £80 per 1,000 words.

MILAP WEEKLY/NAVIN WEEK
Masbro Centre, 87 Masbro Road, London W14 0LR.
Tel/fax: 020 7385 8966
Editors: Ramesh Soni/Ramesh Kumar.
Weekly news publications for Indian, Pakistani and Bangladeshi people. Published in Hindi (Navin) and Urdu (Milap).
Illustrations: B&W only. News pictures concerning topical immigrant matters, pictures of leading Asian personalities.
Text: News stories; all matters of interest to immigrant Asian communities.
Overall freelance potential: Good for those in touch with relevant communities.
Fees: By negotiation.

NEW INTERNATIONALIST
55 Rectory Road, Oxford OX4 1BW.
Tel: 01865 728181. Fax: 01865 793152. E-mail: ni_ed@newint.org
Co-Editors: (UK) Katharine Ainger, Vanessa Baird, David Ransom, Dinyar Godrej.
Monthly magazine covering global issues from a mainly Southern (Africa, Asia, Latin American) perspective.
Illustrations: B&W and colour. Pictures to illustrate news stories and topical features on subjects such as social justice, human rights, environmental issues, poverty, sustainable development, etc.
Text: Illustrated stories and features on relevant topics as above.
Overall freelance potential: Good.
Editor's tips: Each editor edits individually themed issues and is responsible for his/her own picture research.
Fees: Pictures, from a minimum of £40 to £250 for front cover.

PCS VIEW
The Public & Commercial Services Union, 160 Falcon Road, Clapham, London SW11 2LN.
Tel: 020 7801 2620. Fax: 020 7801 2822. E-mail: editor@pcs.org.uk
Editor: Sharon Breen.
Monthly publication for members of the PCS Union, the biggest civil service union. Also has large private sector membership.
Illustrations: News pictures of trade union activity, especially involving members of PCS. Other topical pictures of current affairs that may impinge on Union members may also be of interest.
Text: No scope.
Overall freelance potential: Good, 75 per cent of pictures come from outside contributors.
Fees: Good; on a rising scale according to size of reproduction.

Railways

HERITAGE RAILWAY
Mortons Heritage Media, PO Box 43, Horncastle, Lincs LN9 6JR.
Tel: 01507 529300. Fax: 01507 529301.
Editor: Robin Jones.
Monthly magazine devoted to railway preservation – steam, diesel and electric.
Illustrations: Mainly colour. Captioned news pictures depicting restoration projects, restored locomotives on their first runs, special events etc, especially from less well-known lines and museums. Mainly UK-based but will also consider overseas coverage of locomotives with a British connection, especially really "stunning and attractive" pictures.
Text: Well-illustrated features on preservation and restoration topics; write with suggestions first.
Overall freelance potential: Very good.
Fees: By negotiation.

INTERNATIONAL RAILWAY JOURNAL
Simmons-Boardman Publishing Corporation, 46 Killigrew Street, Falmouth, Cornwall TR11 3PP.
Tel: 01326 313945. Fax: 01326 211576. E-mail: irj@railjournal.co.uk
Editor: David Briginshaw. **News Editor:** Keith Barrow.
Monthly publication for the principal officers of the railways of the world (including metro and light rail systems), ministers and commissioners of transport, railway equipment manufacturers and suppliers.
Illustrations: Digital files preferred. Pictures of new line construction projects, electrification projects, track or signalling improvements, new locomotives, passenger coaches and freight wagons. Interesting pictures of railway operations from far-flung corners of the world. No steam or nostalgia material. Covers: colour shots tied in with the theme of a particular issue.
Text: Features on any sizeable contracts for railway equipment; plans for railway developments, eg new line construction, track or signalling improvements; almost anything which involves a railway spending money or making improvements and techniques. No padding or speculation.
Overall freelance potential: Quite good for the right business-oriented material.
Fees: Rising scale according to size of pictures; text, £120 per 1,000 words.

RAIL
EMAP Active Ltd, Bretton Court, Bretton, Peterborough PE3 8DZ.
Tel: 01733 264666. Fax: 01733 282720. E-mail: rail@emap.com
Editor: Nigel Harris.
Fortnightly magazine dealing with modern railways.
Illustrations: Mostly colour, some B&W. Digital files preferred. Single photographs and up-to-date

news pictures on any interesting railway topic in Britain, particularly accidents and incidents of all kinds. Covers: Colour shots with strong impact.
Text: Illustrated articles of up to 1,500 words on any railway topic. Check recent issues for style.
Overall freelance potential: Excellent.
Editor's tips: Topicality is everything for news coverage. For other pictures try to get away from straightforward shots of trains; be imaginative. Always looking for something different.
Fees: Pictures range from £25–£70; illustrated articles around £90–£150. Will pay more for high-impact special pics that give the magazine a commercial advantage.

RAIL EXPRESS
Foursight Publishing, 20 Park Street, King's Cliffe, Peterborough PE8 6XN.
Tel: 01780 470086. Fax: 01780 470060. E-mail: picturedesk@railexpress.co.uk
Editor: Philip Sutton.
Monthly magazine for modern railway enthusiasts.
Illustrations: Mainly colour, digital or transparency. Any good or unusual photographs of the contemporary railway scene, but really need to be of current and newsworthy interest (new locomotives, new colour schemes, etc). Some scope for historic diesel/electric coverage.
Text: Suggestions for articles welcome, from anyone with good background knowledge of the subject, especially traction. Consult with the editor first.
Overall freelance potential: The magazine features lots of photography and always needs more.
Editor's tips: Topicality is the key, and images should always be taken in sunshine.
Fees: From basic rate of £20 per picture.

RAILNEWS
Railnews Ltd, East Side Offices, King's Cross Station, London N1 9AP.
Tel: 020 7278 6100. Fax: 020 7278 6145. E-mail: newsdesk@railnews.co.uk
Editor: Paul Whiting.
Monthly newspaper for people in the rail industry, covering the modern railway scene in the UK.
Illustrations: Digital media preferred, B&W and colour prints accepted. Railway news pictures, unusual pictures of events, operations, activities, with good captions.
Text: No scope.
Overall freelance potential: Good.
Editor's tips: Approach before submitting.
Fees: By negotiation.

RAILWAY MAGAZINE
IPC Media Ltd, Blue Fin Building, 110 Southwark Street, London SE1 0SU.
Tel: 020 3148 4683. Fax: 020 3148 8521. E-mail: railway@ipcmedia.com
Editor: Nick Pigott.
Monthly for all rail enthusiasts, covering both main line and heritage railways, modern and historic.
Illustrations: Mostly colour, digital files preferred. News pictures concerning the current rail network, as well as images from recent heritage events, galas or rail tours. Also pictures of new liveries, new trains on test, accidents/derailments, and rare or unusual workings. Previously unpublished material from the 1940s onwards always of interest for historical features. Top quality non-news pictures may be used for spreads and/or occasional calendars. Captions should be supplied on individual slide mounts or prints, not on separate caption sheet. For digital e-mail thumbnails (10 images max) in first instance; CDs (50 images max) must have thumbnail sheet.
Text: Well-researched illustrated articles on any British railway topic, current or historic; discuss ideas with the editor first.
Overall freelance potential: Excellent.
Editor's tips: News pictures must be recent – no more than six weeks old.
Fees: From £15 minimum for news pictures, to £50+ for larger reproductions.

STEAM RAILWAY
EMAP Active Ltd, Bushfield House, Orton Centre, Peterborough PE3 5UW.
Tel: 01733 237111. E-mail: steam.railway@emap.com
Editor: Danny Hopkins.
Four-weekly magazine for the steam railway enthusiast. Closely concerned with railway preservation.
Illustrations: Mostly colour; archive B&W. Accurately captioned photographs depicting steam trains and railways past and present, preserved railway lines, and railway museums (topical subjects especially welcomed).
Text: Illustrated articles on relevant subjects.
Overall freelance potential: Most of the photographic content is contributed by freelances.
Editor's tips: Material should be lively, topical and newsworthy, although some nostalgic or historic material is accepted. Always query the editorial team before submitting.
Fees: By arrangement.

TODAY'S RAILWAYS UK
Platform 5 Publishing, 3 Wyvern House, Sark Road, Sheffield S2 4HG.
Tel: 0114 255 2625. Fax: 0114 255 2471. E-mail: editorial@platform5.com
Editor: Peter Fox.
Monthly covering the contemporary British railway scene, aimed at both rail professionals and enthusiasts.
Illustrations: Digital files preferred. News pictures relating to current or planned UK rail operations, accompanied by detailed captions or stories. Stock material may be of interest – send detailed lists in the first instance.
Text: Feature suggestions always considered, but only from writers who have in-depth knowledge of their subject.
Overall freelance potential: Limited, as much is obtained from industry sources.
Editor's tips: Always contact editor before submitting as many stories may already be covered.
Fees: Pictures from £12.50; text £50 per page.

TRACTION
Warners Group Publications plc, The Maltings, West Street, Bourne, Lincs PE10 9PH.
Tel: 01778 391160. Fax: 01778 425437. E-mail: davidb@warnersgroup.co.uk
Managing **Editor:** David Brown.
Monthly magazine dedicated to classic diesel and electric locomotives.
Illustrations: Mostly colour; B&W archive material. Photographs of classic diesels and electrics operating on British railways from the 1940s to the present day. Particular interest in archive shots from the earlier eras up to the early 1970s.
Text: Limited scope at present.
Overall freelance potential: Good.
Fees: From £15–£50 according to size of reproduction.

Religion

CATHOLIC HERALD
Herald House, 15 Lamb's Passage, Bunhill Row, London EC1Y 8TQ.
Tel: 020 7448 3600. Fax: 020 7256 9728. E-mail: editorial@catholicherald.co.uk
Editor: Luke Coppen.
Weekly newspaper reflecting on Catholicism/Christianity and its place in the wider world, plus church news.
Illustrations: Colour and B&W. Digital files preferred. Principal need for news photographs of events involving churches, clerics or prominent Catholics.

Text: Articles of up to 1,200 words on the social, economic and political significance of the church domestically and internationally, plus spiritual and reflective writings.
Overall freelance potential: Better for features than other material.
Fees: By arrangement but not high.

THE CATHOLIC TIMES
Gabriel Communications Ltd, First Floor, St James Buildings, Oxford Street, Manchester M1 6FP.
Tel: 0161 488 1700. Fax: 0161 237 6690. E-mail: kevin.flaherty@the-universe.net
Editor: Kevin Flaherty.
Weekly newspaper covering Catholic affairs.
Illustrations: B&W and colour. Topical pictures of Catholic interest. Also off-beat devotional shots.
Text: News stories and short features. 900 words maximum.
Overall freelance potential: Very good.
Fees: Text around £40 per 1,000 words; pictures by negotiation.

CHURCH OF ENGLAND NEWSPAPER
Central House, 142 Central Street, London EC1V 8AR.
Tel: 020 7417 5800. Fax: 020 7216 6410. E-mail: cen@churchnewspaper.com
Editor: Colin Blakely.
Weekly newspaper covering Anglican news and views.
Illustrations: B&W and colour. Colour print and digital accepted. Will consider any news pictures that relate to the Church of England.
Text: News stories, plus features that relate Christian faith to politics, the arts and everyday life. Up to 1,000 words, but submit ideas only in the first instance.
Overall freelance potential: Good for those with Church connections.
Fees: £20 – £40 per published picture; text about £40 per 1,000 words.

CHURCH TIMES
G.J.Palmer & Sons Ltd, 13-17 Long Lane, London EC1A 9PN.
Tel: 020 7776 7450. E-mail: news@churchtimes.co.uk
Editor: Paul Handley.
Weekly newspaper covering Church of England affairs.
Illustrations: B&W and colour. Digital files preferred. Up-to-the-minute news pictures of Anglican events and personalities. Detailed captions essential.
Text: Short articles on current religious topics; up to 1,000 words.
Overall freelance potential: Fair.
Editor's tips: It is preferred that people in pictures are engaged in activities rather than just looking at the camera.
Fees: Photographs according to use, average £70; text £100 per 1,000 words.

Science & Technology

BBC FOCUS
Bristol Magazines Ltd, 14th Floor, Tower House, Fairfax Street, Bristol BS1 3BN.
Tel: 0117 927 9009. Fax: 0117 934 9008. E-mail: cericrump@originpublishing.co.uk
Editor: Paul Parsons. **Art Editor:** Jess Hibbert. **Picture Editor:** Ceri Crump.
Popular science monthly relating to all BBC science content. Aimed at both adults and teenagers.
Illustrations: Digital files preferred. Will consider colour photo essays on popular science, technology, space exploration, medicine and the environment. Contact art editor in the

first instance.
Text: Interesting features on subjects above always considered. Submit a synopsis first.
Overall freelance potential: Fair.
Editor's tips: Only top quality material is considered; study the magazine before submitting.
Fees: Negotiable; generally good.

CHEMISTRY AND INDUSTRY

Society of Chemical Industry, 15 Belgrave Square, London SW1X 8PS.
Tel: 020 7598 1500. Fax: 020 7235 9410. E-mail: enquiries@soci.org
Editor: Neil Eisberg.
Fortnightly science and business magazine covering chemistry and related sciences, and the chemical, healthcare, food, biotech, environment and water industries.
Illustrations: Mostly colour. Digital files preferred. Photographs of chemical factories, chemistry research and environmental pollution, food, plants, water, people and places.
Text: News stories and articles from contributors with the requisite technical background.
Overall freelance potential: Limited as regards photography.
Editor's tips: Always contact the editor before preparing any submission.
Fees: £300 per 1,000 words for text; photographs by negotiation.

EDUCATION IN CHEMISTRY

The Royal Society of Chemistry, Burlington House, Piccadilly, London W1J 0BA.
Tel: 020 7437 8656. Fax: 020 7437 8883. E-mail: eic@rsc.org
Editor: Kathryn Roberts.
Bi-monthly publication for teachers, lecturers in schools and universities, concerning all aspects of chemical education.
Illustrations: Digital files preferred. Pictures that deal with chemistry in the classroom, laboratories or the chemical industry. Covers: Pictures relating to specific articles inside.
Text: Features concerned with chemistry or the teaching of it. Under 2,500 words.
Overall freelance potential: Limited.
Fees: By agreement.

NEW SCIENTIST

Reed Business Information, Lacon House, 84 Theobalds Road, London WC1X 8RR.
Tel: 020 7611 1201. Fax: 020 7611 1280. E-mail: alison.lawn@rbi.co.uk
Editor: Jeremy Webb. **Art Editor:** Alison Lawn.
Weekly magazine about science and technology for people with some scientific or technical education and also for the intelligent layman.
Illustrations: Digital files preferred. Pictures on any topic that can be loosely allied to science and technology. Particularly interested in news photographs related to scientific phenomena and events. Covers: usually connected with a feature inside.
Text: News and features on scientific/technical subjects that might appeal to a wide audience.
Overall freelance potential: A lot of freelance work used, but consult the magazine before submitting.
Fees: Photographs on a rising scale according to size of reproduction. Text £150 per 1,000 words.

T3

Future Publishing Ltd, 2 Balcombe Street, London NW1 6NW.
Tel: 020 7042 4000. Fax: 020 7042 4471. E-mail: stuart.james@futurenet.co.uk
Editor: Mike Brook. **Art Editor:** Stuart James.
Monthly technology and gadget magazine aimed primarily at young men.

Illustrations: Digital files preferred. Always interested in pictures of new technology and new designs for consumer durables, especially exclusive shots of latest developments, pre-production models, new releases etc. Also general stock of any technology-related subject.
Text: Mainly staff produced but exclusive news items on new products always of interest.
Overall freelance potential: Fair
Fees: By negotiation. Will pay top rates for exclusives.

Sport

AIR GUNNER
Archant Specialist, 3 The Courtyard, Denmark Street, Wokingham, Berkshire RG40 2AZ.
Tel: 011897 71677. Fax: 011897 72903. E-mail: mail@nigelallen.net
Managing Editor: Nigel Allen.
Monthly magazine for all airgun enthusiasts.
Illustrations: Illustrated news items, and stock shots of small field animals (rats, rabbits) and pest species of birds (pigeons, magpies, crows). Covers: colour, usually commissioned, but a speculative picture might be used.
Text: Articles on any aspect of airgun use, 700–1,000 words, and accompanied by a good selection of transparencies.
Overall freelance potential: Good for file photos and well illustrated articles.
Fees: In the region of £60 per published page.

ALL OUT CRICKET
TriNorth Ltd, The Brit Oval, Kennington, London SE11 5SS.
Tel: 020 7820 4190. E-mail: aff@alloutcricket.co.uk/matt@alloutcricket.co.uk
Editors: Andy Afford, Matthew Thacker.
Official magazine of the Professional Cricketer's Association. Published 10 times a year.
Illustrations: Digital files preferred. Assignments available to shoot individual cricketers or teams for profiles – submit details of experience and areas covered by e-mail in the first instance. No scope for stock images, which are supplied via agency contract.
Text: Suggestions for profiles and features always considered.
Overall freelance potential: Fair.
Fees: By negotiation.

ATHLETICS WEEKLY
Descartes Publishing, 83 Park Road, Peterborough PE1 2TN.
Tel: 01733 898440. Fax: 01733 898441. ISDN: 01733 349199.
E-mail: jason.henderson@athletics-weekly.co.uk
Editor: Jason Henderson.
Weekly news magazine for the competitive and aspiring athlete. Focuses on events and results.
Illustrations: Colour. Digital files preferred. Coverage of athletics events at grass roots level, such as area championships, rather than top events (the latter are supplied by agency photographers). Always interested in anything out of the ordinary, such as well-known athletes off the track or in unusual situations.
Text: No scope.
Overall freelance potential: Fair.
Editor's tips: Freelances aware of what is happening locally can often obtain coverage missed by the nationals and agencies – top athletes "dropping in" to take part in local events etc.
Fees: According to size of reproduction, from £15 – £30. Published pictures frequently gain extra sales via reader requests.

BADMINTON

iSPORTgroup, No.4 The Spinney, Chester Road, Poynton, Cheshire SK12 1HB.
Tel: 07973 544719. E-mail: rachel.pullan@isportgroup.com
Editor: Rachel Pullan.
The only magazine in the UK devoted to badminton. Published quarterly.
Illustrations: Colour. Will consider good action coverage, sports fashion, health material.
Text: Little scope for writing on the sport itself, but may consider articles on sports fashion, health, fitness and diet. 750–1,000 words.
Overall freelance potential: Limited.
Fees: By agreement.

BOXING MONTHLY

Topwave Ltd, 40 Morpeth Road, London E9 7LD.
Tel: 020 8986 4141. Fax: 020 8986 4145. E-mail: mail@boxing-monthly.demon.co.uk
Editor: Glyn Leach.
Heavily illustrated publication for boxing enthusiasts, covering both professional and amateur boxing.
Illustrations: B&W and colour. Coverage of boxing at all levels, including the amateur scene.
Text: Knowledgeable articles, features, interviews, etc. on any aspect of the boxing scene. Always contact the editor in the first instance.
Overall freelance potential: Excellent scope for boxing specialists, and for good amateur boxing coverage.
Fees: By negotiation.

CLIMBER

Warners Group Publications plc, The Maltings, West Street, Bourne, Lincs PE10 9PH.
Tel: 01778 392425. Fax: 01778 394748. E-mail: climbercomments@warnersgroup.co.uk
Editor: Bernard Newman.
Monthly magazine dealing with world-wide climbing from Lakeland fells to Everest. Highly literate readership. Contributors range from "unknowns" to top climbers like Chris Bonington.
Illustrations: First ascents and newsworthy events but, in the main, used only with text. Covers: action shots of climbers or dramatic mountain pictures.
Text: Features on rock climbing, Alpinism, high altitude climbing, mountain skiing (not downhill racing). 1,500–2,000 words.
Overall freelance potential: Good; 90 per cent of articles and 100 per cent of pictures come from freelances, but many are regulars.
Editor's tips: This is a specialist field and is full of good writer/photographers. There is potential for the freelance to break in, but the magazine is heavily commissioned and usually well stocked with material.
Fees: Variable.

DARTS WORLD

World Magazines Ltd, 28 Arrol Road, Beckenham, Kent BR3 4PA.
Tel: 020 8650 6580. Fax: 020 8650 4343. E-mail: dartsworld@blueyonder.co.uk
Editor: Tony Wood.
Monthly magazine for darts players and organisers.
Illustrations: B&W and colour. Pictures on any darts theme, action shots and portraits of leading players. Good colour material also required for the annual Darts Player.
Text: Features on all darts subjects.
Overall freelance potential: Most of the copy and pictures comes from freelances.
Editor's tips: The darts-playing environment is often dim and smoky, which can make it difficult to produce bright, interesting pictures. Photographers who can come up with colourful shots that catch the eye are welcomed.
Fees: Good, on a rising scale according to size of reproduction or length of feature.

DIVE
Dive International, 1 Victoria Villas, Richmond, Surrey TW9 2GW.
Tel: 020 8332 8401. Fax: 020 8332 9307. E-mail: simon@dive.uk.com
Editor: Simon Rogerson. **Art Editor:** David Lloyd.
Monthly magazine for divers and underwater enthusiasts.
Illustrations: Top-quality underwater photography, usually published within photojournalistic features. Most interested in material that tells a story and involves people, with images showing divers in action.
Text: Features as above.
Overall freelance potential: Excellent for underwater specialists.
Editor's tips: Good quality material from British waters stands a good chance of being published, as this is harder to find than that from clearer waters abroad.
Fees: £150 per published page.

F1 RACING
Haymarket Publishing Ltd, Teddington Studios, Broom Road, Teddington TW11 9BE.
Tel: 020 8267 5163. Fax: 020 8267 5022. E-mail: drew.gibson@haymarket.com
Editor: Matt Bishop. **Picture Editor:** Drew Gibson.
Glossy monthly devoted to Formula One motor racing.
Illustrations: All coverage of Formula One, past and present; those with collections of relevant material should send lists. Commissions available to experienced portrait and reportage photographers who can deliver high quality whatever the circumstances – contact picture editor to show portfolio.
Text: Will always consider ideas for any F1 related material, which should always be discussed with the editor before submission.
Overall freelance potential: Good.
Editor's tips: Write or e-mail first, don't phone.
Fees: Set rates, from £60 minimum to £230 full page, £320 dps, £400 cover.

FIELDSPORTS
BPG (Stamford) Ltd, Roebuck House, 33 Broad Street, Stamford, Lincs PE9 1RB.
Tel: 01780 766199. Fax: 01780 754774. E-mail: m.barnes@bournepublishinggroup.co.uk
Editor: Mike Barnes.
Heavily-illustrated quarterly for the serious game shooter who also enjoys a spot of fishing in the summer months.
Illustrations: Colour transparencies and digital images accepted. High-quality images depicting all aspects of game shooting and fishing, for general illustration purposes. Commissioned photography generally handled by regulars.
Text: Will consider illustrated articles from contributors who really know their subject and can write in depth with real enthusiasm.
Overall freelance potential: Fair.
Editor's tips: Readers are not casual sportsmen but people who spend heavily on the sport and have a real passion for it.
Fees: By negotiation.

FOURFOURTWO
Haymarket Leisure Magazines Ltd, Teddington Studios, Broom Road, Teddington, Middlesex TW11 9BE.
Tel: 020 8267 5339. Fax: 020 8267 5354. E-mail: 442pictures@haymarket.com
Editor: Hugh Sleight. **Picture Editor:** Jeff Beasley.
Monthly magazine aimed at the adult soccer fan.
Illustrations: Mainly colour. Especially interested in exclusive or unusual shots of footballers and football people. Always interested to know of good stock collections, both current and historic. Commissions possible for photographers with at least some sports experience – submit samples of

work via e-mail in the first instance.
Text: Some scope for specialists.
Overall freelance potential: Quite good but best for specialists.
Fees: According to size of reproduction, based on page rate of £200. Text £100–£175 per 1,000 words.

GOLF MONTHLY
IPC Media Ltd, Blue Fin Building, 110 Southwark Street, London SE1 0SU.
Tel: 020 3148 5000. Fax: 020 3148 8130. E-mail: golfmonthly@ipcmedia.com
Editor: Michael Harris. **Art Editor:** Paul Duggan.
Monthly international consumer magazine for golfers.
Illustrations: Digital files preferred. Mainly for use as illustrations to articles. Small market for one-off pictures from golf tournaments of golf-related events.
Text: Illustrated features on instruction and other golf-related topics. Also in-depth profiles of leading world players. Around 2,000 words, but not critical.
Overall freelance potential: Most of the magazine is commissioned. Room for more material of the right type from freelances.
Editor's tips: This is an international magazine so material must have a wide appeal. No features of a parochial nature.
Fees: By agreement.

GOLF WORLD
EMAP Active Ltd, Bushfield House, Orton Centre, Peterborough PE2 5UW.
Tel: 01733 237111. Fax: 01733 288025. E-mail: paul.ridley@emap.com
Editor: TBA. **Art Director:** Paul Ridley.
Monthly publication for golfers, covering all aspects of the sport.
Illustrations: Digital files preferred. Unusual golfing pictures always of interest.
Text: Profiles of leading golfers and general or instructional features. 1,500–2,000 words.
Overall freelance potential: Around 20 per cent comes from freelance sources.
Fees: By agreement.

INTERNATIONAL RUGBY NEWS
Independent Magazines Ltd, Independent House, 191 Marsh Wall, London E14 9RS.
Tel: 020 7005 5000. Fax: 020 7005 5075. E-mail: intrugbynews@indmags.co.uk
Editor: John Edwards.
Monthly rugby magazine covering all levels of the sport.
Illustrations: Almost exclusively colour. Coverage at the top level is usually obtained from agency sources, so scope for the freelance is mostly at local and "grass roots" level, including school tournaments.
Text: Articles and local match reports may be considered, but always query the editor first.
Overall freelance potential: Fair.
Editor's tips: The different picture with really good action, at whatever level, will always be of interest.
Fees: By negotiation.

MARTIAL ARTS ILLUSTRATED
Martial Arts Ltd, Revenue Chambers, St Peter Street, Huddersfield, West Yorkshire HD1 1EL.
Tel: 01484 435011. Fax: 01484 422177. E-mail: martialartsltd@btconnect.com
Editor: Bob Sykes.
Monthly magazine covering all forms of Oriental fighting and self-defence techniques.
Illustrations: Will always consider single pictures or sets depicting well-known martial artists, club events, tournament action and aspects of technique.
Text: Well-illustrated articles on any relevant subject – profiles of leading figures and individual clubs, interviews, technique sequences and self-defence features.

Overall freelance potential: Excellent for those with access to the martial arts scene.
Editor's tips: Always write in the first instance with suggestions.
Fees: Should be negotiated before submission, as many contributions are supplied free of charge.

MATCH
EMAP Active Ltd, Bushfield House, Orton Centre, Peterborough PE2 5UW.
Tel: 01733 237111. Fax: 01733 288150. E-mail: ian.foster@emap.com
Editor: Ian Foster.
Weekly publication for younger readers, looking at the whole spectrum of soccer. Aimed at the 8–16 age group.
Illustrations: Digital files preferred. Action shots all agency-supplied, but will consider unusual non-action images featuring top players. Usually bought only after consultation with the editor.
Text: Profiles and interviews concerning personalities in the soccer field. Length by arrangement.
Overall freelance potential: Limited – most is staff or agency produced.
Fees: By agreement.

RACING PIGEON PICTORIAL INTERNATIONAL
The Racing Pigeon Co Ltd, Unit G5, The Seedbed Centre, Wyncolls Road, Colchester, Essex CO4 9HT.
Tel: 01206 843456. E-mail: racing123@btconnect.co.uk
Editor: Lee Fribbins.
Monthly magazine for pigeon fanciers. Provides in-depth articles on methods, successful fanciers, scientific information, etc.
Illustrations: Pictures to illustrate features, plus some one-off pictures of pigeons, pigeon lofts, pigeon fanciers and related subjects.
Text: Features on subjects as above, from contributors with serious knowledge of the sport. 1,500 words.
Overall freelance potential: Around 10–15 per cent of the pictures come from freelance photographers. Articles are mostly by specialist writers.
Editor's tips: Short, colourful, exotic articles with good illustrations stand a reasonable chance.
Fees: £20 per published page minimum.

RUGBY WORLD
IPC Media Ltd, Blue Fin Building, 110 Southwark Street, London SE1 0SU.
Tel: 020 3148 4702. E-mail: kevin_eason@ipcmedia.com
Editor: Paul Morgan. **Art Editor:** Kevin Eason.
Britain's biggest selling monthly rugby magazine giving general coverage of Rugby Union.
Illustrations: Digital files preferred. Main scope is for regional/local coverage, since the top level matches are covered by regulars. Photographs of Cup matches, County championships, personalities, off-beat shots, etc. Covers: Good action shots of top players.
Text: Good articles with different angles are always of interest.
Overall freelance potential: Dependent on quality and appeal.
Fees: On a rising scale according to size of reproduction or length of text.

RUNNER'S WORLD
Natmag-Rodale, 6th Floor, 33 Broadwick Street, London W1F 0DQ.
Tel: 020 7339 4400. Fax: 020 7339 4420. E-mail: russell.fairbrother@natmag-rodale.co.uk
Editor: Andy Dixon. **Art Editor:** Russell Fairbrother.
Monthly publication for running enthusiasts.
Illustrations: Pictures relating to sports, recreational and fitness running. Consult art editor before submitting.
Text: Feature material considered, but only by prior consultation with the editor.
Overall freelance potential: Fair.
Fees: By agreement.

RUNNING FITNESS

Kelsey Publishing, 1st Floor, South Wing, Broadway Court, Broadway, Peterborough PE1 1RP.
Tel: 01733 347559. Fax: 01733 891342. E-mail: rf.ed@kelseypb.co.uk
Editor: David Castle.
Monthly magazine for active running enthusiasts, those who run for health or recreation.
Illustrations: Coverage of competitions and running events at local or regional level, off-beat pictures, and general stock shots of runners. Both racing and training pictures are welcome. Some scope for general atmospheric pictures incorporating runners and athletic-looking subjects in picturesque and inspirational settings. Possible commission scope for "fashion" features. Covers: usually by commission – interested in hearing from photographers who can bring a creative approach to the subject.
Text: Illustrated articles of a practical nature, giving advice on training, diet, etc., and on unusual or exciting running events worldwide 1,000–1,500 words. Features of an inspirational nature also welcome – well-written and illustrated pieces on elite athletes, or other sportspeople who run as part of their training. Discuss ideas with the editor first.
Overall freelance potential: Good.
Fees: From a minimum of £20 up to £80 for a full page; text £70 per 1,000 words.

SGB UK

Datateam Publishing Ltd, London Road, Maidstone ME16 8LY.
Tel: 01622 699140. Fax: 01622 757646. E-mail: rknowles@datateam.co.uk
Editor: Rebecca Knowles.
Monthly magazine for the UK sports retail trade.
Illustrations: B&W and colour. Topical pictures concerning the retail trade, usually to illustrate specific news stories, features and new products.
Text: Illustrated features and news stories on anything to do with the sports retail industry, including manufacturer and retailer profiles etc.
Overall freelance potential: Limited.
Fees: Text, £150 per 1,000 words; pictures by negotiation.

THE SCOTTISH SPORTING GAZETTE

BPG (Stamford) Ltd, Roebuck House, 33 Broad Street, Stamford, Lincs PE9 1RB.
Tel: 01780 766199. Fax: 01780 766416. E-mail: m.barnes@bournepublishinggroup.co.uk
Editor: Mike Barnes.
Annual publication to market Scottish shooting, fishing, stalking and allied services. Aimed at the upper income bracket in the UK, Europe and America.
Illustrations: Digital files preferred. High quality scenic photography, plus pictures of shooting, fishing, stalking, live game animals, whisky production, antique Scottish weapons, tartans, castles and hunting lodges. Covers: exceptional colour pictures of game animals or action sporting shots.
Text: Features on shooting, fishing and stalking in Scotland or articles on other topics that are particularly Scottish, as above. 600–2,000 words.
Overall freelance potential: Good.
Editor's tips: Pictures and text must be unusual, not the normal anecdotes associated with this field. Material should have a good Scottish flavour. It does not have to be essentially sporting, but should be allied in some way.
Fees: Open to negotiation.

THE SHOOTING GAZETTE

IPC Country & Leisure Media. Editorial: PO Box 225, Stamford, Lincolnshire PE9 2HS.
Tel: 01780 485350. Fax: 01780 754774. E-mail: will_hetherington@ipcmedia.com
Editor: Will Hetherington.
Britain's only monthly magazine covering exclusively game and rough shooting, wildlife, countryside.
Illustrations: Pictures for general illustration, including countryside scenes, hunting, shooting,

fishing, farming, birds and animals – quarry and non-quarry species.
Text: Well-illustrated articles from those with specialist knowledge, and profiles or interviews. Up to 2,000 words.
Overall freelance potential: Good.
Fees: By negotiation.

SHOOTING TIMES AND COUNTRY MAGAZINE
IPC Media Ltd, Blue Fin Building, 110 Southwark Street, London SE1 0SU.
Tel: 020 3148 4741. Fax: 020 3148 8104. E-mail: steditorial@ipcmedia.com
Editor: Camilla Collinson.
Weekly magazine concentrating on all aspects of quarry shooting (game, pigeon, rough shooting, wildfowling and stalking). Also covers clay shooting, other fieldsports and general country topics.
Illustrations: Digital files preferred. Good photographs of shooting subjects plus gundogs, wildlife, rural crafts, country food. Some scope for good generic photographs of British counties, showing known landmarks. Covers: shots should be vertical in shape with room for title at the top.
Text: Illustrated features on all aspects of quarry shooting and general country topics as above. In the region of 900 words.
Overall freelance potential: Excellent; plenty of scope for new contributors.
Editor's tips: The magazine likes to keep pictures on file as it is not always possible to know in advance when a picture can be used. For features, remember that the readers are real country people.
Fees: Colour inside £10–£60 according to size; covers £70–£90. Features £40 per 500 words.

SKI & BOARD
The Ski Club of Great Britain, The White House, 57-63 Church Road, Wimbledon Village, London SW19 5SB.
Tel: 0845 4580780. Fax: 0845 4580781. E-mail: editor@skiclub.co.uk
Editor: Arnie Wilson.
Published four times a year. Official magazine of the Ski Club of Great Britain, covering the sport at all levels.
Illustrations: Digital files preferred. Pictures for general illustration and for special gallery section, holiday skiing, ski-touring, racing and equipment, good adventure/action pics, shots illustrating snowcraft and particular techniques. Also good, attractive pictures of specific ski resorts and ski slopes in season. Covers: good colour action with one or more skiers.
Text: Some scope for general articles about skiing, and on techniques. Very interested in Adventure articles, especially with pics.
Overall freelance potential: Quite good.
Fees: By arrangement.

THE SKIER AND SNOWBOARDER MAGAZINE
Mountain Marketing Ltd, PO Box 386, Sevenoaks, Kent TN13 1AQ.
Tel: 0845 310 8303. E-mail: frank.baldwin@skierandsnowboarder.com
Editor: Frank Baldwin.
Published five times a year: July, Sep/Oct, Nov/Dec, Jan/Feb, Mar/Apr. Covers all aspects of skiing and snowboarding.
Illustrations: Good action pictures and anything spectacular, odd or humorous that summons up the spirit of skiing. Also a special "Photo File" section in which photographers can submit up to three favourite shots backed by text which tells the reader about the set-ups/techniques used, linked with a short biog of the photographer.
Text: Original ideas for illustrated features always welcome. Possible scope for resort reports and news items.
Overall freelance potential: Very good.
Fees: By negotiation.

SNOOKER SCENE

Hayley Green Court, 130 Hagley Road, Hayleygreen, Halesowen B63 1DY.
Tel: 0121 585 9188. Fax: 0121 585 7117. E-mail: clive.everton@talk21.com
Editor: Clive Everton.
Monthly publication for snooker players and enthusiasts.
Illustrations: Snooker action pictures and coverage related to tournaments, or material of historical interest.
Text: Features on snooker and billiards. 250–1,000 words.
Overall freelance potential: Small.
Fees: By arrangement.

SNOWBOARD UK

Freestyle Publications Ltd, Alexander House, Ling Road, Tower Park, Poole, Dorset BH12 4NZ.
Tel: 01202 735090. Fax: 01202 733969. E-mail: markmcg@freepubs.co.uk
Editor: Mark McGettigan.
Magazine covering the sport of snowboarding. Published eight times a year during the winter sports season from September to April.
Illustrations: Digital files preferred. Good action coverage of the sport always required; should be colourful, innovative and stylish. Interested in any freestyle or alpine shots from anywhere in the world.
Text: Short, heavily-illustrated articles on any aspect of the sport.
Overall freelance potential: Excellent; the magazine is very photo-based.
Editor's tips: The magazine, which also supplies shots to other publications, is keen to build up a pool of photographers who can be relied upon to produce quality coverage of the sport.
Fees: Variable; according to use and nature of material.

SPIN

WW Magazines Ltd. Editorial: Sunnyhill House, 3/7 Sunnyhill Road, London SW16 2UG.
Tel: 020 8696 6204. E-mail: editors@spincricket.com
Editor: Duncan Steer. **Art Director:** Matthew Levett.
Monthly cricket magazine focusing on the game at international level. Aims for a modern and youthful approach to the sport.
Illustrations: No scope for match coverage, but keen to see material documenting the lifestyle and culture that exists around the game, especially anything exotic or unusual that is rarely seen. Also interested in hearing from freelances who can supply top quality photo essays and stories on other aspects of the sport.
Text: Text with pictures is welcomed, but should be kept short and snappy in tabloid style.
Overall freelance potential: Good opportunities for unusual cricket coverage.
Fees: By negotiation.

SPORTING SHOOTER

Archant Specialist, Jubilee House, 2 Jubilee Place, London SW3 3TQ.
Tel: 020 7751 4917. E-mail: james@sportingshooter.co.uk
Editor: James Marchington.
Monthly aimed at sports shooters and gamekeepers.
Illustrations: Digital files preferred. Will consider good stock images depicting pigeon, clay and pheasant shooting, deer stalking, gun dogs, gamekeeping and relevant wildlife. Some commissions possible to photograph specific features.
Text: also very interested in illustrated articles on shooting topics
Overall freelance potential: Good.
Editor's tips: The magazine has a very specific style so always call to discuss ideas first.
Fees: By negotiation.

SWIMMING TIMES

41 Granby Street, Loughborough, Leicestershire LE11 3DU.
Tel: 01509 632230. Fax: 01509 632233. E-mail: swimmingtimes@swimming.org
Editor: Peter Hassall.
Official monthly magazine of the Amateur Swimming Association and Institute of Swimming
Teachers and Coaches. Covers all aspects of swimming including diving, synchro-swimming, water
polo, etc.
Illustrations: Digital files preferred. News pictures of swimmers at major events and any off-beat
or particularly interesting shots of swimming-related activity.
Text: Human interest stories about individual swimmers.
Overall freelance potential: Limited.
Fees: Negotiable.

THE NON-LEAGUE PAPER

The Football Paper Ltd, Tuition House, St George's Road, Wimbledon, London SW19 4DS.
Tel: 020 8971 4333. Fax: 020 8971 4366. ISDN: 020 8605 2391. E-mail:
leaguenewsdesk@bhtmedia.com
Editor: David Emery. **News Editor:** John Lyons. **Picture Editor:** Sam Emery.
Weekly tabloid covering the non-League soccer scene, published every Sunday.
Illustrations: Digital files required. Always interested in hearing from capable football
photographers able to produce regular coverage of their local teams, but must have the
ability/facilities to send material direct via modem on the Saturday night. Submit details of
experience and area covered in the first instance.
Text: No scope – all staff or agency produced.
Overall freelance potential: Much is produced by freelance regulars but replacements are often
needed.
Fees: According to assignment and/or use.

TODAY'S GOLFER

EMAP Active Ltd, Bushfield House, Orton Centre, Peterborough PE3 5UW.
Tel: 01733 237111. Fax: 01733 288014. E-mail: andy.calton@emap.com
Editor: Andy Calton.
Monthly for golfing enthusiasts.
Illustrations: Digital files preferred. Stock shots of leading players and courses, and anything off-
beat, considered on spec.
Text: Instructional material; player profiles; equipment features; course tests.
Overall freelance potential: Limited.
Fees: By negotiation.

THE WISDEN CRICKETER

Wisden Cricket Magazines Ltd, 1.4 Shepherds Building, Charecroft Way, London W14 0EE.
Tel: 020 7471 6900. Fax: 020 7471 6901. E-mail: twc@wisdengroup.com
Editor: John Stern. **Art Director:** Nigel Davies.
Monthly publication aimed at all cricket lovers. Concentrates on the game at first-class and
especially international level.
Illustrations: Mainly colour. Exceptional photographs of the above always considered.
Text: Scope for exclusive news stories and features. But check first before submitting. 400–2,500
words.
Overall freelance potential: Fair.
Fees: On a rising scale according to size of pictures or length and significance of article.

Trade

AM

EMAP Automotive Ltd, Media House, Lynchwood, Peterborough Business Park, Peterborough PE2 6EA.
Tel: 01733 468259. Fax: 01733 468350. E-mail: stephen.briers@emap.com
Editor: Stephen Briers.
Fortnightly publication for the motor industry, mainly franchised dealers.
Illustrations: Digital files preferred. News photographs covering the motor trade generally. Some scope for commissions to photograph industry figures and premises.
Text: News items and news features of interest to industry executives.
Overall freelance potential: Good for those with contacts in the trade and local freelances.
Fees: By negotiation.

THE BOOKSELLER

VNU Entertainment Media UK Ltd, 5th Floor, Endeavour House, 189 Shaftesbury Avenue, London WC2H 8TJ.
Tel: 020 7420 6006. Fax: 020 7420 6103.
Editor-in-Chief: Neill Denny.
Weekly trade magazine for booksellers, publishers, librarians and anyone involved in the book industry. Covers trade trends and events, authors, etc.
Illustrations: B&W and colour. Digital files preferred. Pictures of bookshops and book-related activities outside London. Busy book fairs, busy book shops, etc. Portraits of authors and book trade figures.
Text: Serious, humorous, analytical, descriptive articles connected with the book trade, plus author interviews.
Overall freelance potential: Only for those freelances who have good access to the book trade.
Fees: Variable; depends on material.

BRITISH BAKER

William Reed Publishing, Broadfield Park, Crawley, West Sussex RH11 9RT.
Tel: 01293 846595. Fax: 01293 846538. E-mail: sylvia.macdonald@william-reed.co.uk
Editor: Sylvia Macdonald.
Weekly business-to-business news magazine covering the entire baking industry.
Illustrations: Interesting photographs relating to working bakeries, especially news items such as shop openings, promotions, charity events, etc. Also good stock shots of bakery products.
Text: Short news stories (300 words) or features (500–1,000 words) on any baking industry topic.
Overall freelance potential: Fair, for those who can supply relevant material.
Fees: £125 per 1,000 words for text; photographs by negotiation.

CABINET MAKER

CMP Information Ltd, Ludgate House, 245 Blackfriars Road, London SE1 9UY.
Tel: 020 7921 8433. Fax: 020 7921 8452. E-mail: rdemelim@cmpinformation.com
Editor: Richard de Melim.
Weekly publication for all those in the furniture and furnishing trade and industry.
Illustrations: Freelances commissioned to cover news assignments in the trade. Some scope for pictures to illustrate features.
Text: Features about companies making furniture for sale to retailers and interior designers. Length from one to four pages (1,000 words plus three pictures makes two pages).
Overall freelance potential: Around 10 per cent contributed, including news coverage.
Editor's tips: Approach the editor or deputy editor for a brief before submitting.
Fees: By agreement.

CATERER & HOTELKEEPER

Reed Business Information Ltd, Fifth Floor, Quadrant House, The Quadrant, Sutton, Surrey SM2 5AS.
Tel: 020 8652 3221. Fax: 020 8652 8973. E-mail: mark.lewis@rbi.co.uk
Editor: Mark Lewis. **Art Editor:** Sarah Thompson. **Picture Librarian:** Sue Hockins.
Weekly magazine for the hotel and catering trade.
Illustrations: News pictures relevant to hotel and catering establishments – openings, extensions, refurbishments, people, etc. Special interest in regional material. Commissions possible to cover establishments, equipment and food.
Text: Specialist articles of interest to the trade, by commission only.
Overall freelance potential: Mainly limited to those with connections within the trade.
Editor's tips: Also welcomes tip-offs concerning the industry, for which a fee of £15–£25 is paid.
Fees: On a rising scale according to size of reproduction or length of text.

CHEMIST AND DRUGGIST

CMP Information Ltd, Riverbank House, Angel Lane, Tonbridge TN9 1SE.
Tel: 01732 377487. Fax: 01732 367065. E-mail: chemdrug@cmpinformation.com
Editor: Gary Paragpuri.
Weekly news publication for retail pharmacists; the pharmaceutical, toiletries and cosmetics industries; pharmaceutical wholesalers, etc.
Illustrations: B&W and colour. Digital files preferred. News pictures concerning individual retailers and retailing related events, plus industry events relating to pharmaceutical companies.
Text: Local news stories relating to community pharmacy.
Overall freelance potential: Limited.
Fees: On a rising scale, according to contribution.

CONTAINERISATION INTERNATIONAL

Informa UK Ltd, 69-77 Paul Street, London EC2A 4LQ.
Tel: 020 7017 4820. Fax: 020 7017 4976. E-mail: robert.evers@informa.com
Editor: John Fossey. **Art Editor:** Robert Evers.
Monthly business-oriented magazine on issues facing the international container transport industry.
Illustrations: Digital files preferred. Unusual pictures of container shipping activities, especially in exotic locations overseas, or interesting/amusing uses for containers.
Text: Well-researched and exclusive articles, preferably on some aspect of the container transport business not covered by staff writers. Around 2,000 words.
Overall freelance potential: Limited.
Fees: By agreement.

CONVENIENCE STORE

William Reed Ltd, Broadfield Park, Crawley, West Sussex RH11 9RT.
Tel: 01293 613400. Fax: 01293 610330. E-mail: david.rees@william-reed.co.uk
Editor: David Rees.
Fortnightly magazine for independent neighbourhood retailers and convenience stores, and their wholesale suppliers.
Illustrations: Digital files preferred. Photographs usually to illustrate specific features; little scope for pictures on their own.
Text: Illustrated features or stories concerning late-night, local, food-based stores. Should ideally feature a retailer who is doing something a bit different, or who has been highly successful in some way.
Overall freelance potential: Modest.
Fees: By negotiation.

DRAPERS
EMAP Retail, Greater London House, Hampstead Road, London NW1 7EJ.
Tel: 020 7812 3700. Fax: 020 7812 3760. E-mail: lauretta.roberts@emap.com
Editor: Lauretta Roberts. **Art Editor:** Heather Reeves.
Weekly news publication for clothing and textile retailers.
Illustrations: Digital files preferred. News pictures of interest to the clothing and fashion trade.
Some scope for portraits and fashion shoots by commission.
Text: Features, fashion and news items of relevance to retailers in the fashion and textile fields.
Overall freelance potential: Limited for news; fair for commissioned work.
Editor's tips: Do not send unsolicited material – call the art editor first.
Fees: Good; on a rising scale according to size of illustration or length of feature.

EUROFRUIT MAGAZINE
Market Intelligence Ltd, 4th Floor, Market Towers, One Nine Elms Lane, London SW8 5NQ.
Tel: 020 7501 3700. Fax: 020 7498 6472. E-mail: michael@fruitnet.com
Editor: Mike Knowles.
Monthly magazine of the European fresh fruit and vegetable trade. Aimed at producers, exporters, importers, merchants and buyers.
Illustrations: Subjects such as harvesting fruit, loading on to ships or lorries, quality checks on fruit, packing etc. Photographs accepted mostly for the magazine's own picture library.
Text: Topical features on fruit and vegetables, e.g. Chilean apples in Europe, French Iceberg lettuce, Egypt's expanding export range, Norway as an alternative market, etc. 1,250–2,000 words.
Overall freelance potential: Quite good. Some regular contributors, but scope for the freelance writer who can also supply pictures.
Editor's tips: It is best to work in close contact with the editorial department to get names of people who would be of interest to the publication.
Fees: Negotiable.

FISH UPDATE
Special Publications, Craigcrook Castle, Craigcrook Road, Edinburgh EH4 3PE.
Tel: 0131 312 4550. Fax: 0131 312 4551. E-mail: bkennedy@fishupdate.com
Editor: Bob Kennedy.
Monthly tabloid for the the UK and Irish commercial fishing industries, but with coverage extending to the rest of Europe.
Illustrations: Digital files preferred. Captioned news pictures covering any subject relating to the UK, Irish and European fishing industries, including fish farming, processing, etc.
Text: Short illustrated news items, and longer features from contributors with suitable knowledge of the industry.
Overall freelance potential: Good, especially for those with connections in the fishing industry.
Fees: By negotiation.

FISHING NEWS
Informa PLC, 4th Floor, Telephone House, 69–77 Paul Street, London EC2A 4LQ.
Tel: 020 7017 4531. Fax: 020 7017 4536. E-mail: tim.oliver@informa.com
Editor: Tim Oliver.
Weekly newspaper for the commercial fishing industry in Britain and Ireland.
Illustrations: B&W and colour. Digital files preferred. Captioned news pictures covering any subject relating to the UK or Irish commercial fishing industries.

Are you working from the latest edition of The Freelance Photographer's Market Handbook? It's published on 1 October each year. Markets are constantly changing, so it pays to have the latest edition

Text: Illustrated news stories always considered.
Overall freelance potential: Very good; a lot of photographs are used.
Fees: Standard £30 per picture.

THE FLORIST & WHOLESALE BUYER
Wordhouse Publishing Group Ltd, 68 First Avenue, Mortlake, London SW14 8SR.
Tel: 020 8939 6470. Fax: 020 8878 9983. E-mail: info@thewordhouse.co.uk
Editor: Caroline Marshall-Foster.
Publication for retail florists, published 10 times a year.
Illustrations: Digital files preferred. News pictures about the trade and other interesting pictures of floristry in the retail context, i.e. special displays, promotions, etc.
Text: Features on anything relating to floristry and retailing, shop profiles, practical aspects, advertising and promotion, etc.
Overall freelance potential: Limited.
Fees: Text, £150 per 1,000 words published; pictures by agreement.

FOOD TRADER FOR BUTCHERS
National Federation of Meat & Food Traders, 1 Belgrove, Tunbridge Wells, Kent TN1 1YW.
Tel: 01892 541412. Fax: 01892 535462. E-mail: graham@nfmft.co.uk
Editor: Graham Bidston.
Official magazine of the National Federation of Meat & Food Traders. Published 10 times a year.
Illustrations: Topical pictures related to news and issues in the meat and related food industry.
Text: Topical features on the food industry, primarily the meat trade. Up to 2,000 words.
Overall freelance potential: Fair for those in close contact with the trade.
Editor's tips: Only exclusive material will be considered.
Fees: By negotiation.

FORECOURT TRADER
William Reed Publishing Ltd, Broadfield Park, Crawley, West Sussex RH11 9RT.
Tel: 01293 610219. Fax: 01293 610330. E-mail: merril.boulton@william-reed.co.uk
Editor: Merril Bolton.
Monthly magazine for petrol station operators.
Illustrations: News pictures relating to petrol stations and the petrol sales business generally.
Text: News and features relating to all areas of petrol retailing.
Overall freelance potential: Fair.
Fees: Text, £120 per 1,000 words; pictures according to use.

FOREST MACHINE JOURNAL
PO Box 7570, Dumfries DG2 8YD.
Tel/fax: 01387 880359. E-mail: editor@forestmachinejournal.com
Editor: Mark Andrews.
Monthly magazine covering all aspects of forestry and timber production – arboriculture, estate management, harvesting, haulage, and recreational use of forests/woodland.
Illustrations: Digital files preferred. Plenty of photographs used, but usually only as accompaniment to features on topics as above.
Text: Always seeking freelances to produce well-illustrated local stories on forestry topics, and for profiles of individual contractors etc. Write or e-mail the editor with suggestions and/or details of areas covered.
Overall freelance potential: Good for complete illustrated features.
Fees: £150 per published page.

H: THE HOTEL MAGAZINE
William Reed Hospitality Ltd, 6th Floor, 103 Regent Street, London W1B 4HL.
Tel: 020 7534 3792. E-mail: joe.mcallister@william-reed.co.uk

Editor: Mark Hayes. **Art Director:** Joe McAllister.
Monthly magazine for independent hoteliers, proprietors of upmarket B&Bs and the managers of hotel chains across the UK.
Illustrations: Opportunities for experienced photographers to carry out commissions to shoot portraits or hotel locations. Contact art director in the first instance.
Text: Ideas and suggestions for topical illustrated articles on the independent hotel trade always welcomed.
Overall freelance potential: Good for freelances who have good experience and/or contacts in the industry.
Fees: In line with NUJ recommendations.

HARDWARE & GARDEN REVIEW
Faversham House Group Ltd, Faversham House, 232A Addington Road, South Croydon CR2 8LE.
Tel: 020 8651 7100. Fax: 020 8651 7117. E-mail: hgr@fav-house.com
Editor: Paul Fanning.
Monthly magazine for the independent hardware, housewares, garden centre and DIY trade.
Illustrations: B&W and colour. Digital files preferred. Trade news pictures and picture stories concerning particular stores and outlets.
Text: Illustrated articles on store redesign, and retailer profiles. Around 1,000 words.
Overall freelance potential: Fair.
Editor's tips: Articles should be exclusive in this field. Always send an outline in the first instance.
Fees: On a rising scale according to size of reproduction or length of text.

INDEPENDENT RETAIL NEWS
Nexus Media Communications, Media House, Azalea Drive, Swanley, Kent BR8 8HY.
Tel: 01322 611240. Fax: 0322 616375. E-mail: john.kirwan@nexusmedia.com
Editor: John Kirwan.
Fortnightly publication for independent, convenience, licensed and CTN retailers. Assists them in being more profitable and aware of new products and campaigns.
Illustrations: Captioned news pictures and picture stories of interest to independent grocery and convenience store traders. Stock images to illustrate people buying goods in independent/corner stores, retail crime, under-age sales, bootlegging, national lottery sales, etc.
Text: Articles and stories relevant to small retailers.
Overall freelance potential: Fair.
Editor's tips: A sample copy of the magazine is available to potential contributors. Always phone first with ideas.
Fees: Photographs according to how sourced, but up to £150 for features and £50-£100 for news stories. For commissioned features £170 per 1,000 words and negotiable for news stories.

MEAT TRADES JOURNAL
William Reed Ltd, Broadfield Park, Crawley, West Sussex RH11 9RT.
Tel: 01293 846567. Fax: 01293 610330. E-mail: ed.bedington@william-reed.co.uk
Editor: Ed Bedington.
Monthly journal for the whole meat and poultry trade.
Illustrations: Digital files preferred. Pictures relating to any current meat trade issue, including legislation, food scares, court cases, etc.
Text: Stories on current issues as above. Illustrated features on current food issues, research, technology, and profiles of individual businesses.
Overall freelance potential: Good for those in a position to cover this industry.
Editor's tips: It is much preferred if material offered is exclusive.
Fees: Negotiable, according to use.

WORLD FISHING
Nexus Media Communications, Media House, Azalea Drive, Swanley, Kent BR8 8HY.
Tel: 01322 611280. Fax: 01322 616324. E-mail: john.barnes@nexusmedia.com
Managing Editor: John Barnes. **Deputy Editor:** Carly Wills.
Monthly journal for the commercial fishing industry. Covers fisheries and related industries from an international perspective.
Illustrations: B&W and colour. Mainly to accompany specific articles, but some scope for scene-setting shots of commercial fishing activity in specific locations worldwide.
Text: Illustrated articles on any commercial fishing topic. Should always contain some international interest. Maximum 1,500 words.
Overall freelance potential: Good for those with connections in the industry.
Fees: By negotiation.

Transport

COACH AND BUS WEEK
Rouncy Media Ltd, 3 The Office Village, Cygnet Park, Peterborough PE7 8GX.
Tel: 01733 293240. Fax: 0845 2802927. E-mail: andrew.sutcliffe@rouncymedia.co.uk
Editorial Director: Andrew Sutcliffe. **News Editor:** Andrew Peace.
Weekly news magazine covering coach and bus operations. Aimed at licensed coach, bus and tour operators.
Illustrations: Digital files preferred. Pictures as illustrations to features mentioned below; coach and bus related news items. Places of interest to coach parties.
Text: Features on coach and bus operators, hotels, ferry operations, resorts and venues, anything that would be of interest to a coach party or an operator. Articles on subjects that an operator might find useful in their day-to-day business. Up to 1,000 words.
Overall freelance potential: Always interested in seeing work from freelances.
Fees: By negotiation.

COMMERCIAL MOTOR
Reed Business Information Ltd, Quadrant House, The Quadrant, Sutton, Surrey SM2 5AS.
Tel: 020 8652 3500. Fax: 020 8652 8969. E-mail: steven.gale@rbi.co.uk
Editor: Andy Salter. **Art Editor:** Steve Gale.
Weekly publication devoted to the road haulage industry. Aimed at vehicle enthusiasts as well as industry readers.
Illustrations: Mostly commissioned; arrange to show portfolio to the art editor first. Possible interest in professional stock photographs of commercial vehicles and aspects of road haulage – send lists of subjects available.
Text: Technical articles on road haulage topics, from expert contributors only.
Overall freelance potential: Only for experienced contributors.
Fees: Day rate around £250–£300 plus expenses. Other material by negotiation.

OLD GLORY
Mortons Heritage Media, PO Box 43, Horncastle, Lincs LN9 6JR.
Tel: 01507 529300. Fax: 01507 529301. E-mail: ctyson@mortons.co.uk
Editor: Colin Tyson.
Monthly devoted to industrial/commercial transport and machinery heritage and vintage restoration including traction engines, tractors, etc.
Illustrations: Digital files preferred. Pictures of all forms of traction engines, tractors, buses, commercial vehicles, fairground machinery and maritime subjects such as old steamboats. News pictures of individual machines, restoration projects, etc. Detailed captions necessary including where and when picture taken. Covers: colourful pictures of traction engines in attractive settings.

Text: Illustrated articles on subjects as above.
Overall freelance potential: A lot of scope for good colour material.
Fees: Pictures £20–£75 dependent on size used.

ROADWAY
Roadway House, 35 Monument Hill, Weybridge, Surrey KT13 8RN.
Tel: 01932 841515. E-mail: roadway@rha.net
Editor: Peter Shakespeare.
Monthly news magazine for the road haulage industry. Official magazine of the Road Haulage Association.
Illustrations: Digital files preferred. Pictures of trucks on motorways, at depots etc. Should be newsworthy or of unusual interest.
Text: Articles on any aspect of the road haulage industry. Length by prior agreement with the editor.
Overall freelance potential: Limited.
Fees: By arrangement.

TOWPATH TALK
Mortons Media Group, Media Centre, Morton Way, Horncastle, Lincs LN9 6JR.
Tel: 01507 523456. E-mail: thoyland@mortons.co.uk
Editor: Tony Hoyland.
Specialist newspaper covering all aspects of Britain's waterways. Published every three weeks.
Illustrations: Digital files preferred. News pictures and picture stories relevant to all forms of waterways and towpath use, including boating, cycling, horse riding, angling or walking.
Text: Will consider news stories and features on anything concerning the UK's waterways, such as the environment, canal restoration and heritage. Also specialist articles on technical matters such as engine maintenance and boat care.
Overall freelance potential: Good.
Fees: According to use.

TRACTOR
Mortons Heritage Media, Newspaper House, Morton Way, Horncastle, Lincs LN9 6JR.
Tel: 01507 529304. Fax: 01507 529495. E-mail: pkelly@mortons.co.uk
Editor: Peter Kelly.
Monthly magazine celebrating the farm tractor and its development.
Illustrations: Mainly colour; archive B&W. Images of interesting classic or vintage tractors, restoration projects, tractor rallies and events. Detailed captions about individual machines and their history always essential. Also archive pictures depicting farm life and machinery from WW1 to the 1960s.
Text: Well-illustrated articles on relevant subjects always considered.
Overall freelance potential: Very good.
Fees: By negotiation.

TRACTOR & MACHINERY
Kelsey Publishing Group. Editorial: 1 Longview Cottage, Bodle Street Green, East Sussex BN27 4RA.
Tel: 01323 833125. E-mail: peterlove@kelsey.co.uk
Editor: Peter Love.
Monthly magazine for tractor enthusiasts, covering classic, vintage and contemporary machines from all parts of the world.
Illustrations: Mainly colour. Digital files preferred. Pictures of tractors in the news, classic and vintage gatherings, unusual and interesting tractors, and related machinery. Captions must include details of type, model and year of tractor and name of driver. Contact editor before preparing a

submission.
Text: Those who can add words to their images are welcomed.
Overall freelance potential: Good.
Fees: By arrangement.

TRUCK & DRIVER
Reed Business Information, Quadrant House, The Quadrant, Sutton, Surrey SM2 5AS.
Tel: 020 8652 3682. Fax: 020 8652 8988. E-mail: phil.brooker@rbi.co.uk
Editor: Brian Weatherley. **Art Editor:** Phil Brooker.
Monthly magazine for truck drivers.
Illustrations: Digital files preferred. Interesting individual trucks, unusual situations involving drivers and their vehicles, news items and some studio work.
Text: Commissioned features on anything of interest to truck drivers. Looks for freelances with ideas.
Overall freelance potential: Very good.
Fees: By negotiation.

Travel

AUSTRALIA & NEW ZEALAND
Merricks Media, Units 3&4, Riverside Court, Lower Bristol Road, Bath BA2 3DZ.
Tel: 01225 786800. Fax: 01225 786801. E-mail: anna.scrivenger@merricksmedia.co.uk
Editor: Anna Scrivenger.
Monthly magazine aimed at both holidaymakers and migrants.
Illustrations: Very limited scope for photography on its own as much is sourced from the travel and migration trade. Pictures only required as part of complete feature packages as below, or possibly for cover use.
Text: Well-illustrated features of around 1,200 – 2,000 words. Real-life stories of those who have emigrated to Australia or NZ, plus coverage of specific locations, cities, activities, food and culture. Should have wide rather than niche appeal. Submit ideas only in the first instance, along with examples of previous work.
Overall freelance potential: Good for experienced travel freelances who can provide the complete package.
Editor's tips: Looking for material that strikes a good balance between inspiration and information.
Fees: Features £180 per 1,000 words inclusive of pictures.

BUSINESS TRAVELLER
Panacea Publishing International Ltd, 2nd Floor, Cardinal House, Albemarle Street, London W1S 4TE.
Tel: 020 7647 6330. Fax: 020 7647 6331. E-mail: editorial@businesstraveller.com
Editor: Tom Otley. **Art Editor:** William Harvey.
Monthly consumer publication aimed at the frequently travelling international and domestic business executive.
Illustrations: Digital files preferred. Pictures to illustrate destination features on a wide variety of cities around the world – request features list of upcoming destinations.
Text: Illustrated features on business travel, but only by prior consultation with the editor.
Overall freelance potential: Around 65 per cent of the magazine is contributed by freelances.
Editor's tips: Submit low-res digital or dupes in the first instance.
Fees: Pictures from £50 up to £180 for a full page; covers £250. Text, £200 per 1,000 words.

CONDE NAST TRAVELLER

The Condé Nast Publications Ltd, Vogue House, Hanover Square, London W1S 1JU.
Tel: 020 7499 9080. Fax: 020 7493 3758. E-mail: cntraveller@condenast.co.uk
Editor: Sarah Miller. **Director of Photography:** Caroline Metcalfe.
Heavily-illustrated glossy monthly for the discerning, independent traveller.
Illustrations: Colour and occasional B&W. Top quality photo-feature material covering all aspects of travel, from luxury hotels and food, restaurant interiors to adventure travel, ecological issues, and reportage, etc. Very stylish and striking B&W photography also sought. Always interested in hearing from experienced photographers who are planning specific trips.
Text: Mostly commissioned from top name writers.
Overall freelance potential: Very good for material of the highest quality.
Editor's tips: The magazine seeks to use material with an original approach. Particularly interested in hearing from photographers who can produce excellent work but who are not necessarily travel specialists.
Fees: Variable depending on what is offered, but top rates paid for suitable material.

FOOD & TRAVEL

Green Pea Publishing, Spectrum House, 4 Ingate Place, Queenstown Road, London SW8 3NS.
Tel: 020 7501 0511. E-mail: edits@foodandtravel.com
Editor: Janine Furness. **Creative Director:** Angela Dukes.
Up-market monthly for affluent couples interested in long-haul travel, weekend breaks and eating out.
Illustrations: Colour. High quality food and travel photography, invariably produced on commission. Specialist photographers are advised to contact the creative director with details of experience and ideas. Limited scope for travel stock material since most is commissioned.
Text: Ideas for articles always considered, but most produced in-house.
Overall freelance potential: Good for specialists; better for travel than for food.
Fees: By negotiation.

FRANCE

Archant House, Oriel Road, Cheltenham, Gloucestershire GL50 1BB.
Tel: 01242 216050. Fax: 01242 216074. E-mail: steve.rayner@francemag.com
Editor: Carolyn Boyd. **Art Editor:** Steve Rayner.
Monthly magazine for Francophiles, with the emphasis on the real France.
Illustrations: Picture stories, and top quality individual pictures to illustrate articles, on French regions, annual events, cuisine, travel, arts, history, shopping, fashion, sport and property. Especially interested in destination, scenic, character and human interest shots, and mood pictures. Covers: pictures that capture the essence of France. Photographs also required for annual calendar – selected early in each new year.
Text: Lively and colourful illustrated features on the life, culture and history of France. Normally around 800–1,200 words, but up to 2,000 words considered. Factual accuracy essential.
Overall freelance potential: Excellent for top quality material.
Editor's tips: Call or e-mail with outlines/summary before submitting material.
Fees: Photographs from £25 up to £100 for cover or DPS. £100 per 1,000 words.

FRENCH MAGAZINE

Merricks Media, Unit 3&4, Riverside Court, Lower Bristol Road, Bath BA2 3DZ.
Tel: 01225 786800. Fax: 01225 786801. E-mail: edit@frenchmagazine.co.uk
Editor: Justin Postlethwaite.
Monthly magazine for regular travellers to France and those with, or seeking, property there.
Illustrations: Digital files preferred. Typical French images for general illustration purposes – historic sites, vineyards, food/restaurants, activities, and homes and interiors etc. Submit lists of subjects available in the first instance. Commissions may be available to photographers with medium format or high-end digital equipment.

Text: Well-illustrated articles always welcomed, especially on gastronomy, buying property and regional features. Around 1,0500 words plus 8-10 illustrations.
Overall freelance potential: Excellent.
Fees: Single pictures according to use; features from £150 per 1,000 words; packages negotiable.

GEOGRAPHICAL
Circle Publishing, One Victoria Villas, Richmond, Surrey TW9 2GW.
Tel: 020 8332 2713. Fax: 020 8332 9307. E-mail: magazine@geographical.co.uk
Editor: Geordie Torr. **Art Director:** David Lloyd. **Picture Researcher:** Liz Fensome
Monthly magazine of the Royal Geographical Society. Covers a wide spread of topics including travel, culture, environment, wildlife, conservation, history and exploration.
Illustrations: Digital files accepted but transparencies preferred. Mainly looking for photo-stories on geographical topics – human, political, ecological, economic and physical. Relevant news pictures always considered.
Text: Well-illustrated articles on any geographical subject, written in an informative but accessible way. Feature proposals should be sent to proposals@geographical.co.uk in the form of a 150-200 word synopsis.
Overall freelance potential: Excellent for the right type of material.
Fees: Negotiable, but in the region of £100 per published page. Single pictures according to use.

GREECE
Merricks Media, Unit 3&4, Riverside Court, Lower Bristol Road, Bath BA2 3DZ.
Tel: 01225 786835. E-mail: greece.edit@merricksmedia.co.uk
Editor: Diana Cambridge.
Bi-monthly for lovers of Greece, both holidaymakers and those considering property in the country.
Illustrations: Attractive stock images of Greek subjects, but especially holiday activities and food and drink. Send lists of coverage available.
Text: Illustrated features on subjects of interest to the visitor or potential home buyer. Submit ideas only in the first instance.
Overall freelance potential: Fair.
Fees: Pictures according to use; features negotiable.

ITALIA
Anthem Publishing Limited, Suite 6, Picadilly House, London Road, Bath BA1 3PL.
Tel: 01225 489984. Fax: 01225 489980. E-mail: debra.hughes@anthem-publishing.com
Editor: Amanda Robinson. **Art Editor:** Debra Hughes.
Highly-pictorial monthly covering regional travel and property in Italy. Also has sister-title Taste Italia focusing on Italian food and drink.
Illustrations: Digital files preferred. Happy to hear from photographers, particularly those based in or regularly visiting Italy, and those with large collections of existing images. Pictures used mainly scenic/landscape and people/local colour images.
Text: little scope as the magazine generates most topics in-house and commissions from known writers.
Overall freelance potential: Very good.
Fees: By negotiation.

THE ITALIAN MAGAZINE
Merricks Media, Units 3&4, Riverside Court, Lower Bristol Road, Bath BA2 3DZ.
Tel: 01225 786800. Fax: 01225 786801. E-mail: fred.dutton@merricksmedia.co.uk
Editor: Fred Dutton.
Monthly focussing on holidaying in Italy and enjoyment of the Italian lifestyle. Aimed at those who admire and appreciate Italian food, drink, culture and style even if they have never visited the country.
Illustrations: Colour. Photographs illustrating the widest range of Italian topics. Open to offers of

high-quality stock or feature photography.
Text: open to suggestions for features or specialist coverage.
Overall freelance potential: Very good.
Editor's tips:
Fees: By negotiation.

ITALY

Poundbury Publishing Ltd, Prospect House, Peverell Avenue East, Poundbury, Dorchester DT1 3WE.
Tel: 01305 756391. Fax: 01305 262760. E-mail: melissa@italymag.co.uk/design@italymag.co.uk
Editor: Melissa Ormiston. **Art Editor:** Paul Tutill.
General interest monthly for lovers of all things Italian.
Illustrations: Digital files preferred. Stock images always required on all aspects of Italian life and culture – send detailed lists in the first instance.
Text: Well-illustrated articles focusing on interesting but less well-known places and regions rather than the popular holiday destinations, or on aspects of Italian lifestyle, culture, crafts and history.
Overall freelance potential: Very good.
Editor's tips: Complete word and picture packages are given preference. In all cases, make first approach by e-mail, with subject lists or ideas.
Fees: From £30 depending on size of reproduction. Text £100 per 1,000 words.

LIVING FRANCE

Archant Life, Archant House, Oriel Road, Cheltenham GL50 1BB.
Tel: 01242 216050. Fax: 01242 216074. E-mail: editorial@livingfrance.com
Editor: Eleanor O'Kane.
Monthly magazine for those thinking of buying property in or moving to France, or hoping to work there.
Illustrations: Digital files preferred. Images reflecting working and living in France – property, French lifestyle, working life in France, retirement in France, children's education. Submit subject lists to deputy editor in the first instance.
Text: Suggestions for articles always considered. Main scope for destination pieces, interviews/profiles with expats in France, practical articles on buying property, living and working in France. E-mail synopsis in the first instance.
Overall freelance potential: Good.
Fees: Individual pictures according to use; illustrated articles £300 for 1,000–2,500 words.

A PLACE IN THE SUN

Brooklands Magazines, Westgate, 120-128 Station Road, Redhill, Surrey RH1 1ET.
Tel: 01737 786800. Fax: 01737 786801. E-mail: matt.havercroft@brooklandsgroup.com
Editor: Matt Havercroft. **Art Editor:** David Boosey.
Glossy monthly for prospective buyers of overseas property. Official magazine of the C4 TV series of the same name.
Illustrations: Mostly by commission, though some stock images are used. Will consider sets of images based around people moving or living abroad, or suggestions for subjects, which could lead to a full-scale commission. Other general commissions also possible – submit details of experience and a few samples in the first instance.
Text: Illustrated feature stories as above.
Overall freelance potential: Good for the more experienced worker.
Fees: By negotiation.

PORTUGAL

Merricks Media, Unit 3&4, Riverside Court, Lower Bristol Road, Bath BA2 3DZ.
Tel: 01225 786819. E-mail: sarah.seamarks@merricksmedia.co.uk
Editor: Sarah Seamarks.

Magazine devoted to Portugal, covering holidays, property, culture, lifestyle, food and drink. Publishes nine issues per year.
Illustrations: Digital files preferred. Will consider stock material depicting aspects of Portugese life, people, activities, etc for use in illustrating stories and features. Also spectacular or unusual landscape shots for the magazine's 'Gallery' pages. Possible opportunities for photographers who are planning to visit the country on other business. Initial contact via e-mail or letter is requested.
Text: Always interested in well-illustrated articles on the country. Write with synopsis or suggestions in the first instance.
Overall freelance potential: Good for complete illustrated articles.
Fees: By negotiation.

REAL TRAVEL
Hedrush Media, 7th Floor, Tower House, Fairfax Street, Bristol BS1 3BN.
Tel: 0117 945 1913. Fax: 0117 927 7984. E-mail: ian@realtravelmag.com
Editor: Ian Waller. **Art Editor:** Tim Bates.
Magazine for "active travellers" rather than holidaymakers.
Illustrations: Pictures of real people experiencing the world on career breaks or gap years or just for adventure, charity work, sporting activity, etc. Also stock pictures of less "touristy" destinations; submit details of coverage available in the first instance.
Text: Will always consider illustrated features focusing on "exciting yet attainable" destinations. From the more experienced contributor, expert advice and travel tips, on practical topics such as health, staying safe, etc.
Overall freelance potential: Good for the right sort of material as described.
Editor's tips: Contributions must have been clearly produced by active travellers from their own personal experience.
Fees: By negotiation.

THE SUNDAY TIMES TRAVEL MAGAZINE
River Publishing Ltd, 14 Leicester Place, London WC2H 7BZ.
Tel: 020 7306 0304 (ext 347). Fax: 020 7306 0314. E-mail: praine@riverltd.co.uk
Editor: Ed Grenby. **Group Photo Editor:** Paola Raine. **Picture Editor:** Vanessa Jones.
Monthly glossy aimed at up-market travellers. Published on behalf of The Sunday Times.
Illustrations: Digital files preferred. Will always consider high-quality travel material on spec, including especially striking single images for use in double-page spreads. Lists of stock material always of interest. Only limited scope for commissions.
Text: Will consider very high-quality illustrated travel features. Should include human interest story elements rather than simple travelogues.
Overall freelance potential: Good for top-quality work.
Fees: Negotiable and according to use.

TRAVELLER
WEXAS International Ltd, 45-49 Brompton Road, London SW3 1DE.
Tel: 020 7589 0500. Fax: 020 7581 8476. E-mail: traveller@wexas.com
Editor: Amy Sohanpaul.
Quarterly publication containing narrative features on unusual and adventurous travel, usually in the developing countries of the world. Aimed at the independent traveller who prefers to travel off the beaten track.
Illustrations: Digital files preferred. High quality documentary travel pictures, usually from developing countries, rarely Europe or North America. Usually required as an integral part of illustrated articles as below, but there is also a six-page photo-essay (action/reportage). No tourist brochure-type shots.
Text: Well-illustrated travel articles from contributors with in-depth knowledge of the area/subject covered. Around 900 words, plus about 10 pictures. Unusual subject matter preferred, including coverage of world hot spots.

Overall freelance potential: Good, but limited by the magazine's frequency.
Editor's tips: Excellent photographic work is essential.
Fees: Photographs, From £50, full-page £80, £150 for cover. Text, £200 per 1,000 words.

WANDERLUST
Wanderlust Publications Ltd, PO Box 1832, Windsor, Berks SL4 1EB.
Tel: 01753 620426. Fax: 01753 620474. E-mail: info@wanderlust.co.uk
Editor: Dan Linstead. **Picture Editor:** Amy Bellew.
Magazine for the "independent-minded" traveller, published eight times a year.
Illustrations: Colour transparency or digital files (should be available at 60MB, no upsizing).
Majority required for use in conjunction with features. Send a summary stock list in the first
instance with a small selection of sample work. Covers: Always looking for bold, bright and
uncluttered images that shout "travel", preferably with strong colours such as blue/yellow or
red/orange.
Text: Well-illustrated features on independent and special interest travel at any level and in any
part of the world. Contributors must have in-depth knowledge of their subject area and be prepared
to cover both good and bad aspects. Short pieces up to 750 words; longer articles from 1,800–2,500
words.
Overall freelance potential: Excellent for complete packages of words and pictures.
Editor's tips: Don't send unsolicited originals; photocopies or prints will do as samples. Detailed
"Notes for Contributors" and "Guidelines for Photographers" can be viewed on website:
www.wanderlust.co.uk.
Fees: Photographs by negotiation and according to use; text £200 per 1,000 words.

Women's Interest

BELLA
H. Bauer Publishing Ltd, Academic House, 24-28 Oval Road, London NW1 7DT.
Tel: 020 7241 8000. Fax: 020 7241 8056.
Editor: Jayne Marsden. **Picture Editor:** Lizzie Rowe.
Weekly magazine for women, covering human interest stories, fashion, cookery and celebrities.
Illustrations: Pictures of celebrities and royalty, off-beat pictures and curiosities considered on
spec. Fashion and food, mostly commissioned.
Text: Some scope for exclusive human interest features and celebrity interviews. Always check with
the editor first.
Overall freelance potential: Limited for speculative work.
Fees: By negotiation.

BEST
National Magazine Company, 72 Broadwick Street, London W1F 9EP.
Tel: 020 7439 5000. Fax: 020 7437 6886.
Editor: Michelle Hather. **Picture Editor:** Alison Thurston.
Weekly magazine for women, covering affordable fashion, health matters, cookery, home
improvements, features etc.
Illustrations: Scope for off-beat, general human interest and curiosity shots, and informal celebrity
material. Commissioned coverage of fashion, food, features, etc.

> *Are you working from the latest edition of The Freelance Photographer's*
> *Market Handbook? It's published on 1 October each year. Markets are*
> *constantly changing, so it pays to have the latest edition*

Text: Articles with a practical slant, aimed at working women.
Overall freelance potential: Quite good.
Fees: Commissioned photography by negotiation; other material according to use.

CLOSER
EMAP Elan Network, Endeavour House, 189 Shaftesbury Avenue, London WC2H 8JG.
Tel: 020 7859 8685. Fax: 020 7859 8685. E-mail: alex.morris@emap.com
Editor: Lisa Burrow. **Picture Editor:** Alex Morris.
Weekly women's magazine with the emphasis on celebrities and true-life stories.
Illustrations: Mainly by commission. Opportunities for experienced photographers to shoot a range of celebrity material, from paparazzi street photography to studio work. Exclusive paparazzi material also considered on spec, but much is sourced from agencies. Photographers in all parts of the UK also needed to shoot portraits to illustrate true-life stories – submit details of experience and area of the country covered.
Text: True-life stories about ordinary people always wanted – submit brief details in the first instance.
Overall freelance potential: Good for those with some experience in these areas.
Fees: Photography by negotiation or according to job. True-life stories, up to £500.

COMPANY
National Magazine Company Ltd, 72 Broadwick Street, London W1F 9EP.
Tel: 020 7439 5000. Fax: 020 7312 3051. E-mail: abi.dillon@natmags.co.uk
Editor: Victoria White. **Picture Editor:** Abi Dillon.
Monthly magazine aimed at up-market young women in their twenties.
Illustrations: Digital files preferred. Photographs to illustrate features on fashion, beauty, relationships, careers, travel and personalities, invariably by commission.
Text: Articles on the above topics, of varying lengths. Also, more topical and "newsy" features.
Overall freelance potential: Fair scope for experienced contributors.
Fees: By negotiation.

COSMOPOLITAN
National Magazine Company Ltd, 72 Broadwick Street, London W1V 2BP.
Tel: 020 7439 5000. Fax: 020 7439 5016. E-mail: joan.tinney@natmags.co.uk
Editor: Louise Court. **Art Director:** Andy Greenhouse. **Picture Editor:** Joan Tinney.
Monthly magazine for women in the 18–34 age group.
Illustrations: Photographs to illustrate features on fashion, style and beauty, by commission only. Some top quality stock situation pictures may be used to illustrate more general features on emotional, sexual or social issues.
Text: Articles of interest to sophisticated young women. Always query the editor first
Overall freelance potential: Only for the experienced contributor to the women's press.
Fees: By negotiation.

ELLE
Hachette Filipacchi (UK) Ltd, 64 North Row, London W1K 7LL.
Tel: 020 7150 7342. Fax: 020 7150 7670. E-mail: marina.ansell@hf-uk.com
Editor: Lorraine Candy. **Associate Picture Editor:** Marina Ansell.
Up-market monthly magazine with the emphasis on fashion.
Illustrations: Mainly colour. Top quality coverage of fashion and style subjects, portraiture and still life, always by commission.
Text: Some scope for top quality feature articles and photojournalism, usually by commission and from established contributors.
Overall freelance potential: Good for contributors experienced at the top level of magazine journalism.
Fees: By negotiation.

ESSENTIALS
IPC Media Ltd, Blue Fin Building, 110 Southwark Street, London SE1 0SU.
Tel: 020 3148 5000. E-mail: stuart_thomas@ipcmedia.com
Editor: Julie Barton-Breck. **Art Director:** Stuart Thomas.
Monthly mass-market magazine for women with the emphasis on practical matters.
Illustrations: Digital files preferred. Health, interior decoration, travel, food, etc. Some commissioned work available.
Text: Practical articles, health, features of interest to women. Synopsis essential in first instance.
Overall freelance potential: Good for experienced contributors to quality women's magazines.
Fees: By negotiation.

FIRST
EMAP Entertainment, Endeavour House, 189 Shaftesbury Avenue, London WC2H 8JG.
Tel: 020 7295 6754 (picture editor). E-mail: first@emap.com
Editor: Jane Ennis. **Picture Editor:** Clara Massie.
Picture-led, topical weekly aimed at "thirty-something mums".
Illustrations: Interested in hearing from serious photojournalists who can offer top level current news pictures, both nationally and internationally. Top quality news picture stories also considered. Special "Eyewitness" section for readers' pictures – news pictures, paparazzi-type shots of celebrities and amusing images can be e-mailed direct to firsteyewitness@emap.com.
Text: No scope.
Overall freelance potential: Very good for high-quality or unique material.
Editor's tips: Think carefully if material is suitable before submitting.
Fees: £100 for published "Eyewitness" contributions; other fees by negotiation and according to use.

GLAMOUR
The Condé Naste Publications Ltd, 6-8 Old Bond Street, London W1S 4PH.
Tel: 020 7499 9080. Fax: 020 7491 2551. lucy.slade@condenast.co.uk
Editor: Jo Elvin. Features **Editor:** Corrie Jackson. Picture Director: Lucy Slade.
Mid-market general interest monthly for the 18-32 age group.
Illustrations: Mostly by commission to shoot features, portraiture, still life and interiors; make an appointment to show portfolio. Possible but limited scope for stock, including celebrity material.
Text: Always interested in celebrity interviews, investigative articles and features on relationships, careers, fashion, health and fitness. Send short synopsis in the first instance.
Overall freelance potential: Good for the experienced worker.
Fees: By negotiation.

GOOD HOUSEKEEPING
National Magazine Company Ltd, National Magazine House, 72 Broadwick Street, London W1V 2BP.
Tel: 020 7439 5000. Fax: 020 7439 5591. E-mail: contact@goodhousekeeping.co.uk
Editor: Louise Chunn. **Picture Editor:** Lauren Meckiff.
General interest magazine for up-market women. Concentrates on home and family life.
Illustrations: Interiors, gardening, food, fashion, travel and reportage. Usually by commission to illustrate specific articles.
Text: Articles of interest to up-market women – interesting homes (with photos), gardening, personality profiles, emotional features, humorous articles, etc.
Overall freelance potential: Good scope for the highest quality material.
Fees: By negotiation.

GRAZIA
EMAP Consumer Media, Endeavour House, 189 Shaftesbury Avenue, London WC2H 8JG.
Tel: 020 7437 9011. Fax: 020 7520 6599. E-mail: deborah.brown@emap.com
Editor: Jane Bruton. Picture Director: Deborah Brown.

Britain's first women's glossy to be published on a weekly basis, offering a mixture of celebrity coverage, real life stories, reportage, fashion and beauty.
Illustrations: Pictures of leading personalities at premieres, parties and generally out and about, plus paparazzi street shots. Pictures also required for news section containing hard news with the focus on women's issues and interests alongside celebrity stories. News pictures can be submitted on spec to grazianewspics@emap.com. Opportunities for experienced workers in portraiture, beauty, still life and interiors; contact the picture director in the first instance with details of prior experience and coverage offered.
Text: Little freelance scope.
Overall freelance potential: Wide range of opportunities for experienced photographers.
Editor's tips: Celebrity coverage must be strictly A list, not C or D list. A short lead time means the magazine goes to press on Friday for sale the following Tuesday.
Fees: By negotiation.

HARPER'S BAZAAR
National Magazine Company Ltd, 72 Broadwick Street, London W1F 9EP.
Tel: 020 7439 5000. Fax: 020 7439 5506.
Editor: Lucy Yeomans. **Art Director:** Tom Usher. **Picture Editor:** Charlotte Schmidt.
Monthly glossy magazine featuring fashion, design, travel, interiors, beauty and health.
Illustrations: Colour and high-quality B&W. Top quality photography to illustrate subjects as above, only by commission.
Text: General interest features of very high quality. 1,500–3,000 words. Only by commission.
Overall freelance potential: Good for those who can produce the right material.
Fees: Good; on a rising scale according to length of feature.

HELLO!
Hello Ltd, Wellington House, 69/71 Upper Ground, London SE1 9PQ.
Tel: 020 7667 8700. Fax: 020 7667 8711. E-mail: pictures@hellomagazine.com
Editor: Ronnie Whelan. **Picture Editor:** Freddie Sloan.
Weekly magazine for women covering people and current events.
Illustrations: Digital files preferred. Pictures and picture stories on personalities and celebrities of all kinds. People in the news and current news events. Off-beat pictures. Dramatic picture stories of bravery, courage or rescue.
Text: Interviews and/or reports to accompany photos.
Overall freelance potential: Excellent for quality material.
Editor's tips: The magazine has short lead times which it likes to exploit to the full – can include late stories in colour up to the Friday of the week before publication.
Fees: By negotiation.

THE LADY
The Lady, 39–40 Bedford Street, Strand, London WC2E 9ER.
Tel: 020 7379 4717. Fax: 020 7836 4620. E-mail: editors@lady.co.uk
Editor: Arline Usden. **Picture Researcher:** Beth Clarke.
Weekly general interest magazine for women.
Illustrations: Digital files preferred. Pictures only required to accompany particular articles. Covers: Images of women 35–50 years; famous faces.
Text: Illustrated articles on British and foreign travel, the countryside, human interest, wildlife, pets, cookery, gardening, fashion, beauty, British history and commemorative subjects. 1,000–1,200 words.
Overall freelance potential: Excellent for complete illustrated articles.
Fees: Photographs £14 mono; £18 colour. Text from £80 per 1,000 words.

LOOK
IPC Media Ltd, Blue Fin Building, 110 Southwark Street, London SE1 0SU.
Tel: 020 3148 5000. E-mail: jo_walker@ipcmedia.com
Editor: Ali Hall. **Picture Editor:** Jo Walker.
Young women's weekly offering a mix of affordable fashion, celebrity style and gossip, and true life stories.
Illustrations: Mostly by commission. Those seeking fashion or portrait work should make an appointment to show their portfolio. Those experienced in "real-life" work should make initial contact by e-mail. Celebrity images or other material that may be relevant to the target readership will be be considered on spec.
Text: Little scope.
Overall freelance potential: Good opportunities for experienced workers in this field.
Fees: By negotiation.

LOVE IT!
News Magazines Ltd, 14 Flood Walk, Chelsea, London SW3 5RG.
Tel: 020 7198 3030. Fax: 020 7198 3070. E-mail: arlene.brown@newsmagazines.co.uk
Editor: Karen Pasquali Jones. **Picture Editor:** Arlene Brown. **Deputy Picture Editor:** Verina Durand.
Real life weekly aimed at younger women.
Illustrations: Freelances around the country needed to shoot reportage, portraits and some studio work. Sample portfolios or CDs should be sent by post or e-mail to the picture desk.
Text: Original and exclusive real life stories always required.
Overall freelance potential: Excellent for the experienced worker.
Fees: Dependent on the nature of the job, but full day rate is £350, more typically £250 For shorter shoots.

MARIE CLAIRE
European Magazines Ltd, Blue Fin Building, 110 Southwark Street, London SE1 0SU.
Tel: 020 3148 5000. E-mail: sian_parry@ipcmedia.com
Editor: Joanna Coles. **Picture Editor:** Sian Parry.
Fashion and general interest monthly for sophisticated women in the 25–35 age group.
Illustrations: Top quality fashion, beauty, portraits, reportage, interiors, still life, etc, usually by commission.
Text: In-depth articles, features and profiles aimed at an intelligent readership. Up to 4,000 words.
Overall freelance potential: Very good for experienced contributors in this field.
Fees: By negotiation.

MORE
EMAP Elan Ltd, Endeavour House, 189 Shaftesbury Avenue, London WC2H 8JG.
Tel: 020 7208 3397. Fax: 020 7208 3595. E-mail: tijen.denizmen@emap.com
Editor: Lisa Smosarski. **Picture Director:** Tijen Denizmen.
Weekly magazine for young women in the 18–24 age group.
Illustrations: Up-to-date news pictures featuring celebrities, formal and informal. Fashion, beauty, health and pictures to illustrate specific articles, always by commission.
Text: Articles and features, often with a practical slant, of general interest to young women. Submit ideas only in the first instance.
Overall freelance potential: Quite good for quality material.
Editor's tips: No unsolicited features – commissions only.
Fees: By negotiation.

MS LONDON
Independent Magazines, Independent House, 191 Marsh Wall, London E14 9RS.
Tel: 020 7005 5000. Fax: 020 7005 2999.
Managing **Editor:** Bill Bloom. **Group Art Editor:** Steve Bowling.
Weekly magazine for young, independent women working in London.
Illustrations: Digital files preferred. Mostly fashion and portraits, some still life and reportage work. Covers: colour fashion and general interest subjects; medium format preferred.
Text: Off-beat, sharply-written features of interest to young, aware, working Londoners. 800–1,500 words.
Overall freelance potential: Around 90 per cent of the magazine comes from freelances.
Editor's tips: Best to send copies of recently-published work plus list of ideas before actual submission.
Fees: By agreement.

NOW
IPC Media Ltd, Blue Fin Building, 110 Southwark Street, London SE1 0SU.
Tel: 020 3148 5000. E-mail: nowpictures@ipcmedia.com
Editor: Helen Johnston. **Picture Editor:** Francesca D'Avanzo.
Weekly entertainment for women with the focus on celebrities and "true-life" stories.
Illustrations: Digital files preferred. Topical coverage of current film and TV stars, both formal and informal shots. Some commissions available to illustrate true-life stories and general features.
Text: Ideas for stories and interviews always considered.
Overall freelance potential: Limited.
Fees: Variable according to the material or assignment; top rates paid for good exclusives.

OK!
Northern & Shell plc, Northern & Shell Building, Number 10 Lower Thames Street, London EC3R 6EN.
Tel: 0871 434 1010. Fax: 0871 520 7766. E-mail: sophie.mutter@express.co.uk
Editor: Lisa Palta. **Picture Director:** Amanda Davis. **Picture Researchers:** Jacqui McLennan, Sophie Mutter.
Weekly, picture-led magazine devoted to celebrity features and news pictures.
Illustrations: Digital files preferred. Shots of celebrities of all kinds considered on spec, especially exclusives or unpublished archive material. Commissions available to experienced photographers – contact picture researcher.
Text: Exclusive stories/interviews with celebrities always of interest.
Overall freelance potential: Excellent for the right type of material.
Fees: Negotiable; depends on nature of the material or assignment.

PICK ME UP
IPC Media Ltd, Blue Fin Building, 110 Southwark Street, London SE1 0SU.
Tel: 020 3148 6440. Fax: 020 3148 8112. E-mail: sidske_vandervos@ipcmedia.com
Editor: June Smith-Sheppard. **Picture Editor:** Sidske Van Der Vos.
True life weekly presenting stories more graphically and in more detail than its rivals. Includes a limited amount of health material, but no celebrities.
Illustrations: Digital files preferred. Happy to hear from capable photographers around the country who are able to shoot stories as they arise. Initial contact should be made in writing, giving details of area covered and of any previous experience in the field.
Text: Suggestions for stories always welcomed, not only UK-based but also from overseas.
Overall freelance potential: Good for experienced contributors in this field.
Editor's tips: More is asked of contributors than is usually the case with real life material.

Photographers will be expected to cover more angles, such as going to where an event took place or covering other aspects of a story.
Fees: Variable depending on what the photographer is required to do and how much travel is involved.

PRIMA
National Magazine Company, 72 Broadwick Street, London W1F 9EP.
Tel: 020 7439 5000. Fax: 020 7312 4100. E-mail: jo.lockwood@natmags.co.uk
Editor: Maire Fahey. **Art Director:** Jacqueline Hampsey. **Picture Editor:** Jo Lockwood. **Picture Researcher:** Matthew Brown.
General interest women's monthly with a strong emphasis on practical subjects. Major topics covered include cookery, gardening, crafts, health, fashion and homecare.
Illustrations: Digital files preferred. Top quality work in the fields of food, fashion, still-life, interiors and portraiture, usually by commission. Some scope for good stock shots of family and domestic situations, food, pets, etc that could be used for general illustration purposes, but query needs before before submitting.
Text: Short, illustrated practical features with a "how-to-do-it" approach.
Overall freelance potential: The magazine relies heavily on freelances.
Fees: Commissioned photography in the region of £400 per day. Other fees according to use.

PSYCHOLOGIES
Hachette Filipacchi (UK) Ltd, 64 North Row, London W1K 7LL.
Tel: 020 7150 7000. Fax: 020 7150 7001. E-mail: liz.simon@hf-uk.com
Editor: Maureen Rice. **Features Editor:** Rebecca Alexander. **Photo Editor:** Liz Simon.
Up-market women's monthly with the focus on "positive living", including topics such as work, health, family and social issues, travel.
Illustrations: Digital files preferred. Interested in both high-quality stock and in commissioning for specific features. Most images used are lifestyle-based, but relaxed and natural. Also opportunities for top-quality portraiture and beauty images. Initial approach should be by e-mail or telephone.
Text: Possible scope for high-quality lifestyle features.
Overall freelance potential: Good for experienced photographers.
Editor's tips: Examine the magazine closely to get a feel for its style.
Fees: By negotiation.

REAL PEOPLE
ACP-NatMag, 33 Broadwick Street, London W1F 0DQ.
Tel: 020 7439 5000. Fax: 020 7339 4650. E-mail: sue.miles@acp-natmag.co.uk
Editor: Samm Taylor. **Picture Editor:** Sue Miles.
Real life weekly for women.
Illustrations: Requires experienced freelances in all parts of the country who may be available to undertake reportage and portrait shoots to illustrate stories. Initial contact by e-mail is preferred, giving brief details of any previous experience.
Text: Real life stories always required.
Overall freelance potential: Excellent for the experienced worker.
Fees: Around £200–£300 per assignment, depending on the nature of the shoot and rights licensed. Up to £500 for real life stories.

RED
Hachette Filipacchi (UK) Ltd, 64 North Row, London W1K 7LL.
Tel: 020 7150 7000. Fax: 020 7150 7001. E-mail: beverley.croucher@hf-uk.com
Editor: Sam Baker. **Art Director:** Jonathan Whitelocke. **Picture Editor:** Beverley Croucher.

Sophisticated monthly aimed at women in their 30s.
Illustrations: High quality commissioned photography covering portraiture, fashion, interior design, food and celebrities. Telephone to make an appointment to drop off portfolio in the first instance. Little scope for stock material.
Text: Ideas always welcome from experienced writers.
Overall freelance potential: Good for the experienced worker.
Fees: By negotiation.

REVEAL
The National Magazine Company Ltd, 72 Broadwick Street, London W1F 9EP.
Tel: 020 7439 5000. E-mail: vanessa.colls@acp-natmag.co.uk
Editor: Michael Butcher. **Picture Editor:** Vanessa Colls.
A "five magazines in one" weekly package, with a mix of celebrities, real-life stories, fashion, lifestyle and TV listings.
Illustrations: Good scope for celebrity shots, especially paparazzi-style pictures. Happy to hear from freelances if they think they have something, but ideally should be an exclusive. Send an e-mail first rather than sending images. Some opportunities for commissions to shoot real-life or lifestyle features.
Text: Good, illustrated real-life stories always being sought; e-mail features.reveal@natmags.co.uk with suggestions.
Overall freelance potential: Excellent for the right type of material.
Fees: Photography by negotiation; £500 upwards for real-life stories.

SHE
National Magazine Company, National Magazine House, 72 Broadwick Street, London W1V 2BP.
Tel: 020 7439 5000. Fax: 020 7439 5350. E-mail: editor@shemagazine.co.uk
Editor: Sian Rees. **Art Director:** Abdul Malique. **Features Editor:** Sarah Gooding.
General interest monthly for the 30-something woman.
Illustrations: Most material by commission for specific articles; anything else only considered by appointment.
Text: Top quality features of interest to intelligent women; suggestions welcomed but always query the editor first.
Overall freelance potential: Little unsolicited material used, but quite good for commissions.
Editor's tips: Please study the content and style before contacting magazine.
Fees: By arrangement.

THAT'S LIFE!
H.Bauer Publishing Ltd, 24-28 Oval Road, London NW1 7DT.
Tel: 020 7241 8000. Fax: 020 7241 8008. E-mail: jim.taylor@bauer.co.uk
Editor: Jo Checkley. **Picture Editor:** Jim Taylor.
Popular women's weekly concentrating on true-life stories and confessions.
Illustrations: Digital files preferred. Mostly commissioned shots of people to accompany stories; photographers who can produce good informal portrait work should write to the picture editor enclosing a couple of samples. Also limited opportunities in fashion, food and still life. Quirky and amusing "readers' pictures" always considered on spec – should be accompanied by a brief story or anecdote.
Text: Personal true-life stories always of interest – shocking, scandalous, embarrassing, tear-jerking, etc. Around 300 words. Contact the editor with suggestions first.
Overall freelance potential: Good.
Fees: Story shoots around £150; readers' pictures £25; other photography by negotiation. £200 for true stories.

WI LIFE

NFWI, 104 New Kings Road, Fulham, London SW6 4LY.
Tel: 020 7731 5777. Fax: 020 7736 4061. E-mail: h&ced@nfwi.org.uk
Editor: Neal Maidment. **Art Editor:** Diane Lilley.
Published eight times a year for Women's Institute members, includes WI news and features.
Illustrations: Digital files preferred. Pictures of WI events, members, craft and cookery projects.
Text: Mostly written in-house.
Overall freelance potential: Modest scope for picture sales.
Editor's tips: Always consult the editor before submitting.
Fees: By agreement.

WOMAN

IPC Media Ltd, Blue Fin Building, 110 Southwark Street, London SE1 0SU.
Tel: 020 3148 5000. E-mail: emma_smith@ipcmedia.com
Editor: Jackie Hatton. **Picture Editor:** Emma Smith.
Weekly magazine devoted to all women's interests.
Illustrations: Most pictures commissioned to illustrate specific features. Some scope for human interest shots which are dramatic, off-beat or unusual.
Text: Interviews with leading personalities, human interest stories. Other features mostly staff-produced. Submit a synopsis in the first instance.
Overall freelance potential: Only for experienced contributors in the field.
Fees: Good; on a rising scale according to size of reproduction or length of articles.

WOMAN AND HOME

IPC Media Ltd, Blue Fin Building, 110 Southwark Street, London SE1 0SU.
Tel: 020 3148 7836. Fax: 020 3148 8120. E-mail: sharon_mears@ipcmedia.com
Editor: Sue James. **Art Director:** Shannon Morton. **Picture Researcher:** Sharon Mears.
Monthly magazine for all women concerned with family and home.
Illustrations: All photography commissioned from experienced freelances, to illustrate subjects including cookery, fashion, beauty, interior design, DIY, gardening, travel, topical issues and personality articles.
Text: Articles on personalities, either well-known or who lead interesting lives. 1,500 words.
Overall freelance potential: Very good for the experienced worker. Including regular contributors, about 50 per cent of the magazine is produced by freelances.
Fees: By negotiation.

WOMAN'S OWN

IPC Media Ltd, Blue Fin Building, 110 Southwark Street, London SE1 0SU.
Tel: 020 3148 5000. Fax: 020 3148 8112. E-mail: fran_jepps@ipcmedia.com
Editor: Karen Livermore. **Picture Editor:** Fran Jepps.
Weekly publishing articles and practical features of interest to women.
Illustrations: Mainly colour. Mostly commissioned to illustrate features on fashion, interior design, crafts, etc.
Text: Mostly staff-produced. Send a brief outline of any proposed feature in the first instance to the features editor.
Overall freelance potential: Fair for commissioned work, but much is produced by regulars.
Fees: Good; on a rising scale according to size of reproduction or length of article.

Are you working from the latest edition of The Freelance Photographer's Market Handbook? It's published on 1 October each year. Markets are constantly changing, so it pays to have the latest edition

---

WOMAN'S WEEKLY
IPC Media Ltd, Blue Fin Building, 110 Southwark Street, London SE1 0SU.
Tel: 020 3148 6628. E-mail: sue_de_jong@ipcmedia.com
Editor: Sheena Harvey. **Art Editor:** Fiona Watson. **Picture Editor:** Sue De Jong.
General interest family-oriented magazine for women in the 35+ age group.
Illustrations: Mostly by commission to illustrate features on fashion, beauty, cookery, decoration, etc.
Text: Practical features on general women's topics, plus human interest stories and celebrity pieces.
Overall freelance potential: Fairly good for the experienced contributor.
Fees: By negotiation.

---

*As a member of the Bureau of Freelance Photographers, you'll be
kept up-to-date with markets through the BFP Market Newsletter,
published monthly. For details of membership, turn to page 9*

NEWSPAPERS

In this section we list the national daily and Sunday newspapers, and their associated magazine supplements. While the supplements may publish a wide range of general interest subject matter, the parent papers are obviously only likely to be interested in hard news pictures and stories of genuine interest to a nationwide readership.

News pictures

Despite the heavy presence of staff and agency photographers at major events, it is still perfectly possible for an independent freelance to get the shot that makes the front page. And when it comes to the unexpected, the freelance is often the only one on the spot to capture the drama.

If you think you have obtained a "hot" news picture or story, the best plan is to telephone the papers most likely to be interested as soon as possible and let them know what you have to offer.

Note that newspapers prefer to work from digital files and will not want to handle transparencies. They will, however, accept colour print or negative if that is all that is available.

In the listings that follow, as well as the main switchboard number you will find direct line telephone numbers which take you directly through to the picture desk of the paper concerned.

There should be little cause to use fax numbers for newspapers these days, but if you do it is advisable to always check the correct number for the department you want. Newspaper offices have numerous fax machines; the numbers listed here are necessarily general editorial numbers and if used without checking might delay your message getting to the department you need.

Other material

There is some scope for other material apart from hard news in most of the papers. Some use the occasional oddity or human interest item as a "filler", while in the tabloids there is always a good market for celebrity pictures.

Finally, of course, there is a market for top quality glamour material of the "Page 3" variety in several of the tabloids.

The supplements operate much like any other general interest magazine. Most of their content is commissioned from well-established photographers and writers, though some will accept exceptional photojournalistic features or exclusives on spec.

Fees

Fees paid by newspapers can vary tremendously according to what is offered and how it is used. However, it can be taken for granted that rates paid by the national papers listed here are good.

Generally, picture fees are calculated on standard rates based on the size of the reproduction, with the minumum fee you might expect from a national newspaper being around £65.

However, for material that is exclusive or exceptional the sky is almost literally the limit. If you think you have something very special and are prepared to offer it as an exclusive, make sure you negotiate a fee, and perhaps get several offers, before committing the material to anyone.

National Daily Newspapers

DAILY EXPRESS
Express Newspapers, 10 Lower Thames Street, London EC3R 6EN.
Tel: 0871 434 1010. Picture desk: 0871 520 7171.
E-mail: expresspix@express.co.uk
Editor: Peter Hill. **Picture Editor:** Neil McCarthy.

DAILY MAIL
The Daily Mail Ltd, Northcliffe House, Derry Street, London W8 5TT.
Tel: 020 7938 6000. Picture desk: 020 7938 6373. Fax: 020 7937 5560.
E-mail: pictures@dailymail.co.uk
Editor: Paul Dacre. **Picture Editor:** Paul Silva.

DAILY MIRROR
Mirror Group Newspapers Ltd, Canary Wharf Tower, 1 Canada Square, London E14 5AP.
Tel: 020 7293 3000. Picture desk: 020 7293 3851. Fax: 020 7293 3983. ISDN: 020 7572 5802.
E-mail: picturedesk@mirror.co.uk
Editor: Richard Wallace. **Picture Editor:** Greg Bennett.

DAILY RECORD
The Scottish Daily Record and Sunday Mail Ltd, One Central Quay, Glasgow G3 8DA.
Tel: 0141 309 3000. Picture desk: 0141 309 3245. Fax: 0141 309 3835. ISDN: 0141 309 4879.
E-mail: a.baird@dailyrecord.co.uk
Editor: Bruce Waddell. **Picture Editor:** Alasdair Baird.

DAILY SPORT
Sport Newspapers Ltd, 19 Great Ancoats Street, Manchester M60 4BT.
Tel: 0161 236 4466. Picture desk: 0161 238 8169. Fax: 0161 236 4535.
E-mail: paul.currie@sportnewspapers.co.uk
Editor: Dave Beevers. **Picture Editor:** Paul Currie.

DAILY STAR
Express Newspapers, 10 Lower Thames Street, London EC3R 6EN.
Tel: 0871 434 1010. Picture desk: 0871 434 7353. Fax: 0871 434 2723.
E-mail: rob.greener@dailystar.co.uk
Editor: Dawn Neesom. **Picture Editor:** Rob Greener.

THE DAILY TELEGRAPH
Telegraph Media Group, Victoria Plaza, 111 Buckingham Palace Road, London SW1W 0SR.
Tel: 020 7931 2000. Picture desk: 020 7931 2660.
E-mail: photo@telegraph.co.uk
Editor: Will Lewis. **Picture Editor:** Stuart Nicol.
TELEGRAPH MAGAZINE
Editor: Michele Lavery. **Picture Editor:** Cheryl Newman.

As a member of the Bureau of Freelance Photographers, you'll be kept up-to-date with markets through the BFP Market Newsletter, published monthly. For details of membership, turn to page 9

FINANCIAL TIMES
The Financial Times Ltd, Number One Southwark Bridge, London SE1 9HL.
Tel: 020 7873 3000. Picture desk: 020 7873 3151. Fax: 020 7873 3073. ISDN: 020 7378 6642.
E-mail: jamie.han@ft.com
Editor: Lionel Barber. **Picture Editor:** Jamie Han.

THE GUARDIAN
119 Farringdon Road, London EC1R 3ER.
Tel: 020 7278 2332. Picture desk: 020 7713 4070. Fax: 020 7239 9951.
E-mail: pictures@guardian.co.uk
Editor: Alan Rusbridger. **Picture Editor:** Roger Tooth.
WEEKEND GUARDIAN
Editor: Merope Mills. **Picture Editor:** Kate Edwards.

THE HERALD
200 Renfield Street, Glasgow G2 3QB.
Tel: 0141 302 7000. Picture desk: 0141 302 6668. Fax: 0141 333 1147. ISDN: 0141 302 2101.
E-mail: pictures@theherald.co.uk
Editor: Charles McGhee. **Picture Editor:** Douglas Salteri.

THE INDEPENDENT
Independent News & Media Plc, Independent House, 191 Marsh Wall, London E14 9RS.
Tel: 020 7005 2000. Picture desk: 020 7005 2830. Fax: 020 7005 2086.
E-mail: picturedesk@independent.co.uk
Editor: Simon Kelner. **Picture Editor:** Lynn Cullen.
THE INDEPENDENT MAGAZINE
Picture Editor: Nick Hall.

THE SCOTSMAN
The Scotsman Publications Ltd, 108 Hollyrood Road, Edinburgh EH8 8AS.
Tel: 0131 620 8620. Picture desk: 0131 620 8555. Fax: 0131 620 8615.
E-mail: tspics@scotsman.com
Editor: Mike Gilson. **Picture Editor:** Andy O'Brien.

THE SUN
News Group Newspapers Ltd, 1 Virginia Street, London E98 1SN.
Tel: 020 7782 4000. Picture desk: 020 7782 4110/4116. Fax: 020 7782 4335.
E-mail: pictures@thesun.co.uk
Editor: Rebekah Wade. **Picture Editor:** John Edwards.

THE TIMES
News International Newspapers Ltd, 1 Pennington Street, London E98 1TT.
Tel: 020 7782 5000. Picture desk: 020 7782 5877. Fax: 020 7782 5449.
E-mail: pictures@thetimes.co.uk
Editor: Robert Thomson. **Picture Editor:** Paul Sanders.
THE TIMES MAGAZINE
Editor: Gill Morgan. **Picture Editor:** Graham Wood.

National Sunday Newspapers

THE INDEPENDENT ON SUNDAY
Independent News & Media Plc, Independent House, 191 Marsh Wall, London E14 9RS.
Tel: 020 7005 2000. Picture desk: 020 7005 2837/2828. Fax: 020 7005 2086.
E-mail: picturedesk@independent.co.uk
Editor: Tristan Davies. **Picture Editor:** Sophie Batterbury.
THE SUNDAY REVIEW
Editor: Bill Tuckey. **Picture Editor:** Hannah Brenchley.

THE MAIL ON SUNDAY
Northcliffe House, 2 Derry Street, Kensington, London W8 5TS.
Tel: 020 7938 6000. Picture desk: 020 7938 7017. Fax: 020 7938 6609.
E-mail: pix@mailonsunday.co.uk
Editor: Peter Wright. **Picture Editor:** Liz Cocks.
YOU MAGAZINE
Editor: Sue Peart. **Picture Editor:** Eve George.
NIGHT & DAY
Editor: Gerard Greaves. **Picture Editor:** Sam Reilly.

NEWS OF THE WORLD
News International Newspapers Ltd, Virginia Street, London E1 9XR.
Tel: 020 7782 4000. Picture desk: 020 7782 4421. Fax: 020 7782 4463.
ISDN: 020 7680 1010/7702 9140. E-mail: nowpicture@newsint.co.uk
Editor: Colin Myler. **Picture Editor:** Paul Ashton.
SUNDAY MAGAZINE
Editor: Mandy Appleyard. **Picture Editor:** David Jester.

THE OBSERVER
The Observer Ltd, 3-7 Herbal Hill, London EC1R 5EJ.
Tel: 020 7278 2332. Picture desk: 020 7713 4304. Fax: 020 7278 7209.
ISDN: 020 7713 7496. E-mail: picture.desk@observer.co.uk
Editor: Roger Alton. **Picture Editor:** Greg Whitmore.
THE OBSERVER MAGAZINE
Editor: Allan Jenkins. **Picture Editors:** Anthony Bell, Anna Bassett.
OBSERVER FOOD MONTHLY
Editor: Nicola Jeal. **Picture Editor:** Anna Bassett.
OBSERVER MUSIC MONTHLY
Editor: Caspar Llewellyn Smith. **Picture Editor:** Matthew Gynn
OBSERVER SPORT MONTHLY
Editor: Tim Lewis. **Picture Editors:** Jim Powell, Steve Bloor.
OBSERVER WOMAN
Editor: Nicola Jeal. **Picture Editor:** Kit Burnet.

THE PEOPLE
Mirror Group plc, 1 Canada Square, Canary Wharf, London E14 5AP.
Tel: 020 7293 3000. Picture desk: 020 7293 3901. Fax: 020 7293 3810.
ISDN: 020 7572 5801 (Easy Transfer); 020 7513 2427 (Foresight).
E-mail: pictures@people.co.uk
Editor: Mark Thomas. **Picture Editor:** Paula Derry.
TAKE IT EASY
Editor: Hannah Tavner. **Picture Editor:** Paula Derry.

SCOTLAND ON SUNDAY
Barclay House, 108 Holyrood Road, Edinburgh EH8 8AS.
Tel: 0131 620 8438. Fax: 0131 620 8491. ISDN: 0131 556 5379/1230.
E-mail: sospics@scotsman.com
Editor: Les Snowdon. **Picture Editor:** Alan Macdonald.

SUNDAY EXPRESS
Express Newspapers, 10 Lower Thames Street, London EC3R 6EN.
Tel: 0871 434 1010. Picture desk: 0871 520 7172. Fax: 0871 434 7300.
E-mail: sundayexpresspix@express.co.uk
Editor: Martin Townsend. **Picture Editor:** Terry Evans.
SUNDAY EXPRESS MAGAZINE
Editor: Louise Robinson. **Picture Editor:** Jane Woods.

SUNDAY HERALD
200 Renfield Street, Glasgow G2 3QB.
Tel: 0141 302 7000. Picture desk: 0141 302 7876. Fax: 0141 302 7815. ISDN: 0141 302 2103.
E-mail: sunday.pictures@sundayherald.com
Editor: Richard Walker. **Picture Editor:** Elaine Livingstone.
SUNDAY HERALD MAGAZINE
Editor: Jane Wright. **Picture Editor:** Leanne Thompson.

THE SUNDAY MAIL
The Scottish Daily Record and Sunday Mail Ltd, 1 Central Quay, Glasgow G3 8DA.
Tel: 0141 309 7000. Picture desk: 0141 309 3434. Fax: 0141 309 3587.
ISDN: 0141 309 4884/4886. E-mail: a.hosie@sundaymail.co.uk
Editor: Allan Rennie. **Picture Editor:** Andy Hosie.

SUNDAY MIRROR
Mirror Group plc, 1 Canada Square, Canary Wharf, London E14 5AP.
Tel: 020 7293 3000. Picture desk: 020 7293 3335/6. Fax: 020 7510 6991.
E-mail: pictures@sundaymirror.co.uk
Editor: Tina Weaver. **Picture Editor:** Mike Sharp.
CELEBS ON SUNDAY
Editor: Mel Brodie. **Picture Editor:** Jo Aspill.

THE SUNDAY POST
D. C. Thomson & Co Ltd, Courier Place, Dundee DD1 9QJ.
Tel: 01382 223131. Fax: 01382 201064. ISDN: 01382 575935.
E-mail: mail@sundaypost.com
Editor: David Pollington. **News Editor:** Tom McKay. **Picture Editor:** Alan Morrison.
POST PLUS MAGAZINE
Editor: Jan Gooderham.

SUNDAY SPORT
Sport Newspapers Ltd, 19 Great Ancoats Street, Manchester M60 4BT.
Tel: 0161 236 4466. Picture desk: 0161 238 8169. Fax: 0161 236 4535.
E-mail: paul.currie@sportnewspapers.co.uk
Editor: Paul Carter. **Picture Editor:** Paul Currie.

THE SUNDAY TELEGRAPH

Telegraph Media Group, Victoria Plaza, 111 Buckingham Palace Road, London SW1W 0SR.
Tel: 020 7538 5000. Picture desk: 020 7538 7369. Fax: 020 7538 7918.
E-mail: stpics@telegraph.co.uk
Editor: Patience Wheatcroft. **Picture Editor:** Bet Lynch.
STELLA
Editor: Anna Murphy.

THE SUNDAY TIMES

Times Newspapers Ltd, 1 Pennington Street, London E98 1ST.
Tel: 020 7782 5000. Picture desk: 020 7782 5666. Fax: 020 7782 5563.
E-mail: pictures@sunday-times.co.uk
Editor: John Witherow. **Picture Editor:** Ray Wells.
THE SUNDAY TIMES MAGAZINE
Editor: Robin Morgan. **Picture Editor:** TBA.

BOOKS

Books represent a substantial and ever-growing market for the photographer. In an increasingly visual age the market for heavily illustrated books continues to expand, with hundreds of new titles being published every year.

In this section we list major book publishers, and specifically those companies that make considerable use of photographic material.

As well as regular publishers, also included here are book packagers. These are companies that offer a complete editorial production service and specialise in producing books that can be sold as finished packages to publishers internationally. The majority of their products are of the heavily illustrated type, and thus these companies can often present a greater potential market for photographic material than do the mainstream publishers.

Making an approach

In this field the difficulty for the individual freelance is that there is no easy way of knowing who wants what and when.

Obviously book publishers only require pictures of specific subjects when they are currently working on a project requiring such material. Much of the time they will rely heavily on known sources such as picture libraries, but this does not mean that there is not good scope for the individual photographer who has a good collection of material on particular subjects, or who may be able to produce suitable work to order.

The solution for the photographer, therefore, is to place details of what he or she has to offer in front of all those companies that might conceivably require material of that type.

The initial approach is simply to send an introductory letter outlining the sort of material that you can supply. A detailed list of subjects can be attached where appropriate.

There is little point however, in sending any photographs at this stage, unless it be one or two samples to indicate a particular style. And one should not expect an immediate response requesting that work be submitted; most likely the publisher will simply keep your details on file for future reference.

Preceding the listings of book publishers is a subject index that should assist in identifying the most promising markets for those areas in which you have good coverage.

In the listings that follow, the major areas of activity for each publisher are detailed under "Subjects". Of course, the larger companies publish on the widest range of subjects and therefore their coverage may be stated as "general", but in most entries you will find a list of specific subject areas. These are by no means a complete list of all the subjects handled by each publisher, but indicate those areas where the company is most active and therefore most likely to be in need of photographic material.

In some entries a "Contact" name is given. However, in a lot of cases it is not possible to give a specific name as larger book publishers usually have large numbers of editorial personnel with constantly shifting responsibilities for individual projects. In addition, many companies frequently use the services of freelance picture researchers. A general approach should therefore simply be addressed to the editorial director.

Rights and fees

Whereas the rights sold in the magazine world are invariably for UK use only, book publishers – and especially packagers – make a good deal of their profit from selling their products to other publishers in overseas markets.

It is therefore quite likely that when work is chosen for use in a particular book the publisher may at some stage request, in addition to British publishing rights, rights for other areas such as "Commonwealth", "North American", "French language", etc. These differing rights will, of course, affect the fees that the photographer receives – the more areas the book sells into, the higher the fees.

Other major factors affecting fees are the size of reproduction on the page and the quantity of the print-run.

Thus there is no easy way to generalise about the sort of fees paid in this field. On the whole, however, fees in book publishing are quite good and comparable with good magazine rates. For packages destined for the international co-edition market they can be substantially higher.

A word about names and imprints

The use by large publishers of a multiplicity of names for different divisions can be quite confusing.

Many famous publishing names, though still in existence, now belong to huge publishing conglomerates. A few are still run as separate companies, but most have effectively become "imprints".

These imprints are used by large publishers for specific sections of their list. In the past many imprints were run as completely separate operations, but in an age of consolidation most have now been incorporated into their parent company. Only relevant imprints are listed here, those that use photography to any extent.

Subject Index

Ryland, Peters & Small
Sheldrake Press
Simon & Schuster
Souvenir Press Ltd

Gardening

Anness Publishing
Antique Collectors' Club Ltd
Breslich & Foss
Kyle Cathie Ltd
Chrysalis Books Group
The Crowood Press
Focus Publishing
W. Foulsham & Co Ltd
Guild of Master Craftsman Publications Ltd
Hodder Headline Ltd
Frances Lincoln Ltd
New Holland Publishers
Octopus Publishing Group Ltd
Orion Publishing Group Ltd
Pan Macmillan
Quarto Publishing plc
Reader's Digest Association Ltd
Ryland, Peters & Small
Souvenir Press Ltd

Health/Medical

Breslich & Foss
Cambridge University Press
Carroll & Brown Publishers
Kyle Cathie Ltd
Chrysalis Books Group
Constable & Robinson
Ebury Publishing
Focus Publishing
W. Foulsham & Co Ltd
Grub Street
Piatkus Books
Quarto Publishing plc
Simon & Schuster
Souvenir Press Ltd
Transworld Publishers

Interior Design

Chrysalis Books Group
Ebury Publishing
Frances Lincoln Ltd
New Holland Publishers
Octopus Publishing Group Ltd
Orion Publishing Group Ltd

Ryland, Peters & Small
Thames & Hudson

Military

Ian Allan Publishing
Amber Books Ltd
Cassell Military
Chrysalis Books Group
Constable & Robinson
The Crowood Press
Robert Hale Ltd
Osprey Publishing
Transworld Publishers
Tempus Publishing Ltd
Sutton Publishing Ltd
Weidenfeld & Nicolson Ltd

Motoring

Ian Allan Publishing
The Crowood Press
Haynes Publishing
Sutton Publishing Ltd

Music

Cambridge University Press
Ebury Publishing
Faber & Faber Ltd
Guinness Publishing Ltd
Robert Hale Ltd
Hodder Headline Ltd
Omnibus Press/Book Sales Ltd
Pan Macmillan
Plexus Publishing Ltd
Thames & Hudson
Virgin Books Ltd

Natural History

Appletree Press
A & C Black (Publishers) Ltd
Cambridge University Press
The Crowood Press
Robert Hale Ltd
Christopher Helm Publishers Ltd
Kingfisher Publications
New Holland Publishers
Orion Publishing Group Ltd
T & A D Poyser
Reader's Digest Association Ltd
Souvenir Press Ltd
Usborne Publishing

Photography

Breedon Books
Chrysalis Books Group
David & Charles Publishing Ltd
Phaidon Press Ltd
Photographer's Institute Press
RotoVision
Thames & Hudson Ltd

Politics/Current Affairs

Bloomsbury Publishing Ltd
Jonathan Cape Ltd
Century
Chatto & Windus
Constable & Robinson
Faber & Faber Ltd
Fourth Estate Ltd
Hutchinson
Pan Macmillan
Yale University Press

Railways

Ian Allan Publishing
Railways – Milepost 92½
Sutton Publishing Ltd
Tempus Publishing Ltd

Science

Amber Books Ltd
Cambridge University Press
Fourth Estate Ltd
Lutterworth Press
Orion Publishing Group Ltd
Transworld Publishers

Sport

A & C Black (Publishers) Ltd
Breedon Books
Jonathan Cape Ltd
The Crowood Press
Ebury Publishing
Focus Publishing
W. Foulsham & Co Ltd
Guinness Publishing Ltd
Robert Hale Ltd
Hodder Headline Ltd
Octopus Publishing Group Ltd
Orion Publishing Group Ltd
Transworld Publishers
Virgin Books Ltd

Travel

AA Publishing
Amber Books Ltd
Appletree Press
Bloomsbury Publishing Ltd
Cambridge University Press
Chatto & Windus
Chrysalis Books Group
Constable & Robinson
The Crowood Press
Ebury Publishing
W. Foulsham & Co Ltd
Robert Hale Ltd
Hutchinson
New Holland Publishers
Octopus Publishing Group Ltd
Orion Publishing Group Ltd
Pan Macmillan
Quarto Publishing plc
Sheldrake Press
Thames & Hudson Ltd

Book Publishers

AA PUBLISHING
Automobile Association, Fanum House, Basingstoke, Hampshire RG21 2EA.
Tel: 01256 491588. Fax: 01256 492440. E-mail: travelimages@theaa.com
Contact: Liz Allen, Head of Picture Library.
Subjects: Travel images for guide books, maps and atlases. Commissions only.

ALBION PRESS LTD
Spring Hill, Idbury, Chipping Norton, Oxfordshire OX7 6RU.
Tel: 01993 831094.
Subjects: Children's, cookery, fine arts, social history.

IAN ALLAN PUBLISHING
Riverdene Business Park, Molesey Road, Hersham, Surrey KT12 4RG.
Tel: 01932 266600. Fax: 01932 266601.
Web: www.ianallanpublishing.com
Subjects: Aviation, military, motoring, railways, road transport.

AMBER BOOKS LTD
Bradley's Close, 74-77 White Lion Street, London N1 9PF.
Tel: 020 7520 7600. Fax: 020 7520 7606. E-mail: terry@amberbooks.co.uk
Web: www.amberbooks.co.uk
Contact: Terry Forshaw.
Subjects: General; aviation, fitness and survival, military, naval, popular science, transport.

ANNESS PUBLISHING LTD
Hermes House 88-89 Blackfriars Road, London SE1 8HA.
Tel: 020 7401 2077. Fax: 020 7633 9499.
Web: www.lorenzbooks.com
Contact: Picture Library Manager.
Imprints: Aquamarine, Hermes House, Lorenz Books, Southwater.
Subjects: Crafts, cookery, gardening, health, reference.

ANOVA BOOKS
10 Southcombe Street, London W14 0RA.
Tel: 020 7605 1400. Fax: 020 7605 1401.
Web: www.anovabooks.com
Imprints: Batsford, Collins & Brown, Conway Maritime Press, Pavilion, Robson.
Subjects: General illustrated; architecture, arts & crafts, aviation, biography, cookery, gardening, health, military, photography, transport.

ANTIQUE COLLECTORS CLUB LTD
Sandy Lane, Old Martlesham, Woodbridge, Suffolk IP12 4SD.
Tel: 01394 389950. Fax: 01394 389999.
Web: www.antique-acc.com
Contact: Diana Steel, Managing Director (by letter only).
Subjects: Antiques, architecture, art, gardening. (Digital not accepted).

Are you working from the latest edition of The Freelance Photographer's Market Handbook? It's published on 1 October each year. Markets are constantly changing, so it pays to have the latest edition

---

APPLETREE PRESS LTD
14 Howard Street South, Belfast BT7 1AP.
Tel: 028 90 243074. Fax: 028 90 246756. E-mail: reception@appletree.ie
Web: www.appletree.ie
Contact: Jean Brown, Desk & Marketing Editor.
Subjects: Irish and Scottish interest; arts & crafts, cookery, nature, UK travel.

A & C BLACK (PUBLISHERS) LTD
38 Soho Square, London W1D 3HB.
Tel: 020 7758 0200. Fax: 020 7758 0222. E-mail: enquiries@acblack.co.uk
Web: www.acblack.com
Imprints: Adlard Coles Nautical, Christopher Helm, Herbert Press, T&AD Poyser.
Subjects: Arts and crafts, children's educational, nautical, ornithology, reference, sport, theatre, ceramics.

BLOOMSBURY PUBLISHING PLC
36 Soho Square, London W1D 3QY.
Tel: 020 7494 2111. Fax: 020 7434 0151.
Web: www.bloomsbury.com
Subjects: General; biography, children's, current affairs, reference, travel.

BREEDON BOOKS PUBLISHING CO LTD
3 The Parker Centre, Mansfield Road, Derby DE21 4SZ.
Tel: 01332 384235. Fax: 01332 292755. E-mail: steve.caron@breedonpublishing.co.uk
Web: www.breedonpublishing.co.uk
Contact: Steve Caron, Managing Director.
Subjects: Archive photography, British heritage and local history, sport (especially football).

BRESLICH & FOSS LTD
2a Union Court, 20-22 Union Road, London, SW4 6JP
Tel: 020 7819 3990. Fax: 020 7819 3998. E-mail: editorial@breslichfoss.com
Contact: Janet Ravenscroft.
Subjects: Arts, children's, crafts, gardening, health, lifestyle.

CAMBRIDGE UNIVERSITY PRESS
The Edinburgh Building, Shaftesbury Road, Cambridge CB2 2RU.
Tel: 01223 312393. Fax: 01223 315052. E-mail: information@cambridge.org
Web: www.www.cambridge.org
Subjects: Archaeology, architecture, art, astronomy, biology, drama, geography, history, medicine, music, natural history, religion, science, sociology, travel.

JONATHAN CAPE LTD
Random House, 20 Vauxhall Bridge Road, London SW1V 2SA.
Tel: 020 7840 8595. Fax: 020 7233 6125.
Web: www.randomhouse.co.uk
Imprint: Yellow Jersey Press (sport).
Contact: Suzanne Dean, Art Director.
Subjects: Biography and memoirs, current affairs, history, sport, travel.

CARROLL & BROWN PUBLISHERS LTD
20 Lonsdale Road, London NW6 6RD.
Tel: 020 7372 0900. Fax: 020 7372 0460. E-mail: mail@carrollandbrown.co.uk
Web: www.carrollandbrown.co.uk
Contact: Chrissie Lloyd, Art Director.
Subjects: General illustrated reference, health, parenting.

KYLE CATHIE LTD
122 Arlington Road, London NW1 7HP.
Tel: 020 7692 7215. Fax: 020 7692 7260. E-mail: vicki.murrell@kyle-cathie.com
Web: www.kylecathie.com
Contact: Vicki Murrell, Editorial Assistant.
Subjects: Beauty, food and drink, gardening, health, reference.

CENTURY
Random House, 20 Vauxhall Bridge Road, London SW1V 2SA.
Tel: 020 7840 8557. Fax: 020 7233 6127.
Web: www.randomhouse.co.uk
Subjects: Biography, current affairs, food and drink.

CHATTO & WINDUS LTD
Random House, 20 Vauxhall Bridge Road, London SW1V 2SA.
Tel: 020 7840 8400. Fax: 020 7233 6117.
Web: www.randomhouse.co.uk
Subjects: General; biography and memoirs, current affairs, history, travel.

THE CROWOOD PRESS LTD
The Stable Block, Crowood Lane, Ramsbury, Marlborough, Wiltshire SN8 2HR.
Tel: 01672 520320. Fax: 01672 520280. E-mail: enquiries@crowood.com
Web: www.crowoodpress.co.uk
Subjects: Angling, aviation, climbing, country interests, crafts, DIY, equestrian, gardening, motoring, military, natural history, sport, travel.

DAVID & CHARLES PUBLISHING LTD
Brunel House, Newton Abbot, Devon TQ12 4PU.
Tel: 01626 323200. Fax: 01626 323317.
Web: www.davidandcharles.co.uk
Contact: Prudence Rogers.
Subjects: Arts and crafts, equestrian, practical art and photography.

EBURY PUBLISHING
Random House, 20 Vauxhall Bridge Road, London SW1V 2SA.
Tel: 020 7840 8400. Fax: 020 7840 8406.
Web: www.eburypublishing.co.uk
Imprints: BBC Books, Ebury Press, Rider, Time Out Guides,Vermilion.
Contact: Rachael Rayner, Editorial Assistant.
Subjects: Biography, cookery, crafts, current affairs, decorating and interiors, health and beauty, history, mind, bidy spirit, music, parenting, sport, travel guides.

FABER & FABER LTD
3 Queen Square, London WC1N 3AU.
Tel: 020 7465 0045. Fax: 020 7465 0034.
Web: www.faber.co.uk
Contact: Design Department.
Subjects: Biography, film, music, politics, theatre, wine.

FOCUS PUBLISHING (SEVENOAKS) LTD
11A St Botolph's Road, Sevenoaks, Kent TN13 2EB.
Tel: 01732 742456. Fax: 01732 743381. E-mail: caroline@focus-publishing.co.uk
Web: www.focus-publishing.co.uk
Contact: Caroline Watson, Publishing Manager.
Subjects: General illustrated; crafts, DIY, food and drink, gardening, health, photography, sport, transport.

W. FOULSHAM & CO
The Publishing House, Bennetts Close, Cippenham, Slough, Berkshire SL1 5AP.
Tel: 01753 526769. Fax: 01753 535003.
Web: www.foulsham.com
Contact: Barry Belasco, Managing Director.
Subjects: Crafts, collecting, cookery, DIY, gardening, health, hobbies, sport, travel.

GRUB STREET PUBLISHING
4 Rainham Close, London SW11 6SS.
Tel: 020 7924 3966. Fax: 020 7738 1009. E-mail: post@grubstreet.co.uk
Web: www.grubstreet.co.uk
Subjects: Aviation history, cookery.

GUILD OF MASTER CRAFTSMAN PUBLICATIONS LTD
86 High Street, Lewes, East Sussex BN7 1XN.
Tel: 01273 477374. Fax: 01273 402849.
Web: www.thegmcgroup.com
Imprint: Photographers' Institute Press
Contact: Anthony Bailey, Chief Photographer.
Subjects: Crafts; gardening, needlework, photography, woodworking.

GUINNESS WORLD RECORDS LTD
3rd Floor, 184 Drummond Street, London NW1 3HP.
Tel: 020 7891 4567. Fax: 020 7891 4501.
Web: www.guinnessworldrecords.com
Contact: Design Department.
Subjects: Guinness World Records book, TV and merchandising, sport and popular music.

HALDANE MASON
PO Box 34196, London NW10 3YB.
Tel: 020 8459 2131. Fax: 020 8728 1216. E-mail: info@haldanemason.com
Web: www.haldanemason.com
Contact: Ron Samuel, Art Director.
Subjects: Children's illustrated non-fiction.

ROBERT HALE LTD
Clerkenwell House, 45-47 Clerkenwell Green, London EC1R 0HT.
Tel: 020 7251 2661. Fax: 020 7490 4958.
Web: www.halebooks.com
Contact: Susan Hale.
Subjects: General; architecture, cookery, crafts, equestrian, gemmology, horology, mind, body and spirit, military, music, natural history, sport, topography, travel. (Digital not accepted).

HARPERCOLLINS PUBLISHERS
77-85 Fulham Palace Road, London W6 8JB.
Tel: 020 8741 7070. Fax: 020 8307 4440.
Web: www.harpercollins.co.uk
Imprints: Collins, Fourth Estate, HarperElement, HarperPress, HarperSport, HarperThorsons.
Subjects: General.

HARVILL SECKER
Random House, 20 Vauxhall Bridge Road, London SW1V 2SA.
Tel: 020 7840 8570. Fax: 020 7233 6117.
Web: www.randomhouse.co.uk
Contact: Lily Richards.
Subjects: General non-fiction.

HAYNES PUBLISHING
Sparkford, Yeovil, Somerset BA22 7JJ.
Tel: 01963 440635. Fax: 01963 440023.
Web: www.haynes.co.uk
Imprints: G.T.Foulis, Patrick Stephens.
Contact: Christine Smith, Adminstration Manager.
Subjects: Cars, motoring and motor racing, motorcycles, motoring biography, DIY.

CHRISTOPHER HELM PUBLISHERS/T&AD POYSER
(Imprints of A&C Black Publishers)
38 Soho Square, London W1D 3HB.
Tel: 020 7758 0200. Fax: 020 7758 0222. E-mail: nredman@acblack.com
Web: www.acblack.com
Contact: Nigel Redman, Commissioning Editor; Sophie Page, Editor.
Subjects: Ornithology and natural history.

HODDER EDUCATION GROUP
338 Euston Road, London NW1 3BH.
Tel: 020 7873 6000. Fax: 020 7873 6325.
Web: www.hodderheadline.co.uk
Contact: Helen Townson.
Subjects: Education including geography, health, history, science, travel.

HODDER HEADLINE LTD
338 Euston Road, London NW1 3BH.
Tel: 020 7873 6000. Fax: 020 7873 6024.
Web: www.hodderheadline.co.uk
Contact: Picture Manager, c/o division.
Imprints: Hachette Children's Books, Headline, Hodder Education, Hodder & Stoughton.
Subjects: General; academic, biography, children's, food and wine, history, music, sport.

HUTCHINSON
Random House, 20 Vauxhall Bridge Road, London SW1V 2SA.
Tel: 020 7840 8564. Fax: 020 7233 6127.
Web: www.randomhouse.co.uk
Contact: Sue Freestone.
Subjects: Biography, current affairs, history, travel.

LAURENCE KING PUBLISHING LTD
361–373 City Road, London EC1V 1LR.
Tel: 020 7841 6900. Fax: 020 7841 6969. E-mail: julia@laurenceking.co.ok
Web: www.laurenceking.co.ok
Contact: Julia Ruxton, Picture Manager.
Subjects: Arts and architecture, design, fashion. (Digital not accepted).

KINGFISHER PUBLICATIONS
New Penderel House, 283-288 High Holborn, London WC1V 7HZ.
Tel: 020 7903 9836. Fax: 020 7242 4979. E-mail: cwestonbaker@kingfisherpub.com
Web: www.kingfisherpub.com
Contact: Cee Weston-Baker.
Subjects: Children's non-fiction, natural history, reference.

FRANCES LINCOLN LTD
4 Torriano Mews, Torriano Avenue, London NW5 2RZ.
Tel: 020 7284 4009. Fax: 020 7485 0490.
Web: www.franceslincoln.com
Contact: Sue Gladstone, Picture Department.
Subjects: General; architecture, art, gardening, travel.

LITTLE, BROWN BOOK GROUP UK
Brettenham House, Lancaster Place, London WC2E 7EN.
Tel: 020 7911 8000. Fax: 020 7911 8100.
Web: www.littlebrown.co.uk
Subjects: General.

THE LUTTERWORTH PRESS
P O Box 60, Cambridge CB1 2NT.
Tel: 01223 350865. Fax: 01223 366951. E-mail: publishing@lutterworth.com
Web: www.lutterworth.com
Contact: Adrian Brink.
Subjects: Antiques, art and architecture, biography, crafts, natural history, reference, religion, science.

NEW HOLLAND PUBLISHERS (UK) LTD
Garfield House, 86-88 Edgware Road, London W2 2EA.
Tel: 020 7724 7773. Fax: 020 7258 1293. E-mail: postmaster@nhpub.co.uk
Web: www.newhollandpublishers.com
Subjects: Biography, crafts, cookery, gardening, history, interior design, natural history, sports and outdoor pursuits, travel.

As a member of the Bureau of Freelance Photographers, you'll be kept up-to-date with markets through the BFP Market Newsletter, published monthly. For details of membership, turn to page 9

OCTOPUS PUBLISHING GROUP LTD
2-4 Heron Quays, London E14 4JP.
Tel: 020 7531 8400. Fax: 020 7531 8650.
www.octopus-publishing.co.uk
Imprints: Cassell Illustrated, Conran Octopus, Gaia Books, Godsfield Press, Hamlyn, Mitchell Beazley, Philip's.
Subjects: Illustrated general reference and non-fiction.

OMNIBUS PRESS/MUSIC SALES LTD
14-15 Berners Street, London W1T 3LJ.
Tel: 020 7612 7400. Fax: 020 7612 7545.
Contact: Chris Charlesworth, Editor; Sarah Bacon, Picture Researcher.
Subjects: Rock, pop and classical music.

ORION PUBLISHING GROUP LTD
Orion House, 5 Upper St Martin's Lane, London WC2H 9EA.
Tel: 020 7240 3444. Fax: 020 7240 4822.
Web: www.orionbooks.co.uk
Contact: Design Department.
Subjects: General; biography, cookery, design, gardening, history, interiors, natural history, popular science, sport, travel.

OSPREY PUBLISHING LTD
Midland House, West Way, Botley, Oxford OX2 0HP.
Tel: 01865 727022. Fax: 01865 727017. E-mail: editorial@ospreypublishing.com
Web: www.ospreypublishing.com
Subjects: Illustrated military history and aviation.

OXFORD UNIVERSITY PRESS
Great Clarendon Street, Oxford OX2 6DP.
Tel: 01865 556767. Fax: 01865 556646.
Web: www.oup.co.uk
Imprints: Clarendon Press, Oxford Paperbacks.
Subjects: General; academic, educational, reference.

PAN MACMILLAN
20 New Wharf Road, London N1 9RR.
Tel: 020 7014 6000. Fax: 020 7014 6001.
Web: www.panmacmillan.com
Imprints: Boxtree, Macmillan, Pan, Picador, Sidgwick & Jackson.
Contact: Bruno Vincent, Editorial Assistant.
Subjects: General; biography, crafts, current affairs, gardening, music, popular history, practical, travel.

PENGUIN GROUP (UK)
80 Strand, London WC2R 0RL.
Tel: 020 7010 3000. Fax: 020 7010 3294. E-mail: kate.brunt@penguin.co.uk
Web: www.penguin.co.uk
Imprints: Allen Lane, Hamish Hamilton, Michael Joseph, Penguin, Viking.
Contacts: Kate Brunt, Samantha Johnson (Picture Editors).
Subjects: General.

PHAIDON PRESS LTD
Regent's Wharf, All Saints Street, London N1 9PA.
Tel: 020 7843 1000. Fax: 020 7843 1010.
Web: www.phaidon.com
Subjects: Architecture, decorative and fine arts, design, photography.

PHOTOGRAPHERS' INSTITUTE PRESS
(Imprint of GMC Publications)
166 High Street, Lewes, East Sussex BN7 1XN.
Tel: 01273 477374. Fax: 01273 402849. E-mail: jamesb@thegmcgroup.com
Web: www.pipress.co.uk
Contact: James Beattie, Books Editor.
Subjects: Photography.

PIATKUS BOOKS LTD
5 Windmill Street, London W1T 2JA.
Tel: 020 7631 0710. Fax: 020 7436 7137. E-mail: info@piatkus.co.uk
Web: www.piatkus.co.uk
Contact: Alice Davis, Managing Editor.
Subjects: Biography, health, leisure, lifestyle, mind body & spirit, popular culture, women's interests.

PLAYNE BOOKS LTD
Park Court Barn, Trefin, Haverfordwest, Pembrokeshire SA62 5AU.
Tel: 01348 837073. Fax: 01348 837063. E-mail: playne.books@virgin.net
Contact: Gill Davies, Editorial Director.
Subjects: General illustrated books for adults and children.

PLEXUS PUBLISHING LTD
25 Mallinson Road, London SW11 1BW.
Tel: 020 7924 4662. Fax: 020 7924 5096. E-mail: info@plexusuk.demon.co.uk
Web: www.plexusbooks.com
Contact: Julia Shone, Editorial Assistant.
Subjects: Biography, fashion, film, music, popular culture.

QUARTO PUBLISHING PLC
The Old Brewery, 6 Blundell Street, London N7 9BH.
Tel: 020 7700 6700. Fax: 020 7700 4191.
Web: www.quarto.com
Contact: Caroline Guest, Assistant Art Director.
Subjects: General; arts and crafts, cookery, gardening, health, home interest, new age, reference, travel.

RAILWAYS - MILEPOST 92½
Newton Harcourt, Leicestershire LE8 9FH.
Tel: 0116 259 2068. Fax: 0116 259 3001. E-mail: studio@railphotolibrary.com
Contacts: Colin Garratt, Director; Colin Nash, Picture Library Manager.
Subjects: Railways worldwide – past and present.

RANDOM HOUSE UK LTD
Random House, 20 Vauxhall Bridge Road, London SW1V 2SA.
Tel: 020 7840 8400. Fax: 020 7233 8791.
Web: www.randomhouse.co.uk
Contact: Design Department.
Illustrated imprints: Jonathan Cape, Century, Chatto & Windus, William Heinemann, Hutchinson, Secker & Warburg.
Subjects: Various; see individual imprints.

READER'S DIGEST ASSOCIATION
11 Westferry Circus, Canary Wharf, London E14 1HE.
Tel: 020 7715 8000. Fax: 020 7715 8181.
Web: www.readersdigest.co.uk
Subjects: General illustrated; cookery, crafts, DIY, encyclopaedias, folklore, gardening, guide books, history, natural history.

ROTOVISION
Sheridan House, 114 Western Road, Hove BN3 1DD.
Tel: 01273 727268. Fax: 01273 727269. E-mail: lizf@rotovision.com
Web: www.rotovision.com
Contact: Liz Farrelly, Commissioning Editor.
Subjects: Design, photography.

ROUTLEDGE
2 Park Square, Milton Park, Abingdon, Oxon OX14 4RN.
Tel: 020 7017 6000. Fax: 020 7017 6699.
Web: www.routledge.com
Contact: Design Department.
Subjects: Academic, professional and reference.

RYLAND PETERS & SMALL LTD
20-21 Jockey's Fields, London WC1R 4BW.
Tel: 020 7025 2200. Fax: 020 7025 2201. E-mail: leslie.harrington@rps.co.uk
Web: www.rylandpeters.com
Contact: Leslie Harrington, Art Director.
Subjects: Body and soul, food and drink, gift, home and garden.

SHELDRAKE PRESS LTD
188 Cavendish Road, London SW12 0DA.
Tel: 020 8675 1767. Fax: 020 8675 7736. E-mail: enquiries@sheldrakepress.co.uk
Web: www.sheldrakepress.co.uk
Contact: Simon Rigge, Publisher.
Subjects: Cookery, history, travel.

SIMON & SCHUSTER
Africa House, 64-78 Kingsway, London WC2B 6AH.
Tel: 020 7316 1900. Fax: 020 7316 0332. E-mail: Editorial.enquiries@simonandschuster.co.uk
Web: www.simonsays.com
Imprints: Martin Books, Pocket Books.
Subjects: Biography, cookery, health, history, self-help.

SOUVENIR PRESS LTD
43 Great Russell Street, London WC1B 3PD.
Tel: 020 7580 9307. Fax: 020 7580 5064. E-mail: souvenirpress@ukonline.co.uk
Subjects: General; archaelogy, art, animals, childcare, cookery, gardening, health, hobbies, plants, practical, sociology. (Digital not accepted).

SUTTON PUBLISHING LTD
MPI Media, Cirencester Road, Chalford, Stroud, Gloucestershire GL6 8PE.
Tel: 01285 760000. Fax: 01285 760001.
Web: www.suttonpublishing.co.uk
Subjects: Archaeology, aviation, biography, canals, general history, military and naval history, railway history, sport history.

TEMPUS PUBLISHING
The Mill, Brimscombe Port, Stroud, Gloucestershire GL5 2QG.
Tel: 01453 883300. Fax: 01453 883233. E-mail: info@tempus-publishing.com
Web: www.tempus-publishing.com
Imprints: Nonsuch, Spellmount, Stadia.
Subjects: History, including local, military, sport, transport history.

THAMES & HUDSON LTD
181a High Holborn, London WC1V 7QX.
Tel: 020 7845 5000. Fax: 020 7845 5050. E-mail: s.ruston@thameshudson.co.uk
Web: www.thamesandhudson.com
Contact: Sam Ruston, Head of Picture Research.
Subjects: Art, architecture, archaeology, anthropology, cinema, fashion, interior design, music, photography, practical guides, religion and mythology, theatre, travel.

TOUCAN BOOKS LTD
3rd Floor, 89 Charterhouse Street, London EC1M 6HR.
Tel: 020 7250 3388. Fax: 020 7250 3123. E-mail: info@toucanbooks.co.uk
Web: www.toucanbooks.co.uk
Contact: Christine Vincent, Picture Manager
Subjects: General illustrated.

TRANSWORLD PUBLISHERS
61-63 Uxbridge Road, London W5 5SA.
Tel: 020 8579 2652. Fax: 020 8579 5479. E-mail: info@transworld-publishers.co.uk
Web: www.transworld-publishers.co.uk
Imprints: Bantam, Doubleday, Expert.
Subjects: General non-fiction; biography, food & drink, health, military, music, popular science, social history, sport, travel.

USBORNE PUBLISHING
83-85 Saffron Hill, London EC1N 8RT.
Tel: 020 7430 2800. Fax: 020 7242 0974. E-mail: mail@usborne.co.uk
Web: www.usborne.com
Contacts: Steve Wright; Mary Cartwright.
Subjects: General children's; crafts, natural history, practical, reference.

VIRGIN BOOKS LTD
Thames Wharf Studios, Rainville Road, London W6 9HA.
Tel: 020 7386 3300. Fax: 020 7386 3360.
Web: www.virginbooks.com
Contacts: Lucy Stevens (design department), Carolyn Thorne (arts, music, lifestyle).
Subjects: General; arts, current affairs, health, lifestyle, music, sport.

WEIDENFELD & NICOLSON LTD
Orion House, 5 Upper St Martin's Lane, London WC2H 9EA.
Tel: 020 7240 3444. Fax: 020 7240 4822.
Web: www.orionbooks.co.uk
Imprints: Cassell Military, Weidenfeld.
Subjects: Biography, history, military.

YALE UNIVERSITY PRESS
47 Bedford Square, London WC1B 3DP.
Tel: 020 7079 4900. Fax: 020 7079 4901. E-mail: emma.wraith@yaleup.co.uk
Web: www.yaleup.co.uk
Contact: Emma Wraith, Picture Manager.
Subjects: Architecture, art, history, politics, sociology.

CARDS, CALENDARS, POSTERS & PRINTS

This section lists publishers of postcards, greetings cards, calendars, posters and prints, along with their requirements. There is some overlap here, with many of the companies listed producing a range of products that fall into more than one of these categories,

With the exception of traditional viewcard producers, who have always offered rather meagre rates for freelance material, fees in this area are generally good. However, only those who can produce precisely what is required as far as subject matter, quality and format are concerned, are likely to succeed.

Market requirements

While digital is generally accepted here, a number of companies continue to express a preference for transparencies – particularly large format such as 6x7cm or 6x9cm.

But whether it's digital or film, the need for material of the highest quality cannot be too strongly emphasised. The market is highly specialised with very specific requirements. If you aim to break into this field, you must be very sure of your photographic technique. You must be able to produce professional quality material that is pin sharp and perfectly exposed with excellent colour saturation.

You must also know and be able to supply *exactly* what the market requires. The listings will help you, but you should also carry out your own field study by examining the photographic products on general sale.

After a period in the doldrums the photographic greetings card has been making something of a comeback in recent years. Neverthless, the big mass-market card publishers still employ mostly art or graphics. Those that do use photography tend to be smaller, specialised companies, many of them publishing a full range of photographic products. These companies also use a lot of work from top photographers or picture libraries, which means that there is greater competition than ever to supply material for these products.

The calendar market is equally demanding, though fortunately there are still large numbers of calendars using photographs being produced every year. Many calendar producers obtain the material they need from picture agencies, but this is not to say that individual photographers cannot successfully break into this field. Once again, though, you must be sure of your photographic technique and be able to produce really top quality work.

Make a point of studying the cards, calendars or posters that you see on general sale or hanging up in places you visit. Don't rely solely on what *you* think would make a good card or calendar picture; familiarise yourself with the type of pictures actually being used by these publishers.

Finally, it is worth noting that whilst many firms will consider submissions at any time, some in the calendar or greetings card market only select material at certain times of the year or when they are renewing their range. So when contemplating an approach to one of these firms, always check first to see if they are accepting submissions at the time.

Rights and fees

Where provided by the company concerned, fee guidelines are quoted. Some companies prefer to negotiate fees individually, depending upon the type of material you offer. If you are new to this field, the best plan is to make your submission (preferably after making an initial enquiry, outlining the material you have available) and let the company concerned make you an offer. Generally speaking, you should not accept less than about £75 for Greetings Card or Calendar Rights.

Remember, you are not selling your copyright for this fee; you are free to submit the same photograph to any *non-competitive* market (for example, a magazine) at a later date. But you should not attempt to sell the picture to another greetings card publisher once you have sold Greetings Card Rights to a competing firm.

ABACUS CARDS LTD
Gazeley Road, Kentford, Newmarket, Suffolk CB8 7RH.
Tel: 01638 552399. Fax: 01638 554082. E-mail: liz.ellis@abacuscards.co.uk
Web: www.abacuscards.co.uk
Contact: Liz Ellis (Art Editor).
Products: Greetings cards.
Will consider top-quality carefully-composed garden scenes, landscapes, winter scenes (British),
pets, action or extreme sports. Limited scope as much is produced in-house or obtained from
libraries.
Formats: Transparencies all formats, or digital files.
Fees: Around £200 for three-year world rights.

CHRIS ANDREWS PUBLICATIONS
15 Curtis Yard, North Hinksey Lane, Oxford OX2 0LX.
Tel: 01865 723404. Fax: 01865 725294. E-mail: chris.andrews1@btclick.com
Web: www.cap-ox.co.uk
Contact: Chris Andrews (Partner).
Products: Calendars, postcards, guidebooks, diaries, address books.
Require atmospheric colour images of recognisable places (towns, villages) throughout central
England, specifically the Cotswolds, Oxfordshire, Cherwell Valley, Thames and Chilterns.
Winterscapes especially welcome. Photographs not required for immediate use may be accepted into
the Oxford Picture Library which is run in parallel.
Formats: Any considered.
Fees: By negotiation.

THOMAS BENNACI
Unit 12, Bessemer Park, 250 Milkwood Road, London SE24 0HG.
Tel: 020 7924 0635. Fax: 020 7924 0636. E-mail: thomasbennaciltd@btconnect.com
Contact: Romano Di Giulio (Manager).
Products: Postcards.
Always interested in new views of London for sale to the tourist market – landmarks, scenes and
buildings that are easily recognisable or interesting to tourists. Images should be bright and lively.
Formats: All considered.
Fees: £50 for postcard rights.

CARD CONNECTION
Park House, Hickleys Court, South Street, Farnham, Surrey GU9 7QQ.
Tel: 01252 892300. Fax: 01252 892339. E-mail: carrie-clatworthy@card-connection.co.uk
Web: www.card-connection.co.uk
Contact: Natalie Turner (Senior Product & Marketing Manager).
Products: Greetings cards, giftwrap, gift bags.
Will consider humorous or cute animal images (domestic or wild), florals, still life, landscapes and
sporting images. Also humorous B&W (or colour for use as B&W) "scenes from daily life".
Formats: Medium format transparencies required for colour products, though very high quality
prints may be considered. Digital also accepted.
Fees: By negotiation, for 2–5 year world greetings card rights.

GB EYE LTD
1 Russell Street, Kelham Island, Sheffield S3 8RW.
Tel: 0114 276 7454. Fax: 0114 272 9599. E-mail: mike@gbeye.com
Web: www.gbeye.com
Contact: Mike Cunsolo (Creative Executive).
Products: Posters, prints and postcards.
Interested in pin-up type images of youth-culture celebrities – contemporary pop stars, young film

and TV actors/actresses, popular young sports stars. Colour or B&W, but must have immediate appeal to the youth market. Also open to new ideas for possible generic subjects – landscapes, animals, humour, etc.
Formats: 35mm transparencies considered but medium format preferred. Digital accepted, 32x45cm at 300dpi.
Fees: Negotiable.

HALLMARK CARDS PLC
Bingley Road, Bradford BD9 6SD.
Tel: 01274 252000. Fax: 01274 252675.
Contact: Mary Crowther (Studio Manager).
Products: Greetings cards, postcards, giftwrap.
Will consider any B&W and colour images suitable for these products.
Formats: All considered.
Fees: Dependent on work and use.

IMAGES & EDITIONS LTD
Bourne Road, Essendine, Nr Stamford, Lincs PE9 4UW.
Tel: 01780 757118. Fax: 01780 754629.
Contact: Charlotte Kemp (Head of Design).
Products: Greetings cards and stationery.
Will consider British landscapes and wildlife, domestic pets (especially cats, dogs, horses), florals.
Formats: Digital files (JPEGS for initial assesssment; then CMYK TIFFs) or transparencies (top quality 35mm acceptable but larger formats preferred).
Fees: By negotiation or on 5 per cent royalty basis, for world rights for greetings cards for three years.

INDIGO ART LTD
Indigo House, Brunswick Place, Liverpool L20 8DT.
Tel: 0151 933 9779. Fax: 0151 922 1524. E-mail: louise@indigoart.co.uk
Web: www.indigoart.co.uk
Contact: Louise Pallister (Design Manager).
Products: Large-scale display prints for use in interior design projects.
Striking colour or B&W images with a modern/contemporary look. Wide variety of styles considered: abstracts, close-ups, experimentation with light, angles or digital manipulation. Also monochrome landscape or lifestyle images. See the Indigo Collection on website for current range of styles.
Formats: Transparencies, prints or high-res scans (50MB preferred).
Fees: On a royalties basis, 10% of wholesale print price.

INFOCADO
Gooch's Court, Stamford, Lincs PE9 2RE.
Tel: 01733 237373. Fax: 01733 237383. E-mail: info@infocado.co.uk
Web: www.infocado.co.uk
Contact: David Pike (Managing Director).
Products: Calendars, greetings cards and prints.
Will consider anything depicting "the true character of Britain". British countryside; architecture and heritage; flowers and gardens; animals both domestic and wild, natural and humorous; transport.
Formats: Any transparency size as long as good quality. Digital also accepted (50MB TIFF). See website for full submission guidelines.
Fees: Subject to negotiation.

INNOVA MILL
Unit 83, Mochdre Industrial Estate, Newtown, Powys SY16 4LE.
Tel: 01686 625100.
Contact: Peter Morrish (Picture Editor).
Products: Desk calendars.
Landscape views required for the "British Highlights" and "Nature's Art", and "Worldwide Panoramas" desk calendars. Pictures of principal British and world countryside, and exotic or spectacular places around the world, always of interest if well-composed and colourful. Preference for scenes without people. Compositions must be suited to fit an elongated landscape shape. Selection mainly during November/December.
Formats: Medium format transparencies; no digital.
Fees: £60 for non-exclusive UK rights.

JUDGES POSTCARDS LTD
176 Bexhill Road, St Leonard's on Sea, East Sussex TN38 8BN.
Tel: 01424 710375. Fax: 01424 438538. E-mail: richard.isaac@judges.co.uk
Web: www.judges.co.uk
Contact: Haley Perez (Product Developer).
Products: Postcards, calendars, greetings cards.
Will consider images of England and Wales, local and regional, appealing to the tourist industry. Must be bright, sunny and vibrant. Landscapes, flowers, animals and any other imagery may be considered.
Formats: Film and digital. Small JPEG files may be sent for viewing purposes. Final digital submission must be to A3 at 300dpi, TIFFs in CMYK (convert RGB before submitting). Prefer unretouched original files.
Fees: Dependent on quality and quantity.

KARDORAMA LTD
PO Box 85, Potters Bar, Herts EN6 5AD.
Tel: 01707 652781.
Contact: Brian Elwood (Managing Director).
Products: Postcards.
Always seeking new views of London – major tourist sights or subjects that tourists would consider typical such as red buses, phone boxes, policemen, taxis, etc. Should be good record shots but with "a hint of romance" and plenty of detail in the main subject. Also, humorous images, any subject or location providing the image needs no explanation, but must be sharp and well exposed under good lighting conditions.
Formats: Digital files preferred (with print copy); 35mm and medium format transparencies also considered.
Fees: Variable, depending on quality of work, subject matter and quantities

KEVIN MAYHEW PUBLISHERS
Buxhall, Stowmarket, Suffolk IP14 3BW.
Tel: 01449 737978. Fax: 01449 737834. E-mail: chriscoe@kevinmayhewltd.com
Contact: Miss Chris Coe (Greetings Card Manager).
Products: Greetings cards.
Images suitable for both religious and secular greetings cards of all kinds – landscapes, seascapes, mountains, water images, florals. Must be strong, bright images with good atmosphere.
Formats: Original transparencies or high-res digital.
Fees: Negotiable, usually around £50–£65 for greetings card rights.

As a member of the Bureau of Freelance Photographers, you'll be kept up-to-date with markets through the BFP Market Newsletter, published monthly. For details of membership, turn to page 9

PINEAPPLE PARK LTD
58 Wilbury Way, Hitchin, Herts SG4 0TP.
Tel: 01462 442021. Fax: 01462 440418. E-mail: sarah@pineapplepark.co.uk
Web: www.pineapplepark.co.uk
Contact: Sarah M Parker (Director).
Products: Greetings cards.
Seek high quality colour images of: 1) Florals – contemporary and traditional needed for female-orientated range of greetings cards. Country kitchen type arrangements including china, country dressers etc also needed. 2) Male subjects, eg collection of wine bottles, sporting items, cars etc for male-orientated greetings cards. 3) Gardens and gardening.
Formats: Transparency only, 35mm upwards. Check website for submission details.
Fees: By negotiation, for worldwide greetings card rights.

PORTFOLIO COLLECTION LTD
105 Golborne Road, London W10 5NL.
Tel: 020 8960 1826. Fax: 020 8960 6570.
Contact: Jayne Diggory (Director).
Products: Greetings cards and posters.
Specialists in creative black and white photography. Strong, contemporary, expressive images – landscapes, cityscapes, people, etc. Also nostalgic images from the '60s and '70s – pop stars, swinging London, flower power, etc.
Formats: Prints from 10x8in up.
Fees: Usually on royalty basis at 12 per cent of distribution price. Flat fees may be negotiated.

NIGEL QUINEY PUBLICATIONS
Cloudesley House, Shire Hill, Saffron Walden, Essex CB11 3FB.
Tel: 01799 520200. Fax: 01799 520100. E-mail: abutterworth@nigelquiney.com
Web: www.nigelquiney.com
Contact: Alison Butterworth (Creative Director).
Products: Greetings cards.
Top quality colour images of animals (domestic and wild) in humorous or interesting situations, and florals – bright, modern, contemporary. Will also consider images suitable for anniversary, new baby, etc.
Formats: 5x4in transparencies and digital files.
Fees: Dependent on product/design, for world rights for five years.

RIVERSIDE CARDS
Jubilee Way, Grange Moor, Wakefield WF4 4TD.
Tel: 01924 840500. Fax: 01924 840600. E-mail: design@riversidecards.com
Web: www.riversidecards.com
Contact: Suzanne Pickles (Design Manager).
Products: Greetings cards.
B&W and colour images of cute domestic animals (kittens, puppies, etc), landscapes, seascapes, countryside scenes, artistic/natural florals, dramatic/atmospheric sunsets and sunrise.
Formats: Any considered including digital files (low-res JPEG for initial submission; high res TIFF required once order confirmed).
Fees: By negotiation.

ROSE OF COLCHESTER LTD
Clough Road, Severalls Industrial Park, Colchester CO4 9QT.
Tel: 01206 844500. Fax: 01206 845872. E-mail: simon@rosecalendars.co.uk
Web: www.rosecalendars.co.uk
Contact: Simon Williams (Publishing Manager).
Products: Calendars for business promotion.

Will consider British and worldwide landscapes and wildlife. Also glamour, classic and supercars, domestic and farm animals, adventure sport. Submit January for annual selection process. **Formats:** Medium and larger formats. Minimum acceptable trasnparency size 6x6cm. XPan considered for landscapes. 35mm acceptable for wildlife. High-end professional scans and digital capture (minimum 8MP camera orgination) also accepted. **Fees:** Negotiable depending on subject matter.

SANTORO GRAPHICS
Rotunda Point, 11 Hartfield Crescent, Wimbledon, London SW19 3RL.
Tel: 020 8781 1100. Fax: 020 8781 1101. E-mail: submissions@santorographics.com
Web: santorographics.com
Contact: Meera Santoro (Projects Director).
Products: Postcards and greetings cards.
Requires striking and attractive images appealing to the typical young poster and card buyer: nostalgic, retro, contemporary, romantic, humorous and cute images of people, animals and situations. B&W a speciality, but colour images in contemporary styles are also sought.
Formats: Any considered, including digital.
Fees: By negotiation for worldwide rights.

AGENCIES

Picture libraries and agencies are in the business of selling pictures. They are not in the business of teaching photography or advising photographers how to produce saleable work – although they can sometimes prove remarkably helpful in the latter respect to those who show promise. Their purpose is strictly a business one: to meet the demand for stock pictures from such markets as magazine and book publishers, advertising agencies, travel operators, greetings card and calendar publishers, and many more.

Many photographers look upon an agency as a last resort; they have been unable to sell their photographs themselves, so they think they might as well try unloading them on an agency. This is the wrong attitude. No agency will succeed in placing pictures which are quite simply unmarketable. In any event, the photographer who has had at least some success in selling pictures is in a far better position to approach an agency.

Agency requirements

If you hope to interest an agency in your work, you must be able to produce pictures which the agency feels are likely to sell to one of their markets. Although the acceptance of your work by an agency is no guarantee that it will sell, an efficient agency certainly will not clutter up its files with pictures which do not stand a reasonably good chance of finding a market.

Agents handle pictures of every subject under the sun. Some specialise in particular subjects – sport, natural history, etc – while others act as general agencies, covering the whole spectrum of subject matter. Any photograph that could be published in one form or another is a suitable picture for an agency.

Even if you eventually decide that you want to place all your potentially saleable material with an agency, you cannot expect to leave every aspect of the business to them. You must continue to study the market, watching for trends; you must continue to study published pictures.

For example, if your speciality is travel material, you should use every opportunity to study the type of pictures published in current travel brochures and other markets using such material. Only by doing this – by being aware of the market – can you hope to continue to provide your agency with marketable pictures.

Nowadays most agencies do a great deal of their business on-line and maintain extensive websites displaying the images they hold. Indeed, many newer agencies are "on-line only" and deal only in digitally-captured or scanned images.

Although agency websites are primarily aimed at potential picture buyers, they are well worth looking at for the photographer considering an approach, since they will give a good indication of the type of subject and style of work the agency handles.

Commission and licensing

Agencies generally work on a commission basis, 50 per cent being the most usual rate – if they receive £100 for reproduction rights in a picture, the photographer gets £50 of this. The more heavily digitised or Web-based agencies have more variable rates, depending on whether photographer or agency is expected to bear the cost of producing high-resolution scans.

The percentage taken may seem high, but it should be remembered that a picture agency, like any other business, has substantial overheads to account for.

There can also be high costs involved in making prospective buyers aware of the pictures that are available. The larger agencies produce lavish colour catalogues featuring selections of their best pictures, while smaller agencies regularly send out flyers. All are involved in constantly maintaining and updating their websites.

Agents do not normally sell pictures outright. As would the individual photographer, they merely sell reproduction rights, the image being licensed to the buyer for a specific purpose. Images may be licensed by size of reproduction, by territory in which they are published, by the medium in which they are reproduced, by time and/or quantity of reproductions, and can be exclusive or non-exclusive. Selling in this way is known as "rights-managed" licensing.

The other form of selling undertaken by some agencies is "royalty-free". Under this method images are sold as part of a collection purchased for a flat fee and pre-licensed for a specified range of uses.

A long-term investment

When dealing with a photographer for the first time, most agencies require a minimum initial submission – which can consist of anything from a few to 500 or more pictures. Most also stipulate that you must keep your material with them for a minimum period of anything from one to five years.

When an agency takes on the work of a new photographer, they are involved in a lot of work – scanning, categorising, filing, key-wording, cross-indexing and more.

The next step will be to make it known to picture buyers that these new pictures are available, perhaps including reproductions of them in any new catalogues or publicity material and getting an initial selection onto the website.

Having been involved in all this work and expense, it is not unreasonable for them to want to be given a fair chance to market the pictures. If the photographer were able to demand the withdrawal of the images after only a few months, the agency will have been involved in a lot of work and expense for nothing.

Dealing with an agency must therefore be considered a long-term investment. Having initially placed, say, a few hundred pictures with an agency, it could be at least several months before any are selected by a picture buyer, and even longer before any monies are seen by the photographer.

Normally, the photographer will also be expected to regularly submit new material to the library. Indeed, only when you have several hundred pictures lodged with the library can you hope for regular sales – and a reasonable return on your investment.

Making an approach

When considering placing work with an agency, the best plan is to make an initial short-list of those that seem most appropriate to your work.

Then contact the agency or agencies of your choice outlining the material you have available. It may also be worth mentioning details of any sales you have made yourself. If an agency is interested they will probably ask that you first post or e-mail some samples to them. Later they may suggest an appointment when you can bring a wider selection material to show them in person.

But remember that there is little point in approaching an agency until you have a sizeable collection of potentially saleable material. Most will not feel it worth their while dealing with a photographer who has only a dozen or so marketable pictures to offer – it just wouldn't be worth all the work and expense involved. And the chance of the photographer seeing a worthwhile return on just a dozen pictures placed with an agency are remote indeed; you'd be lucky to see more than one cheque in ten years!

In the listings that follow you'll find information on more than 100 agencies seeking work from new contributors: the subjects they handle, the markets they supply, the formats they stock, their terms of business (including any minimum submission quantity and minimum retention period), and their standard commission charged on sales.

Prefacing the listings you'll find an Agency Subject Index. This is a guide to agencies which have a special interest in those subjects, though many other agencies may also cover the same subjects within their general stock.

Remember: simply placing material with an agency doesn't guarantee sales. And no agency can sell material for which there is no market. On the other hand, if you are able to produce good quality, marketable work, and can team up with the right agency, you could see a very worthwhile return from this association.

An asterisk against an agency name in the main listings indicates membership of the British Association of Picture Libraries & Agencies (BAPLA).

Subject Index

Aerial

Geo Aerial Photography
Skyscan Photolibrary

Agriculture

Alvey & Towers
Ecoscene
NHPA Ltd
Oxford Scientific (OSF) Ltd
Panos Pictures
Papilio
Royal Geographical Society Picture Library

Architecture

Acestock.com
Ancient Art & Architecture Collection
Arcblue
E & E Picture Library
Heritage Trail Image Library
Images of Birmingham Photo Library
Red Cover Limited
View Pictures Ltd
Elizabeth Whiting & Associates

Botanical/Gardening

FLPA – Images of Nature
Garden Picture Library
Garden World Images
NHPA Ltd
Oxford Scientific (OSF) Ltd
Papilio
Red Cover Limited
Elizabeth Whiting & Associates

Business/Industry

Alvey & Towers
E-Picture Library
Eye Ubiquitous
Leslie Garland Picture Library
Robert Harding World Imagery
Images of Birmingham Photo Library
Impact Photos
Link Picture Library
Newscast
Photolibrary.com

Panos Pictures
Picturebank Photo Library Ltd
SCR Photo Library
StockScotland.com
Still Moving Picture Company
TopFoto

Food/Drink

Bubbles Photo Library
E-Picture Library
Food Features
Foodanddrinkphotos.com
Fresh Food Images
Red Cover Limited
Stockfood Ltd
Travel Ink
Elizabeth Whiting & Associates

General (all subjects)

Acestock.com
Adams Picture Library
Alamy Images
Art Directors/TRIP Photo Library
Corbis
Eye Ubiquitous
Getty Images
Robert Harding World Imagery
JS Library International
Pictoreal
Pictures Colour Library
TheImagefile.com
TopFoto

Geography/Environment

Sylvia Cordaiy Photo Library
Ecoscene
Eye Ubiquitous
FLPA – Images of Nature
Impact Photos
Link Picture Library
NHPA Ltd
Oxford Scientific (OSF) Ltd
Panos Pictures
Papilio
Picturebank Photo Library Ltd
Royal Geographical Society Picture Library
SCR Photo Library

187

Glamour

Bodysnappers.com
Camera Press Ltd
Picturebank Photo Library Ltd

Historical

Ancient Art & Architecture Collection
Bridgeman Art Library
Heritage Trail Image Library
Popperfoto.com
Royal Geographical Society Picture Library

Landscapes

Arcangel Images
Arcblue
Cornish Picture Library
Jason Friend Image Library
Loop Images
NHPA Ltd
Oxford Scientific (OSF) Ltd
Still Moving Picture Company
StockScotland.com

Music

Arena PAL
Camera Press Ltd
Capital Pictures
Famous
Jazz Index Photo Library
Lebrecht Music & Arts Photo Library
Redferns Music Picture Library
Retna Pictures Ltd
S.I.N.

Natural History

FLPA – Images of Nature
NHPA Ltd
Oxford Scientific (OSF) Ltd
Papilio

News/Current Affairs

Camera Press Ltd
Express Syndication
Getty Images News & Sport
London Media Press
Rex Features Ltd
Scoopt

Solarpix
World Picture News

People/Lifestyle

Acestock.com
E-Picture Library
Images of Birmingham Photo Library
PYMCA
Picturebank Photo Library Ltd
Photolibrary.com
Photofusion Picture Library
Retna Pictures Ltd
S.I.N.
TheImagefile.com

Personalities/Celebrities

Big Pictures
Camera Press Ltd
Capital Pictures
Eyevine
Express Syndication
Famous
Getty Images News & Sport
London Media Press
Monitor Picture Library
Newscast
Nunn Syndication
Retna Pictures Ltd
Rex Features Ltd
S.I.N.
Scoopt
Solarpix
Writer Pictures

Science/Technology

Camera Press Ltd
Leslie Garland Picture Library
Oxford Scientific (OSF) Ltd
Picturebank Photo Library Ltd
Science Photo Library

Social Documentary

Arkreligion
John Birdsall Social Issues Photo Library
Bubbles Photo Library
Collections
E & E Picture Library
Eye Ubiquitous
Impact Photos

Link Picture Library
PYMCA
Panos Pictures
Photofusion Picture Library
World Religions Photo Library

Sport

Action Images Ltd
Airsport Photo Library
Alvey & Towers
Cut and Deal Ltd
Getty Images News & Sport
Kos Picture Source Ltd
PA Photos/Empics Sport
Photolibrary.com
Skishoot – Offshoot
Skyscan Photolibrary
Solarpix
Still Moving Picture Company
StockShot

Transport

Acestock.com
Alvey & Towers
Edinburgh Photographic Library
The Flight Collection
Heritage Trail Image Library
Impact Photos
Milepost 92½
Skyscan Photolibrary
TRH Pictures/Cody Images
Travel Ink

Travel/Tourist

Acestock.com
Alvey & Towers
Andes Press Agency
Sylvia Cordaiy Photo Library
Eye Ubiquitous
E-Picture Library
Fresh Food Images
Jason Friend Image Library
Images of France
Kos Picture Source Ltd
Photolibrary.com
Picturebank Photo Library Ltd
Pictures Colour Library
Royal Geographical Society Picture Library
Skishoot – Offshoot
Spectrum Colour Library
Still Moving Picture Company
StockShot
TheImagefile.com
TopFoto
Travel Ink
The Travel Library
World Pictures

Underwater

FLPA – Images of Nature
Sylvia Cordaiy Photo Library
Kos Picture Source Ltd
Oxford Scientific (OSF) Ltd
Papilio

ACESTOCK.COM*
Satellite House, 2 Salisbury Road, Wimbledon, London SW19 4EZ.
Tel: 020 8944 9944. E-mail: john@acestock.com
Web: www.acestock.com
Contact: John Panton (Director).
Specialist subjects/requirements: General: Architecture, business, concepts, industry, nature/environment, people/lifestyles, science/medical, sports/leisure, still-life, technology, transport, wildlife, world travel.
Markets supplied: Advertising; design; publishing.
Formats accepted: All formats; digital preferred. Top quality portfolio work only.
Usual terms of business: No minimum initial submission: 200 accepted images. Minimum retention period: 3 years.
Commission: 50 per cent.
Additional information: Submit 100 low-res images for initial assessment.

ACTION IMAGES*
Image House, Station Road, Tottenham, London N17 9LR.
Tel: 020 8885 3000. Fax: 020 8267 2035. E-mail: info@actionimages.com
Web: www.actionimages.com
Contact: Neil Sullivan (Managing Editor).
Specialist subjects/requirements: High quality sports pictures, especially of any unusual or spectacular incident.
Markets supplied: Newspapers, magazines, books, etc.
Formats accepted: Digital only; minimum 18MB files.
Usual terms of business: No minimum initial submission, but phone first to discuss possible submissions.
Commission: Negotiable.
Additional information: Operates as the specialist sports arm of the Reuters news agency.

ADAMS PICTURE LIBRARY*
Studio 1, Canalot Studios, 222 Kensal Road, London W10 5BN.
Tel: 020 8964 8007. Fax: 020 8960 8609. E-mail: info@adamspicturelibrary.com
Web: www.adamspicturelibrary.com
Contact: Dave Jarvis, Tamsyn Jarvis (Partners).
Specialist subjects/requirements: All subjects except hot news.
Markets supplied: All markets including advertising, publishing, calendars and posters.
Formats accepted: All formats, but digital files preferred (A4 at 300dpi).
Usual terms of business: Minimum initial submission: 100 images. Minimum retention period: 5 years; 1 year's notice required for withdrawal.
Commission: 50 per cent (for exclusive images).

AIRSPORT PHOTO LIBRARY
East Farm Studio, Nordelph, Downham Market, Norfolk PE38 0BG.
Tel: 01366 324346; 07703 542804 (mobile). E-mail: library@airsport-photo.co.uk
Web: www.airsport-photo.co.uk
Contact: David Wootton (Proprietor).
Specialist subjects/requirements: All forms of airsports: ballooning, hang gliding, paragliding, skydiving, kiting, bungee jumping, microlighting, light aircraft, etc.
Markets supplied: Editorial, advertising, books, internet.
Formats accepted: Colour transparencies/digital.
Usual terms of business: No minimum initial submission but like to see at least 20 to begin with.
Commission: 50 per cent.
Additional information: Pictures should be bright, colourful and dramatic to show the sports at their best. Phone or e-mail before submitting. The library also specialises in commercial aerial photography.

ALAMY IMAGES*

127 Milton Park, Abingdon, Oxon OX14 4SA.
Tel: 01235 844640. Fax: 01235 844650. E-mail: memberservices@alamy.com
Web: www.alamy.com
Contact: Alan Capel (Head of Content); Alexandra Bortkiewicz (Director of Photography).
Specialist subjects/requirements: Quality images of all subjects – business, lifestyle, travel, vacations, sports, food, abstracts, concepts, still life, science, wildlife, people, celebrities, historical, reportage.
Markets supplied: Advertising, design, corporate and publishing worldwide.
Formats accepted: Digital files only, usually 48–70MB uncompressed RGB JPEG. See website for full technical requirements.
Usual terms of business: Submit initial test CD of 10–15 images; if accepted no minimum submission applies.
Commission: 65 per cent to photographer.
Additional information: Photographers must supply their own digital files and keywording. Alamy do not edit photographers' submissions but files are checked for technical accuracy before being allowed online. For initial approach first register at the website.

ALVEY & TOWERS*

The Springboard Centre, Mantle Lane, Coalville, Leicestershire LE67 3DW.
Tel/fax: 01530 450011. E-mail: office@alveyandtowers.com
Web: www.alveyandtowers.com
Contact: Emma Rowen (Library Manager).
Specialist subjects/requirements: Agriculture, business, industry, leisure, people, transport and travel. Specialist modern railway library incorporating all aspects of this particular industry.
Markets supplied: Advertising, books, magazines, corporate brochures, calendars, audio visual.
Formats accepted: All formats, digital and transparency.
Usual terms of business: On application.
Commission: 40 per cent.
Additional information: It is essential that potential contributors make contact prior to making any submission in order to discuss precise requirements. Digital submission guidelines available via e-mail. Transparencies must be mounted and numbered with captions on accompanying sheet of paper, not on mounts.

ANCIENT ART & ARCHITECTURE COLLECTION LTD

Suite 1, 410-420 Rayners Lane, Pinner, Middlesex HA5 5DY.
Tel: 020 8429 3131. Fax: 020 8429 4646. E-mail: library@aaacollection.co.uk
Web: www.aaacollection.com
Contact: Michelle Williams (Librarian).
Specialist subjects/requirements: Historical art and artifacts mainly from pre-history up to the Middle Ages; everything which illustrates the civilisations of the ancient world, its cultures and technologies, religion, ideas, beliefs and development. Also warfare, weapons, fortifications and military historical movements. Statues, portraits and contemporary illustrations of historically important people – kings and other rulers.
Markets supplied: Mainly book publishers, but including magazines and TV.
Formats accepted: Digital files only, at 30MB minimum.
Usual terms of business: Minimum retention period: 3 years. 24 months notice of return.
Commission: 50 per cent.
Additional information: All submissions must be accompanied by return sae.

As a member of the Bureau of Freelance Photographers, you'll be kept up-to-date with markets through the BFP Market Newsletter, published monthly. For details of membership, turn to page 9

ANDES PRESS AGENCY*
26 Padbury Court, London E2 7EH.
Tel: 020 7613 5417. Fax: 020 7739 3159. E-mail: photos@andespressagency.com
Web: www.andespressagency.com
Contact: Valeria Baker.
Specialist subjects/requirements: Latin America, including the Caribbean; world religions.
Markets supplied: Books, newspapers, magazines.
Formats accepted: 35mm and medium format transparencies.
Usual terms of business: Minimum initial submission: 100 transparencies. Minimum retention period: 3 years.
Commission: By negotiation.

ARCANGEL IMAGES LTD
Apartado 528, Calle Las Mimosas 85, Campo Mijas, Mijas Costa, 29649, Malaga, Spain.
Tel: 0871 218 1023. E-mail: submissions@arcangel-images.com
Web: www.arcangel-images.com
Contact: Michael Mascaro (Director).
Specialist subjects/requirements: creative and fine art imagery, from nudes to landscapes and with the emphasis on digital capture. Will consider all types of images and styles, from general high-quality stock to personal fine art work.
Markets supplied: Book publishing, music industry, design companies, etc.
Formats accepted: Colour and B&W. Digital files only (minimum 17MB, preferred 30-40MB).
Usual terms of business: Minimum initial submission: 20 accepted images. Minimum retention period: 3 years.
Commission: 50 per cent.
Additional information: British/Spanish company with head office in Spain. Prefer initial approach by e-mail with a few sample images (totalling no more than 500KB) or a link to a personal website.

ARCBLUE*
93 Gainsborough Road, Richmond, Surrey TW9 2ET.
Tel: 020 8940 2227. Fax: 020 8940 6570. E-mail: info@arcblue.com
Web: www.arcblue.com
Contact: Peter Durant (Library Manager).
Specialist subjects/requirements: Modern contemporary architecture and built environment. Also interiors and landscape.
Markets supplied: General publishing, advertising and design.
Formats accepted: B&W and colour transparencies; digital files preferred (50MB, RGB, 300dpi).
Usual terms of business: Minimum initial submission: 30 images. Minimum retention period: 2 years.
Commission: 50 per cent.
Additional information: Prefer to see coherent sets of images that work together as well as individually. Send sample set of images in the first instance, by mail or e-mail, preferably 6–20 images in digital format or tearsheets/photocopies.

ARENA PAL*
1st Floor, 55 Southwark Street, London SE1 1RU.
Tel: 020 7403 8542. Fax: 020 7403 8561. E-mail: enquiries@arenapal.com
Web: www.arenapal.com
Contact: Biddy Hayward (Managing Director).
Specialist subjects/requirements: Performing arts and the entertainment industry – theatre, dance, jazz, TV, music, opera, circus, festivals and venues.
Markets supplied: All media including publishing, arts bodies, advertising, design companies.
Formats accepted: B&W and colour, all formats. Digital files preferred.

Usual terms of business: No minimum initial submission, but expect around 100 images. Minimum retention period: 3 years.
Commission: 50 per cent.
Additional information: Incorporates the former Performing Arts Library. Looks for photographers with a well-presented portfolio and a solid base in the performing arts. Also acts as a photographer's agent.

ARKRELIGION.COM*
57 Burdon Lane, Cheam, Surrey SM2 7BY.
Tel: 020 8642 3593. Fax: 020 8395 7230. E-mail: images@artdirectors.co.uk
Web: www.arkreligion.com
Contact: Helene Rogers (Partner).
Specialist subjects/requirements: All religions worldwide, mainstream to alternate, ceremonies from birth to death, festivals and important events, people (priests, pilgrims, worshippers), artefacts, churches/temples, holy books, worship, meals and food, daily rituals.
Markets supplied: Advertising and editorial.
Formats accepted: All formats, but digital preferred (minimum 50MB 8-bit TIFF).
Usual terms of business: Minimum initial submission: 100 images. Minimum retention period: 3 years.
Commission: 50 per cent.
Additional information: Photographers' Guidelines can be viewed on the website.

ART DIRECTORS/TRIP PHOTO LIBRARY*
57 Burdon Lane, Cheam, Surrey SM2 7BY.
Tel: 020 8642 3593. Fax: 020 8395 7230. E-mail: images@artdirectors.co.uk
Web: www.artdirectors.co.uk
Contact: Bob Turner (Partner).
Specialist subjects/requirements: All subjects and all locations. Art Directors supplies images mainly for advertising; TRIP handles general travel material and in-depth, extensive coverage of all religions.
Markets supplied: Advertising and editorial.
Formats accepted: All formats; digital preferred (minimum 50MB 8-bit TIFF).
Usual terms of business: Minimum initial submission: 100 images. Minimum retention period: 3 years.
Commission: 50 per cent.
Additional information: Ask for Photographers' Guidelines or view them on website.

BIG PICTURES*
50-54 Clerkenwell Road, London EC1M 5PS.
Tel: 020 7250 3555. Fax: 020 7250 0033. E-mail: picturedesk@bigpictures.co.uk
Web: www.bigpictures.co.uk/www.mrpaparazzi.com
Contact: Chris Pettitt (Picture Desk).
Specialist subjects/requirements: Current, well-known and preferably A-list celebrities, mainly informal paparazzi material.
Markets supplied: News media and magazines worldwide.
Formats accepted: Digital files preferred.
Usual terms of business: No minimum submission. Minimum retention period: Exclusive worldwide sales licence for 90 days.
Commission: 50 per cent, or outright purchase.
Additional information: Urgent images can be quickly uploaded via the agency's "Mr Paparazzi" website.

JOHN BIRDSALL SOCIAL ISSUES PHOTO LIBRARY*

89 Zulu Road, Nottingham NG7 7DR.
Tel: 0115 978 2645. Fax: 0115 978 5546. E-mail: photos@johnbirdsall.co.uk
Web: www. johnbirdsall.co.uk
Contact: Anna Grapes (Photo Library Manager).
Specialist subjects/requirements: Social issues – education, older people, children, young people and families, health and the NHS, disability, housing and homelessness, environment.
Markets supplied: Charities, national and local government, social services, educational book and magazine publishers.
Formats accepted: Digital, minimum 26MB. Caption, keyword and origin contained in IPTC header or file info.
Usual terms of business: No minimum submission. Minimum retention period: Negotiable.
Commission: 50 per cent.
Additional information: Model released images preferred.

BODYSNAPPERS.COM*

Urban Photography, Jack's Place, Corbet Place, Hanbury Street, London E1 6NH.
Tel: 0870 446 9696. Fax: 0870 446 0166. E-mail: info@bodysnappers.com
Web: www. bodysnappers.com
Contact: Angie Noon (Sales Manager).
Specialist subjects/requirements: Glamour or nude images of men's and women's bodies – pictures where the body of the person is the main subject (not fashion shots or products shots). Subjects can be semi-nude, nude or abstract. Lingerie/underwear shots also acceptable.
Markets supplied: Advertising, design, general publishing.
Formats accepted: Digital; JPEG or TIFF.
Usual terms of business: Minimum initial submission: 10 images. Minimum retention period: Negotiable.
Commission: 60 per cent to photographer.
Additional information: There is a £25 annual registration fee. Contributors can register, upload images and descriptions, and manage their accounts, all online.

BRIDGEMAN ART LIBRARY*

17-19 Garway Road, London W2 4PH.
Tel: 020 7727 4065. Fax: 020 7792 8509. E-mail: info@bridgeman.co.uk
Web: www.bridgeman.co.uk
Contact: Adrian Gibbs (Collections Manager).
Specialist subjects/requirements: American, European and Oriental paintings and prints, antiques, antiquities, arms and armour, botanical subjects, ethnography, general historical subjects and personalities, maps and manuscripts, natural history, topography, transport, etc.
Markets supplied: Publishing, advertising, television, greetings cards, calendars, etc.
Formats accepted: Mainly colour, some B&W. Minimum 5x4in transparencies or 50MB digital files (RGB TIFF).
Usual terms of business: No minimum initial submission. Retention period negotiable.
Commission: 50 per cent.

BUBBLES PHOTO LIBRARY*

3 Rose Lane, Ipswich IP1 1XE.
Tel: 01473 288605. E-mail: info@bubblesphotolibrary.co.uk
Web: www.bubblesphotolibrary.co.uk
Contact: Sarah Robinson, Loisjoy Thurstun (Partners).
Specialist subjects/requirements: Babies, children, pregnancy, mothercare, child development, education (especially aspects of multiculturalism), teenagers, old age, family life, women's health and medical, still lives of food, vegetables, herbs, etc.
Markets supplied: Books, magazines, newspapers and advertising.

Formats accepted: Colour and B&W. All formats, digital files preferred (A3 at 300dpi)
Usual terms of business: Minimum initial submission: 100 images. Regular contributions
expected. Minimum retention period: 3 years.
Commission: 50 per cent.
Additional information: Attractive women and children sell best. Always looking for
multicultural and multiracial children/adults. Photographers must pay close attention to selecting
models that are healthy-looking and ensure that backgrounds are uncluttered. Best clothes to wear
are light coloured and neutral fashion.

CAMERA PRESS LTD*
21 Queen Elizabeth Street, London SE1 2PD.
Tel: 020 7378 1300. Fax: 020 7407 2635. E-mail: j.wald@camerapress.com
Web: www.camerapress.com
Contact: Jacqui Ann Wald (Managing Editor).
Specialist subjects/requirements: Mainly celebrity, pop, photo reportage, personality portraits.
Also material suitable for women's magazines and general interest features, humour, travel, and
some general stock.
Formats accepted: B&W and colour. Digital preferred but scanning still undertaken.
Usual terms of business: By mutual agreement.
Commission: 50 per cent.

CAPITAL PICTURES*
85 Randolph Avenue, London W9 1DL.
Tel: 020 7286 2212. E-mail: sales@capitalpictures.com
Web: www.capitalpictures.com
Contact: Phil Loftus (Manager).
Specialist subjects/requirements: Celebrities and personalities from the worlds of showbusiness,
film and TV, rock and pop, politics and royalty.
Markets supplied: UK and international magazines, newspapers, etc.
Formats accepted: Digital only.
Usual terms of business: Minimum initial submission: 100 images. Minimum retention period:
1 year.
Commission: 50 per cent.

COLLECTIONS*
13 Woodberry Crescent, London N10 1PJ.
Tel: 020 8883 0083. Fax: 020 8883 9215. E-mail: sal.shuel@btinternet.com
Web: www.collectionspicturelibrary.com/www.collectionspicturelibrary.co.uk
Contact: Brian, Sal and Simon Shuel (Directors).
Specialist subjects: The British Isles and Ireland.
Markets supplied: All, particularly on the editorial side.
Formats accepted: All formats, digital (min 26MB) or transparency, and B&W prints.
Usual terms of business: By arrangement; "easy going and on the side of the contributor."
Commission: 50 per cent.
Additional information: The library aims to stock quality pictures of as many places, things,
happenings on these islands as possible.

CORBIS*
11 Salusbury Road, London NW6 6RG.
Tel: 020 7731 9995. Fax: 020 7644 7645. E-mail: info@corbis.com
Web: www.corbis.com
Contact: Vanessa Kramer (Director of Artistic Relations).
Specialist subjects/requirements: General library handling most subjects, on both a licensed and
royalty-free basis.

Markets supplied: Advertising, publishing, design, etc.
Formats accepted: Colour and historic B&W. Digital files only, minimum 17MB (digital capture) or 33MB (scans) for editorial images. Larger file sizes required for advertising, fashion and royalty-free images.
Usual terms of business: Minimum initial submission variable. Minimum retention period: 3 years.
Commission: 20–50 per cent, depending on client and use.
Additional information: For contributor submission information see http://studioplus.corbis.com

SYLVIA CORDAIY PHOTO LIBRARY*
45 Rotherstone, Devizes, Wiltshire SN10 2DD.
Tel: 01380 728327. Fax: 01380 728328. E-mail: info@sylvia-cordaiy.com
Web: www.sylvia-cordaiy.com
Contact: Sylvia Cordaiy (Proprietor).
Specialist subjects/requirements: Worldwide travel, world heritage sites, architecture, exploration, wildlife, places, domestic animals and livestock, marine biology, environmental issues.
Markets supplied: General publishing, text books, travel books, cards and calendars, brochures, exhibitions, advertising.
Formats accepted: All formats including digital (minimum 50MB TIFF).
Usual terms of business: Minimum initial submission: 100 images. Minimum retention period: 3 years.
Commission: 50 per cent.
Additional information: Prefers Fuji film stock for transparencies. Only top quality images considered and all must be accurately captioned.

CORNISH PICTURE LIBRARY*
40b Fore Street, St Columb Major, Cornwall TR9 6RH.
Tel: 01637 880103/01503 250673. E-mail: paul@imageclick.co.uk
Web: www.imageclick.co.uk
Contact: Paul Watts (Proprietor).
Specialist subjects/requirements: Cornwall and the West Country (Devon, Dorset, Somerset, Wiltshire, Isles of Scilly, Channel Isles) – landscapes, historic sites, gardens, people, activities, attractions, wildlife.
Markets supplied: Magazines, books, tourism, etc.
Formats accepted: Digital files from 6MP cameras upwards, minimum 16MB TIFF; must be colour correct preferably with Adobe 1998 profile. Medium format or larger transparencies accepted, top quality 35mm considered. B&W archive (pre-1960) images of Cornwall.
Usual terms of business: No minimum submission. Minimum retention period: 3 years.
Commission: 50 per cent.
Additional information: Contact by e-mail or letter with details of subjects covered before sending submission. Browse website for more info and to view images already held; very similar images not required, only better shots or different views. Contributors' guidelines available on request.

CREATIVE IMAGE LIBRARY*
Brook Cottage, Hale Oak Road, Weald, Sevenoaks, Kent TN14 6NQ.
Tel: 01892 723388. E-mail: binny@creativeimagelibrary.com
Web: www.creativeimagelibrary.com
Contact: Binny Cuddiford (Partner).
Specialist subjects/requirements: Quality images of wildlife, farm animals, landscapes, cottages, cars, lifestyle. Material suitable for the greetings card, calendar and poster market.
Markets supplied: calendars, greetings cards, posters, magazines, book publishers etc.
Formats accepted: Digital files only, 48 MB files minimum.
Usual terms of business: No minimum initial submission. Minimum retention period: 2 years.

Commission: 50 per cent.
Additional information: Images must be of a style and content suitable for the card/calendar market - see website for examples. Please do not submit on spec - always e-mail in the first instance to discuss submissions.

CUT AND DEAL LTD
Suite 299, 2 Landsdowne Row, London SW18 3SX.
Tel: 07951 537370. E-mail: submissions@cutanddeal.com
Web: www.cutanddeal.com
Contact: Glen Conybeare (Director).
Specialist subjects/requirements: Images relating to gambling of all kinds. Gambling locations, gaming subjects and sports betting, including images of sports that people bet on such as horse racing, dog racing, football, basketball, cricket, golf, rugby, etc.
Markets supplied: Design industry, advertising, general publishing.
Formats accepted: Digital. Uncompressed files at least 10MB.
Usual terms of business: Minimum initial submission: 25 images.
Commission: 50 per cent.
Additional information: Potential contributors should submit 5 sample images (or a link to a website) with details of what other subjects can be provided.

THE DEFENCE PICTURE LIBRARY LTD
14 Mary Seacole Road, The Millfields Business Park, Plymouth PL1 3JY.
Tel: 01752 312061. Fax: 01752 312063. E-mail: dpl@defencepictures.com
Web: www.defencepictures.com
Contact: David Reynolds (Director), Andrew Chittock (Picture Editor).
Specialist subjects/requirements: Military images covering all aspects of the armed forces worldwide, in training and on operations. Pictures of UK and international forces across the globe are always of interest.
Markets supplied: Publishers, advertising agencies, national media.
Formats accepted: 35mm and medium format; high-resolutions TIFFS.
Usual terms of business: Minimum initial submission: 50 quality images. Minimum retention period: 5 years.
Commission: 50 per cent.
Additional information: The library is the UK's leading specialist source of military and defence images.

E & E PICTURE LIBRARY*
Beggars Roost, Woolpack Hill, Brabourne Lees, Nr Ashford, Kent TN25 6RR.
Tel/fax: 01303 812608. E-mail: info@picture-library.freeserve.co.uk
Web: www.heritage-images.co.uk (see E&E)
Contact: Isobel Sinden (Proprietor).
Specialist subjects/requirements: Religions – prayer, ritual, services, festivals, ceremonies, art, architecture, objects, clergy, vestments, saints, pilgrims, holy places, manuscripts, illustrations, ancient Biblelands, stained glass. Also: Architecture and buildings; places of interest, heritage. Death (ceremonies, funerals, burials, graveyards, etc). Eccentricities/oddities (historical, military, literary, artistic, religious and secular); transport; industrial archaeology; places; nature; water.
Markets supplied: General publishing, newspapers, TV, merchandising.
Formats accepted: Digital files preferred; transparencies accepted.
Usual terms of business: Minimum initial submission: 50 images; less if specialist subject matter. Minimum retention period: 5 years.
Commission: 50 per cent.

E-PICTURE LIBRARY
Horizon House, Route de Picaterre, Alderney, Guernsey GY9 3UP.
Tel: 01481 824200. E-mail: mail@hrzn.com
Web: www.e-picturelibrary.net
Contact: Mark Osborne-Burns (Managing Director).
Specialist subjects/requirements: People images (couples, singles, families, children), including people in business, lifestyle, sport. Images of models and real people, model released if possible. Also scenics, wildlife, pets, horses, travel, food, industry.
Markets supplied: General publishing, advertising, etc.
Formats accepted: Digital files (50MB+), or transparencies subject to scanning fees.
Usual terms of business: Minimum initial submission: None stated. Minimum term of agreement: 1 year.
Commission: Variable according to stock quantities – see website.
Additional information: Full scanning, retouching and keywording service available. See website for more information.

ECOSCENE*
Empire Farm, Throop Road, Templecombe, Somerset BA8 0HR.
Tel: 01963 371700. E-mail: sally@ecoscene.com
Web: www.ecoscene.com
Contact: Sally Morgan (Proprietor).
Specialist subjects/requirements: Environmental issues worldwide including agriculture, conservation, energy, pollution, transport, sustainable development.
Markets supplied: Books, magazines, organisations, etc.
Formats accepted: Digital files at 50MB.
Usual terms of business: Minimum initial submission: 100 quality images. Minimum retention period: 4 years.
Commission: 55 per cent to photographer.
Additional information: Contributors' guidelines available on request – can also be found on the library's website along with details of specific current requirements.

EPICSCOTLAND*
Unit 5, Hathaway Business Centre, 21-29 Hathaway Street, Glasgow G20 8TD.
Tel: 0141 945 0000. Email: info@epicscotland.com
Web: www.epicscotland.com
Contact: Sarah Chandler (Picture Library Manager).
Specialist subjects/requirements: All aspects of Scotland and Scottish life.
Markets supplied: Newspapers, magazines, publishers, design agencies.
Formats accepted: Mainly colour, all formats. Digital if above 20MB and of high quality.
Usual terms of business: No minimum terms.
Commission: 50 per cent.
Additional information: No submitting without prior contact. Digital files must be checked by e-mail before submission.

EXPRESS SYNDICATION
The Northern & Shell Building, 10 Lower Thames Street, London EC3R 6EN.
Tel: 0870 211 7884. Fax: 0870 211 7871. E-mail: adam.williams@express.co.uk
Web: www.expresspictures.com
Contact: Adam Williams (Syndication Manager).
Specialist subjects/requirements: Current news, features and personalities.
Markets supplied: Magazines and newspapers, UK and overseas.
Formats accepted: B&W and colour, all formats.
Usual terms of business: Minimum retention period: 90 days.
Commission: 50 per cent.

Additional information: Represents the Daily and Sunday Express, Daily Star and OK! magazine as well as freelance photographers and other agencies.

EYE UBIQUITOUS & HUTCHISON*
65 Brighton Road, Shoreham, West Sussex BN43 6RE.
Tel: 01273 440113. Fax: 01273 440116. E-mail: library@eyeubiquitous.com
Web: www.eyeubiquitous.com
Contacts: Paul Seheult (Proprietor), Stephen Rafferty (Library Manager).
Specialist subjects/requirements: Material suitable for the travel/tourist industry (scenics, resorts, beaches, major sights), plus general stock and social documentary material (people, lifestyles, work, environment, etc). Also incorporates the Hutchison Picture Library offering in-depth documentary coverage of indigenous cultures worldwide.
Markets supplied: Publishing markets, travel industry, UK and European advertising agencies.
Formats accepted: Digital or colour transparency (generally prefer Fuji material).
Usual terms of business: Suggested minimum submission 200 images, but terms open to discussion.
Commission: 40 per cent.
Additional information: The collections are run as separate entities, though contributing photographers may have work with more than one.

EYEVINE
3 Mills Studios,Three Mill Lane, London E3 3DU.
Tel: 020 8709 8709. E-mail: info@eyevine.com
Web: www.eyevine.com
Contact: Graham Cross (Director).
Specialist subjects/requirements: Portraiture, news and reportage.
Markets supplied: Worldwide editorial publishing (newspapers, magazines, books etc).
Formats accepted: Digital files preferred, minimum 30MB RGB JPEG. Colour/B&W print or transparency also accepted.
Usual terms of business: Minimum initial submission: 1 image. Minimum retention period: 3 years.
Commission rate: 50 per cent.
Additional information: Although a news, feature, personalities and assignments agency we are only looking to take on portraiture at this stage. See website for further information.

FLPA – IMAGES OF NATURE*
Pages Green House, Wetheringsett, Stowmarket, Suffolk IP14 5QA.
Tel: 01728 860789. Fax: 01728 860222. E-mail: pictures@flpa-images.co.uk
Web: www.flpa-images.co.uk
Contact: Jean Hosking, David Hosking (Directors).
Specialist subjects/requirements: Natural history and weather phenomena: birds, clouds, fish, fungi, insects, mammals, pollution, rainbows, reptiles, sea, snow, seasons, trees, underwater, hurricanes, earthquakes, lightning, volcanoes, dew, rain, fog, etc. Ecology and the environment. Horse, dog and cat breeds.
Markets supplied: Book publishers, advertising agencies, magazines.
Formats accepted: Digital files at 50MB (contact agency for guidelines).
Usual terms of business: Minimum initial submission: 20 images for evaluation. Minimum retention period: 4 years.
Commission: 50 per cent.
Additional information: Competition in the natural history field is fierce, so only really sharp, well-composed pictures are needed. Sales are slow to start with, and a really keen photographer must be prepared to invest money in building up stock to the 1,000 mark.

FAMOUS*
13 Harwood Road, London SW6 4QP.
Tel: 020 7731 9333. Fax: 020 7731 9330. E-mail: info@famous.uk.com
Web: www.famous.uk.com
Contact: Rob Howard (Managing Director).
Specialist subjects/requirements: Celebrity photographs, especially personalities in the TV, movie, music, fashion and Royal fields. Taken in any situation: red carpet, paparazzi, party, performance, studio and at home.
Markets supplied: General press and publishing.
Formats accepted: Digital only.
Usual terms of business: No minimum submission or retention period.
Commission: 50 per cent.
Additional information: Always looking for photographers who can supply relevant pictures fast.

THE FLIGHT COLLECTION*
Quadrant House, The Quadrant, Sutton, Surrey SM2 5AS.
Tel: 020 8652 8888. Fax: 020 8652 8933. E-mail: qpl@flightglobal.com
Web: www.theflightcollection.com
Contact: Kim Hearn (Head of Picture Library).
Specialist subjects/requirements: All aspects of aviation – civil, military, helicopters, airports, crew, aircraft interiors, maintenance, etc.
Markets supplied: Books, magazines, advertising, exhibitions, etc.
Formats accepted: Mainly colour; B&W historical. All formats accepted; digital preferred (minimum 20MB, corrected and captioned).
Usual terms of business: Minimum initial submission: 50 images for inspection. Minimum retention period: 2 years.
Commission: 50 per cent.
Additional information: Call first for "wants" list.

FOOD FEATURES*
Stream House, West Flexford Lane, Wanborough, Guildford, Surrey GU3 2JW.
Tel: 01483 810840. Fax: 01483 811587. E-mail: frontdesk@foodpix.co.uk
Web: www.foodfeatures.net
Contact: Steve Moss, Alex Barker (Partners).
Specialist subjects/requirements: Food and drink, especially images involving people – dining, cooking, dinner parties, al fresco, chefs, etc.
Markets supplied: Publishing, advertising, etc.
Formats accepted: Digital files preferred, 30MB minimum, 50MB preferred. 35mm transparencies acceptable for location shots but larger formats preferred.
Usual terms of business: No minimum initial submission. Minimum retention period: 3 years.
Commission: By agreement.

FOODANDDRINKPHOTOS.COM*
Studio 4, Sun Studios, 30 Warple Way, London W3 0RX.
Tel: 020 8740 6610. Fax: 020 8762 9994. E-mail: info@foodanddrinkphotos.com
Web: www.foodanddrinkphotos.com
Contact: Simon Reed (Submissions Manager).
Specialist subjects/requirements: All food and drink related photography, all styles, both

Are you working from the latest edition of The Freelance Photographer's Market Handbook? It's published on 1 October each year. Markets are constantly changing, so it pays to have the latest edition

traditional and more conceptual.
Markets supplied: Editorial, advertising and design.
Formats accepted: Transparencies or digital files (minimum 25MB).
usual terms of business: Minimum initial submission: 20 images. Minimum retention period: 3 years.
Commission rate: 50 per cent.
Additional information: Transparencies scanned for free and digitised to high resolution.

FRESH FOOD IMAGES
2nd Floor, 7 Woodfield Road, London W9 2BA.
Tel: 020 8877 1123. Fax: 020 8877 9787. E-mail: creative@freshfoodimages.co.uk
Web: www.freshfoodimages.co.uk
Contact: Library Manager.
Specialist subjects/requirements: Food and wine related images. High quality, original material on all aspects from farming, fishing, country trades, markets and vineyards to raw ingredients, finished dishes, chefs, restaurants and kitchens.
Markets supplied: Publishing, advertising, etc.
Formats accepted: Digital files required, shot on 10MP camera or high-end scans at 50MB.
Usual terms of business: Minimum initial submission: 50+ images for initial evaluation.
Minimum retention period: 3 years.
Commission: 50 per cent.
Additional information: Formerly the Anthony Blake Photo Library, now part of the international Photolibrary Group. Only stocks images of the very highest standard. See www.freshfoodimages.co.uk/photographers.html for full submission details.

JASON FRIEND IMAGE LIBRARY
151 Shields Road, Newcastle Upon Tyne NE6 1DP.
Tel: 0845 094 0479. Fax: 07020 973452. E-mail: mail@jasonfriend.co.uk
Web: www. jasonfriend.co.uk
Contact: Jason Friend (Managing Director).
Specialist subjects/requirements: Travel subjects from all locations around the world – landscape, cityscape, people, food, wildlife, transport, etc. Always looking for fresh takes on popular and iconic subjects. Particularly interested in images from the UK (especially London), USA, Canada, New Zealand, Australia and Antarctica.
Markets supplied: Editorial (books, magazines, newspapers), card/calendar/poster publishers.
Formats accepted: Digital files only, minimum 48MB. Digitally originated images should be shot on a SLR with a least 6 megapixels. All files supplied must be cleaned, captioned and keyworded.
Usual terms of business: Minimum initial submission: 50 images. Minimum retention period: 3 years.
Commission: 65 per cent to contributor.
Additional information: The library is based around the work of award-winning photographer Jason Friend and operates online only. Initial contact should be via e-mail. Stock is also marketed in New Zealand via www.jasonfriend.co.nz

GARDEN PICTURE LIBRARY*
Unit 12, Ransome's Dock, 35 Parkgate Road, London SW11 4NP.
Tel: 020 7228 4332. Fax: 020 7924 3267. E-mail: lee@gardenpicture.com
Web: www.gardenpicture.com
Contact: Lee Wheatley (Creative Director).
Specialist subjects/requirements: Gardens, plants (mainly cultivated), people and animals in the garden, practical gardening, food al fresco, outdoor living, flower shows, floral still life, and garden features.
Markets supplied: General publishing, greetings cards and calendars, advertising and design.
Formats accepted: All formats. Digital media preferred – contact for specifications.

Usual terms of business: Minimum initial submission: 100 images.
Commission: 50 per cent.
Additional information: Submission guidelines available on request or via website.

GARDEN WORLD IMAGES*
Grange Studio, Woodham Road, Battlesbridge, Wickford, Essex SS11 7QU.
Tel: 01245 325725. Fax: 01245 429198. E-mail: info@gardenworldimages.com
Web: www.gardenworldimages.com
Contact: Tyrone McGlinchey, Lisa Smith (Partners).
Specialist subjects/requirements: All aspects of horticulture, plants, vegetables, fruit, herbs, trees, gardens, pools, patios, etc. Also gardening action shots, people doing things, step-by-step, making patios, etc. Creative abstract images. Also fauna.
Markets supplied: Publishing, calendars, seed catalogues, etc.
Formats accepted: Digital images preferred, minimum 50MB.
Usual terms of business: Minimum initial submission: 50 images. No minimum retention period.
Commission: 50 per cent.
Additional information: Plant portraits must be identified with Latin name.

LESLIE GARLAND PICTURE LIBRARY
"High Pasture", Yarrow, Falstone, Hexham, Northumberland NE48 1BG.
Tel/fax: 01434 240324. E-mail: pictures@lesliegarland.co.uk
Web: www.lesliegarland.cwc.net
Contact: Leslie Garland ARPS (Proprietor).
Specialist subjects/requirements: General coverage of Europe; all subjects, though especially industry, engineering, science and technology.
Markets supplied: Advertising, books, brochures, exhibitions, magazines, etc.
Formats accepted: Medium format or larger transparencies preferred, exceptional 35mm considered depending on subject matter.
Usual terms of business: Minimum initial submission: 25 accepted images. Minimum retention period: 3 years.
Commission: 50 per cent.
Additional information: All pictures must be of top quality professional standard with comprehensive captions. View contributor guidelines etc on net before submitting.

GEO AERIAL PHOTOGRAPHY*
4 Christian Fields, London SW16 3JZ.
Tel/fax: 020 8764 6292 or 0115 981 9418. E-mail: geo.aerial@geo-group.co.uk
Web: www.geo-group.co.uk
Contact: John Douglas (Director), Kelly White (Consultant).
Specialist subjects/requirements: Worldwide oblique aerial photographs.
Markets supplied: Books, magazines, advertising, etc.
Formats accepted: Digital files preferred, 35mm or larger format transparencies accepted.
Usual terms of business: Negotiable.
Commission: 50 per cent.
Additional information: Locations must be identified in detail. Do not send samples of work but contact by letter first.

GETTY IMAGES*
101 Bayham Street, London NW1 0AG.
Tel: 020 7267 8988. Fax: 020 7267 6540. E-mail: editor@gettyartists.com
Web: http://creative.gettyimages.com
Contact: Picture Editor.
Specialist subjects/requirements: Conceptual and general stock photography on all subjects.
Markets supplied: Advertising, publishing, design agencies, etc.

Formats accepted: B&W and colour, all formats.
Usual terms of business: On application, for rights-managed and royalty-free sales.
Commission: Variable.
Additional information: The Getty Images Creative division incorporates several major collections including The Image Bank, Stone, Photonica and Photodisc. For contributor information see www.gettyimages.com/contributors

GETTY IMAGES NEWS & SPORT*
116 Bayham Street, London NW1 0AG.
Tel: 0800 376 7981. E-mail:
hugh.pinney@gettyimages.com/steve.rose@gettyimages.com/georges.dekeerle@gettyimages.com
Web: http://editorial.gettyimages.com
Contact: Editors – Hugh Pinney (news), Steve Rose (sport), Georges de Keerle (entertainment).
Specialist subjects/requirements: Contemporary news, sport and entertainment images.
Markets supplied: Newspapers, magazines, television, etc.
Formats accepted: 35mm and digital (for news).
Usual terms of business: Minimum retention period: 3 years.
Commission: 50 per cent.

ROBERT HARDING WORLD IMAGERY*
58-59 Great Marlborough Street, London W1F 7JY.
Tel: 020 7478 4146. Fax: 020 7478 4161. E-mail: submissions@robertharding.com
www.robertharding.com
Contact: Fraser Hall (Library Manager).
Specialist subjects/requirements: People, lifestyle, industry, travel.
Markets supplied: Publishers, advertising agencies, design groups, calendar publishers, etc.
Formats accepted: All formats; digital preferred (48MB non-interpolated for scans, 30MB non-interpolated for digital capture).
Usual terms of business: Minimum initial submission: 200 images. Minimum retention period: 7 years; 12 months notice of withdrawal.
Commission: As per contract; usually 40% to photographer.

THE HERITAGE TRAIL IMAGE LIBRARY
The Studio, 24 Bristol Way, Sleaford, Lincolnshire NG34 7AE.
Tel: 01529 303691. E-mail: laurie@theheritagetrail.co.uk
Web: www.theheritagetrail.co.uk
Contact: Laurie Jonas (Proprietor).
Specialist subjects/requirements: All aspects of British heritage – historic sites, architecture, industrial buildings, castles, churches, follies, statues, country houses, bridges, waterways, railways, aviation, maritime, military etc.
Markets supplied: General publishing, tourism industry.
Formats accepted: Digital only.
Usual terms of business: Minimum initial submission: Up to 20 thumbnail images via e-mail or CD to assess style, quality and subject matter. Minimum retention period: 5 years.
Commission: 50 per cent.
Additional information: Initial contact by e-mail preferred. Detailed submission requirements and full contractual information can be viewed on the website.

IMAGES OF BIRMINGHAM PHOTO LIBRARY
Tel: 0121 288 7222. E-mail: craig@imagesofbirmingham.co.uk
Web: www.imagesofbirmingham.co.uk
Contact: Craig Holmes (Proprietor).
Specialist subjects/requirements: The city of Birmingham and its environs, plus other regions in the Midlands including Coventry, Warwick, Stratford-on-Avon, Stafford, Wolverhampton (and Black

Country), Shropshire, Worcester, Nottingham, Leicester and Derby. Also images of people at work and play within the region (must be model released).
Markets supplied: Advertising, design agencies, general publishing.
Formats accepted: Digital only, minimum 25MB JPEG/TIFF.
Usual terms of business: Minimum initial submission: 25–30 varied images. Minimum retention period: 3 years.
Commission: 50 per cent.
Additional information: Images must be of excellent quality, show the region in a positive light and be suitable for advertising usage.

IMAGES OF FRANCE
4 Beoley Paper Mill, Redditch, Worcestershire B98 8PX.
Tel: 01527 61409. E-mail: info@imagesfrance.com
Web: www.imagesfrance.com
Contact: David Martyn Hughes (Proprietor).
Specialist subjects/requirements: All aspects of France and French life.
Markets supplied: Travel industry, advertising, general publishing.
Formats accepted: Digital capture files only; no scans. Images taken on 6MP cameras and above.
Usual terms of business: No minimum initial submission. Minimum retention period: 1 year. Exclusivity not required.
Commission: 50 per cent.
Additional information: Check the website first to see what kind of images the library sells. Initial contact should be made by e-mail stating what stock a photographer has to offer.

IMAGESTATE*
18–20 St John Street, London EC1M 4NX.
Tel: 020 7734 7344. Fax: 020 7434 0673. E-mail: submissions@imagestate.com
Web: www.imagestate.com
Contact: Hannah Lamb (Manager).
Specialist subjects/requirements: General contemporary stock – lifestyle, business, industry, landscapes, travel, leisure, etc
Markets supplied: Advertising and publishing.
Formats accepted: Mainly colour, some B&W, transparency, negative and print, but digital files preferred at 50MB.
Usual terms of business: Minimum initial submission dependent on quality. Minimum retention period: 5 years.
Commission: Subject to contract.
Additional information: The agency sells both rights-managed and royalty-free stock. Model releases essential for people pictures.

IMPACT PHOTOS*
18-20 St John Street, London EC1M 4NX.
Tel: 020 7251 5091. E-mail: library@impactphotos.com
Web: www.impactphotos.com
Contact: Deborah Jones (Picture Library Assistant).
Specialist subjects/requirements: Worldwide coverage of people in their environment – agriculture, industry, health, religion, transport, modernisation, education, social issues and travel.
Markets supplied: Newspapers, magazines, book, charities, etc.
Formats accepted: Digital on CD preferred (50MB RGB TIFF uncompressed at 300dpi). Also 35mm transparencies.
Usual terms of business: No minimum initial submission. Minimum retention period: 3 years.
Commission: 50 per cent.
Additional information: Digital contributors should also supply low-res images for quick edit.

J.S. LIBRARY INTERNATIONAL
101a Brondesbury Park, London NW2 5JL.
Tel: 020 8451 2668. Fax: 020 8459 8517/0223. E-mail: sales@jslibrary.com
Web: www.jslibrary.com/www.jslibraryprints.com
Contact: John Shelley (Proprietor).
Specialist subjects/requirements: All subjects.
Markets supplied: Newspapers, magazines, book publishers, etc.
Formats accepted: Digital files preferred (JEPG/TIFF, minimum 10-25MB). Plus all transparency formats.
Usual terms of business: No minimum initial submission, but regular submissions of large quantities recommended to maximise sales. Minimum retention period: 5 years.
Commission: 50 per cent.
Additional information: The agency website also has an extensive gallery section where photographers can display single images or portfolios of work.

JAZZ INDEX PHOTO LIBRARY*
26 Fosse Way, London W13 0BZ.
Tel: 020 8998 1232. E-mail: christianhim@jazzindex.co.uk
Web: www.jazzindex.co.uk
Contact: Christian Him (Principal).
Specialist subjects/requirements: Jazz, blues and contemporary music. Good atmospheric shots of musicians (do not have to be well-known). Both contemporary and archive material of interest.
Markets supplied: Newspapers, book publishers, videos, television.
Formats accepted: All transparency formats; B&W, prints or negs; digital at 300dpi.
Commission: 50 per cent.
Usual terms of business: No minimum submission.
Additional information: Always interested in jazz photos from the '50s, '60s or '70s. Contributors must phone first to enquire if material is suitable.

KOS PICTURE SOURCE LTD*
PO Box 52854, 7 Spice Court, Ivory Square, London SW11 3UU.
Tel: 020 7801 0044. Fax: 020 7801 0055. E-mail: images@kospictures.com
Web: kospictures.com
Contact: Chris Savage (Library Manager).
Specialist subjects/requirements: Water-related images from around the world. International yacht racing, all watersports, seascapes, underwater photography, and general travel.
Markets supplied: Advertising, design, publishing.
Formats accepted: 35mm and digital files (min 20MB).
Usual terms of business: No minimum initial submission. Minimum retention period: 2 years.
Commission: Variable.

LEBRECHT MUSIC & ARTS PHOTO LIBRARY*
3 Bolton Road, London NW8 0RJ.
Tel: 020 7625 5341. Fax: 020 7625 5341. E-mail: pictures@lebrecht.co.uk
Web: www.lebrecht.co.uk
Contact: Elbie Lebrecht (Proprietor).
Specialist subjects/requirements: All aspects of music (classical, opera, jazz, rock), the performing arts and literature. Instruments, composers, musicians, singers, writers, artists, playwrights, philosophers. Interiors and exteriors of concert halls and opera houses, statues and tombs of famous composers in the UK and abroad.
Markets supplied: Specialist magazines, national press, record companies, book publishers.
Formats accepted: B&W and colour. Digital submissions preferred (300dpi 50MB TIFF).
Usual terms of business: No minimum initial submission or retention period.
Commission: 50 per cent.

LINK PICTURE LIBRARY*
41A The Downs, London SW20 8HG.
Tel: 020 8944 6933. E-mail: library@linkpicturelibrary.com
Web: www.linkpicturelibrary.com
Contact: Orde Eliason (Proprietor).
Specialist subjects/requirements: General documentary coverage of countries worldwide, but particularly Africa – communications, culture, education, environment, health, industry, people and politics. Special interest in South Africa, South East Asia, India and Israel.
Markets supplied: Newspapers, general publishing.
Formats accepted: Digital files preferred, at 300dpi for A4 output. 35mm transparencies also stocked.
Usual terms of business: Minimum initial submission: 50 images. Minimum retention period: 3 years.
Commission: 50 per cent.
Additional information: Intial submission should be low-res images on CD.

LONDON MEDIA PRESS
11a Printing House Yard, London E2 7PR.
Tel: 020 7613 2548. Fax: 020 7729 9209. E-mail: pictures@london-media.co.uk
Web: www. london-media.co.uk
Contact: Rick Hewett, Andrew Buckwell (Directors).
Specialist subjects/requirements: News pictures, picture stories and features for worldwide syndication, especially celebrity/paparazzi material.
Markets supplied: National and international newspapers and magazines.
Formats accepted: Digital only.
Usual terms of business: No minimum initial submission. Minimum retention period: None stated.
Commission: 60 per cent to contributor.
Additional information: Freelance shift work frequently available.

LOOP IMAGES
The Studio, 61 Park Road, Woking, Surrey GU22 7BZ.
Tel/fax: 01483 830120. E-mail: paul@loopimages.com
Web: www.loopimages.com
Contact: Paul Mortlock (Library Manager).
Specialist subjects/requirments: Contemporary Britain photography (material shot in England, Scotland, Ireland and Wales) – landscape, cityscape, lifestyle, architecture, history, heritage, culture and the arts. Particular need for good town/city imagery.
Markets supplied: Magazine/book/newspaper publishers, design and ad agencies, travel and tourism industry in UK/US and Europe.
Formats accepted: Digital only – A4 300dpi TIFF (26-30MB) as library master.
Usual terms of business: Minimum initial submission: 50 images. Minimum retention period: Negotiable, but usually 2 years.
Commission rate: 50 per cent.
Additional information: Looking for quality material, not fillers.

MILEPOST 92¼*
Newton Harcourt, Leicestershire LE8 9FH.
Tel: 0116 259 2068. Fax: 0116 259 3001. E-mail: studio@railphotolibrary.co.uk
Web: www.railphotolibrary.co.uk
Contact: Colin Nash (Library Manager).
Specialist subjects/requirements: Railways – all aspects, national and international, contemporary and archive.
Markets supplied: Advertising, publishing, design, corporate railways.

Formats accepted: 35mm, medium format or digital (min 25MB JPEG/TIFF). Archive B&W.
Usual terms of business: Minimum initial submission: 25 pictures. No minimum retention period.
Commission: 50 per cent.
Additional information: All material must be of the highest quality. Transparencies must be mounted and captioned with brief, accurate details.

MONITOR PICTURE LIBRARY*
The Forge, Harlow Road, Roydon, Nr Harlow, Essex CM19 5HH.
Tel: 01279 792700. Fax: 01279 792600. E-mail: elly@monitorpicturelibrary.com
Web: www.monitorpicturelibrary.com
Contact: Elly White (Picture Editor).
Specialist subjects/requirements: Photographs of personalities from politics, business, sport, entertainment, royalty. Both current and archive material of interest.
Markets supplied: National and international press, television, advertising, publishers, etc.
Formats accepted: B&W and colour. 35mm, medium format and digital (high-res TIFF).
Usual terms of business: No minimum submission.
Commission: 50 per cent, but may make outright purchase offer for suitable material.

NHPA LIMITED*
29-31 Saffron Hill, London EC1N 8SW.
Tel: 020 7421 6003. Fax: 020 7421 6006. E-mail: nhpa@nhpa.co.uk
Web: www.nhpa.co.uk
Contact: Lee Dalton (Picture Editor).
Specialist subjects/requirements: Worldwide wildlife, domestic animals and pets, plants and gardens, landscapes, agriculture and environmental subjects. Endangered and appealing wildlife of particular interest.
Markets supplied: Books, magazines, advertising and design, cards and calendars, electronic publishing, exhibitions, etc (UK and overseas).
Formats accepted: Digital files preferred, transparencies accepted.
Usual terms of business: Minimum initial submission: 200 images.
Commission: 50 per cent.
Additional information: Pictures should be strong, active and well-composed. Write before submitting material. Full submissions guidelines available on website.

NATURAL SCIENCE PHOTOS*
PO Box 397, Welwyn Garden City, Herts AL7 9BA.
Tel: 01707 690561. Fax: 01707 690738. E-mail: natasha@naturalsciencephotos.com
Web: www.naturalsciencephotos.com
Contact: Natasha Jones (Partner).
Specialist subjects/requirements: All types of living organisms including wildlife of every description, domestic animals and fowl, botany, ecology, geology, geography, climate and effects, astronomy, pollution and effects, indigenous people and their ways of life, countryside topics and scenics, latter mostly without artifacts. Also angling, both sea and freshwater.
Markets supplied: Books, magazines, newspapers, calendars, audio-visual, television and advertising, UK and overseas. Some inter-agency deals.
Formats accepted: Digital files preferred, transparencies accepted.
Usual terms of business: No minimum submission. Standard contract allows for 3 years retention and is non-exclusive.
Commission: 50 per cent.
Additional information: All material to be clearly captioned and well documented – English and scientific names, locality and photographer; also any useful additional information.

NEWSCAST LTD*
The Coach House, 4 Cannon Hill, London N14 7HG.
Tel: 020 8886 5895. Fax: 020 8882 8334. E-mail: photo@newscast.co.uk
Web: www.newscast.co.uk
Contact: Ricky McIntosh (Media Relations Manager).
Specialist subjects/requirements: Images relevant to business and corporate activities worldwide. Portraits of business people, politicians, company buildings and company activities.
Markets supplied: Magazines, newspapers and broadcasting media worldwide.
Formats accepted: Digital files preferred, minimum 18MB JPEG.
Usual terms of business: No minimum initial submission. Minimum retention period: 2 years.
Commission: 50 per cent.
Additional information: This is an entirely Web-based syndication service. For image security the website is password-protected and all images watermarked.

NUNN SYNDICATION*
PO Box 56303, London SE1 2TD.
Tel: 020 7357 9000. Fax: 020 7231 3912. E-mail: production@nunn-syndication.com
Web: www.nunn-syndication.com
Contact: Robin Nunn (Managing Director).
Specialist subjects/requirements: All aspects of the British royal family, including state occasions, foreign tours, informal shots, etc. Also foreign royalty and general celebrities.
Markets supplied: General publishing.
Formats accepted: 35mm transparencies.
Usual terms of business: No minimum terms specified.
Commission: 40 per cent.

ONIMAGE
2 Independent Place, London E8 2HE.
Tel/fax: 020 7249 8384. E-mail: info@onimage.co.uk
Web: www.onimage.co.uk
Contact: Andre Pinkowski (Managing Director).
Specialist subjects/requirements: Contemporary and evocative imagery with a distinctive visual style and character.
Markets supplied: Advertising, design agencies, magazine publishing.
Formats accepted: Digital files preferred, shot on at least a 12.5MP camera or scans of near drum scan quality at 50MB (for 35mm). Colour negative and transparency also accepted for in-house scanning.
Usual terms of business: Minimum initial submission: 30 images. Minimum retention period: 3 years.
Commission: 50 per cent.
Additional information: Potential contributors are advised to look at the website to gain an idea of the type and style of material required.

OXFORD SCIENTIFIC (OSF) LTD*
Network House, Station Yard, Thame, Oxfordshire OX9 3UH.
Tel: 01844 262370. Fax: 01844 262380. E-mail: creative@osf.co.uk
Web: www.osf.co.uk
Contact: Gilbert Woolley (Creative Director).
Specialist subjects/requirements: High quality wildlife photography, plus the environment, botanical, science, travel, pollution and conservation, landscapes, agriculture, high-speed photography, special effects, underwater, creative plant shots, indigenous people, pets.
Markets supplied: Magazines, book publishers, advertising/design companies, merchandising etc.
Formats accepted: All formats, including 5x4in and panoramic transparencies, but digital files preferred.

Usual terms of business: Minimum initial submission 100 images. Minimum retention period: 5 years.
Commission: Negotiable.
Additional information: See website for full submission guidelines.

PA PHOTOS/EMPICS SPORT*
Pavilion House, 16 Castle Boulevard, Nottingham NG7 1FL.
Tel: 0115 844 7447. Fax: 0115 844 7448. E-mail: photographers@empics.com
Web: www.paphotos.com
Contact: Neal Simpson (Photographic Director); Simon Galloway (Sports Picture Desk Manager).
Specialist subjects/requirements: Sport; most interested in the unusual, not run-of-the-mill coverage. The agency has an electronic picture desk and wire service for extensive syndication.
Markets supplied: Newspapers, magazines, advertising agencies, governing bodies, etc.
Formats accepted: Digital, 35mm colour neg and transparency.
Usual terms of business: No minimum terms.
Commission: 50 per cent.
Additional information: Empics Sport is now a part of the PA Group. Always happy to consider any unusual, exclusive and historical sports material.

PANOS PICTURES*
1 Honduras Street, London EC1Y OTH.
Tel: 020 7253 1424. Fax: 020 7253 2752. E-mail: pics@panos.co.uk
Web: www.panos.co.uk
Contact: Adrian Evans (Director).
Specialist subjects/requirements: Documentary coverage of the Third World and Eastern Europe, focusing on social, economic and political issues and with special emphasis on environment and development. Also agriculture, education, energy, health, industry, landscape, people, religions.
Markets supplied: Newspapers and magazines, book publishers, development agencies.
Formats accepted: B&W and colour, 35mm or digital files.
Usual terms of business: No minimum initial submission or retention period.
Commission: 50 per cent.
Additional information: 50 per cent of all profits from the library are covenanted to the Panos Institute, an international development studies group.

PAPILIO
155 Station Road, Herne Bay, Kent CT6 5QA.
Tel: 01227 360996. E-mail: library@papiliophotos.com
Web: www.papiliophotos.com
Contact: Justine Pickett or Robert Pickett (Directors).
Specialist subjects/requirements: All aspects of natural history worldwide, including plants, insects, birds, mammals and marine life.
Markets supplied: Books, magazines, advertising, etc.
Formats accepted: Digital preferred (shot as RAW in camera, minimum 18MB TIFF after conversion).
Usual terms of business: Minimum initial submission: 100 images. Minimum retention period: 5 years.
Commission: 50 per cent.
Additional information: Digital files preferred, but contact first before sending digital submissions to obtain full detailed requirements.

PAUL BEARD PHOTO AGENCY
PBPA House, 33 Sanctuary Close, St John's, Worcester WR2 5PY.
Tel: 01905 749959. E-mail: postmaster@photographers-united.com
www.photographers-united.com

Contact: Paul Beard (Proprietor).
Specialist subjects/requirements: General stock images. Especially interested in model-released pictures of people, both portraits and situation pictures.
Markets supplied: Magazines, books, design groups, advertising agencies.
Formats accepted: Digital files only, minimum 18MB JPEG.
Usual terms of business: No minimum submission or specified retention period.
Commission: 50%
Additional information: The majority of sales are now made through Alamy.

PHOTOFUSION PICTURE LIBRARY*
17a Electric Lane, Brixton, London SW9 8LA.
Tel: 020 7733 3500. Fax: 020 7738 5509. E-mail: library@photofusion.org
Web: www.photofusionpictures.org
Contact: Liz Somerville (Library Manager).
Specialist subjects/requirements: All aspects of contemporary life with an emphasis on environmental and social issues. Specialist areas include children, disability, education, environment, the elderly, families, health, housing & homelessness, plus people generally.
Markets supplied: UK book and magazine publishing, newspapers, charities, annual reports, etc.
Formats accepted: Digital files preferred (minimum 30MB TIFF), transparencies and prints accepted.
Usual terms of business: Minimum initial submission: 100 images. Minimum retention period: 3 years.
Commission: 50 per cent.

PHOTOLIBRARY*
4th Floor, 83–84 Long Acre, London WC2E 9NG.
Tel: 020 7836 5591. Fax: 020 7379 4650. E-mail: creative@photolibrary.com
Web: www.photolibrary.com
Contact: Lucette Kenay (Group Creative Director).
Specialist subjects/requirements: High-end, creative imagery primarily oriented to advertising and business-to-business markets. Mainly travel, lifestyle, business, nature and sport.
Markets supplied: Advertising, design agencies, business.
Formats accepted: Digital (50MB TIFF), transparency and negative.
Usual terms of business: Minimum initial submission: Up to 50 images for initial assessment. Minimum retention period: 5 years.
Commission: 50 per cent.
Additional information: The Photolibrary Group represents a wide range of individual stock agencies and offers worldwide distribution with offices in 10 countries. Releases always required for people, animals and property. See website for full details.

PHOTOSHOT*
29-31 Saffron Hill, London EC1N 8SW.
Tel: 020 7421 6000. Fax: 020 7421 6006. E-mail: charles@uppa.co.uk
Web: www.photoshot.com
Contact: Charles Taylor (Managing Director).
Specialist subjects/requirements: Photoshot consists of seven distinct collections – UPPA (news, royalty, business, politics and the judiciary); Starstock (celebrity, entertainment and music), World Illustrated (culture, environment and heritage); Talking Sport (sport); Photoshot Creative (creative/lifestyle, both RF and RM); World Pictures (travel), NHPA (nature/wildlife; see separate listing).
Markets supplied: Newspapers, magazines, book publishers, broadcasting, advertising, etc.

Formats accepted: All formats, digital preferred.
Usual terms of business: Variable.
Commission: Usually 50 per cent.
Additional information: See website for futher details on individual collections.

PICTOREAL
26 Spring Meadow, Tipton, West Midlands DY4 7BA.
Tel: 0121 520 7881. E-mail: info@pictoreal.com
Web: www.pictoreal.com
Contact: Lee Dirden (Director).
Specialist subjects/requirements: General – objects, people and places, with an emphasis on UK-themed subject matter. For both royalty-free and rights-managed sale.
Markets supplied: General publishing, advertising, design agencies, etc.
Formats accepted: Digital.
Usual terms of business: No minimum initial submission. Minimum retention period: None stated.
Commission: 35 per cent royalty-free, 40 per cent rights-managed, depending on subject quality and quantity supplied.
Additional information: No cost to contributors for upload, transparency scanning, storage or admin fees. Contributors can choose whether to sell via royalty-free or rights-managed only. For initial submission requirements see website.

PICTUREBANK PHOTO LIBRARY LTD*
Parman House, 30–36 Fife Road, Kingston-upon-Thames, Surrey KT1 1SY.
Tel: 020 8547 2344. Fax: 020 8974 5652. E-mail info@picturebank.co.uk
Web: www.picturebank.co.uk
Contact: Martin Bagge (Managing Director).
Specialist subjects/requirements: Worldwide travel and tourism, UK cities and countryside, people (glamour, families, children, ethnic peoples), environment, animals (domestic and wild), business, industry and technology.
Markets supplied: Magazines, calendars, travel industry, advertising, etc.
Formats accepted: Digital files preferred, 50MB+.
Usual terms of business: Minimum initial submission: 100 images. Minimum retention period: 5 years.
Commission: Variable – maximum 50 per cent.

PICTURES COLOUR LIBRARY*
10 James Whatman Court, Turkey Mill, Ashford, Kent ME14 5SS.
Tel: 01622 609809. Fax: 01622 609806. E-mail: karen@picturescolourlibrary.co.uk
Web: www.picturescolourlibrary.co.uk
Contact: Karen McCunnall (Submissions Manager).
Specialist subjects/requirements: General, but with strong emphasis on travel and travel-related images.
Markets supplied: Magazines, newspapers, travel companies, advertising and design.
Formats accepted: All formats, but digital preferred (minimum file size 50MB).
Usual terms of business: Minimum initial submission: 500 images. Minimum retention period: 3 years.
Commission: 50 per cent.

POPPERFOTO.COM
Paul Popper Ltd, The Old Mill, Overstone Farm, Overstone, Northampton NN6 0AB.
Tel: 01604 670670. Fax: 01604 670635. E-mail:inquiries@popperfoto.com
Web: www.popperfoto.com
Contact: Ian Blackwell (Sales Director).

Specialist subjects/requirements: General library of 14+ million images – historical/modern archive material and stock. No longer accepting contributing photographers but interested in buying photographs outright, particularly vintage social history, family archives, or general historical collections.
Markets supplied: All media worldwide including books, newspapers, magazines, TV and advertising.
Formats accepted: All formats, B&W and colour.
Usual terms of business: Outright purchase only.
Commission: N/A.

PYMCA*
2nd Floor, St John's Building, 43 Clerkenwell Road, London EC1M 5RS.
Tel: 020 7251 8338. E-mail: info@pymca.com
Web: www.pymca.com
Contact: James Lange (Library Manager).
Specialist subjects/requirements: All images related to youth and subcultures, from the past (1940s/50s) to the present day, UK and abroad. Areas of particular interest: street fashions; lifestyle; social documentary; music/clubbing; recreational sport; related incidental imagery.
Markets supplied: General publishing, editorial, advertising, design, music industry etc.
Formats accepted: All formats, B&W and colour, digital files preferred (min 28MB TIFF).
Usual terms of business: Minimum initial submission: 20 pictures. Minimum retention period: 3 years.
Commission: 50 per cent.
Additional information: Particularly interested in model-released work, music and historical youth culture images.

RED COVER LIMITED*
Unit 7, Aura House, 53 Oldridge Road, London SW12 8PP.
Tel: 020 8772 1110. Fax: 020 8772 3113. E-mail: info@redcover.com
Web: www.redcover.com
Contact: Sally Griffiths (Managing Director).
Specialist subjects/requirements: Architecture, interiors, gardens and food.
Markets supplied: International publishing, advertising, design.
Formats accepted: Colour transparencies, all formats, and digital images.
Usual terms of business: Minimum initial submission: 20–50 images. Minimum retention period: 4 years.
Commission: 50 per cent.
Additional information: The agency markets complete features as well as single images. For initial viewing only, scanned images may be submitted on CD or via e-mail.

REDFERNS MUSIC PICTURE LIBRARY*
7 Bramley Road, London W10 6SZ.
Tel: 020 7792 9914. Fax: 020 7792 0921. E-mail: info@redferns.com
Web: www.redferns.com
Contact: Dede Millar (Partner).
Specialist subjects/requirements: All forms of popular music from the 1920s onwards, but with special concentration on the past 40 years. Also related subjects such as musical instruments, dance, stage shows.
Markets supplied: Newspapers, magazines, books, record companies, advertising and design companies.
Formats accepted: B&W and colour. Digital submissions preferred, but accept 35mm and medium format.
Usual terms of business: Negotiable.
Commission: 45 per cent.

RETNA PICTURES LTD*
Units 1a & 1b, Farm Lane Trading Estate, 101 Farm Lane, London SW6 1QJ.
Tel: 0845 034 0645. Fax: 0845 034 0646. E-mail: info@retna.co.uk
Web: www.retna.co.uk
Contact: Steve Hodgson.
Specialist subjects/requirements: Lifestyle images: men, women, couples, family life, health and beauty, leisure, babies, children, teenagers, business and food. Celebrity/music images: portraiture, studio and events photography.
Markets supplied: Newspapers, magazines, books, record companies, advertising.
Formats accepted: B&W and colour, any format but digital files preferred.
Usual terms of business: Minimum initial submission: 40–50 images. Minimum retention period: 3 years.
Commission: Negotiable, depending on material.
Additional information: Lifestyle images must be fully model-released. On-site studio available (www.retnaphotostudio.co.uk).

REX FEATURES*
18 Vine Hill, London EC1R 5DZ.
Tel: 020 7278 7294. Fax: 020 7696 0974. E-mail: photogs@rexfeatures.com
Web: www.rexfeatures.com
Contact: Mike Selby, (Editorial Director), Gretchen Viehmann (Chief Editor).
Specialist subjects/requirements: Human interest and general features, current affairs, personalities, entertainment news, animals (singles and series), humour, travel.
Markets supplied: UK national newspapers and magazines, book publishers, audio visual, television and international press. Daily worldwide syndication.
Formats accepted: B&W and colour. All formats including digital.
Usual terms of business: No minimum submission. Preferred minimum retention period: 2 years.
Commission: 50 per cent.

ROYAL GEOGRAPHICAL SOCIETY PICTURE LIBRARY*
1 Kensington Gore, London SW7 2AR.
Tel: 020 7591 3060. Fax: 020 7591 3001. E-mail: images@rgs.org
Web: www.rgs.org/images
Contact: Library Manager.
Specialist subjects/requirements: Exploration and geographical coverage, both historic and current. Travel photography from remote destinations: indigenous peoples and daily life, landscapes, environmental and geographical phenomena, agriculture, crafts, human impact on the environment.
Markets supplied: Commercial publishing and academic research.
Formats accepted: All formats. Digital files preferred; minimum 17MB digital capture, 50MB scans. Historic B&W.
Usual terms of business: Minimum initial submission: 250 pictures. Minimum retention period: At least 2 years.
Commission: 50 per cent.

SCR PHOTO LIBRARY
Society for Co-operation in Russian and Soviet Studies, 320 Brixton Road, London SW9 6AB.
Tel: 020 7274 2282. Fax: 020 7274 3230. E-mail: ruslibrary@scrss.org.uk
Web: www.scrss.org.uk
Contact: J Cunningham (Librarian).
Specialist subjects/requirements: Pictures from Russia and all Republics of the former Soviet Union. General/everyday scenes, landscapes, architecture, towns and cities, politics, arts, industry,

agriculture, science, etc.
Markets supplied: General.
Formats accepted: All formats.
Usual terms of business: No minimum submission. Minimum retention period: 2 years.
Commission: 50 per cent.

S.I.N. (SYNDICATED INTERNATIONAL NETWORK)*

89a North View Road, Crouch End, London N8 7LR.
Tel: 020 8348 8061. Fax: 020 8340 8517. E-mail: sales@sin-photo.co.uk
Web: www.sin-photo.co.uk
Contact: Marianne Lasson (Proprietor).
Specialist subjects/requirements: Rock and pop music and performers. Also youth culture from all eras, including clubbing, festivals, raves, street fashion, skateboarding, etc.
Markets supplied: Music industry and general publishing.
Formats accepted: Colour and B&W.
Usual terms of business: No minimum initial submission. Minimum retention period: 3 years.
Commission: 55 per cent to photographer.
Additional information: Material must be of a very high standard; prefers initial submissions on CD-ROM.

SCIENCE PHOTO LIBRARY*

327-329 Harrow Road, London W9 3RB.
Tel: 020 7432 1100. Fax: 020 7286 8668. E-mail: rose@sciencephoto.co.uk
Web: www.sciencephoto.com
Contact: Rosemary Taylor (Director).
Specialist subjects/requirements: All types of scientific, industrial and medical imagery, from micrography to astronomical photography. Also includes photographs of equipment, laboratories, factories and relevant personalities.
Markets supplied: Books, magazines, advertising, design, corporate, audio visual.
Formats accepted: Analogue and digital accepted (contact for details).
Usual terms of business: No minimum submission. Minimum retention period: 5 years.
Commission: 50 per cent.
Additional information: All photographs must be accompanied by full caption information, but preferably in non-technical language.

SCOOPT

Scoopt Ltd, Hillington Park Innovation Centre, 1 Ainslie Road, Glasgow G52 5RU.
Tel: 0845 888 7627. E-mail: contact@scoopt.com
Web: www.scoopt.com
Contact: Kyle MacRae (Managing Director).
Specialist subjects/requirements: Newsworthy images of all kinds – hard news, local news, celebrity sightings, etc.
Markets supplied: news media worldwide.
Formats accepted: All formats, film or digital.
Usual terms of business: No minimum initial submission. Minimum retention period: exclusive worldwide sales licence for 12 months.
Commission: 40 per cent to photographer.
Additional information: Images considered "hot" are actively marketed to the media. Less newsworthy images go into gallery section only viewable by registered media users. The agency is now owned by Getty Images.

SKISHOOT– OFFSHOOT*

Hall Place, Upper Woodcott, Whitchurch, Hants RG28 7PY.
Tel: 01635 255527. Fax: 01635 255528. E-mail: pictures@skishoot.co.uk

Web: www.skishoot.co.uk
Contact: Claire Randall (Manager).
Specialist subjects/requirements: Skishoot: skiing and snowboarding, ski resorts in Europe, Asia and North America. Offshoot: major cities and tourist areas in France. Special interest in beaches and local colour.
Markets supplied: Travel industry, general publishing, and advertising.
Formats accepted: Digital files preferred, but also 35mm and medium format transparencies.
Usual terms of business: Minimum initial submission: 50 images. No minimum retention period.
Commission: 50 per cent.

SKYSCAN PHOTOLIBRARY*
Oak House, Toddington, Cheltenham GL54 5BY.
Tel: 01242 621357. Fax: 01242 621343. E-mail: info@skyscan.co.uk
Web: www.skyscan.co.uk
Contact: Brenda Marks (Library Manager).
Specialist subjects/requirements: Anything aerial – air to ground; aircraft; general aviation; aerial sports (skydiving, ballooning, etc).
Markets supplied: Editorial, advertising, design, calendars.
Formats accepted: B&W and colour. All formats. Digital files of 28+MB (preferably 50+MB).
Usual terms of business: Minimum initial submission: 20+ images. Minimum retention period: 2 years.
Commission: 50 per cent.
Additional information: Also operates a brokerage service which is sometimes more appropriate than agency terms. Photographs are retained by the photographer; picture requests are initiated and negotiated by Skyscan and fees split 50/50.

SOLARPIX
C/Iris, Edificio Excelsior Port B, No 3, Nueva Andalucia, Marbella 29600, Malaga, Spain.
Tel :+34 952 811768. Fax: +34 952 819294. E-mail: info@solarpix.com
Web: www.solarpix.com
Contacts: Mark Beltran and Richard Atkins (Photographers and Company Directors).
Specialist subjects: Celebrity personalities from film and TV, rock and pop, politics and royalty. Also fashion, news, sport, corporate assignments and general interest features.
Markets supplied: UK daily and Sunday newspapers, celebrity gossip magazines, general magazines and foreign syndication to over 40 countries worldwide.
Formats accepted: digital only.
Usual terms of business: No minimum initial submission.
Commission: 60 per cent.

SPECTRUM COLOUR LIBRARY
18-20 St John Street, London EC1M 4NX.
Tel: 020 7251 5091. E-mail: nathan.grainger@heritage-images.co.uk
Web: www.impactphotos.com
Contact: Nathan Grainger (Research Coordinator).
Specialist subjects/requirements: Travel, people, culture, places, natural history.
Markets supplied: Advertising, magazines, newspapers, book publishing, travel brochures.
Formats accepted: Digital files preferred, at 50MB.
Usual terms of business: No minimum submission. Minimum retention period: 5 years.
Commission: By negotiation.
Additional information: The library is managed by Heritage Image Partnership and stock is displayed through the Impact Photos website.

STILL MOVING PICTURE COMPANY
1c Castlehill, Doune FK16 6BU.
Tel: 01786 842790. E-mail: info@stillmovingpictures.com
Web: www.stilldigital.co.uk
Contact: John Hutchinson (Director).
Specialist subjects/requirements: All Scottish subjects; scenics, travel, commerce, industry, wildlife, sport and culture.
Markets supplied: Publishing, advertising, tourism, etc.
Formats accepted: Digital files only.
Usual terms of business: No minimum initial submission or retention period.
Commission: 50 per cent.
Additional information: Now operating entirely digital service through www.stilldigital.co.uk.

STOCKFOOD LTD*
88 Kingsway, London WC2B 6AA.
Tel: +49 89 747 202 22 (Munich); 020 7841 1063 (UK sales). E-mail: photographer@stockfood.com
Web: www.stockfood.com
Contact: Petra Thierry, Julia Sander (Photographers & Art Department, Munich).
Specialist subjects/requirements: All types of food and drink imagery, including people eating and drinking and other food-related lifestyle pictures.
Markets supplied: Advertising, design, magazine and book publishing, etc.
Formats accepted: Digital and colour transparency.
Usual terms of business: Minimum initial submission: 100 images. Minimum retention period: 5 years (exclusive representation required).
Commission: Commission to photographer 40% per cent for rights-managed, 30 per cent royalty-free.
Additional information: With its head office in Munich, Germany, the agency has representation in 60 countries and is the largest source of food-related imagery in the world. All initial photographer contact should be made via the website. UK address is sales office only.

STOCKSCOTLAND.COM*
Croft Studio, Croft Roy, Crammond Brae, Tain IV19 1JG.
Tel/fax: 01862 892298. E-mail: info@stockscotland.com
Web: www.stockscotland.com
Contact: Hugh Webster (Library Manager).
Specialist subjects/requirements: All aspects of Scotland and Scottish life – landscapes, castles, Highland games, natural history, industry, whisky, people, lifestyles, etc.
Markets supplied: General publishing, advertising, travel industry.
Formats accepted: B&W and colour, all formats. High-res scans (30Mb+).
Usual terms of business: No minimum initial submission. Minimum retention period: 3 years.
Commission: 50 per cent.
Additional information: Images should be edited rigorously before submission. Do not send lots of very similar images. For more submission details see website.

STOCKSHOT
2b St Vincent Street, Edinburgh EH3 6SH.
Tel: 0131 557 6688. Fax: 0131 556 8282. E-mail: info@stockshot.co.uk
Web: www.stockshot.co.uk
Contact: Bridget Clyde (Library Manager).
Specialist subjects/requirements: Skiing and other winter sports; adventure sports; adventure travel.

Markets supplied: Publishers, newspapers, advertising, tour operators and travel companies.
Formats accepted: 35mm transparencies.
Usual terms of business: No minimum terms.
Commission: 50 per cent.
Additional information: Seek quality rather than quantity, with dynamic, unusual angles etc.
Only limited scope for new contributors.

TRH PICTURES/CODY IMAGES*
2 Reform Street, Beith KA15 2AE.
Tel: 0845 2235451. Fax: 0845 2235452. E-mail: tn@trhpictures.co.uk
Web: www.codyimages.com
Contact: Ted Nevill (Director).
Specialist subjects/requirements: All aspects of aviation, defence, transport (shipping, railways,
road) and space exploration – worldwide, historical and modern.
Markets supplied: Books, magazines, newspapers, multi-media, etc.
Formats accepted: B&W and colour, all formats, digital files preferred.
Usual terms of business: Minimum initial submission: 200 images. Minimum retention period:
3 years.
Commission: 50 per cent.
Additional information: Ring first to discuss submission and agency requirements.

THEIMAGEFILE.COM
PO Box 241, Chertsey, Surrey KT16 0YZ.
Tel: 0870 224 2454. Fax: 0870 224 2455. E-mail: membership@theimagefile.com
Web: www.theimagefile.com
Contact: James Duncan (Director).
Specialist subjects/requirements: All major commercial subjects.
Markets supplied: Advertising, design agencies, general publishing.
Formats accepted: Digital only.
Usual terms of business: No minimum initial submission or retention period.
Commission: 75 per cent to photographer, but because of the personalised facilities offered (se
below) there is a monthly subscription charge of £25 (discount to BFP members: 20%).
Additional information: Contributing photographers have their own account through which they
set their own prices for images sold. They are able to deal direct with purchasers if they wish and
also obtain commissions. Other facilities include direct uploading of images and real time payment
tracking.

TOPFOTO*
PO Box 33, Edenbridge, Kent TN8 5PF.
Tel: 01732 863939. Fax: 01732 860215. E-mail: admin@topfoto.co.uk
Web: www.topfoto.co.uk
Contact: John Balean (Stock Manager).
Specialist subjects/requirements: Industry and social issues.
Markets supplied: Editorial markets.
Formats accepted: Digital only, 300dpi at A4, IPTC captioned.
Usual terms of business: Minimum initial submission: 1000 images. Minimum retention period: 3
years.
Commission: 50 per cent.

TRAVEL INK*
The Old Coach House, 14 High Street, Goring-on-Thames, Berkshire RG8 9AR.
Tel: 01491 873011. Fax: 01491 875558. E-mail: info@travel-ink.co.uk
Web: www.travel-ink.co.uk
Contact: Frances Honnor (Library Manager), Felicity Bazell (Picture Researcher).

Specialist subjects/requirements: All aspects of travel and tourism, from destinations to forms of transport, food, things to buy, famous sights, hotel shots to native lifestyles. All countries including the UK. Particularly interested in travel lifestyle images.
Markets supplied: Travel industry, magazines, books, newspapers, advertising etc.
Formats accepted: All formats including digital (minimum 18MB).
Usual terms of business: Minimum initial submission: 200 images. Minimum retention period: 3 years.
Commission: 40 per cent to photographer.
Additional information: If submitting digital send initial sample of 10 images on CD.

THE TRAVEL LIBRARY*
Unit 7, The Kiln Workshops, Pilcot Road, Crookham Village, Fleet, Hants GU51 5RY.
Tel: 01252 627233. Fax: 01252 812399. E-mail: info@travel-library.co.uk
Web: www.travel-library.co.uk
Contact: Chris Penn (Image Production Manager).
Specialist subjects/requirements: Top quality tourist travel material covering destinations worldwide.
Markets supplied: UK tour operators and travel industry, advertising, design and corporate.
Formats accepted: Digital preferred, RAW files saved and submitted as TIFF (minimum 24MB). Transparencies only accepted in exceptional circumstances.
Usual terms of business: Minimum initial submission: 100 images. Minimum retention period: 5 years.
Commission: 50 per cent.

TREVILLION IMAGES
75 Jeddo Road, London W12 9ED.
Tel: 020 8740 9005. E-mail: info@trevillion.com
Web: www.trevillion.com
Contact: Michael Trevillion (Creative Director).
Specialist subjects/requirements: All subject matter, but style must be "atmospheric, fine-art style", both classic and contemporary. See existing work on website for guidance.
Markets supplied: Editorial, newspapers, advertising, design, posters, etc
Formats accepted: Colour and B&W print, digital (minimum 25MB files).
Usual terms of business: No minimum initial submission. Minimum retention period: 3 years. Commission rate: 50 per cent.
Additional information: See website for full submission guidelines.

VIEW PICTURES LTD*
14 The Dove Centre, 109 Bartholomew Road, London NW5 2BJ.
Tel: 020 7284 2928. Fax: 020 7284 3617. E-mail: dg@dennisgilbert.com/kate@viewpictures.co.uk
Web:.www.viewpictures.co.uk
Contact: Dennis Gilbert (Director), Kate Ledwith (Picture Researcher).
Specialist subjects/requirements: Top quality images of modern architecture and interior design, with the emphasis on recently-completed projects by leading architects. Classic modern buildings and historic structures also represented.
Markets supplied: Book and magazine publishers, advertising agencies, graphic designers.
Formats accepted: Digital and medium/large format colour transparency.
Usual terms of business: Minimum initial submission: None stated. Minimum retention period: Negotiable.
Commission: 50 per cent.
Additional information: Seeks only top quality work from experienced architectural photographers. Commissions may also be available.

ELIZABETH WHITING & ASSOCIATES*
70 Mornington Street, London NW1 7QE.
Tel: 020 7388 2828. Fax: 020 7388 7587. E-mail: ewa@elizabethwhiting.com
Web: www.ewastock.com
Contact: Liz Whiting (Director).
Specialist subjects/requirements: Home interest topics – architecture, interiors, design, DIY, crafts, gardens, food. Some travel and scenic material.
Markets supplied: Book and magazine publishers, advertising, design companies.
Formats accepted: Digital files preferred (minimum 50 MB); colour transparencies accepted.
Usual terms of business: No minimum initial submission, but a contract is only entered into if both parties envisage a long-term commitment. Minimum retention period: 1 year.
Commission: 50 per cent.

WORLD PICTURE NETWORK
62 White Street, 3rd Floor, New York 10013, USA.
Tel: +1 212 871 1215. Fax: +1 212 925 4569. E-mail: info@worldpicturenews.com
Web: www.worldpicturenews.com
Contact: Annika Engvall (Senior Editor).
Specialist subjects/requirements: International news and photojournalism for on-line supply.
Markets supplied: National and international magazines, newspapers, broadcasting organisations.
Formats accepted: Digital.
Usual terms of business: No minimum terms.
Commission: 50 per cent.
Additional information: Originally established in London, HQ is now in New York. Business is conducted entirely on-line and photographers must first register on the website. Contributors must be familiar with scanning procedures, able to process images quickly and have the facility to up-load on-line. For further information see website.

WORLD PICTURES*
29-31 Saffron Hill, London EC1N 8SW.
Tel: 020 7421 6004. Fax: 020 7421 6006. E-mail: mail@worldpictures.co.uk
Web: www.worldpictures.co.uk
Contact: David Brenes (Director).
Specialist subjects/requirements: Travel material: cities, resorts, hotels worldwide plus girls, couples and families on holiday suitable for travel brochure, magazine and newspaper use.
Markets supplied: Tour operators, airlines, design houses, advertising agencies.
Formats accepted: Digital files, 50MB.
Usual terms of business: No minimum submission but usually like the chance of placing material for minimum period of 2 years.
Commission: 50 per cent.

WORLD RELIGIONS PHOTO LIBRARY*
54 Putney Park Lane, London SW15 4HQ.
Tel/fax: 020 7720 6951. E-mail: copix@clara.co.uk
Web: www.worldreligions.co.uk/www.copix.co.uk
Contact: Christine Osborne (Proprietor).
Specialist subjects/requirements: World religions and beliefs, rites of passage, sacred sites, places of worship and pilgrimage, people practising their chosen belief. Travel and lifestyle images from specialist regions: Middle East and Gulf States, developing countries of Africa, South, South East and Central Asia.
Markets supplied: educational publishers, magazines, newspapers travel industry

and internet.
Formats accepted: Digital files with file information inserted.
Usual terms of business: Minimum initial submission: 40 JPEG images on CD for assessment, followed by ability to deposit 300 suitable images. Minimum retention period: 3 years.
Commission: 50 per cent.
Additional information: Images with inadequate caption information will not be considered.

WRITER PICTURES LTD*
90 Temple Park Crescent, Edinburgh EH11 1HZ.
Tel: 020 8241 0039. E-mail: info@writerpictures.com
Web: www. writerpictures.com
Contact: Alex Hewitt (Partner).
Specialist subjects/requirements: Photographs of authors and writers, mainly editorial-style portraiture.
Markets supplied: Publishing industry, news media.
Formats accepted: Digital preferred, minimum 25MB, but transparencies/negs always considered.
Usual terms of business: No minimum initial submission. Minimum retention period: 1 year.
Commission: 50 per cent.
Additional information: Commissions to photograph individual writers may also be available.

SERVICES

This section lists companies providing products and services of use to the photographer. A number of those listed offer discounts to BFP members. To obtain the discounts indicated, members should simply produce their current membership card. In the case of mail order transactions, enclose your membership card with your order, requesting that this be returned with the completed order or as soon as membership has been verified. But in all cases, ensure that your membership card is valid: the discount will not be available to those who present an expired card.

Courses & Training

THE BFP SCHOOL OF PHOTOGRAPHY
Focus House, 497 Green Lanes, London N13 4BP.
Tel: 020 8882 3315. Fax: 020 8886 3933. E-mail: course@thebfp.com
Web: www.thebfp.com
Offers a two-year correspondence course in freelance photography and photojournalism. May be undertaken by either post or e-mail.
Discount to BFP members: On application.

NATIONAL COUNCIL FOR THE TRAINING OF JOURNALISTS (NCTJ)
The New Granary, Station Road, Newport, Saffron Walden, Essex CB11 3PL.
Tel: 01799 544014. Fax: 01799 544015. E-mail: info@nctj.com
Web: www.nctj.com
Official training body for the journalism industry. Offers basic journalism training through its accredited colleges/universities and by distance learning. Short mid-term courses are available in various disciplines for journalists wishing to progress their career.

TRAVELLERS' TALES
92 Hillfield Road, London NW6 1QA.
E-mail: info@travellerstales.org
Web: www.travellerstales.org
Training agency dedicated to travel photography and writing, offering masterclasses in London and overseas. Tutors are top travel photographers, editors and writers. Courses suitable for beginners and semi-professionals. Course details and booking via website.

Equipment Hire

ANGLIA CAMERAS
15-15a St Matthew's Street, Ipswich IP1 3EL.
Tel/fax: 01473 258185. E-mail: info@angliacameras.fsnet.co.uk
Web: www.anglia-cameras.co.uk
Hire of AV equipment, overhead projectors, screens, etc.

CALUMET PHOTOGRAPHIC
Promandis House, Bradbourne Drive, Tilbrook, Milton Keynes MK7 8AJ.
Tel: 08706 030303. Fax: 01908 366322.
Web: www.calumetphoto.co.uk
Branches: London, Aberdeen, Belfast, Birmingham, Bristol, Edinburgh, Glasgow, Liverpool, Manchester and Nottingham.
Comprehensive equipment hire service featuring cameras, lenses, lighting, tripods, backgrounds, digital & AV equipment & accessories.
Discount to BFP members: 15%

EDRIC AUDIO VISUAL LTD
Oak End Way, Gerrards Cross, Bucks SL9 8BR.
Tel: 01753 481400. Fax: 01753 887163.
Web: www.edric-av.co.uk
Also at Manchester: 0161 773 7711; Bristol: 01454 201313; Birmingham: 0121 359 4666.
Hire and sale of AV equipment, film production and video production equipment.

FILM PLUS
Unit 5, Westway Centre, St Marks Road, London W10 6JG.
Tel/fax: 020 8969 0234. E-mail: neil@filmplus.com
Web: www.filmplus.com
Professional rental and sales. Digital, lighting and camera equipment hire. Film and hardware sales. Also studio hire.
Discount to BFP members: 10%

THE FLASH CENTRE
68 Brunswick Centre, Bernard Street, London WC1N 1AE.
Tel: 020 7837 6163. Fax: 020 7833 4882. E-mail: hire@theflashcentre.co.uk
2 Mount Street Business Centre, Birmingham B7 5RD.
Tel/fax: 0121 327 9220.
2nd Floor, Mill 1, Mabgate Mills, Mabgate, Leeds LS9 7DZ.
Tel: 0113 247 0937. Fax: 0113 247 0038.
Web: www.theflashcentre.com
Hire of electronic flash and digital photographic equipment.

Equipment Repair

BOURNEMOUTH PHOTOGRAPHIC (REPAIR) SERVICES LTD
251 Holdenhurst Road, Bournemouth, Dorset BH8 8DA.
Tel: 01202 301273. Fax: 01202 301273
Professional repairs to all makes of equipment. Full test facilities including modern electronic diagnostic test equipment.
Discount to BFP members: 5% off labour charges (cash sales).

CAM SERV
9 Talbot Street, Leek, Staffordshire ST13 5JT.
Tel: 01538 387481. E-mail: camservltd@btconnect.com
Repairs to all makes of cameras, camcorders, flash units, etc.
Discount to BFP members: 20%.

THE CAMERA REPAIR CENTRE
47 London Road, Southborough,Tunbridge Wells, Kent TN4 0PB.
Tel: 01892 619136. Fax: 01892 540362.
Web: www.camerarepaircentre.co.uk
Repairs to all makes of photographic equipment, including camcorders and digital.

CENTRAL CAMERAS
35 Bentley New Drive, Reedswood, West Midlands WS2 8SB.
Tel: 01922 626919/0783 7465556.
General photographic repairs (not AV). Specialist in 35mm cameras, lenses and medium format
equipment.
Discount to BFP members: 10% of labour costs.

COUSINS & WRIGHT
5 The Halve, Trowbridge, Wiltshire BA14 8SB.
Tel: 01225 754242.
Camera and photographic equipment servicing and repair.

THE FLASH CENTRE
68 Brunswick Centre, Bernard Street, London WC1N 1AE.
Tel: 020 7883 4737. Fax: 020 7833 4882. E-mail: service@theflashcentre.co.uk
2 Mount Street Business Centre, Birmingham B7 5RD.
Tel/fax: 0121 327 9220.
2nd Floor, Mill 1, Mabgate Mills, Mabgate, Leeds LS9 7DZ.
Tel: 0113 247 0937. Fax: 0113 247 0038.
Web: www.theflashcentre.com
Specialists in electronic flash service and repair.

A J JOHNSTONE & CO LTD
395 Central Chambers, 93 Hope Street, Glasgow G2 6LD.
Tel: 0141 221 2106. Fax: 0141 221 9166. E-mail: ajjohnstone@btconnect.com
Web: www.ajjohnstone.co.uk
All equipment repairs, including AV equipment. Authorised service centre for Canon, Olympus and
Nikon. Canon and Nikon warranty repairs.
Discount to BFP members: 10%.

T J KENYON LTD
Unit 1, Bowmans Trading Estate, Bessemer Drive, Stevenage, Herts SG1 2DL.
Tel: 01438 313411. Fax: 01438 7438 743551. E-mail: tjkrepairs@aol.com
Comprehensive, nationwide photographic repairs and servicing, including large, medium and 35mm
cameras, lenses, digital cameras, scanners, camcorders and computer equipment.

SENDEAN
9-12 St Anne's Court, London W1F 0BB.
Tel: 020 7439 8418. E-mail: mail@sendeancameras.com
General repair service. Estimates free.
Discount to BFP members: 10%.

Insurance

AUA INSURANCE
De Vere House, 90 St Faiths Lane, Norwich NR1 1NL.
Tel: 01603 623227. Fax: 01603 665516. E-mail: sales@aua-insurance.com
Web: www.aua-insurance.com
Insurance for professional, semi-professional and freelance photographers. Comprehensive package policies covering equipment, liabilities, loss of income, professional negligence, etc.
Discount to BFP members: 10%.

ENTERTAINMENT & LEISURE INSURANCE SERVICES LTD
PO Box 100, Ouseburn, York YO26 9SZ. E-mail: info@eandl.co.uk
Tel: 0870 4022 710. Fax: 0870 4022 600.
Web: www.eandl.co.uk
Specialist photographic insurance scheme covering private, domestic or commercial photo equipment. 5% online discount.

GLOVER & HOWE LTD
12 Chapel Street North, Colchester, Essex CO2 7AT.
Tel: 01206 814502. Fax: 01206 814501. E-mail: info@gloverhowe.co.uk
Web: www.gloverhowe.co.uk
Insurance for photographic equipment and associated risks, for the amateur, semi-pro or professional.
Discount to BFP members: 10%.

GOLDEN VALLEY INSURANCE
The Olde Shoppe, Ewyas Harold, Herefordshire HR2 0ES.
Tel: 01981 240536. Fax: 01981 240451. E-mail: gvinsurance@aol.com
Web: www.photographicinsurance.co.uk
Comprehensive insurance cover for all photographic, video and sound recording equipment, binoculars and telescopes, computers, home office/studio, all accessories etc.
Discount to BFP members: 10%.

MARTIN HALE BRISTOL LTD
Aztec Centre, Aztec West, Almondsbury, Bristol BS32 4TD.
Tel: 01454 203610. Fax: 01454 203611. E-mail: info@martinhalebristol.co.uk
Web: www.martinhalebristol.co.uk
Comprehensive insurance cover for professional photographers in one flexible package.
Discount to BFP members: 5%.

INDEMNITYGUARD
Pavilion Insurance Management Ltd, Pavilion House, Mercia Business Village, Coventry CV4 8HX.
Tel: 02476 851000. Fax: 02476 851080. E-mail: sales@indemnityguard.co.uk
Web: www.indemnityguard.co.uk/bfp
Professional indemnity insurance for photographers and videographers, offering a range of cover levels. Instant quotes, cover, renewals and changes available online.
Discount to BFP members: 10%.

Are you working from the latest edition of The Freelance Photographer's Market Handbook? It's published on 1 October each year. Markets are constantly changing, so it pays to have the latest edition

---

MORGAN RICHARDSON LTD
Freepost CL4071, Westgate Court, Western Road, Billericay, Essex CM12 9ZZ.
Tel: Freecall 0800 731 2940.
Specialist "Policy Portfolio" and "Photographers' Economy" insurance for photographers. Tailored packages. Professional indemnity automatically insured up to £50,000.
Discount to BFP members: 10%

PHOTOGUARD
Pavilion Insurance Management Ltd, Pavilion House, Mercia Business Village, Coventry CV4 8HX.
Tel: 02476 851000. Fax: 02476 851080. E-mail: sales@photoguard.co.uk
Web: www.photoguard.co.uk/bfp
Specialist insurance cover for photographers and their equipment, offering a range of flexible options. Instant quotes, cover, renewals and changes available online.
Discount to BFP members: 10%.

TOWERGATE CAMERASURE
Funtley Court, Funtley Hill, Fareham, Hampshire PO16 7UY.
Tel: 0870 4115511. Fax: 0870 4115515. E-mail: camerasure@towergate.co.uk
Web: www.towergatecamerasure.co.uk
Range of specialist insurances for amateur, semi-professional and professional photographers, including comprehensive cover for equipment, studios, work in progress and legal liabilities (public, products and employer's).
Discount to BFP members: Up to 40%, subject to minimum premium requirements.

WEALD INSURANCE BROKERS LTD
Falcon House, Black Eagle Square, Westerham, Kent TN16 1SE.
Tel: 01959 565678; freephone 0800 074 7016. Fax: 01959 569988.
Web: www.weald-insurance.co.uk
Comprehensive specialist insurance policies for professional and semi-pro photographers.
Discount to BFP members: 15% (subject to no claims).

Postcard Printers

ABACUS (COLOUR PRINTERS) LTD
Lowick House, Lowick, Near Ulverston, Cumbria LA12 8DX.
Tel: 01229 885361/885381. Fax: 01229 885348. E-mail: sales@abacusprinters.co.uk
Web: www.abacusprinters.co.uk
Quality printers specialising in colour postcards & greetings cards. Minimum quantity 500.

BUTTERFLY CARDS
25 Princes Road, Teddington, Middlesex TW11 0RL.
Tel/fax: 020 8943 1496. E-mail: info@butterflycards.co.uk
Web: www.butterflycards.co.uk
Design, artwork and printing of publicity cards, postcards, greetings cards.
Discount to BFP members: 5%.

JUDGES POSTCARDS LTD
176 Bexhill Road, St Leonards on Sea, East Sussex TN38 8BN.
Tel: 01424 420919. Fax: 01424 438538.
Web: www.judges.co.uk
Printers of postcards, greetings cards and calendars. Minimum quantity: 100.
Discount to BFP members: 10%.

THE POSTCARD COMPANY
51 Gortin Road, Omagh BT79 7HZ.
Tel: 028 8224 9222. Fax: 028 8224 9886. E-mail: sales@thepostcardcompany.com
Web: www.thepostcardcompany.com
Printers of postcards, greetings cards and product cards. No minimum quantity.

THE SHERWOOD PRESS (NOTTINGHAM) LTD
Hadden Court, Glaisdale Parkway, Glaisdale Drive West, Nottingham NG8 4GP.
Tel: 0115 928 7766. Fax: 0115 928 0271. E-mail: sales@sherwood-press.co.uk
Web: www.sherwood-press.co.uk
Quality printers specialising in the production of greetings cards, fine art prints, postcards and calendars.

THOUGHT FACTORY
Group House, 40 Waterside Road, Hamilton Industrial Park, Leicester LE5 1TL.
Tel: 0116 276 5302. Fax: 0116 246 0506. E-mail: sales@thoughtfactory.co.uk
Web: www.thoughtfactory.co.uk
Minimum quantity: 250. Price: £54 + VAT.
Discount to BFP members: 10%.

Processing & Finishing

ACTPIX LTD
Units 3 & 4, East Street Enterprise Park, Rhayader, Powys LD6 5ER.
Tel: 01597 810003. Fax: 01597 811265. E-mail: info@actpix.com
Web: www.actpix.com
Full digital services include drum scanning, retouching, RAW file conversion, FTP, file storage and inkjet printing.
Discount to BFP members: 5% on orders over £150.

ANDREWS IMAGING
Leacon Road, Ashford, Kent TN23 4FB.
Tel: 01233 620764. Fax: 01233 645618. E-mail: info@andrewsimaging.co.uk
Web: www.andrewsimaging.co.uk
Comprehensive range of film and digital processing, scanning and printing services.

ANGEL PRINTS
29 Upper Street, Islington, London N1 0PN.
Tel: 020 7359 9210. E-mail: sales@angelprints.co.uk
Web: www.angelprints.co.uk
Digital imaging specialists. Processing and printing of C41 and B&W, plus full-range printing from memory cards, CD, Zip or floppy. Also image editing and transfers to cards, T-shirts, mugs, etc.

AVONCOLOUR IMAGING
131 Duckmoor Road, Ashton Gate, Bristol BS3 2BJ.
Tel: 01179 633456. Fax: 01179 635186. E-mail: info@avoncolour.co.uk
Web: www.avoncolour.co.uk
Full service imaging centre. E6, C41, mounting, laminating, machine and hand printing in colour and B&W, digital printing.
Discount to BFP members: Up to 10%. Tel: Ron Munn.

BLUE MOON DIGITAL LTD
Davina House, 5th Floor, 137-149 Goswell Road, London EC1V 7ET.
Tel: 020 7253 9993/4. Fax: 020 7253 9995. E-mail: info@bluemoondigital.com
Web: www.bluemoondigital.com
Full B&W, colour and digital imaging service including printing, processing and duplicating. Other services include mounting, CD/DVD burning and website design.

BLUESKYIMAGES LTD
The Old Chapel, Barnes Green, Brinkworth, Wiltshire SN15 5AH.
Tel: 01666 510251. E-mail: info@blueskyimages.co.uk
Web: www.blueskyimages.co.uk
Top-quality film scanning from 35mm up to 5x4in. Also printing services, from film or digital.

CC IMAGING
7 Scala Court, Leathley Road, Leeds LS10 1JD.
Tel: 0113 244 8329. Fax: 0113 244 0115. E-mail: info@ccimaging.co.uk
Web: www.ccimaging.co.uk
Comprehensive colour and B&W processing and printing services. E6 specialists. Specialist digital photographic print service. Full mounting and finishing services. Digital scanning, retouching and printing.
Discount to BFP members: 15%.

CPL GRAPHICS & DISPLAY
Head Office: 14 Vale Rise, Tonbridge, Kent TN9 1TB.
Tel: 0870 787 0045. Fax: 01732 366863. E-mail: info@cpl-graphics.com
Web: www.cpl-graphics.com
Specialist printer services aimed solely at photographers. Professional and personal service where the photographer can talk directly to the person printing their work.
Discount to BFP members: 10% on orders over £100.

COLCHESTER COLOUR IMAGING
7 Brunel Court, Severalls Park, Colchester, Essex CO4 9XW.
Tel: 01206 751241. Fax: 01206 855134.
Web: www.colchester-colour.co.uk
Colour and B&W processing, electronic imaging.
Discount to BFP members: 5%.

DUNNS IMAGING GROUP PLC
Chester Road, Cradley Heath, West Midlands B64 6AA.
Tel: 01384 564770. Fax: 01384 637165. E-mail: enquiries@dunns.co.uk
Web: www.dunns.co.uk
Comprehensive colour and B&W processing, digital photographic printing, scanning and image management services. Also schools and package printing.

GENESIS IMAGING
The Depot, 2 Michael Road, Fulham, London SW6 2AD.
Tel: 020 7731 2227. Fax: 020 7731 8778. E-mail: info@genesis-digital.net
Web: www.genesis-digital.net
E6, C41, B&W processing, colour and B&W hand prints and print runs, dupes, pro digital mini-lab and X-pan services, digital image retouching, digital film writing, large format (Lambda) printing, on-line ePrints and prints from digital media cards, RAW camera file conversion, CMYK file conversion and proof print, drum and flatbed scanning, mounting and laminating.
Discount to BFP members: 10%.

HMD GROUP PLC
Olympia House, 4 Garnett Close, Watford, WD24 7JY.
Tel: 01923 237012. Fax: 01923 817421. E-mail: fran@hmdgroup.com
Web: www.hmdgroup.com
Comprehensive colour and B&W processing services, digital printing.
Discount to BFP members: 15%.

HOME COUNTIES COLOUR SERVICES LTD
Suite 1, Ground Floor, Chaucer House, Biscot Road, Luton LU3 1AX.
Tel: 01582 731899. Fax: 01582 402410. E-mail: sales@hccs.co.uk
Web: www.hccs.co.uk
Photographic processing services for photographers, including digital.
Discount to BFP members: On volume work only; open to negotiation.

KAY MOUNTING SERVICE
4c, Athelstane Mews, London N4 3EH.
Tel: 020 7272 7799. Fax: 020 7272 9888. E-mail: kay.mounting@lineone.net
Mounting, canvas-bonding and heat-sealing. Specialists in Diasec bonding behind acrylic, mounting to aluminium, canvas, Foamex, etc.
Discount to BFP members: 10%

ONE VISION IMAGING LTD
Herald Way, Binley, Coventry CV3 2NY.
Tel: 0845 862 0217. Fax: 024 76 444219. E-mail: info@onevisionimaging.com
Web: www.onevisionimaging.com
Comprehensive colour processing and digital imaging services.

PEAK IMAGING
Unit 6, Flockton Park, Holbrook Avenue, Halfway, Sheffield S20 3PP.
Tel: 0870 126 6100. Fax: 0114 224 3205. E-mail: info@peak-imaging.com
Web: www.peak-imaging.com
Mail order pro-am photographic and digital imaging centre.
Discount to BFP members: 10% on pro lab services.

PINEWOOD PHOTOGRAPHIC CENTRE
Stills Road, Pinewood Studios, Pinewood Road, Iver Heath, Buckinghamshire SL0 0NH.
Tel: 01753 656229. E-mail: vicky.joy@pinewoodgroup.com
Web: www.pinewoodphoto.com
Professional photo lab with full range of conventional and digital services. B&W, colour, printing, scanning and processing. Services include physical and on-line storage and free daily collection to and from London.
Discount to BFP members: 20%.

PRIMARY COLOUR
The Depot, 2 Michael Road, Fulham, London SW6 2AD.
Tel: 020 7731 2227. Fax: 020 7731 8778. E-mail: sales@primary-colour.com
Web: www.primary-colour.com
E6, C41, B&W processing, colour and B&W hand prints and print runs, dupes, pro digital mini-lab and X-pan services, digital film writing, large format (Lambda) printing, fine art archival inkjet printing, prints from digital media cards, drum and flatbed scanning, mounting and laminating.
Discount to BFP Members: 10%.

PROFOLAB IMAGING LTD
Unit 4, Surrey Close, Granby Industrial Estate, Weymouth, Dorset DT4 9TY.
Tel: 01305 774098. Fax: 01305 778746. E-mail: info@profolab.co.uk
Web: www.profolab.co.uk
E6, C41 processing and printing up to 30x40in and digital services.

QUICK IMAGING PHOTOSTICKERS
12 Alston Road, Solihull B91 2RQ.
Tel/fax: 0121 703 3123. E-mail: photostickers@btconnect.com
Web: www.quickimagingphotostickers.50megs.com
Full range of professional laboratory services, plus photoleaflets and photostickers.
Discount to BFP members: 10% against cwo.

RUSSELL PHOTO IMAGING
17 Elm Grove, Wimbledon, London SE19 4HE. E-mail: dave@russellsphoto.co.uk
Tel: 020 8947 6177. Fax: 020 8944 2064.
Web: www.russellsphoto.co.uk
Comprehensive colour processing services; 2-hour E6 processing, C41, dupes, copy trans, copy negs, machine and hand line printing, exhibition printing and mounting service. Digital services; scanning, digital printing. Traditional B&W services.
Discount to BFP members: 5%.

SCL
16 Bull Lane, Edmonton, London N18 1SX.
Tel: 020 8807 0725. Fax: 020 8807 2539. E-mail: davids@sclimage.net
Web: www.sclimage.net
Comprehensive colour and B&W processing plus full range of digital output services.

THE VAULT IMAGING LTD
1 Dorset Place, Brighton BN2 1ST.
Tel: 01273 670667. Fax: 01273 688733. E-mail: info@thevaultimaging.co.uk
Web: www.thevaultimaging.co.uk
Comprehensive professional processing, scanning and printing services. Specialists in large format printing on a selection of premium papers and canvas, giclee and photo art archival prints.

Specialised Equipment & Materials

CALUMET PHOTOGRAPHIC
Promandis House, Bradbourne Drive, Tilbrook, Milton Keynes MK7 8AJ.
Tel: 08706 030303. Fax: 01908 366322.
Web: www.calumetphoto.co.uk
Branches: London, Aberdeen, Belfast, Birmingham, Bristol, Edinburgh, Glasgow, Liverpool, Manchester and Nottingham.
Professional photographic equipment for studio and location work. Complete range of standard and specialist films, papers and chemicals.

COLORAMA PHOTODISPLAY LTD
Ace Business Park, Mackadown Lane, Kitts Green, Birmingham B33 0LD.
Tel: 0121 783 9931. Fax: 0121 783 1674. E-mail: info@coloramaphotodisplay.co.uk
Web: www.coloramaphotodisplay.co.uk
Suppliers of Colorama background paper and background support products including Colorama Background Paper, Colorswirl, Rainbow, Colormatt, Colorgloss, Cove-lock infinity coving systems.

THE FLASH CENTRE
68 Brunswick Centre, Bernard Street, London WC1N 1AE.
Tel: 020 7837 5649. Fax: 020 7833 4882. E-mail: sales@theflashcentre.co.uk
2 Mount Street Business Centre, Birmingham B7 5RD.
Tel/fax: 0121 327 9220.
2nd Floor, Mill 1, Mabgate Mills, Mabgate, Leeds LS9 7DZ.
Tel: 0113 247 0937. Fax: 0113 247 0038.
Web: www.theflashcentre.com
Specialist suppliers of electronic flash systems, SLR and medium format digital cameras, and associated colour management and image output services.

JESSOPS
Head Office: Jessop House, 98 Scudamore Road, Leicester LE3 1TZ.
Tel: 0116 232 0033. Fax: 0116 232 0060.
Web: www.jessops.com
Specialist suppliers of all photographic and digital imaging equipment including Portaflash portable studio flash, a full range of darkroom equipment and accessories.

KENRO LTD
Greenbridge Road, Swindon, Wilts SN3 3LH.
Tel: 01793 615836. Fax: 01793 513561. E-mail: sales@kenro.co.uk
Web: www.kenro.co.uk
Wide variety of accessories including camera bags, batteries and chargers, Marumi filters, digital camera converter lenses, flash and lighting kit, background supports, reflector kits, lightboxes and viewers, memory cards.

KENTMERE PHOTOGRAPHIC LTD
Staveley, Kendal, Cumbria LA8 9PB.
Tel: 01539 821365. Fax: 01539 821399. E-mail: sales@kentmere.co.uk
Web: www.kentmere.co.uk
Manufacturers of the Kentmere range of B&W photographic papers. Comprehensive range of large and small format photobase ink jet media. Specialist films for roll-up, pop-up and backlit display applications.
Discount to BFP members: 25%.

S.W. KENYON
PO Box 71, Cranbrook, Kent TN18 5ZR.
Tel: 01580 850770. Fax: 01580 850225. E-mail: swkenyon@btinternet.com
Web: www.swkenyon.com
K-Line dulling sprays for reducing glare on objects to be photographed.

OCEAN OPTICS
7 Bush House Arcade, Aldwych, London WC2B 4PA.
Tel: 020 7240 8193. Fax: 020 7240 7938. E-mail: optics@oceanoptics.co.uk
Web: www.oceanoptics.co.uk
Specialist suppliers of underwater photography equipment.

SILVERPRINT LTD
12 Valentine Place, London SE1 8QH.
Tel: 020 7620 0844. Fax: 020 7620 0129. E-mail: sales@silverprint.co.uk
Web: www.silverprint.co.uk
Specialist suppliers of B&W materials. Importers of Maco and Foma fibre-based and RC papers and a wide range of other papers, toners, liquid emulsions, tinting and retouching materials. Products for archival mounting, and archival storage boxes and folio cases. Mail order service.

JAMIE WOOD LTD
Unit 17, Oaks Farm Workshops, Blackboys Road, Framfield, East Sussex TN22 5PN.
Tel: 01825 890990. E-mail: jamiewood@birdtables.com
Web: www.birdtables.com
Makers of photographic hides and suppliers of photo electronic equipment.
Discount to BFP members: 5%.

Storage & Presentation

ABLE DIRECT CENTRE LTD
5 Mallard Close, Earls Barton, Northampton NN6 0LS.
Tel: 0870 444 2733. Fax: 0870 444 2766.
Web: www.able-labels.co.uk
ABLE-LABELS – printed self-adhesive labels.

ARROWFILE
PO Box 7, Wetherby LS23 7EP.
Tel: 0870 607 2048. Fax: 0870 241 2198. E-mail: customerservices@arrowfile.com
Web: www.arrowfile.com
Archival photographic storage and presentation specialists. The Arrowfile System organises, stores and protects varying photo sizes, negs, slides, and CDs all in one single binder album.

BRAYTHORN LTD
Phillips Street, Aston, Birmingham B6 4PT.
Tel: 0121 359 8800. Fax: 0121 359 8412. E-mail: sales@braythorn.co.uk
Web: www.braythorn.co.uk
Suppliers of cardboard mailing tubes and polythene envelopes. Minimum quantities: 1000 envelopes, 100 tubes.
Discount to BFP members: 10%.

CHALLONER MARKETING LTD
Raans Road, Amersham, Buckinghamshire HP6 6LL.
Tel: 01494 721270. Fax: 01494 725732. E-mail: info@challoner-marketing.com
Web: www.challoner-marketing.com
Suppliers of Fly-Weight envelope stiffener. Minimum quantity: 100.
Discount to BFP members: 5% on orders over 5,000.

DW GROUP LTD
Unit 7, Peverel Drive, Granby, Milton Keynes MK1 1NL.
Tel: 01908 642323. Fax: 01908 640164. E-mail: sales@dw-view.com
Web: www.photopages.com
Filing and presentation systems, masks for all formats, mounts, wallets, storage cabinets, lightboxes, display boxes, viewing booths, viewtowers, ultra-slim light panels. Also CD-ROM production and replication, CD printers and replication systems, floppy disk duping, poster prints.
Discount to BFP members: 10%.

NICHOLAS HUNTER LTD
Unit 8, Oxford Business Centre, Osney Lane, Oxford OX1 1TB.
Tel: 01865 727292. Fax: 01865 200051. E-mail: enquiries@photofiling.com
Web: www.photofiling.com
Plastic wallets for presentation of prints, slides and negatives.
Discount to BFP members: 5% if cwo; 10% on orders over £100.

KENRO LTD
Greenbridge Road, Swindon, Wilts SN3 3LH.
Tel: 01793 615836. Fax: 01793 513561. E-mail: sales@kenro.co.uk
Web: www.kenro.co.uk
Professional and retail photo albums and frames, CD storage products, strut mounts and folders, lightboxes and viewers, storage and presentation accessories for digital and film.

LONDON LABELS LTD
20 Oval Road, London NW1 7DJ.
Tel: 020 7267 7105. Fax: 020 7267 1165.
Self-adhesive labels for 35mm slides, printed with name, address or logo. Also plain labels.

RICHFORDS
E M Richford Ltd, Curzon Road, Chilton Industrial Estate, Sudbury, Suffolk CO10 2XW.
Tel: 01787 375241. Fax: 01787 310179. E-mail: sales@richstamp.co.uk
Web: www.richstamp.co.uk
Rubber stamps and inks, including stamps made to order and specialist quick-drying inks.

RUSSELL PHOTO MARKETING
17 Elm Grove, Wimbledon, London SE19 4HE. E-mail: info@russellphotomarketing.co.uk
Web: www.russellphotomarketing.co.uk
Tel: 020 8947 6171. Fax: 020 8944 2064.
D&F Maxima etc. Albums and accessories. Frames to size wood/metal, many colours.
Discount to BFP members: 5% on orders over £150.

SECOL LTD
Howlett Way, Thetford, Norfolk IP24 1HZ.
Tel: 01842 752341. Fax: 01842 762159. E-mail: rp@secol.co.uk
Web: www.secol.co.uk
Wide range of photographic storage and display products including sleeves, filing sheets, storage boxes, black card masks, mounting systems, portfolio cases and portfolio boxes.
Discount to BFP members: 10% on prepaid orders of £100 or more.

SLIDEPACKS
1 The Moorings, Aldenham Road, Bushey, Herts WD23 2NR.
Tel: 01923 254790. Fax: 01923 254789. E-mail: sales@slidepacks.com
Web: www.slidepacks.com
Binders, folders, mounts and wallets for transparency presentation, storage and filing. Custom-made service also available. Also supply labels, lightboxes, lupes and other accessories.

Studio Hire & Services

ALPHA STUDIOS
43a Lodge Lane, London N12 8JG.
Tel: 020 8445 5040. Fax: 0870 137 4641. E-mail: office@alphastudios.co.uk
Web: www.alphastudios.co.uk
Two fully-equipped studios with good daylight, Bowens flash equipment, additional facilities and free parking. Available evenings and weekends by arrangment.
Discount to BFP members: 10% off standard hire rates.

BASE MODELS
PO Box 6709, Bournemouth BH8 0BW.
Tel: 0845 2255015. Fax: 01202 524193. E-mail: info@basemodels.co.uk
Web: www.basemodels.co.uk
Commercial, fashion and glamour models. Full commercial studio hire facilities.
Discount to BFP members: 10%.

CHALK FARM STUDIOS
10A Belmont Street, London NW1 8HH.
Tel: 020 7482 1001. Fax: 020 7267 3179. E-mail: chalkfarmstudios@btconnect.com
Web: www.chalkfarmstudios.co.uk
Three studios for hire with daylight and blackout facilities, Elinchrom flash and tungsten.
Discount to BFP members: 17%

CHARNWOOD STUDIO
A37 The Springboard Centre, Mantle Lane, Coalville, Leicestershire LE67 3DW.
Tel: 01530 450012. E-mail: studio@alveyandtowers.com
Web: www.charnwoodstudio.co.uk
1000 square feet of fully equipped studio for hire, including lights, backgrounds and digital camera if required.
Discount to BFP members: 10%.

HOLBORN STUDIOS
49/50 Eagle Wharf Road, London N1 7ED.
Tel: 020 7490 4099. Fax: 020 7253 8120. E-mail: studiomanager@holborn-studios.co.uk
Web: www.holborn-studios.co.uk
15 studios to hire, plus very comprehensive equipment hire.
Discount to BFP members: 10% on full week bookings.

LEWIS & KAYE (HIRE) LTD
3b Brassie Avenue, London W3 7DE.
Tel: 020 8749 2121. Fax: 020 8749 9455. E-mail: props@lewisandkaye.eclipse.co.uk
Web: www.lewisandkaye.co.uk
Large collection of silver, glass, china and objets d'art for hire as studio props.
Discount to BFP members: 10% where hire charge is £500 or over.

Web Services

DIGITAL RAILROAD
UK Office: Tel: 01225 479672. E-mail: mshonfeld@digitalrailroad.net
Web: www.digitalrailroad.net
Web service enabling photographers to manage, market and sell images from their own branded archive. Subscribers may also use the linked Marketplace service, where images can be placed on a single database for sale direct to visiting picture buyers.
Discount to BFP members: 15%.

AMAZING INTERNET LTD
82 Heath Road, Twickenham, Middlesex TW1 4BW.

Tel: 020 8607 9535. E-mail: contact@amazinginternet.com
Web: www.amazinginternet.com
Website solutions for photographers. Range from fully updateable portfolio websites to large photo library systems, plus full e-commerce facilities and online sales modules for wedding and social photographers.
Discount to BFP members: 10%.

CONTACT
Surrey House, 31 Church Street, Leatherhead, Surrey KT22 8EF.
Tel: 01372 220330. Fax: 01372 220340. E-mail: mail@contact-uk.com
Web: www.contact-uk.com
Low cost web portfolio portal with international art buyer usage, plus optional annual source book.

INTERNATIONAL PHOTONET LTD
The Mallings, 112 Malling Street, Lewes, East Sussex BN7 2RJ.
Tel: 01273 488094. Fax: 01273 488095. E-mail: info@international-photonet.com
Web: www.international-photonet.com
On-line searchable resources centre for professional photographers and labs worldwide. Comprehensive services, from sourcing commissions to gallery and portfolio display facilities. Also digitisation and image shipping/dispatch services.

MEDIA TRADING SERVICES LTD
1 Abbey Street, Eynsham, Oxfordshire OX29 4TB.
Tel: 0845 370 3711. Fax: 01865 883550. E-mail: sales@mediatradingservices.co.uk
Web: www.mediatradingservices.co.uk
Bespoke web design services to photographers and artists, from standard sites to complex code driven solutions. On-line ordering and printing services and a full on-line portfolio search are available.
Discount to BFP members: On application.

SIGNUM TECHNOLOGIES LTD
Dunraven House, 5 Meadow Court, High Street, Witney, Oxfordshire, OX28 6ER.
Tel: 01933 776929. Fax: 01933 776939. E-mail: signum@signumtech.com
Web: www.signumtech.com
SureSign digital watermarking plug-ins for Photoshop, for copyright protection and notification.

SPANSOFT
8 Juniper Hill, Glenrothes, Fife KY7 5TH.
Tel/fax: 01592 743110. E-mail: support@spansoft.org
Web: www.spansoft.org
Slide Librarian shareware package for cataloguing transparency collections on PC.

THIRD LIGHT
St John's Innovation Centre, Cowley Road, Cambridge CB4 0WS.
Tel: 01223 475674. Fax: 0700 340 1284. E-mail: sales@thirdlight.com
Web: www.thirdlight.com
Provider of Image Management System (IMS), a web-based picture library and e-commerce system enabling photographers to store, display and sell images via internet galleries.

USEFUL ADDRESSES

ASSOCIATION OF MODEL AGENTS
11–29 Fashion Street, London E1 6PX.
Tel: 020 7422 0699. Fax: 020 7247 9230.

ASSOCIATION OF PHOTOGRAPHERS (AOP)
81 Leonard Street, London EC2A 4QS.
Tel: 020 7739 6669. Fax: 020 7739 8707. E-mail: general@aophoto.co.uk
Web: www.the-aop.org

BRITISH ASSOCIATION OF PICTURE LIBRARIES AND AGENCIES (BAPLA)
18 Vine Hill, London EC1R 5DZ.
Tel: 020 7713 1780. Fax: 020 7713 1211. E-mail: enquiries@bapla.org.uk
Web: www.bapla.org

BRITISH INSTITUTE OF PROFESSIONAL PHOTOGRAPHY (BIPP)
Fox Talbot House, Amwell End, Ware, Hertfordshire SG12 9HN.
Tel: 01920 464011. Fax: 01920 487056. E-mail: info@bipp.com
Web: www.bipp.com

BUREAU OF FREELANCE PHOTOGRAPHERS (BFP)
Focus House, 497 Green Lanes, London N13 4BP.
Tel: 020 8882 3315. Fax: 020 8886 3933. E-mail: info@thebfp.com
Web: www.thebfp.com

CHARTERED INSTITUTE OF JOURNALISTS (CIOJ)
2, Dock Offices, Surrey Quays Road, London SE16 2XU.
Tel: 020 7252 1187. Fax: 020 7232 2302. E-mail: memberservices@cioj.co.uk
Web: www.cioj.co.uk

DESIGN & ARTISTS COPYRIGHT SOCIETY (DACS)
33 Great Sutton Street, London EC1V 0DX.
Tel: 020 7336 8811. Fax: 020 7336 8822. E-mail: info@dacs.org.uk
Web: www.dacs.org.uk

THE GUILD OF PHOTOGRAPHERS
Moorlinch Vinyard, Moorlinch, Somerset TA7 9DD.
Tel: 0870 2409242. Fax: 01278 723217. E-mail: info@photoguild.co.uk
Web: www.photoguild.co.uk

MASTER PHOTOGRAPHERS ASSOCIATION (MPA)
Jubilee House, 1 Chancery Lane, Darlington, Co Durham DL1 5QP.
Tel: 01325 356555. Fax: 01325 357813. E-mail: enq@mpauk.com
Web: www.thempa.com

NATIONAL ASSOCIATION OF PRESS AGENCIES (NAPA)
41 Lansdowne Crescent, Leamington Spa, Warwickshire CV32 4PR.
Tel: 01926 420566. Web: www.napa.org.uk

NATIONAL UNION OF JOURNALISTS (NUJ)
Headland House, 308-312 Gray's Inn Road, London WC1X 8DP.
Tel: 020 7278 7916. Fax: 020 7837 8143. E-mail: info@nuj.org.uk
Web: www.nuj.org.uk

PHOTO IMAGING COUNCIL (PIC)
Orbital House, 85 Croydon Road, Caterham, Surrey CR3 6PD.
Tel: 01883 334497. Fax: 01883 334490. E-mail: pic@admin.co.uk
Web: www.pic.uk.net

PHOTO MARKETING ASSOCIATION INTERNATIONAL (PMA)
Wisteria House, 28 Fulling Mill Lane, Welwyn, Herts AL6 9NS.
Tel: 0870 240 4542. Fax: 01438 716572. E-mail: tchapman@pmai.org
Web: www.pmai.org

PRESS ASSOCIATION
292 Vauxhall Bridge Road, London SW1V 1AE.
Tel: 020 7963 7000; Picture Desk: 020 7963 7155. Fax: 020 7963 7191.
Web: www.pressassociation.co.uk

REUTERS
Reuters Building, South Colonnade, Canary Wharf, London E14 5EP.
Tel: 020 7542 7949 (picture desk UK news); 020 7542 8088 (international). E-mail:
lon.pictures@reuters.com
Web: http://pictures.reuters.com

ROYAL PHOTOGRAPHIC SOCIETY (RPS)
Fenton House, 122 Wells Road, Bath BA2 3AH.
Tel: 01225 325733. Fax: 01225 448688. E-mail: rps@rps.org
Web: www.rps.org

SWPP & BPPA
6 Bath Street, Rhyl LL16 3EB.
Tel: 01745 356935. Fax: 01745 356953. E-mail: info@swpp.co.uk
Web: www.swpp.co.uk

INDEX

A

B

C

L

M

N

R

S

Join the BFP today and get next year's Handbook hot from the press!

As a member of the Bureau of Freelance Photographers, you'll be kept right up to date with market requirements. Every month, you'll receive the BFP *Market Newsletter*, a unique publication telling you what picture buyers are looking for now. It will keep you informed of new markets – including new magazines – as they appear and the type of pictures they're looking for. It also serves to keep *The Freelance Photographer's Market Handbook* up to date between editions, since it reports important changes as they occur.

And as part of membership, you receive the Handbook automatically each year as it is published. For details of some of the other services available to members please see page 9.

Membership currently costs just £49 a year. To join, complete the form below and post with your remittance to the BFP. You'll receive your first Newsletter and membership pack within about 14 days.

Please enrol me as a member of the Bureau of Freelance Photographers for 12 months. I understand that if, once I receive my initial membership pack, I decide that membership is not for me, I may return it within 21 days for a full refund.

❏ I enclose cheque/po value £49 *(or £65 Overseas rate*)*

❏ Debit my MASTERCARD/VISA/SWITCH no_____

Expiry Date_____ Issue No (Switch only)_____ in the sum of £49.

NAME _____

ADDRESS _____ BLOCK CAPS PLEASE

_____

_____ Postcode_____

Post to:
Bureau of Freelance Photographers, H07
Focus House, 497 Green Lanes, London N13 4BP.

*Overseas applicants must send cheque/draft drawn on a UK bank; or pay by credit card

Also published by BFP Books

The Freelance Photographer's Project Book is a major new publication from BFP Books. It is designed to help photographers find fresh markets for their work by giving them the inside information on breaking into different sectors of the market. Each of the 20 chapters, or "projects", is written by an experienced and successful freelance who specialises in the market concerned. Each contributor provides the newcomer with the benefit of their long experience in approaching these specific markets.

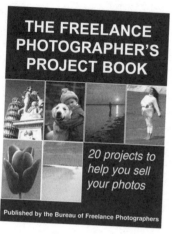

Subjects include Selling family photos; Selling outdoor photos; Selling wildlife photos; Selling country photos; Selling garden photos; Selling boating photos; Selling to photo magazines; Selling to local papers; Selling travel photos; Selling architectural photos; Selling generic photos; Selling transport photos; Selling to home magazines; Selling through libraries; Selling cards & calendars; and Selling stock with articles.

The final two projects cover Mounting an exhibition and Producing a book.

The contributors have been chosen not only for their expertise in their chosen subject but also their ability to impart this knowledge with clarity and precision. A short summary of the contributor's background and experience is appended to each project.

The book is fully illustrated with examples of pictures that sell, all provided by the contributors themselves.

The Freelance Photographer's Project Book will provide invaluable information for anyone who has ever thought of selling their pictures but does not know where to start. Whatever the subject, the Project Book offers a fast track to success.

144 pages Hardback £22.50

Get a special previous user's discount when you order next year's Handbook direct

Each year's *Handbook* contains hundreds of amended listings as well as new entries. To take the magazine section alone, during the course of the year, new publications launch while existing titles fold. In addition, editors change which often leads to a change in picture requirements. Similar important changes occur in every other section of the book.

It's vital to keep up-to-date, therefore, by working from the latest edition. The *Handbook* is published in October each year, and you can order next year's edition from September onwards. By using this form, you'll benefit from a special previous user's discount, saving you £3 on the usual direct-from-the-publishers price. While the normal price is £16.95 (£14.95 plus £2 p&p), you pay only £13.95.

Complete the details below for your copy of next year's *Freelance Photographer's Market Handbook*.

NB. Offer closes 31 December 2008

Please send me a copy of **The Freelance Photographer's Market Handook 2009** at the special Previous User's Discount price of £11.95 plus £2.00 p&p.

☐ I enclose cheque/po value £13.95 including £2.00 p&p.

☐ Debit my MASTERCARD/VISA/SWITCH no_____

Expiry Date_____ Issue No (Switch only)_____in the sum of £13.95

NAME _____ BLOCK CAPS

ADDRESS _____ PLEASE

_____

_____ Postcode_____

Post to:
BFP BOOKS
Focus House, 497 Green Lanes, London N13 4BP.
*Overseas readers must send cheque/draft drawn on a UK bank; or pay by credit card

H08